PUTIN'S COUNTERREVOLUTION

PUTIN'S COUNTERREVOLUTION

SERGEY ALEKSASHENKO

BROOKINGS INSTITUTION PRESS
Washington, D.C.

Copyright © 2018
THE BROOKINGS INSTITUTION
1775 Massachusetts Avenue, N.W., Washington, D.C. 20036
www.brookings.edu

The Brookings Institution is a private nonprofit organization devoted to research, education, and publication on important issues of domestic and foreign policy. Its principal purpose is to bring the highest quality independent research and analysis to bear on current and emerging policy problems. Interpretations or conclusions in Brookings publications should be understood to be solely those of the authors.

Library of Congress Cataloging-in-Publication data are available.
ISBN 978-0-8157-3276-1 (pbk. : alk. paper)
ISBN 978-0-8157-3277-8 (ebook)

9 8 7 6 5 4 3 2 1

Typeset in Ehrhardt MT

Composition by Elliott Beard

Contents

SIX

Preventing Competition 149

LIST OF FIGURES

LIST OF TABLES

Preface and Acknowledgments

I have been fortunate in my lifetime to have participated in a great Russian revolution that transformed a totalitarian state with a planned economy into a market-economy state grasping for democracy. From 1989 to 1998, I served in various state positions, including as deputy minister of finance, from 1993 to 1995, and as first deputy chairman of the Russian Central Bank, from 1995 to 1998, before moving to the private sector. This perspective afforded me a ringside seat to witness the many traumatic upheavals Russia was undergoing, but by the end of the 1990s it seemed to me that despite all the setbacks, Russia was moving steadily toward its goal of becoming a democratic and prosperous nation.

And then the train went off the tracks. A series of incidents led me to suspect that the reforms that had been enacted were far less durable than I thought. Subsequent events confirmed the uncertain nature of the gains, which had seemed at least roughly capable of continuing. By 2013 the Russian economy had stopped growing and Russian business had lost the will to invest for growth.

This is an unnatural mood for business. If the growth impulse is gone, it means that something well out of the ordinary has happened. And yet it's impossible to locate the precise moment that things went wrong. The changes in the country happened gradually over the course of the years that Vladimir Putin has been in power, beginning with his very first day in office.

Many books analyzing the developments in Russia in the last two decades have been published recently. And the authors have often put Vladimir Putin at the epicenter of their explorations, understanding well his role in modern Russia. Steven Lee Myers's biography of Putin takes readers through many episodes of Putin's life, trying to explain how the personality, views, and environment of the "new tsar" came to be shaped. We watch as Putin meets many of the people who would later become his team in the Kremlin. Meticulous research by Karen Dawisha has fleshed out the details of Putin's life in the 1990s, during Russia's and Putin's own critical years. Then the life of the great country underwent a serious transformation as the future president entered the state bureaucracy, where he faced many temptations and certain previously unknown problems, leading him to make decisions whose rationale remained unclear for many until today. A cheerful book by Mikhail Zygar, written from the perspective of an entrenched Kremlin insider, tries to lift the curtain and shed light on the logic and motivation of many of Putin's decisions. Fiona Hill and Cliff Gaddy have constructed a deep psychological portrait demonstrating how the outlook of the person shaped through service in the KGB, the Soviet secret police, has influenced Russian domestic and foreign policy. Masha Gessen and Garry Kasparov offer stories of great emotional breadth, whose many actors create an electric, multicolored mosaic of modern Russia.

Each of those books gives us a piece of unique information. Sometimes the authors' views are very similar, sometimes they present us with different explanations of events and driving forces, but all build their stories around the person of Vladimir Putin, struggling to understand his views and goals, dreams and limitations. I am much less interested in this aspect. Instead, in this book I concentrate on what happened to Russia as a country. It is very important to recognize how weak and unprotected the political system in an emerging democracy can be, as well as in countries with long-established democracies. Today we see the heads of certain Eastern European states following Putin's path, arrogating increasingly more political power to themselves while limiting the rights and freedoms of their opponents and using the bully pulpit to call them out as enemies of the nation. The demolition of the political institutions and the system of checks and balances does not happen overnight, but the steady trajectory leading toward this disappointing finale is obvious, raising well-founded concern over those countries' future. Even in the United States, a country with stable and sound democratic institutions, we see a president fighting with the free media and not hiding his desire to bring the law enforcement agencies to heel and make them personally loyal to him. And once again we may find similarities to Vladimir Putin's early years in power.

In mid-October 2015, Michael McFaul invited me to Stanford University to speak at the Freeman Spogli Institute for International Studies, of which he is director. As usual, I was asked to speak about the Russian economy and why it was in such a sorry state. As I was preparing my response to these seemingly simple questions (the decline in the price of oil, Russia's main export; Western sanctions), I realized I would also need to speak about politics, about institutions, about what had happened in Russia in the twenty-first century under the presidency of Vladimir Putin. After my talk, Michael asked whether I might consider writing a book to take up these interconnected matters at length. Three years later, this book is the fruit of that conversation.

My purpose was to explore what happened to Russia in the years following the dissolution of the Soviet Union and, especially, from Putin's first election to the presidency: how Russia went from a country facing the future with hope to a rogue state menacing its neighbors. To do so, it is necessary to examine what, how, and when Putin did what he did during his tenure—how even while declaring good intentions he made decisions that did not seem to fit into any kind of plan or rational sequence and, in aggregate, turned Russia's course 180 degrees. As the leader of a country with weak institutions and beset with a variety of problems, Putin, like many figures who have gained power in turbulent times and found themselves facing similar situations, followed the well-worn path of strengthening personal power as a seemingly better choice. Step by step, he grabbed additional power, reducing the powers of other branches of government and shifting the balance in his favor. As Russia was just emerging from the extended and painful transition from a Soviet republic and trying to get back on its feet after the severe financial crisis of August 1998, no one could or wanted to resist Putin's desire to expand presidential power. Regions, political parties, businessmen, and the judiciary watched silently as the president removed his opponents one after the other from the political scene, relying exclusively on brute force and abuse of the law. And all this happened with unusual speed: by the end of his first presidential term, Vladimir Putin could truthfully have said, "L'état, c'est moi."

We don't know what sort of country Vladimir Putin wanted to build when he first entered the Kremlin. It's possible he had no strategic plan at all, or any clear vision for the future for his country. But he did have principles on which he based his decisions, and each of them led him unerringly to increase his personal powers and to restrict the rights and freedoms of Russian citizens. As a politician, Putin has achieved his goal: he has been in power for eighteen years, for fourteen of them as an elected president, and it's not clear what could keep him from continuing to govern, surpassing Joseph Stalin's record of staying in power. But as president, Putin has been a failure. Over the past decade, from 2008 to the time of writing, the economy has nearly stopped growing, which means that Russians' quality of life has stopped improving as well.

The momentum for the transformation that Yeltsin bequeathed to Russia has been completely extinguished by Putin's many decisions during his long tenure. The country's trajectory has changed dramatically over that time, and today Russia has lost all sign of the path to prosperity and well-being. Human rights, the rule of law, transparency in government, and basic democratic principles have been sent packing. In this great reversal we can read tidal forces moving against the hard-fought achievements of his predecessor as Putin's counterrevolution becomes cemented in place.

Recent years have demonstrated how weak and unprotected the political system can be. And it is important to recognize that radical changes may happen not overnight but in multiple minor steps, one small change after another.

I would like to thank the many people who directly or indirectly helped me write this book, and whose support helped me move forward with it. I must start with Mikhail Sergeyevich Gorbachev and Boris Nikolaevich Yeltsin, who led Russia out of its historical dead end and thanks to whom we know the right path forward. I also thank my teacher, Yevgeny Grigorievich Yasin, who not only acquainted me with the foundations of economics as my professor at Moscow State University but also taught me to think critically, to collect and analyze facts, and to draw conclusions.

I am endlessly grateful to all those who took the time to talk with me and tell me much of what helped me to write this book: Aleksandr Voloshin, Andrey Klepach, Mikhail Khodorkovsky, Vyacheslav Brecht, Tamara Morshchakova, Viktor Zhuykov, Ekaterina Mishina, Elena Novikova, Vladimir Radchenko, Valery Kogan, Dmitry Ushakov, Peter Aven, Vladimir Gusinsky, Alfred Kokh, Anatoly Chubais, Sergey Dubinin, Mikhail Kolpakov, Irena Lesnevskaya, Dmitry Zimin, Andrey Samodin, Liz Wood, Harvey Baltzer, Liliya Shevtsova, Fiona Hill, Angela Stent, Tobi Gati, Dmitry Simes, Vladimir Ryzhkov, Aleksey Venediktov, Sergey Petrov, Sergey Zenkin, Boris Zimin, Aleksandr Kynev, Bulat Stolyarov, Mikhail Berger, and Kirill Telin.

I am especially grateful to the Kommersant Publishing House for free access to the wonderful archive of their publications and the high-quality search engine that allowed me to refresh my recollections of many facts and find excellent quotes for my book. I thank Sergey Vasilyev, Viktor Kolomiets, and Video International; Lev Gudkov and the Levada Center; Anatoly Karachinsky and Medialogia; and Sergey Shpilkin and Nikolay Kondrashov for the information they provided to me.

Special thanks go to Maria Snegovaya, who helped me during the early stages of writing, and notably to Alena Lavrenyuk for her invaluable assistance in making this book happen.

This book could not have appeared without the support of Evgenia Kara-Murza, Sara Buzadzhi, Leon Geyer, and Daniel Kennelly, who helped finetune my English, and the team at the Brookings Institution Press, led by Bill Finan, Elliott Beard, and Marjorie Pannell, who guided me through the unknown territory of moving from manuscript to a printed book. I cannot forget the good work of Patricia Goodman and Paul Ross, who read the very first draft of this book and inspired me to finalize it.

Last but not least, I thank my family, who supported me not only throughout the entire time I worked on this book but also long before it: my parents,

Alevtina Sergeyevna and Vladimir Pavlovich, for raising me the way they did; my wife, Ekaterina, who was able to relieve me of daily routine, giving me a chance to focus on my work, whatever it was; my older children, Artem and Sergey, who gently prodded me to move along the chosen path; and my younger son, Alexey, who stoically put up with my long absences.

Chronology of Putin's Russia

BEFORE VLADIMIR PUTIN BECAME PRESIDENT

DECEMBER 25, 1991   USSR ceases to exist. Russia becomes an independent state.

OCTOBER 1993   Political conflict increases in Russia. Attempt at a military coup d'état fails.

DECEMBER 1993   Russian constitution is adopted on a referendum.

DECEMBER 1993   Elections to the State Duma take place.

DECEMBER 1995   Elections to the State Duma take place.

JULY 1996   Boris Yeltsin is reelected president of Russia for a second term.

JULY 1998   Vladimir Putin is nominated head of the FSB, the Russian secret police.

FEBRUARY 1999   The Kremlin starts fighting with Prosecutor General Yury Skuratov, using the FSB as a tool.

MAY 1999   The Kremlin starts fighting with Vladimir Gusinsky, using the courts and the prosecutor general's office as tools.

AUGUST 1999   Boris Yeltsin nominates Vladimir Putin Russian prime minister and names him his political successor.

DECEMBER 1999 Elections to the State Duma take place.

DECEMBER 31, 1999 Boris Yeltsin resigns as president of Russia. Valdimir Putin becomes acting president.

MARCH 2000 Vladimir Putin is elected president of Russia.

PUTIN'S FIRST PRESIDENTIAL TERM

MAY 7, 2000 Vladimir Putin is inaugurated president of Russia.

MAY 17, 2000 Putin announces a federal reform, assigning himself the right to fire governors and removing governors and heads of regional legislatures from the Federation Council.

JUNE 2000 Gusinsky is arrested. He exchanges his property for freedom.

AUGUST 2000 The *Kursk* submarine disaster. The Kremlin removes Berezovsky from managerial control over TV Channel One.

JULY 2001 The law on political parties is adopted, requiring state registration and establishing quantitative requirements. Regional parties are prohibited.

JULY 2001 A ban on national referenda in the years when federal elections take place is established.

NOVEMBER 2001 The Kremlin's judicial reform is approved legally. The judiciary comes under the Kremlin's control. Top levels of the juduciary are purged.

DECEMBER 2001 The United Russia party is established after a merger of the Unity bloc and the Fatherland–All Russia party.

JANUARY 2002 TV-6, a company owned by Berezovsky, is liquidated by court order.

JUNE 2002 Electoral reform is adopted through laws. The vertical subordination of electoral commissions is established.

JULY 2002 The law on resistance to extremist activity is adopted.

DECEMBER 2002 The vote threshold for political parties to have representation in the State Duma is raised from 5 percent to 7 percent (effective beginning in 2007).

JUNE 2003 The independent television broadcaster TVS is liquidated.

OCTOBER 25, 2003 Mikhail Khodorkovsky, Yukos's CEO and main shareholder, is arrested. (His partner, Platon Lebedev, is arrested on July 2, 2003.) The demolition of Yukos and nationalization of its assets begin.

NOVEMBER 2003 The Rose Revolution takes place in Georgia, frightening Putin.

DECEMBER 2003 In elections to the State Duma, United Russia wins a majority of votes. First massive electoral fraud occurs.

MARCH 2004 Vladimir Putin is reelected president of Russia for a second term.

PUTIN'S SECOND PRESIDENTIAL TERM

JUNE 2004 Freedom of assembly is removed from the constitution and compulsory state preapproval of gatherings is imposed by law.

SEPTEMBER 1, 2004 More than 1,000 people are taken hostage in a school in the North Ossetian city of Beslan.

SEPTEMBER 13, 2004 Putin declares full-scale political reform, including the removal of majority districts from State Duma elections, a ban on electoral blocs, the replacement of gubernatorial elections with presidential nominations, and restrictions on the establishment of political parties.

DECEMBER 2004 The Orange Revolution takes place in Ukraine.

JANUARY 2005 The Constitutional Court accepts waiving of the limitation period for the Yukos trial.

AUGUST 2005 Putin's crony Yury Kovalchuk obtains beneficial control of Gazprom-Media (formerly Media-Most).

OCTOBER 2005 The Kremlin enforces RAO UES selling its stake in REN-TV (an independent broadcaster); Kovalchuk becomes the final controlling shareholder in 2007.

DECEMBER 2005 The Constitutional Court accepts the removal of direct gubernatorial elections.

JULY 2006 Citizens holding dual passports or residence permits in other countries lose their right to be elected to office.

JULY 2006 Political parties are not allowed to put members of other political parties on their electoral lists.

DECEMBER 2006   A long-term ban on the election of persons previously convicted of a crime is established by law.

DECEMBER 2006   The relocation of the Constitutional Court to St. Petersburg is adopted by law.

DECEMBER 2007   In elections to the State Duma, United Russia wins 70 percent of seats.

FEBRUARY 2008   Putin transfers ownership of the federal television channel Petersburg–Channel 5 to Kovalchuk.

MARCH 2008   Dmitry Medvedev is elected president of Russia.

DMITRY MEDVEDEV'S PRESIDENTIAL TERM

MAY 2008   Vladimir Putin becomes prime minister of Russia.

MAY 2008   Roskomnadzor, the state agency given control of the dissemination of information through media and over the internet, is established

DECEMBER 2008   The length of the Russian presidential term is extended to six years and that of a State Duma seat to five years.

JUNE 2009   The Constitutional Court loses its right to elect the chief justice, who henceforth will be chosen by the president.

JUNE 2010   The state media-monitoring agency is empowered to require media owners to remove information from their websites.

NOVEMBER 2010   The Constitutional Court loses its right to remove the chief justice by a vote.

JANUARY–FEBRUARY 2011   The Arab Spring takes place.

SEPTEMBER 24, 2011   Vladimir Putin announces his decision to run for reelection as president.

DECEMBER 2011   In the State Duma elections, United Russia wins 49.3 percent of votes on universal voting but 53 percent of the seats.

DECEMBER 2011   The streets of Moscow see massive political protests.

DECEMBER 2011   Dmitry Medvedev announces certain political liberalization measures: gubernatorial elections are reestablished and the requirements to establish a political party are eased.

MARCH 2012   Vladimir Putin is reelected president of Russia for a third term.

APRIL 2012 The federal registration agency is granted the right to freeze the process of establishing political parties.

APRIL 2012 Medvedev incorporates a "municipal filter" in gubernatorial elections.

MAY 6, 2012 Police disperse an approved political demonstration in Bolotnaya Square in the heart of Moscow.

PUTIN'S THIRD PRESIDENTIAL TERM

JUNE 2012 Procedures for organizing public assemblies and demonstrations are toughened, with administrative arrest for the organizers of unsanctioned gatherings imposed by the law.

FEBRUARY 2013 The Constitutional Court accepts changes to the law on public demonstrations.

MAY 2013 Citizens owning foreign assets lose the right to be elected to office.

DECEMBER 2013 The prosecutor general's office obtains the right to request blocking of websites without a court order.

FEBRUARY 2014 Majority electoral districts are reestablished for elections to the State Duma.

JANUARY–FEBRUARY 2014 The Euromaidan is launched in Kyiv. Ukrainian president Viktor Yanukovych is ousted from power and flees to Russia.

MARCH 2014 Russia invades Ukraine and annexes the Crimean Peninsula.

APRIL 2014 Military conflict in eastern Ukraine begins.

MAY 2014 Regional legislatures receive the right to eliminate direct elections of city mayors and heads of municipal units.

JULY 2014 Criminal penalties are legally approved for the organizers of unsanctioned marches, demonstrations, and picketing, with the possibility of administrative arrest for participans in nonsanctioned public events.

AUGUST 2014 The Russian Supreme Arbitration Court is liquidated. Justices are purged from the Supreme Court.

MAY 2015 The law on undesirable organizations is approved, allowing extrajudicial liquidation of international and foreign organizations.

JULY 2015 The Constitutional Court assigns itself the right to block the execution of European Court of Human Rights decisions in Russia.

JULY 2015 Restrictions on internet search systems are imposed.

JUNE 2016 Restrictions on the activity of news aggregators on the internet are imposed (verification requirements and removal on request of the government control agency).

JULY 2016 Electronic messaging systems are required to provide their decryption instruments on request of the FSB.

SEPTEMBER 2016 In elections to the State Duma, United Russia wins 75 percent of seats.

NOVEMBER 2016 LinkedIn is blocked in Russia.

MAY 2017 BlackBerry Messenger, Line, and VChat are blocked in Russia. The messaging systems IMO and WeChat are temporarily blocked.

JULY 2017 Restrictions are placed on messaging systems' activity, to include identification by phone number and blocking on request of the governmental control agency.

NOVEMEBER 2017 "Lugovoy's law" is extended.

MARCH 2018 Vladimir Putin is reelected president of Russia for a fourth term.

APRIL 2018 Telegram is blocked in Russia.

PUTIN'S FOURTH PRESIDENTIAL TERM

One

ECONOMIC ROLLER COASTER: 2000–17

Vladimir Putin was fortunate as a politician. He became Russia's prime minister in August 1999, when the country's economy had just emerged from the serious financial crisis of August 1998 and was entering a lengthy period of rapid growth. From 1999 to 2008, the Russian GDP grew 94 percent, or an average annual growth rate of slightly less than 7 percent. In dollar terms, the Russian economy grew 8.5 times. Had Russia been able to maintain similar growth rates for another ten to fifteen years, we would now be talking about the "Russian miracle." After the start of the worldwide recession in mid-2008, however, the Russian economy lost its momentum and essentially stagnated, growing just 5.5 percent in aggregate over the next ten years (see figure 1-1).

Many attribute Russia's economic achievements during the period of 1999–2008 to Vladimir Putin and his economic policies, with the "lost decade" that followed explained away as the result of various unfavorable external factors, such as the global recession of 2008–09, the decline in oil prices from more than U.S. $110 per barrel in 2011–13 to an average of $52 per barrel in 2015 and $43 per barrel in 2016, Western financial sanctions against

1

FIGURE 1-1. **Russian Economic Growth, 1998–2018**

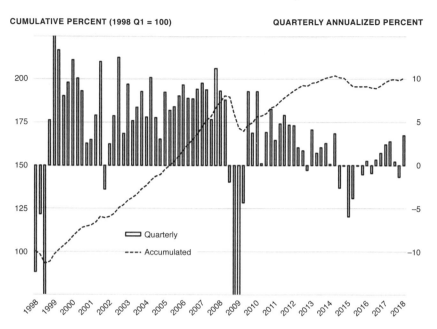

Source: Rosstat, "Ofitsial'naya statistika. Natsional'nyye scheta. Valovoy vnutrenniy product" [Official statistics. National Accounts. Gross Domestic Product] (http://www .gks.ru/wps/wcm/connect/rosstat_main/rosstat/ru/statistics/accounts/#).

Russia imposed in response to the Russian aggression against Ukraine, and the slowing Chinese economy. Others add changes to Putin's economic policies to this list of causes. These explanations are not entirely convincing, nor do they suggest what should be done to get the Russian economy growing again. If the economic policy of 1999–2008 was right, then a return to the methods of that decade should have given the Russian economy a fresh start. Even if the economy grew at only half its former rate of 7 percent, that would still constitute a decent achievement.

An analysis of Russia's economic policy during Putin's entire eighteen-year reign, however, reveals no major differences in the principles and instruments the government applied to the economy in different periods. Nor was there anything particularly liberal about the economic policy of Russia during 1999–2008 that could account for the rapid economic change of that period.

During his first term as president, Vladimir Putin supported the passage of several laws that significantly changed the rules of the game—but their actual contribution to the growth spurt was secondary. The new Tax Code, for example, simplified the tax system and established a flat 13 percent personal income tax, a standard subsequently adopted by many Eastern European countries. The Land Code institutionalized private ownership of land, a move that no doubt spurred economic activity in the Russian agricultural sector, which has been growing at an average rate of 3.5 percent a year since 1999. But the agricultural sector accounts for just 2.5–3.5 percent of Russian GDP, so its annual contribution to economic growth is insignificant. The Duma—the lower house of parliament—adopted a new Labor Code that made the labor market a little more flexible. Energy reform infused the energy sector with additional investments. Social service benefits were monetized, and pension reform introduced the saving component that initially gave a substantial boost to the domestic corporate bond market (though this part of the pension reform subsequently was terminated by the government in 2013).

However important all these decisions were individually, they did not add up to a coordinated reform package.[1] Therefore they did not seriously contribute to Russia's economic growth gains during Putin's first eight years as president. Moreover, none of these reforms were rolled back in 2008–17, nor were any economic counterreforms adopted in 2008–17 that could have weighed significantly on the Russian economy.

Instead, a detailed analysis of the Russian economy from 1999 to 2008 paints a picture of uneven growth affecting disparate sectors rather than a steadily rising tide lifting all boats. Annual growth rates ranged from 2.5–3.0 percent in the second half of 2000 to more than 10 percent growth in some periods. The growth was not distributed equitably across all economic sectors: different sectors acted as the drivers of growth at different times. Within this ten-year period of growth, three different stages can be ascertained, each having its own factors promoting economic growth: 1999–2001, 2001–05, and 2005–08.[2]

RISE AND DECLINE OF GROWTH RATES

The first stage, 1999–2001, bore the characteristics of a classic export and import substitution boom brought on by a sharp devaluation of the national currency in the financial crisis of August 1998.[3] The ruble's devaluation significantly increased the competitiveness of many Russian products on domestic and especially foreign markets. It's not an accident that the sectors that grew most during this period, such as the automobile industry, had unused capacity reserves or else were export-oriented, thus benefiting from lower costs in dollar-equivalent terms. Some examples of the latter were the chemical, metallurgy, and fertilizer production industries.

By 2001 the effects of the devaluation had tapered off as a factor contributing to economic growth, but already by 2000 a new growth-enhancing factor connected to the delayed effects of privatization had kicked in. The post-Soviet redistribution of property was completed by the late 1990s, and the new owners had survived a difficult time of political and economic upheaval. However, the foundations of the new economic system remained unchanged, and businesses realized that nothing threatened their interests and property rights. This realization led to a drastic improvement in managerial efficiency at privatized enterprises, giving rise to a class of efficient owners. Improved efficiency was especially noticeable in the raw materials export sector. A 50 percent increase in oil production for the period 2000–05 illustrates the success of that sector, at a time when privately owned companies were responsible for 80 percent of Russian oil production. In contrast, gas production—95 percent of which was controlled by the state-owned Gazprom holding—grew less than 10 percent. Increases in coal, iron ore, aluminum, steel, and copper production ranged from 17 percent to 29 percent between 1999 and 2005, while nickel production at Norilsk Nickel increased 35 percent between 2000 and 2007. In addition to raw materials production itself, the internal demand generated by the raw materials sector also served as a positive economic driver.

But this period came to an end with the breakup of the oil and gas company Yukos, which had been acquired from the state during the privatization push by Mikhail Khodorkovsky's Menatep Group. The politically motivated arrest of Khodorkovsky and the subsequent forced bankruptcy and nationalization of Yukos undermined the trust big businesses had in political structures—the same trust that had served as a basis for long-term economic forecasting and development programs in the early to mid-2000s. Moreover, once global oil prices began rising rapidly in 2003, the Russian Finance Ministry changed the taxes on oil revenues: since 2006, most of the oil revenue surpluses (up to 85 percent) have gone to the federal budget and have been allocated to fiscal reserves, where they cannot stimulate economic activity. Thus the contributions of the raw materials sector to economic growth has declined steadily since 2005 even as the prices of raw materials have continued to increase.

Fortunately for the Russian economy, the third stage was also a time of wide-open foreign capital markets. Investors recovered from their 1998 losses; the Russian budget was running surpluses, thanks to rising oil prices, and the country's credit ratings improved dramatically. From 2005 to the middle of 2008, Russian external corporate debt (for the financial and real sector combined) increased by almost $400 billion. The financing for foreign mergers and acquisitions to bring Russian companies to foreign markets accounted for approximately half of that amount, leaving about $55–$60 billion annually to finance domestic economic growth (an average of 4.3 percent of GDP for 2006–08).

Much as in other emerging economies, external financing primarily went to nontradable sectors of the Russian economy, such as construction, trade, finance, and market services. These were the key economic growth drivers at this stage, against the backdrop of increased raw materials prices, which overheated the Russian economy. However, the global financial crisis drastically curtailed access to external financing; moreover, some of the previously received loans had to be repaid (this was especially painful for banks), which stemmed the growth these loans had supported.

Two related conclusions can be drawn from all of the above. First, the rapid economic growth in the decade of 1999–2008 did not apply equally to all sectors and was sustained by a succession of unconnected factors over a long period. Hence the idea entertained in some quarters that Putin masterminded the economic growth of the 2000s through certain policy changes simply is not supportable. Second, the factors propelling the Russian economy forward between the 1998 financial crisis and the global recession of 2008–09 were unique and unlikely ever to be repeated in the same form.

The upheavals in the global economy that triggered the crisis in Russia in 2008 were so profound, however, that the government had an easy time attributing all its problems to external factors. And to some extent, this attribution was correct. The dramatic decline in demand for raw materials was indeed a powerful factor in the crisis (railroad shipments declined more than 20 percent in two months at the end of 2008 compared to the previous months; oil and gas shipments fell 7 percent and 20 percent respectively in the fourth quarter of 2008 relative to late 2007; and gas exports fell as much as 60 percent in the first quarter of 2009 relative to 2008 levels). But the decline in demand proved to be short-lived. The global financial system rebounded in the spring of 2009, boosting the global economy as a whole. Russia felt the change as well. After hitting its nadir in April 2009, the country's economy gradually began to improve.

The recovery was slow and uncertain. From mid-2008 to the spring of 2009 the Russian economy fell by 10 percent. Only in early 2012 was it able to surpass its precrisis maximum from mid-2008, but the growth rate soon fell below 2 percent, even though oil prices consistently topped $100 a barrel after January 2011 and the Russian invasion of Ukraine and the Western economic sanctions were not yet in sight. The decline in oil prices beginning in mid-2014 dealt a painful blow to the Russian economy. Export revenues fell precipitously, which drastically reduced contributions to the federal budget, which relied heavily on oil production and export proceeds.[4] Declining oil prices and Western financial sanctions imposed in August 2014 led to a devaluation by half of the ruble by the end of 2014. Russia's countersanctions against the West—specifically the food imports ban—had an adverse impact on the Russian population, driving inflation up to 18 percent.

In the midst of a new crisis, the Russian economy was in a slump, although a much less profound one than in 2008: the drop from the precrisis maximum in mid-2014 to the crisis minimum in mid-2016 was "merely" 3.6 percentage points, as opposed to the ten percentage point drop during the 2008 worldwide financial crisis. Several factors accounted for the gentler fall. First, in contrast to the 2008 crisis, the demand for Russian raw materials continued to grow,[5] and the Russian mining industry grew at an annual rate of 1.5 percent. Second, in contrast to its 2008 practice, the Central Bank of Russia refrained from selling currency reserves at the be-

ginning of 2015, which sent the right signals to the economy, allowing it
to make less painful adjustments to the changed environment. Third, in
2012 Russia embarked on a massive campaign to rearm its military, which
was financed from the country's fiscal reserves. As a result, arms production grew 12–15 percent annually, propping up the whole manufacturing
sector. Fourth, agricultural harvests were at record highs three years in a
row (2015–17), lending momentum to food industry and grain exports. But
while the 2014–16 economic slump was less profound than the 2008–09
one, it lasted for eight successive quarters—much longer than the earlier
recession. The average annualized growth rate that Russia has struggled to
achieve since the second half of 2016 remain below 1.5 percent, indicating
that the forces that slowed the Russian economy from 2012 to 2014 are still
in effect. Moreover, moving from an economic decline to a growth trajectory is not a sign of recovery per se, since growth is the normal state for any
economy.[6] As Russia is an emerging economy, a full-scale economic recovery can be expected only when its economic growth starts running ahead
of global economic growth indicators. But only the most hopeless optimists
could promote this scenario now.

THE LOST DECADE

From a financial perspective, the Russian economic slowdown that first
clearly manifested in 2012 can be attributed to a decline in investment activity, and that in turn has a significant political dimension. Private investment has been steadily decreasing, and the statistical totals have been
sustained by means of grand-scale infrastructure projects paid for out of
the federal budget; some examples are the APEC summit in Vladivostok in
2012, the Sochi Olympics in 2014, the 2018 soccer World Cup, the Crimean
infrastructure, including the Kerch Strait Bridge, and the modernization
of the defense industry. These investments indeed improved the statistics
and hence the optics for investing, but they did nothing to expand economic potential or sustain growth.

Business requires investment. Private enterprise inherently gravitates
toward expansion into new markets and increased efficiency. To realize these

goals, businesses have to invest in growth. It's abnormal for businesses not to do so; nevertheless, such abnormal behavior often appears quite justifiable and rational in Russia.

Businesspeople contemplating growth and investment want to guarantee that they will be the ones to reap the benefits of their investments (whether by profit-taking or by enjoying the company's rising value). To protect their property, businesspeople need independent courts to secure equal protection for all, regardless of power or position or wealth. And to protect their interests, business owners need political competition to ensure that elected officials represent their interests. For political competition to work, business owners should have the opportunity to support politicians who are willing to protect their interests. And to do that, there must be a system of political checks and balances preventing narrow interest groups from monopolizing state power or resources. Business owners also benefit from independent media capable of revealing the malfeasance and corruption of politicians and government officials.

Today's Russia lacks all these things, but just twenty years ago the country seemed as if it had broken the communist deadlock and begun to build political institutions that would eventually yield a stable democracy. The lost decade for the Russian economy is a logical outcome of the political processes that have been unfolding in Russia since 2000. The country's movement toward democracy has stopped. The system of checks and balances was replaced by President Putin's power vertical, in which the president and his administration assign themselves the majority of government powers. Basic state institutions such as political competition, separation of powers, an independent judiciary, a federative state structure, and independent media have been virtually eradicated in Russia. This has created an unfavorable investment climate and has undermined property rights, which are at the basis of all economic activities. As a result, businesses were unwilling to invest in growth, bringing about the economic slowdown and stagnation.

Instead, Russia ended up with a nigh-omnipotent secret police, the FSB, whose permissiveness significantly exceeds that of the KGB, its Soviet predecessor. It ended up with a ruling political party eerily reminiscent of the Soviet Communist Party, with the presidential administration playing the role of the Central Committee and a circle of Putin's lieutenants and cronies acting as the Politburo. It ended up with a parliament where discussions aren't supposed to happen and whose future composition is known long before the elections. And finally, Russia has ended up with a parallel justice system that is prepared to sustain any charges against any individual if that's what the higher-ups want. Once again, Russian jails are home to hundreds of political prisoners, and Russian courts prosecute people for dissenting opinions.

———————

Vladimir Putin is both author and beneficiary of this gradual evolution of the country. In the course of his eighteen years in power, Vladimir Putin and his administration, the Kremlin, have made a plethora of choices, each of which has pushed Russia a little bit farther from the goal pursued by Putin's predecessor, President Boris Yeltsin.

In his brilliant memoirs Albert Speer, Hitler's architect and later Reich minister of armaments and war production, described his personal transformation by quoting the British physicist Sir James Hopwood Jeans: "The course of a railway train is uniquely prescribed for it at most points of its journey by the rails on which it runs. Here and there, however, it comes to a junction at which alternative courses are open to it, and it may be turned on to one or the other by the quite negligible expenditure of energy involved in moving the points." This metaphor fits perfectly the history of Putin's Russia: none of his decisions were radical or energetic enough to upend the country's transformation all at once, but Putin's actions have moved enough points along the way to shift the train gradually onto a track going in the opposite direction. This book is about those junctions—about the decisions that changed Russia and undermined its transformation and its economy. The early buds of democracy were first frozen and finally destroyed, to be replaced by authoritarian rule.

———————

In the closing days of 1999, a little-known figure became the acting president of Russia, and many of his later actions and decisions were shaped by his experiences during a very brief political maturation period.

Though Vladimir Putin easily won the presidential elections of 2000, he saw himself as fighting multiple enemies to do so. In battling real or imagined threats to his rule, Putin destroyed, piece by piece, Russia's unstable democracy, as well as its foundational checks and balances. Free speech fell first before his repressive tactics. Putin undermined the formation of the federative state in Russia by depriving the regions of any real power or finances and by depriving the Russian people of the ability to elect regional governors and city mayors. He put the judiciary system in Russia under his personal control and created a dual-track legal process in the country in which the courts are prepared to do the bidding of the government. He obtained control of the Russian parliament and regional legislatures. Block by block, Vladimir Putin built his "vertical of power"—the hierarchical management system that concentrates all powers in the hands of the president.

An important term that appears in many contexts is *siloviki,* from the Russian root "*sila,*" whose meaning combines "power," "force," "might," and "violence." The *siloviki* are a very important group in modern Russia that has colonized multiple governmental agencies, usually denoted by "law enforcement," that are empowered to use violence on behalf of governmental bodies—the police, the prosecutor general's office, the Investigation Committee, the Antidrug Service, and, most powerful of all, the FSB, or secret police. In general, *siloviki* make up the military-security services and promote a narrative of Russia under attack from internal and external forces, against which Russia must defend itself. This narrative has contributed strongly over the years to the formation of Russia's current defense posture, economic weakness, and an absconded rule of law. Vladimir Putin, lacking any public political experience before becoming president, looked for other ways to defend his authority, and settled on the exercise of raw power to deal with his opponents. In Putin's Russia, *siloviki* have de facto free rein to use their agencies' resources for personal benefit or violate the law to put pressure on ordinary people, political opponents, or business competitors; in many cases they do so not just for personal benefit but to fulfill orders handed down from the Kremlin or a local boss. Thus the history of Putin's Russia in the twenty-first century is very much aligned with the rise to power of the *siloviki,* replacing the oligarchs as Putin's inner circle of associates.

Doing business in Russia is risky. It's easy to lose one's property. In the final two chapters of the book I reflect on the effects of Putin's counterrevolution on Russian business and try to explain why Putin himself is powerless to defend business owners in Russia, even in cases in which he understands the injustices to which they are subject.

The stories recounted in this book speak to the enormous pressure placed on business owners by the Russian government: in all but one case, the business owners lost everything. Some of the companies in this narrative were big, others were small. Some were owned by Russian businessmen, others were major international companies. In all cases the Russian courts accepted the actions of the government agencies and provided no relief to the business owners; the imprisonment of the owners of private businesses became a standard means of seizing the business. All of these losses transpired during the rule of Vladimir Putin, who was personally involved in some of them. No parallel situation arose in the 1990s under Boris Yeltsin as president.

What these changes bode for the future of Russian economy is to some large degree unknown but can be speculated about, a task taken up in the conclusion.

One important disclaimer: I do not discuss Russian foreign policy, including the annexation of Crimea, the military conflict in eastern Ukraine, or the influence of Western sanctions on the Russian economy. I omitted discussing this face of events not because the events are of no importance but because doing so would have amounted to a distraction from my analysis of what happened with Russia.

Notes to Chapter 1

1. Such a comprehensive reform plan was prepared in the first half of 2000 at Putin's request by the task force headed by later economic minister German Gref. In 2010 Gref's deputy, Mikhail Dmitriev, said the plan was implemented by fewer than 40 percent, while its ideas on political reforms were not even included in the final version. Dmitri Krylov, "Progamma-2000 — Chto sdelano" [Program-2000: What was done] (https://iq.hse.ru/news/177674728.html).

2. Of course, no periodization is completely accurate; various factors come into play and stop working at different times, and many factors can be in play at the same time. Nevertheless, it is possible to highlight the most powerful factors in operation at a given time.

3. The crisis of August 1998 came about as the result of several economic factors that influenced the Russian economy at the same time: the Asian crisis, which exploded in the fall of 1997; the decline in oil prices, which started at the beginning of 1998; and the inability of the Russian government to impose tax discipline and collect taxes. As well, a couple of political factors affected the situation: parliament was controlled by the left opposition and rejected many legislative initiatives of the government, which blocked the IMF program, and in March 1998 President Yeltsin replaced his longtime political partner, Prime Minister Viktor Chernomyrdin, with the unknown Sergey Kirienko, who failed to get the support of parliament and public opinion.

4. In 2013, revenues from the production and export of hydrocarbons amounted to 50 percent of the overall revenues of the Russian federal budget, while VAT and excises on imported goods amounted to another 13.3 percent. See Federal Treasury of Russia, "Information on the Execution of Budgets of the Budgetary System of the Russian Federation" (http://roskazna.ru/en/budget-execution/the-information-on-execution-of-budgets-of-budgetary-system-of-the-russian-federation/6884/).

5. Crude oil exports grew 10 percent and coal exports grew 21 percent in physical terms in 2015–17.

6. History reveals only a few examples of a country's economy declining for more than two years in a row when it was not subjected to powerful factors such as wars, falling prices for major exports, debt crises, or a loss of macroeconomic stability.

Two

TRANSFORMATION DERAILED

The Decline of Democratic Reforms
and the Ascent of Putin

In the 1990s, Russia was going through the economic, societal, and governance transformation that had been set in motion even before Yeltsin became president of Russia and before the dissolution of the Soviet Union

To be successful, leaps from totalitarian systems toward democracy must be supported by structural reforms accepted by the electorate, not merely procedural changes. Boris Yeltsin worked on a very large stage: he sought to bring Russia in line with other democratic polities by relying on market reforms as the principal lever of transformation. His drive to change the very basis of the society also meant building from scratch the institutions by which society operates. The newborn institutions were weak, and their interactions were accompanied by friction occasionally severe enough to paralyze the process of governance. Nevertheless, by the end of Yeltsin's era the institutional framework in Russia had been created that procured the stability of the political system after the devastating financial crisis of 1998.

THE GRADUAL OPENING OF RUSSIA

While Boris Yeltsin is the towering figure most often associated with democratic reform in a Russia newly independent of a defunct Soviet Union, the actions of his predecessor, Mikhail Gorbachev, the last general secretary of the CPSU and the first and only president of the Soviet Union, to a large degree set the course. Looking for a way to accelerate economic growth and improve social conditions, Gorbachev introduced perestroika, or restructuring, an umbrella policy approach whose specific provisions included the limited private ownership of certain businesses; political reforms, including the first multicandidate elections; greater democratization; and the all-important glasnost, or openness, which increased personal freedoms enormously. Gorbachev's radical political reforms destabilized the balance of political forces and opened the door to strong nationalism while simultaneously paving the way to a true multiparty system. At the same time, his hesitations in effecting an economic transition resulted in the downward spiraling of the economy, which actually collapsed. The putsch attempt in August 1991, implemented by the proponents of the old system, accelerated the political process and de facto resulted in the demolishing of the Soviet Union. Conditions were thus at hand for the presidents of Belarus, Ukraine, and Russia (Yeltsin) to sign in December 1991 the accords dissolving the Soviet Union. Gorbachev resigned December 25. His efforts toward democratization and reforms would be picked up and further implemented by Yeltsin in a society gripped by rancor and nationalist fervor and elated by the continuing experience of freedoms so recently unknown.

As Russia's first president, Boris Yeltsin brought a complex mix of training and character traits to the business of moving Russia along the path of democratic reform. Though instinctively inclined toward reform, and perhaps the one figure capable of attracting and uniting like-minded, competent younger technocrats to oversee the different ministries, he was also the product of the Soviet nomenklatura system, an apparatchik, for whom personal connections were paramount to political advancement, but no one could be trusted very long, and the authority of a leader at any level went unchallenged. The result was a highly personalized presidency with uncertain, volatile, and temporary power-sharing arrangements. When Yeltsin first came to power, he relied not on the more senior representatives of the Soviet nomenklatura but instead on democratically oriented individuals who arose out of civil society. Though they had little to no experience with state or economic management, a deficit that later led to many problems with long tails, they were idealists: their beliefs and actions were motivated by the imperative of breaking sharply from the communist past and creating a new, democratic Russia.

Under Yeltsin, Russia saw the consistent (though largely intuitive and situational) development of a democratic (republican) government, based on checks and balances. The regions, or oblasts, acted as a counterweight to the federal center, as they were in control of the upper chamber of parliament, the Federation Council. The State Duma, the lower chamber of parliament—where Yeltsin never had a stable majority—acted as a counterweight to the president and the government. The judicial system, which enjoyed more power and freedom under Yeltsin, could challenge the decisions of the president, the government, and parliament. The media were released from state control to compete with one another and to support various political forces in the country. Though Yeltsin wielded great presidential power, he did not try to acquire more by restricting the authority of other institutions or branches of government.

The transformation of the Soviet Union was an unprecedented phenomenon in human history. The largest country in the world by territory and third largest in population disintegrated into fifteen parts. Of course, the collapse of major states had occurred in the past—ancient Rome, the empire of Genghis Khan, the British Empire—but these processes took years to decades. The collapse of the USSR in a historical sense occurred almost instantaneously—within several months. But in addition to its speed, the transformation of the USSR was distinguished by the fact that at the same time, enormous changes were taking place in other areas of life, all part of the transformation of a totalitarian Soviet state into a relatively democratic republic and the emergence of a market economy on the ruins of a planned one.

Russia, as well as other post-Soviet countries, could hardly inherit any part of the Soviet Union's governance system. Having chosen the path of democracy, Russia had to build from scratch all pillars of the new system, from its constitution and legislation to the parliament, federation, and judicial system.

Russia did not inherit from the Soviet Union any political structuring of society, and Yeltsin considered it appropriate to maintain factionalism within the power system, in both the legislative and the executive branches. Sure that Russia had to move forward on the path to democracy but uncertain of the steps, he solicited opinions from different aides he knew to be vehemently opposed to each other's views. During the Yeltsin era the Kremlin actively sought to build situational coalitions and use different combinations of partners to accomplish its political objectives. As an intuitive politician, however, Yeltsin could tolerate minor losses so long as he was consistently driving toward a larger strategic goal.

The factionalism Yeltsin actively encouraged worked against stability of personnel and policy, while his poor health and a disinclination to become directly involved in day-to-day decision-making allowed power to leach out of the center and into the hands of his political opponents. One by one, the first wave of democrats left the inner circle of the Russian president. Those departing included the acting prime minister and leader of the economic reforms Yegor Gaidar; Secretary of State Gennady Burbulis; presidential chief of staff Sergey Filatov and his deputy, Sergey Krasavchenko; Yeltsin's legal adviser and one of the main authors of the new constitution, Sergey Shahrai; and the long-serving foreign minister, Andrey Kozyrev, leaving none of the early architects of Russia's post-Soviet policies in place. They were replaced by more pragmatic functionaries who were focused more on defending their own political positions than on transforming the country.

The December 1995 parliamentary elections underscored the declining popularity of Yeltsin and his reformist efforts. Despite having adequate resources, the pro-reform, democratic factions in the Duma failed to unify and were unable to fend off strong challenges from conservative factions. The top vote-getter was the Communist Party of the Russian Federation, refreshed under the leadership of Gennady Zyuganov, leader of the opposition to the reforms. The CPRF took 22 percent of the seats, while the Liberal Democratic Party of Russia under the leadership of the ultranationalist Vladimir Zhirinovsky took almost 12 percent of the seats in the Duma. The various communist factions and their allies could now muster a vote total in Duma approaching a majority.

Yeltsin entered the June–July 1996 presidential contest at the back of the pack. His approval rating stood at around 4 percent at the beginning of the campaign, and many experts believed victory was practically guaranteed for the leader of the communist forces, Gennady Zyuganov. Fears of the communists coming to power in Russia and of the subsequent rollback of reforms led Russia's top figures in the business world to unite in support of Yeltsin, acting as sponsors and organizers of his campaign. This group included most prominently Vladimir Gusinsky, founder of the Media-Most empire of independent newspapers and television stations, and Boris Berezovsky, whose wealth came from seizing control of assets during the flawed privatization process. Through control of the media, they were able to present the electoral choice as one between Yeltsin and totalitarianism. Driven by these tailwinds in the popular press, Yeltsin, only slightly ahead of his rivals on the first round of voting, significantly widened the gap on the second round, taking 54 percent to Zyuganov's 40 percent, and was reelected president for a new term.

The intense election campaign, which stretched on for several months, undercut the health of the Russian president; he suffered a heart attack and underwent a quintuple bypass procedure in November 1996. After that, Yeltsin began to step back from an active role, transferring a significant part of his responsibilities into the hands of an informal association known as "the Family," which included most notably his daughter, Tatyana; presidential chief of staff Valentin Yumashev; his deputy, Alexander Voloshin, who became presidential chief of staff in 1999; and businessmen Boris Berezovsky and Roman Abramovich.

Shortly after the 1996 election, it became clear that Yeltsin would not run for a third presidential term in 2000, and the main political actors quickly set their eyes on the prize. By the spring of 1997 the field had consolidated into four political camps:

1. The communists retained their strong position in the State Duma, where, together with their allies (the Agrarian Party), they controlled about half of the seats.[1]

2. The governors of the largest and most economically powerful Russian regions, headed by Moscow mayor Yury Luzhkov, wanted to obtain more power in the federative country and to secure a bigger slice of the budget. By then the governors and chairs of the regional legislatures

were members of the Federation Council, the upper chamber of the Russian parliament.

3. The government, headed by Viktor Chernomyrdin, which relied on the support of the CEOs of the biggest industrial enterprises.

4. The "liberals," led by Anatoly Chubais and Boris Nemtsov, who had been nominated by Boris Yeltsin as the two first deputy prime ministers of the Russian government and to a large extent shaped the reform agenda.

None of the camps was powerful enough to defeat its opponents and consolidate power in its own hands. It was in the fight to gain traction that the country's political resources, distributed among counterbalancing institutions, came under the control of these groups as they pursued their personal goals. Individuals were able to seize control over institutions and thus personally determine those institutions' conduct. A major institution captured early by the oligarchs was the media, whose content was tilted to reflect the competing interests of different powerholders. As a result, conflicts, negotiations, and agreements between institutions became personalized, and democracy in Russia became very fragile. The seeds were sown for the derogation of the democracy-building effort in Russia.

REMOVING ALLIES

Several months after Yeltsin's victory in the presidential race, Russia's political and economic life was in a stable mood. Inflation was going down and the economy had started recovering, which allowed the government to concentrate on structural reforms. The business tycoons who had helped secure Yeltsin's second term got their prizes as well: under Anatoly Chubais's privatization regime, the government implemented a dubious loans-for-shares scheme that transferred into their hands the most lucrative pieces of state property. In exchange, the two major television channels, controlled by Gusinsky and Berezovsky, were supportive of the Kremlin and the government.

But this normalization did not last long: in the summer of 1997 the oligarchs, who had previously been united, were riven over a tasty prize. The triggering event was the privatization of a 25 percent stake in the national telecommunications holding Svyazinvest, one of the last big chunks of property the government intended to privatize. As was customary for the large privatization auctions in Russia between 1995 and 1996, the results were agreed upon in advance by the oligarchs, who avoided competing with one another. The government knew about this collusion, but Chubais, a free-market advocate and the person in charge of the privatization process, felt it was a price that had to be paid to obtain the support of Big Business in fighting "the hydra of communism." Gusinsky and Berezovsky allied (joined by Alfa group and Spanish Telefonica), forming a front company to purchase the Svyazinvest shares, but their rival, Uneximbank chief Vladimir Potanin, whose own consortium included the international financier George Soros, violated the agreement and outbid them.

In one swoop, oligarchic unity was destroyed. Gusinsky did not accept that the process had been conducted fairly, for Potanin, who had stepped down from his position as deputy prime minister to enter the auction, had access to budgetary resources unavailable to other bidders, a result of significant federal customs funds being held in an account at Uneximbank. Chubais, for his part, decided to roll back his previous policy, declaring that businessmen had to begin living according to the new rules, and refused to revise the auction results.[2] Humiliated, Gusinsky threw his support to Moscow's mayor Yury Luzhkov, who held conservative views and had been speaking openly of his presidential aspirations. At the same time, Gusinsky's media holdings, which included the highly influential television channel NTV, changed its attitude and started regularly criticizing the government. In the autumn of 1997, the Russian media published financial documents proving that Chubais and some of his colleagues, also members of the government, had received large payouts for an unwritten book about the history of the Russian privatization effort. This situation was untenable for Yeltsin, who fired Chubais from his post as finance minister, leaving his position as deputy prime minister untouched, and dismissed others involved in the scandal from the government. Although Yeltsin himself continued to trust Chubais, the latter's political position was severely weakened by the episode. The public support for the "liberal camp," led by Chubais, fell off, and its political influence has not been restored in the ensuing years. The liberals were the most pro-democracy political bloc in Russia supportive of Yeltsin's policies. As they lost their role in checking and balancing the aggressiveness of the three other camps, the consolidation of power moved forward.

When Boris Yeltsin, anticipating leaving the Kremlin in 2000, began to look for a politician to succeed him, there were no best choices. Although he had close and friendly relations with Prime Minister Chernomyrdin, whom many saw as Yeltsin's natural successor, the Russian president in the spring of 1998 began to have doubts about Chernomyrdin's ability to consolidate the government; at the same time, Yeltsin was becoming more and more jealous of Chernomyrdin's rising political popularity. In March 1998 Yeltsin decided to cut the knot and opted for another unpredictable decision: he fired Chernomyrdin's government, removing the second powerful piece from the political chessboard, a figure who had played an important role in building political stability in the country. After that he had no allies but only opponents in the political arena—communists and governors—who started the hunt for the top position in the country.

Yeltsin's authority was further weakened by the severe economic crisis, which owed partly to the decline in world oil prices but mostly to weak fiscal discipline. In August 1998 Russia devalued its currency and defaulted on its debts. This caused a severe political crisis, as a result of which Yeltsin made significant concessions to the leftists, appointing Yevgeny Primakov the next prime minister. Primakov, a former member of Gorbachev's Politburo and inner circle, strongly criticized the economic reforms of 1990s and was supported by the communists. As it turns out, Yeltsin in choosing Primakov unwittingly contributed to an alliance between the government and the Duma.

By the end of 1998 it had become clear that the economy was swiftly emerging from the crisis: first, the bitter pills swallowed in August 1998 finally proved to have been good medicine, and second, Primakov's government didn't veer from the path laid down by his predecessors, steadily implementing the painful measures. Contrary to expectations, Primakov did not advocate a return to a more Soviet-like economic policy but instead undertook strong macroeconomic stabilization efforts both conventional and unconventional, such as the freezing of wages and pensions, significantly reducing the budget deficit, and restructuring both domestic and foreign state debt. Although Primakov's policy looked more like that of the technocrats, the left-wing majority of the Duma saw it as a victory for their side. The need to make significant decisions on a daily basis to address the consequences of the financial crisis, as well as Yeltsin's diminished role, made Primakov an even stronger political figure. At a certain point, Primakov himself began to consider the possibility of becoming the next Russian president, and mentioned that idea to Yeltsin and others. "I'm prepared to act as president for two years, and then maybe Stepashin could replace me," he said.

Intentionally or not, he attracted opponents of the current president, who came to view him as a potential replacement for Yeltsin. By the beginning of 1999, the Federation Council had joined the alliance of the left-wing Duma majority and the government. Regional governors, being members of the Federation Council, were looking for solutions to many of their regions' problems in Moscow. In a country where the budgets of most of the regions depended on transfers from the federal budget, the principle of "he who has the gold makes the rules" was in full effect. The governors were visiting the Kremlin less and less often, turning instead to the prime minister.

In the fall of 1998, the Russian prosecutor general Yury Skuratov secretly opened an investigation into charges of corruption against the head of the Administrative Department of the Presidential Administration and Yeltsin's daughter.[3] The investigation was based on documents provided by a Swiss official, but as the Russian prosecutor general's office asked its counterpart in Switzerland to conduct searches, the media learned of the case. The Kremlin decided to fire Skuratov. The presidential request to dismiss the prosecutor general had be approved by the Federation Council, which had come together in opposition to the president and was strongly against this idea—only six out of 178 voted to approve Skuratov's dismissal, while 142 voted against it. That was one of Yeltsin's most stunning rebukes. Recognizing favorable political winds, Skuratov addressed the Duma, looking for more political support. The lower chamber passed a resolution (lacking any legal force) supporting him, with 233 deputies (out of 450) voting in favor.

On April 21, 1999, Aleksandr Voloshin, then presidential chief of staff, addressed the Federation Council on Yeltsin's behalf, arguing for the prosecutor general's dismissal, but his speech was unconvincing, and he was unable to give clear answers to questions.[4] The Federation Council vote against the president once again (79-61). The following day Voloshin accused Prime Minister Primakov, the Federation Council chairman, and Yury Luzhkov, Moscow's mayor, of orchestrating the president's defeat in the matter of the prosecutor general's dismissal. Voloshin blamed Primakov, saying he had begun an open campaign for power: "The failure to remove Skuratov from office strengthens Primakov, who is already transparently working on his own behalf." He promised "to take serious measures" against the Duma and the government if they continued to "destabilize the situation."

Voloshin was right. Luzhkov and most influential regional governors had definitively turned against Yeltsin. The day after the Federation Council vote they established their own political bloc.[5] The governors openly declared their intentions: to form a party capable of winning the State Duma elections in December 1999. "We want to become a shield [protecting Russia] that will gain a majority in the Duma, and then be able to form a government," said Tatarstan's president and regional heavyweight Mintimer Shaimiev.[6] Personal ambitions and jealousy prevented the governors from elevating one person from among their ranks (they had eighteen co-chairs), and they couldn't pass over the current prime minister in their search for a new leader. In the evening of the day the governors' bloc was established, Luzhkov held a two-hour meeting with Primakov, forging an alliance that would pose the greatest threat to the Kremlin in the following months.

In parallel with the consolidation of regional elites in opposition to Yeltsin, in the spring of 1999 the left-wing majority in the Duma launched another offensive against Yeltsin, attempting to impeach the president. The impeachment process was initiated in the Duma in May 1998; five accusations, largely political in nature, were made against Yeltsin.[7] This may have been why the left-wing majority hesitated for a long time before bringing the matter to a vote, being unsure it would receive the necessary support. By April 1999, these doubts had begun to fade. On April 21 the State Duma overcame the resistance of the presidential administration[8] and adopted changes to its regulations governing the voting procedure. This gave the green light to officially discuss impeachment in the Duma session on May 13, 1999.

The political situation was strained to the breaking point. A confrontation between the president and the coalition of both chambers of parliament, the government, and the governors was inevitable. There was now a loaded pistol on the political stage, and it would have to go off.

WINNER TAKES ALL

It was a decisive moment in the political struggle between the two sides, with both prepared to wage a final battle. Nevertheless, it was the Kremlin that emerged victorious, using tactics that its opponents had failed to foresee. From that point on, first the political initiative and then the support of the population began to turn in favor of the Kremlin.

Two days before the impeachment vote,[9] Yeltsin dismissed Prime Minister Primakov and appointed Sergey Stepashin, first deputy prime minister and former interior minister, in his place. This step marked the beginning of the transfer of power to the political successor of the incumbent Russian president. The main problem was that the Kremlin had no clear successor, and the range of potential candidates was small. Boris Yeltsin's popularity was at an abysmal level. Most politicians and experts believed that, with the Luzhkov-Primakov alliance gaining strength, Yeltsin had lost the will to continue the political struggle and intended to quietly retire from power at the end of his term in mid-2000. The only candidates Yeltsin and the Family could look to were two men under direct command of the president, the head of the police and the head of the secret police—Sergey Stepashin and Vladimir Putin.[10]

In his memoirs, Boris Yeltsin said he chose Putin from the very beginning and that the promotion of Stepashin was a ruse. Yeltsin's daughter draws a different picture: after his nomination as prime minister, Stepashin turned out to be weak and indecisive. Though Stepashin was a longtime ally of Yeltsin who had served in various positions, Yeltsin was unpleasantly surprised by his poor arguments when asked to guess "what the boss thinks." Putin seemed much sounder, with clear views that he was ready to defend, and was not afraid to contradict the president. It was the latter who won the sui generis primaries and thus became prime minister in August 1999, when Boris Yeltsin named him his political successor. On the same day, Vladimir Putin announced his acceptance of Yeltsin's proposal and declared he would run for president in 2000.

PUT YOURSELF IN PUTIN'S SHOES

As Russia's first democratically elected president, Yeltsin had both to introduce democratic reforms to a country that had not known democracy in living memory and to show the populace what the presidency of a democratic country should look like. But after the severe political crisis of 1993, the presidency in Russia was overly strengthened in the new constitution, which gave the incumbent additional powers and provided fewer checks and balances for other institutions. But as the strategic goal for Yeltsin was to lead Russia out of its communist past and transform it into a normal democratic country, facing resistance from the parliament, regions, judiciary, or media, Yeltsin did not try to redistribute political power in his favor, being prepared to make concessions and compromises and even accept tactical defeats to achieve his strategic aims.

The Russian president has a constitutional right to nominate and fire *siloviki,* including heads of the police and secret police services, at his own discretion, as well as to change the structure of the governmental firing and nominating of ministers and deputy prime ministers in agreement with the prime minister. This change represented perhaps the most significant fault line in the system of checks and balances under which the newly democratized country was struggling to get on its feet. Yeltsin's practice of seeking countervailing opinions from his ministerial and administrative appointees also led to shifting or absent policies, weakening any sense of a coherent policy. In his second presidential term (starting in mid-1996) Yeltsin introduced an unofficial exercise of presidential power by unelected people—family members and advisers—that became the default way of running the country whenever he was incapacitated.

By May 1999, Yeltsin and his inner circle had been backed into a corner. The president had no support from either chamber of parliament; the regional leaders had all come together to disparage him and his politics; and the prime minister and the mayor of the country's capital had joined forces to create a political group that sought total victory in the upcoming parliamentary and presidential elections. Yeltsin was left with two choices: he could either accept the appearance of a political opponent who would come to power, or he could try to transfer power to a successor. Yeltsin saw the first option as a personal political defeat—a communist revenge that would erase everything he had done to transform the country. What is more, the sharp criticisms his opponents leveled at him and members of his family raised serious concerns about their physical safety. Being a man unaccustomed to defeat, Yeltsin chose the second path. He believed that the transfer of power to his successor would ensure the continuance of his transformation of Russia.

In the spring of 1999, Vladimir Putin was the director of the Russian secret police, which was just emerging from the fog of the post-Soviet period. The future president was right in the thick of things and, of course, took part in heated discussions in the regnant atmosphere of hostility and hatred for one's opponents; he considered real and imaginary threats, developed plans to fight his opponents, and sought methods to defeat his enemies.[11] As the head of a powerful agency, one with expertise in spying, gathering compromising information, and intimidating, blackmailing, and pressuring targets, Putin was confident that the ends justified the means. He therefore used the power of the secret police to attack the opposition from all sides. The Kremlin, seeing no other effective means of fighting back, accepted these methods and decided to build victory on the basis of violent suppression of its opponents.

In accepting Yeltsin's offer, Putin clearly began to consider his future position. An almost random confluence of events had brought Putin to the top of the political pyramid—in three years he had climbed the Russian bureaucratic pyramid from a lowly position as ex-deputy mayor of the second-biggest city in the country to the prime ministerial position. He had never been a politician, participated in elections, or sought a political career. His limited experience in public politics was not a success: in 1996 he was in charge of the election headquarters of his boss, St. Petersburg mayor Anatoly Sobchak, who failed to win a second term in office. The political consultants surrounding Putin, and Yeltsin himself, assured him he wouldn't have to do any campaigning. But for Putin, this was a cause for even greater concern: if as an unknown functionary he could become president of the country, what were his battle-hardened opponents capable of? And how would he be able to hold on to power, surrounded by so many enemies and threats?

Putin didn't like losing any more than Yeltsin did. With a clear understanding of who his opponents were, and who could threaten the stability of his presidency when he came to power, Putin immediately began to fight them, attempting to co-opt or weaken competitors and eliminate former allies who posed credible threats. His use of power against his opponents was not constrained by any boundaries. Putin had limited understanding of the art of political life and negotiating skills but good knowledge of how to fight his adversaries. He started using a stick-and-carrot policy, along with credible threats to his chief rivals, to secure his position, and he succeeded in part because of the absence of an effective anchoring of the presidency in other institutions of governance. In each of his actions against adversaries, Putin limited their independence and constrained their constitutional rights while extending his presidential authorities. All that contributed to eroding the institutions of the republic and the federation, loosening the supports for democracy and undermining the basis for sustainable long-term economic growth.

Notes to Chapter 2

1. "Vybory — 1995: Itogi i uroki" [Elections 1995: Results and lessons]. Nasledie
.ru, March 3, 1995.

2. Petr Aven, "Anatoliy Chubays: 'Asimmetrichnyy otvet' (1997–1998 gg.)" [Anatoly Chubais: "Asymmetric answer" (1997–1998)], Snob.ru, January 28, 2016.

3. At the same time, in January 1999, the prosecutor general's office initiated a
criminal case against Boris Berezovsky on suspicion of embezzling funds from
Aeroflot, thereby acquiring yet another powerful and influential opponent.

4. Inertia drew out the business of the prosecutor general's dismissal for several
more months, but it was no longer a key element of the political process. The Kremlin
appointed Yury Chayka acting prosecutor general, and Skuratov was banned from entering his workplace or making any official decisions (though he continued to receive a
salary, which was delivered by courier to his house each month). On October 13, 1999,
the matter of Skuratov's dismissal was again brought up for a vote in the Federation
Council, and the Kremlin lost again: even fewer senators voted aye than in April—52
in total. But this no longer seemed of great concern to anyone. On December 1, 1999,
the Constitutional Court of Russia ruled that the president had the right to temporarily remove the prosecutor general from office without the approval of the Federation
Council if a criminal case was opened against him or her. Three weeks after Vladimir
Putin was elected president, the Federation Council approved the dismissal of Skuratov (133-10 in favor).

5. "Kto ob'edinyaetsya" [Who is uniting], *Kommersant* 69, April 23, 1999, p. 3.

6. Irina Holmskaya, "Vot i 'Vsya Rossiya'" [That's "All Russia"], *Kommersant* 69,
April 23, 1999, first page.

7. The disintegration of the USSR, the dissolution of the parliament in 1993, the
war in Chechnya, the collapse of the army, and the genocide of the Russian people.

8. According to Aleksandr Voloshin, the Kremlin had no chance of achieving a
positive outcome for itself through a vote on this issue, but, thanks to the situational
majority in the Council of the State Duma, for several weeks it was able to block the
imposition of this issue at the general meeting of the chamber. A YouTube video of Voloshin speaking at the Moscow School of Civic Education in 2013 is available at www.
youtube.com/watch?v=9ijsxdfe0hq.

9. Impeachment failed. Five charges were presented for a vote by the Duma. The
maximum number of aye votes went to the war in Chechnya—283, which was seventeen fewer than required.

10. In Russia, the police come under federal authority; regional and local police are
structural units of the Ministry of Interior (MVD). Later in this book, "police" is used
as a synonym for the MVD or "militia" (the name for the Russian police before 2011).

"Secret police" is used synonymously with "FSB" (Federal Security Service), whose Soviet predecessor was the KGB.

11. At a certain point, according to Yeltsin's daughter, Prime Minister Primakov did attempt to remove Putin from his position as director of the secret police for his refusal to intercept the telephone conversations of the leader of the opposition party, but he couldn't gain Yeltsin's support on the matter. Tatiana Yumasheva, "Kak Primakov pytalsya uvolit' Putina" [How Primakov tried to dismiss Putin], LiveJournal.ru, March 15, 2010.

Three

THE KEY ELEMENT OF CONTROL

Freedom of Speech

We've never had free speech in Russia, so I don't really understand what there is to "trample on."
—Vladimir Putin[1]

Reform would have been impossible in the USSR without freedom of speech. Right from the start, Soviet territories were cut off from the rest of the world by the Iron Curtain. The Soviet system rigorously restricted citizens' access to information about all events, whether domestic or foreign, past or present. Soviet leaders believed that limiting people's access to information was the key to maintaining a stable system and a docile population. Individual expression could always be twisted to show that citizens were harming the state, and dissent was punished without due process.

In February 1986, before any sign of reform had appeared on the horizon, Mikhail Gorbachev said, "Greater transparency [*glasnost*] is an essential measure for us. . . . Without transparency, there can be no democracy, no political initiatives from the masses or participation in government." Though legal censorship wasn't abolished in the USSR until August 1,

29

1990, Gorbachev's words in the spring of 1986 marked a clear policy shift. Previously banned works, including Aleksandr Solzhenitsyn's account of the system of labor camps, *Gulag Archipelago*, and Boris Pasternak's anti-socialist-realism novel *Doctor Zhivago*, were published without reprisals. Movie theaters began screening films that had been gathering dust on shelves for more than a decade. In the fall of 1986 the Soviet Union stopped blocking Voice of America, Radio Liberty, BBC, and Deutsche Welle broadcasts. By the spring of 1989, there was complete freedom of speech in the USSR.

Indeed, free speech played an important role at significant turning points in the at first gradual, then more rapid collapse of the Soviet system. For example, in November 1987 the entire country learned about a candidate for Politburo membership, Boris Yeltsin, and heard his critique of the current state of affairs. In the spring of 1989, again thanks to freedom of speech, the USSR held its first (and last) competitive elections, for the Congress of People's Deputies, the Soviet parliament. In June 1991, Boris Yeltsin became president of the Russian Federation, with support from many independent media outlets, which provided voters with detailed coverage of his campaign.

It was thus entirely appropriate, though coincidental, that one of the first laws passed by the Russian parliament after the dissolution of the USSR was the law "On the Mass Media." This law established the main principles to guide the work of the media and created what were deemed at the time secure foundations for their independence. On the strength of this law, many new federal and local newspapers, magazines, and television corporations emerged in the 1990s. When the Soviet Union fell in 1991, 3,353 magazines and 4,863 newspapers were published in Russia, representing a wide range of viewpoints. By 1996 there were 27,000 print publications.[2]

Freedom of speech on television lagged only slightly behind freedom of expression in print media.[3] All television channels in the USSR were state-owned, and even the arrival of perestroika and glasnost didn't break up that monopoly. In January 1994, Yeltsin privatized one federal television station after an informal tender with two participants. This was followed by the appearance of the television channel NTV, which focused on news and political analysis. At the end of 1994, Yeltsin transformed the biggest state-owned federal television channel to the joint-stock company ORT (Obshchestvennoye Rossiyskoye Televideniye, Public Russian TV) and, though retaining a 51 percent stake in it for the government, handed over its management to journalists. In January 1997, yet another private channel, REN-TV, began national broadcasts, airing many news and politics programs. Cable television was widespread in newly constructed urban homes by the mid-1990s, and the first Russian satellite television system, NTV+, was launched in February 1999.

Thus, despite Putin's assertion, there was widespread free speech in Russia, dating even to late Soviet times.

The situation today is quite different. Reporters Without Borders in 2018 ranked Russia 148 (out of 180 countries evaluated) on its Press Freedom Index, describing the country as having a "stifling atmosphere for journalists."[4] Several journalists were in jail; others had been murdered. The path from the free expression of dissent to the risky business of practicing free speech shows the complex intertwining of politics and law in post-2000 Russia. The Kremlin's relentless pursuit of news and popular media underscores the centrality of free speech to a democratic republic and thus the Putin regime's need to wind it back into the state, to absorb the media within its power vertical.

ENEMY NUMBER ONE: THE MEDIA TYCOON

The Russian media had two major problems at the beginning of the 1990s: a politically polarized society (divided over questions of maintaining the Soviet Union, the introduction of market reforms, and the role of parliament versus that of the president), and a lack of financial resources (due to hyperinflation and no advertising market). These problems had two major consequences: first, media companies needed to find "sponsors"—budgetary financing (particularly at the regional level) or wealthy businessmen—to support them, and second, the powerful Russian businessmen (oligarchs) who emerged in the 1990s began using their media to support their interests in commercial disputes and influencing government policy. The most powerful figure in the Russian media was undoubtedly Vladimir Gusinsky, whose central business holding, Media-Most, included the popular NTV. The latter was a pet project on which he lavished time and attention, sometimes down to the smallest detail.

From the start, NTV was a pro-presidential company, extensively covering Yeltsin's goals for reform and supporting the politicians working to implement those goals. This is not to say that NTV slavishly praised state officials; the anchors didn't hesitate to discuss controversial issues or criticize the government, which was good for attracting new viewers. The satirical show *Kukly* (Puppets) mercilessly skewered senior Russian politicians for their missteps and foibles. Nonetheless, there was never any real doubt about where the channel's sympathies lay. The situation changed radically after Gusinsky lost a bid to buy shares in Svyazinvest in mid-1997: NTV began to sharply criticize the government and the liberals within it, destroying their political support and popularity.

The Kremlin's attitude toward Gusinsky and his media holdings shifted dramatically over the course of 1998. Media-Most began to turn its critical eye on the Kremlin, where "the Family" was acquiring an ever-larger role in decision-making. In the Kremlin, meanwhile, doubts about Gusinsky's loyalty were growing, with enthusiastic assistance from Boris Berezovsky, whose relationship with Gusinsky was marked by competitiveness and jealousy. When the political crisis hit in the fall of 1998, Gusinsky thought that President Yeltsin had lost all genuine authority and placed his bets on Moscow's Mayor Luzhkov, whose influence was growing. After Luzhkov formed an alliance with Prime Minister Primakov, the pair received "most favored politician" treatment from NTV and Media-Most in general.

The Kremlin's "total war" against political opponents began at the same time as the active search for Yeltsin's successor got under way in the spring of 1999. The Kremlin's main target and most powerful adversary was naturally the Luzhkov-Primakov alliance, as the pair had made no secret of their political ambitions. Though Primakov was removed from his position as prime minister, he remained very popular in Russia, and his chances at the presidency had not significantly decreased. The Kremlin needed to undermine his popularity, which was bolstered by Gusinsky's media resources.

The attacks on Gusinsky started in May 1999, three months before Yeltsin zeroed in on Putin, and were initiated by the presidential administration. Media-Most had taken on a great deal of debt to finance its expansion. Gusinsky's underlying business strategy was to build a major company whose shares could be sold to investors, but he lacked the time to do so. The financial crisis of 1998 made shares in any Russian company impossible to sell. Media-Most received the bulk of its loans from banks and companies with state ties; Gazprom was its largest creditor.[5] This leverage put Gusinsky in jeopardy, which he first felt when the state-owned bank VEB, at the Kremlin's request, refused to extend a loan previously granted to Media-Most. Aleksandr Voloshin, presidential chief of staff, defended this action by arguing that it was unacceptable for a media company funded by the state or state-owned companies to criticize the current government or support its opponents.[6] Gusinsky tried to repay the loan by transferring government bonds to VEB, but the bank refused to accept them as repayment, and the banking accounts of Media-Most and NTV+ were frozen by court order. This marked the first time the Kremlin used court orders to attack a business, but not the last: they became the main instrument used to pursue Gusinsky. At this stage, however, it seems that the Kremlin didn't want to take over Gusinsky's company, only to pressure him into changing his position.

This attack ceased temporarily in the summer of 1999, when the Kremlin was focused on the final stage of "Operation Successor." Moreover, for a time, Gusinsky believed he could come to an agreement with Vladimir Putin after the latter's appointment as prime minister.[7] This hope proved illusory, however, largely because NTV continued to assert its independence from the Kremlin, actively criticizing the government in connection with the outbreak of the Second Chechen War. Putin, who was personally leading the Russian military operation in Chechnya, saw this as unacceptable and characterized all criticism of the war effort as an attempt on behalf of Russia's enemies to undermine his personal authority.

Aside from the fact that Russian military actions in Chechnya this time were better planned and executed, the Kremlin was also able to shift public opinion in its favor. While most Russians had an extremely negative view of the actions of the Russian authorities in the First Chechen War (1994–96), during the second campaign the sympathies of the people were with the Russian military. This was in part a completely understandable public reaction to the terrorist attacks that had occurred in several Russian cities, including Moscow, killing hundreds of civilians. But to a much greater extent the change in public opinion was the result of the Kremlin's active role in directing media coverage of the military operations. The authorities were both better and more efficient at supplying official information in a timely manner; they also deployed significant resources against critical journalists.

Gusinsky's NTV was the only federal television channel providing independent coverage of the war and the only one frequently criticizing the actions of the Russian military. From his days in the FSB, Putin had information that the CIA and Islamic radicals from Saudi Arabia supported the Chechen rebellion, and he saw attempts by the Russian media to provide fair and balanced coverage of the military conflict as an obstruction of national interests.[8] In this landscape, the Kremlin extensively condemned such coverage as anti-Russian and unpatriotic. The adversarial nature of the relationship between Gusinsky and the authorities intensified after NTV reported on the failed bombings of residential buildings in Ryazan (110 miles east of Moscow), including some evidence that the bombings had been staged by the FSB. Putin, a graduate of the FSB's predecessor, the Soviet KGB, considered these reports an attack on the FSB and on himself personally.

The final break between Putin and Gusinsky occurred after their meeting in September 1999. In the spring of 1999, the government gave $100 million in subsidies to ORT, and Gusinsky asked Putin to provide similar funding to NTV so that the station could cover the run-up to the Duma elections of December 1999. Putin, according to Gusinsky, promised nothing during their meeting, saying only that he "would think about it, would settle it later." The next day Putin called Berezovsky and accused Gusinsky of blackmailing him by threatening that NTV would campaign against him in the elections if the government didn't provide funding.[9]

After this episode, Gusinsky was public enemy number one, both to the Family and to Putin personally, who brought the might of the state to bear against the businessman. State-owned banks closed their credit lines with Most Bank, owned by Gusinsky. The Russian Central Bank imposed restrictions on the bank's daily activities, and in the late autumn of 1999 it publicly proposed selling the bank for a symbolic $1 to the state-owned VTB bank. The loss of the bank robbed its parent company, Media-Most, of financial support and put it in an extremely vulnerable position. The Kremlin immediately took advantage of this: state-owned banks and companies that had issued loans to Media-Most began demanding repayment, simultaneously employing court orders to block the bank accounts of Gusinsky's companies.

During the December 1999 Duma elections, the Kremlin was engaged in a fight with the communists and the Fatherland–All Russia (OVR) political bloc, headed by Luzhkov and Primakov. The election results fully reflected the unstable political situation in the country. The communists, while officially winning the election, lost about a third of their seats in the lower chamber of the Russian parliament, as well as their ability to create even a "situational" majority. The OVR bloc, which had led the polls since the summer, unexpectedly fell behind at the finish line, receiving only half the votes it had counted on just a month before.[10] The pro-Kremlin bloc, Unity, coming in second in the proportional vote and only 1 percent behind the communists, was not able to secure more than nine (out of 225) seats in majoritarian districts, and its overall presence in the Duma was less than 20 percent.

Surprisingly to many, the Kremlin agreed to establish a parliamentary majority with the communists, the Liberal Democratic Party of Russia, and a group of independent deputies. As a result, OVR received no serious representation in the Duma's leadership and recognized its political defeat, declining to nominate a presidential candidate for the March 2000 elections. The position of OVR's leader, Luzhkov, was dramatically weakened, while his partner, former prime minister Primakov, retired from active political life. (Putin later promoted him to the chairmanship of the Russian Chamber of Commerce.[11])

The defeat of the Luzhkov-Primakov alliance stripped Gusinsky of political support. Nonetheless, he directed his media to attack Putin and his entourage, including the FSB, which had already become a major supplier of staff to President Putin. Gusinsky, in his own words, hadn't fully comprehended the drastic changes in the political situation. He still believed that owning the most powerful information resource in the country was the best way to guarantee his security.[12] By this point, Putin had made the decision to remove Gusinsky from the political scene. To accomplish this goal, he promised "to put him in his place," and accepted that this would require Gusinsky to be stripped of control over his media holdings.

Five weeks after Putin's inauguration, Gusinsky was arrested on trumped-up charges. He faced a choice: imprisonment or the sale of Media-Most to Gazprom. He opted for freedom and signed a promise to sell his assets.[13] The battle for control of NTV continued for a few more months; the Kremlin used a wide range of tools, from unfounded criminal charges and falsification of court rulings to raids and seizure by force. It was an unequal fight. By mid-April 2001 the Kremlin had established full control over Gusinsky's media holdings, with Gazprom being its new owner of record.

Vladimir Gusinsky left Russia in 2000 and has yet to return.

The Kremlin allowed NTV to maintain a significant degree of editorial independence until the end of 2002. However, after the terrorist attack in Moscow in October 2002, when more than 900 people were taken hostage in the Dubrovka Theater and 174 died during the assault on the building orchestrated by the FSB, Putin personally launched a new attack against the television channel. He accused NTV, without evidence, of reporting from the scene and broadcasting over live television the movements of the commandos just before they stormed the building. At Putin's demand, the management of the television company was replaced, putting NTV programming firmly under the control of the Kremlin.

TOO DANGEROUS TO HAVE SUCH A FRIEND

Boris Berezovsky, *l'enfant terrible* of Russian politics, was undoubtedly one of the most noteworthy and powerful players on the scene in the second half of the 1990s. It's difficult to come to a single, unitary conclusion about his actions; he was a talented opportunist in both business and politics. He was also skilled at thinking unconventionally and at gaining wide support for his plans.

That was how he managed to gain control over Russia's largest television channel in 1994. The popularity of the state-owned Channel One was dropping, and the advertising market had not yet developed enough to support a channel with a news-heavy broadcast schedule. The state, stuck in a permanent budget crisis, could no longer support several federal television channels and accepted Berezovsky's idea to create a public-private partnership by giving him a 49 percent stake in ORT in exchange for private funding for the company's activity. Boris Yeltsin's daughter Tatyana Yumasheva described the deal: "The government had little understanding of television at that point, of how it could influence viewers. Berezovsky did understand. He was one of the first to realize what it could do. . . . His business colleagues, somehow agreeing [with Berezovsky] that he understood politics better than they did, entrusted him with the management of Channel One. And so he gained a powerful means of influence."[14]

Although Berezovsky did have close ties to the Kremlin, frequently taking part in discussions and planning political initiatives, he was also eager to be a creative force rather than just a participant, and sought to carve out an independent place for himself in the history of Russian politics. He wasn't afraid to criticize the Kremlin's plans behind closed doors, or even publicly oppose them. According to Yeltsin's daughter, Berezovsky made his first serious attempt to influence political decisions prior to the events in Chechnya in 1994. He was horrified when he saw that the government was going to try to resolve the conflict in Chechnya through armed intervention. Berezovsky was steeped in nineteenth-century Russian history, especially that detailing the empire's wars in the Caucasus, and he brought several books on the subject to Aleksandr Korzhakov (head of the presidential security service), Viktor Ilyushin (senior aide to the president), and anyone else he could access. In these meetings, he predicted the terrible outcomes of the approaching conflict: it would last years, if not decades; it would be a catastrophe for Russia; it would spill out of Chechnya across the entire region, and so on. No one took him seriously. Nearly everyone who reported to the president on the Chechen situation and who had analyzed various possible scenarios believed that a Russian military operation in Chechnya would bring the region under control in a matter of weeks or, at worst, a few months.[15]

In the spring of 1998 Berezovsky convinced a charismatic Russian general, Aleksandr Lebed, to run against the Kremlin-backed incumbent in the Krasnoyarsk region gubernatorial elections. Lebed won the race with a margin of 20 percent. "Berezovsky triumphed. The president's administration and the White House [residence of the Russian government] . . . suffered an ignominious defeat," wrote Yumasheva.[16]

After Putin's official appointment as prime minister in late August 1999, Berezovsky managed with great difficulty to convince Voloshin, presidential chief of staff, to sponsor the establishment of a new political bloc before the Duma elections that the new leader could rely on. Voloshin didn't see this as a top priority, but Berezovsky wouldn't let the matter rest. He visited ten different regions and found several influential governors who opposed

Moscow's Mayor Luzhkov and ex-prime minister Primakov. These governors agreed to join the efforts of the Kremlin to set up the Unity bloc, whose successful showing in the 1999 Duma elections allowed the Kremlin to tip the balance of power in the Duma in its favor.

In addition to his role in the founding of Unity, Berezovsky played a decisive part in the coverage of the election campaigns. Under his management the ORT television channel was unequivocally on the Kremlin's side and mounted a vigorous attack against the OVR political bloc and its leaders, Luzhkov and Primakov. ORT programs used such dirty tricks that Yeltsin's daughter strongly objected: "I found it unacceptable for the government to be using such methods. But Sasha [Voloshin] couldn't be dissuaded; he thought he had to do everything he could to make sure that neither of them came to power."[17]

After the Duma elections, the political forces in Russia underwent rapid realignment. Berezovsky, like Gusinsky, failed to grasp the reality of the shifting political landscape. The Kremlin dialed back its involvement with Berezovsky, who wasn't aware that Putin and his advisers were developing the idea of the power vertical and thought he could continue playing an active political role. It was indeed a dangerous game he was playing. Berezovsky decided to demonstrate his power and do everything he could to complicate Putin's victory in the presidential race. He launched a campaign on ORT "against everyone,"[18] which could have led to the elections being declared invalid.[19] Putin furiously castigated Berezovsky's gambit: "There are some political figures who are trying to push this society, the population, into undermining the elections. . . . To what end? To make the situation in the country worse, the economic situation worse. . . . This position is destructive and lacking in foresight."[20]

On the one hand, Berezovsky had extensive connections to the Russian political elite, controlled a major national television channel, and had been a key figure in laying the foundations of Putin's path to power. On the other hand, in the eyes of the new Russian president, Berezovsky's resources and creativity made him a real danger.

Putin and the Kremlin grew tired of Berezovsky, of his constant desire to nudge events in a direction beneficial to him. The presidential administration was prepared to cut off all ties, owing to the oligarch's extensive political interventions and his unwillingness to settle into place in the power vertical already established within the Kremlin.[21] But they still needed Berezovsky, if only to finish dismantling Gusinsky's media empire. Although the prosecutor general's office and Minister of Information Lesin[22] were the main forces behind this attack, Berezovsky couldn't pass up the chance to weaken his competition—but he never stopped to consider whether he might be the next target. According to Voloshin, "Two or three months before the events of that summer [Gusinsky's arrest], Berezovsky asked the prosecutor general to investigate Gusinsky's ties to Chechen militants and terrorists."[23]

In mid-2000, Berezovsky's main political instrument was ORT, and Putin moved quickly to establish control over this resource. Berezovsky managed ORT, but the state owned a controlling stake in the company (51 percent), while Berezovsky owned 49 percent. It was therefore simple enough to remove Berezovsky—just a matter of waiting for the right moment. The trigger for the attack on Berezovsky was the *Kursk* submarine accident in August 2000. The Russian navy initially failed to give Putin a full briefing on the situation, and the president continued his vacation at his seaside residence in Sochi for several days after the incident before returning to Moscow.[24] Such inappropriate behavior at a time of tragedy aroused strong criticism throughout Russian society, and ORT became a leading voice in the backlash. None of this criticism was unfounded. The navy had lied publicly about the causes of the catastrophe and had refused to accept foreign assistance when it proved unable to save the crew on its own. But it was unacceptable to Putin that a television channel owned by the state and funded from its coffers would dare to criticize his actions and behavior as commander in chief. As Yeltsin's daughter put it, "[Putin], in the end, finally got fed up with it. And Aleksandr Voloshin, whom it is practically impossible to upset, also got so furious he was ready to eat him [Berezovsky] alive."[25]

Putin was entirely unwilling to accept the personal criticism, which he saw as a betrayal, and demanded that Berezovsky be stopped. Voloshin explained the Kremlin's logic: "Everything has to come to an end sometime. The situation surrounding the *Kursk* accident was so dramatic, and the position of the journalists under Berezovsky's control was so odious, that it was clear: Berezovsky's informal control of [ORT] couldn't continue. . . . That was my only goal in meeting with Berezovsky—to explain to him that his management of ORT was over . . . and I did. . . . I only requested that he stop managing the journalists. . . . That was all we wanted. Everything we asked for, we got in the end—Berezovsky was deprived of his influence and was never able to get it back. . . . After all, Berezovsky's authority was unofficial. He would call journalists, call Ernst [the CEO of ORT]. And these phone calls had never been formalized in any way in the charter [of the company]." "Berezovsky was so upset by the loss of [ORT] that he wanted to hear it from the president directly, and asked me to set up a meeting with Mr. Putin. I said that I couldn't promise it, but that I would tell Putin. I did, and to my surprise, he agreed: 'Go ahead, set it up. I'll tell him personally what I think.' They met, very briefly. . . . The president confirmed that Berezovsky was no longer to have any influence over [ORT] or the channel's journalists."[26]

While Voloshin repeatedly emphasized that he and Putin only spoke about "ending the influence" Berezovsky wielded at ORT, another participant in the process, Roman Abramovich, was more straightforward: "I was asked to buy those shares [the stake in ORT belonging to Berezovsky]." "If the president or Voloshin had asked me not to buy [ORT] shares, or if I had sensed that they were opposed, I wouldn't have gone anywhere near it."[27] One year later ORT was rebranded as Channel One, which removed the very important word "public" from its name.

Berezovsky didn't like losing and decided to try to get revenge by using another television channel, TV-6, which he had bought previously. In April 2001 he hired many former NTV journalists who had refused to work under Gazprom. TV-6 was quickly transformed from an entertainment channel into a political one, and its ratings doubled, topping 16 percent of all Russian television viewers by the end of 2001. But for the Kremlin, this was just another indicator that Berezovsky was a dangerous political opponent and that the information space in the emerging autocratic regime needed to be controlled by the state. In September 2001, the pension fund Lukoil-Garant, which owned a 15 percent stake in TV-6, filed a lawsuit to liquidate the company, though neither the shareholder itself nor any of the counterparties had any financial claims against the company. By mid-January 2002, TV-6 had been liquidated by court order.[28]

Berezovsky made one more attempt. In mid-2002 he set up a new channel, TVS, which was to be funded by several Russian businessmen, none of whom owned enough shares to exercise unilateral control. The TV-6 journalists migrated there, but this project failed within a year of its launch for lack of funding and conflict among shareholders. That was the last attempt to establish a federal news television channel independent of the state. From this point on, Russian news television became fully controlled by the Kremlin (see figure 3-1).

In November 2000, criminal charges were brought against Berezovsky.[29] He left Russia and never returned, dying in the U.K. in 2013. Though Berezovsky tried to influence Russian political life from abroad, his clout swiftly dissipated to the point that he ceased to be a real political player in Russia. Putin had successfully removed Berezovsky, his closest ally early in his political life, from the Family and from the political chessboard.

FIGURE 3-1. **Death of Independent Television: Shares of News Channels Viewed by the Moscow Television Audience**

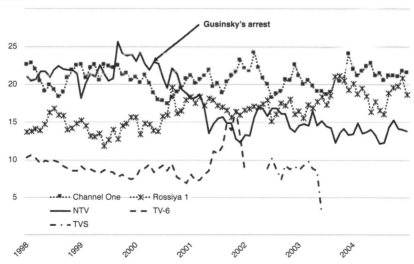

Source: Data provided by Video International.

NEW FEARS

By the middle of his first presidential term, Vladimir Putin had consolidated political power in Russia, but this did not ease his anxieties about the stability of his reign. The Kremlin had grown accustomed to fighting and found it difficult to shift into a different gear; Putin's staff continued to warn him of new threats.

After becoming president, Putin was eager to demonstrate that he was taking an active role; he traveled frequently around the country and held a great number of meetings. However, his administration soon noticed that the state-run media were not used to such a fast tempo of presidential events and were failing to keep the population informed of Putin's activities. To address this problem, the Kremlin's chief of staff began to hold weekly meetings with the editors in chief of state media outlets, where he covered the president's plans, upcoming trips, and initiatives currently in the works at the Kremlin. The nature of these meetings began to change gradually in the first half of 2003: the attendees "began to receive political assignments, they started to go after people," one former Kremlin expert reported. "It was said that we had enemies, and ways of using information to take them down were discussed. The transformation happened without me noticing it, either."[30] The Kremlin's efforts to shape the news and information landscape gradually became a campaign against free speech.

During his second presidential term, Putin recognized that he had failed to co-opt the liberal politicians, led by former prime minister Mikhail Kasyanov and the 1997–98 deputy prime minister Boris Nemtsov. Having supported Putin during his first presidential term, the liberals began to criticize him after Khodorkovsky's arrest and the nationalization of Yukos. As the liberals lost elections to the Duma in 2003—partly because of a poorly managed electoral campaign and partly because of vote tabulation fraud—they had no other way to demonstrate but to hold public rallies and meetings protesting Putin's policy and actions.

The Rose Revolution in Georgia in the autumn of 2003, the Orange Revolution in Ukraine in 2004–05, and the Tulip Revolution in Kyrgyzstan in March–April 2005 shocked Putin; he was still talking about these events a decade later.[31] His entire worldview had been shaken to its foundations:

legitimate governments had been overthrown by the crowd. Aside from the presence of "the hand of the West"[32] in all these cases, he perceived that independent television channels had played an important role in consolidating the political opposition. The fear of a Russian color revolution was fueled by the protest actions commencing in 2005, dubbed the "Marches of Dissent." These protests united opposition groups from both the right and the left that were not represented in the State Duma.[33] Fearing the threat of a similar popular uprising in Russia, the Kremlin stepped up its pressure on the political opposition and attacks on information resources not controlled by the state.

THERE IS NO HIM WITHOUT CRONIES

Television is still viewed as the main source of news for a majority of the Russian population, while for more than a half of Russians television remains the sole source of information (see figure 3-2). By the mid-2000s, second-tier television players had begun gaining popularity; their coverage of political life provided a broader range of opinions, and, unlike the state-controlled television channels, they didn't have to pull their punches when it came to giving airtime to critical viewpoints. Therefore, gaining control over the country's newly emerging popular independent television channels became a priority for the Kremlin, which was focused on avoiding the threat of a color revolution.

But the Kremlin also recognized that the nationalization of these media sources would not be a good idea. Doing so would be costly to the public treasury and would also increase competition among state officials, possibly leading to a split in the ruling elite. By the mid-2000s the Russian economy was booming, and the growing advertising market was finally able to provide a sufficient revenue base for television channels. As in many other industries, one of Putin's personal friends rose to the top of the media sector. Yury Kovalchuk obtained beneficial ownership of Gazprom-Media Holding, which had absorbed Gusinsky's media assets (including NTV), and began to build his media empire.[34]

REN-TV was the most active privately owned channel in terms of political

FIGURE 3-2. Consumption of News Sources in Russia

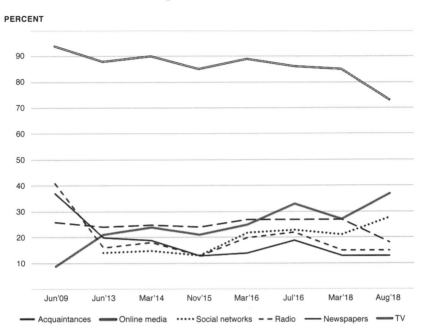

PERCENT

Source: Levada Center, "Kanaly informatsii" [Information channels] (Moscow, September 13, 2018) (https://www.levada.ru/2018/09/13/kanaly-informatsii/).

news coverage by mid-2000. Until 2000, the main shareholder of REN-TV was the oil company Lukoil. After Putin came to power, Lukoil wanted the channel to stop broadcasting political news, sparking a serious conflict with the channel's management that ended only when Lukoil agreed to sell its 70 percent stake. According to the agreement, a group of individuals headed by one of the leading reformers of the 1990s, Anatoly Chubais, was to buy the shares. In reality, however, the shares were purchased by the subsidiaries of the energy monopoly RAO UES, of which the state owned a 51 percent stake and Chubais was the CEO.

Chubais, even though he was the manager of a large state monopoly,[35] at that time never concealed the closeness of his ties with the liberals, whose activities REN-TV covered in detail. After starting its attack on the liberals, whom Putin suspected of organizing a color revolution in Russia, the Kremlin began to pressure Chubais to change the profile of REN-TV. The urging gradually evolved into an order to sell the company. To increase pressure on

Chubais, a special law was passed prohibiting RAO UES from owning media outlets. In October 2005, REN-TV was sold to a consortium of investors,[36] and its managers, Irena and Dmitry Lesnevsky, were forced out. Immediately thereafter the key employees of the channel's information service were laid off, and the number of entertainment programs on the broadcasting schedule rose sharply. By 2007 a controlling stake in REN-TV had been transferred to Kovalchuk.

Before the end of Putin's second term, Kovalchuk's National Media Group (NMG) acquired management rights over another major television channel previously owned by the St. Petersburg city authorities, Petersburg–Channel 5.[37] Three months earlier the channel had received national status by Putin's presidential decree—that is, its signal was now broadcast throughout the country, and, with the transition to digital television under way in Russia, it was included in the television package delivered to all households in the country for free.

From 2008, when Dmitry Medvedev became president, all Russian television channels with news broadcasts were under the Kremlin's control, either directly through state ownership, as in the case of Channel One and Rossiya, or indirectly through ownership by state-controlled companies, as with NTV, or by Putin's cronies, such as REN-TV and Petersburg–Channel 5. Independent television companies were scared to air political or news stories, concentrating on local issues only. This provided the Kremlin with total control over the information space and seemingly allowed it to relax its grip: there were now no credible challenges to the integrity of the television information blockade. As Putin said, "There is no way back to the TV that existed in those times [the 1990s]. That time has passed. It does not exist anymore. It will not come back. Forget it."[38]

SELF-CENSORSHIP

Though the traditional media outlets—radio, newspapers, and magazines—in Russia obviously could not compete with television and didn't pose a significant threat to the Kremlin's propaganda supremacy, any strong criticism of the Russian authorities was immediately followed by a Kremlin-based attack against its source.

In September 2002, the *Limonka* newspaper, published by the leader of the National Bolshevik Party, Eduard Limonov, was closed by court order. The Ministry of Press and Mass Communications claimed the newspaper had abused its media freedoms and violated the law "On the Mass Media." It was alleged that *Limonka* articles were intended to incite intolerance and hatred and included war propaganda and calls for the violent seizure of power and for changing the constitution.

In November 2002, FSB officers entered the offices of the newspaper *Versiya*, seized its computers, and halted publication. According to the managers of *Versiya*, the FSB's aim was to prevent the publication of a story about the Dubrovka Theater terrorist attack that contained an analysis of the actions and errors of the special forces during the storming of the building.

In February 2003, the editor in chief of the newspaper *Novye Izvestiya* (owned by Berezovsky) and his deputy editor faced criminal charges for embezzlement and were dismissed from their positions. The criminal case was transferred to the court eighteen months later, which sent the case back for further investigation; beyond that its fate is currently unknown.

In July 2003, Duma member and deputy editor of *Novaya Gazeta* Yury Shchekochikhin was fatally poisoned. He was known for his investigations into illegal activities by law enforcement agencies. The results of the autopsy and details of Shchekochikhin's illness were classified and hidden from his family.

In September 2004, on orders from the Kremlin, the editor in chief of the newspaper *Izvestia*, Raf Shakirov, was dismissed. The reason for his dismissal was the publication of an issue completely dedicated to the events in the Ossetian town of Beslan, the largest terrorist attack in Russia up to then. In that incident more than 1,200 people, mostly children, were seized and held hostage at a local school. As a result of the ill-planned storming of the school building, 333 people were killed, including 186 children. The Kremlin tried to hide the scale of the tragedy in every way, fearing mass protests. The publication in Moscow of a story about the attack, including many photographs, by one of the country's most prominent newspapers was apparently too much for the authorities to bear.

In many respects, singling out dissident media outlets for punishment was an effective solution. By this time the Russian judicial system had completely lost its independence and was unwilling to protect either the media or individual journalists. Businessmen who owned media resources did not want to suffer the fate of Mikhail Khodorkovsky and were prepared to dismiss managers and journalists at the slightest hint of displeasure from the Kremlin. However, this system of media control was reactive in nature: it could only respond to publications and reports after they had already seen the light of day. The Kremlin wanted to prevent damaging reports and dissident publications from appearing at all.

The ideal solution to this problem, of course, would have been to restore the kind of censorship the USSR had maintained. But after a decade and a half, Russian society had grown accustomed to life without such a system, and no one could figure out a way around that problem. Total censorship is also very costly, as it necessitates maintaining an omnipresent security apparatus tasked with eliminating all public dissent, hardly a viable prospect in today's open technology-driven world. What is more, total censorship might lead to total suppression of critical viewpoints. This was not desirable, as it would eliminate all safety valves for the controlled venting of public frustrations. Recognizing this, the Kremlin decided to go another route: enacting numerous vague legal regulations that encouraged the media to engage in self-censorship or to backtrack if a news report went too far. This "rule by law" approach became one of the most frequently used instruments of the Kremlin in imposing various restrictions. By keeping the legislature under its full control, the Kremlin could pass a law in a matter of days, allowing it to immediately punish opponents for criminal violations. In the case of the media, the goal was to spread uncertainty and fear among journalists, forcing them to keep their mouths shut.

One of the most important milestones on this course was the law "On Countering Extremist Activity," adopted in the summer of 2002. The law contained a very broad and vague definition of "extremism," making it a convenient tool for selective application by state media-monitoring agencies and the courts. According to this law, the state has the right to withdraw a media outlet's license if that outlet receives two warnings within a year for violating restrictions on the dissemination of extremist information. At the same time the law imposed criminal penalties (including imprisonment) for supporting, financing, or participating in extremist activity. Later, this article (no. 282) of the Criminal Code would be regularly invoked to punish dissent.

Another law adopted in July 2003 gives the state the right to suspend the activities of media outlets if they violate election law. According to this law, ordinary media coverage of campaign events can be deemed a violation of the law if the election commission believes that a journalist "crossed the line between journalism and direct participation in the election campaign of any candidate." Journalistic publications can also be classified as unpaid advertisements on behalf of a candidate. According to a law adopted in July 2006, the activities of a media outlet can be suspended if the outlet's materials "publicly justify terrorism and other extremist materials." Such vague wording means the law can be used to prohibit any criticism of the Kremlin or of the government.

By mid-2007, the Kremlin was in full control of the information space in Russia, a necessary step for maintaining stability and retaining power in the country. During Dmitry Medvedev's presidency (May 2008–May 2012), the Kremlin continued to amend legislation to encourage self-censorship by the media. The weekly meetings of the presidential administration with managers of state-controlled media became compulsory for editors of all the major media outlets. At those meetings, Kremlin officials listed "taboo" topics. A "stop list" was drawn up at these meetings for Russian television channels: this was a list of people (mainly political opposition leaders and experts critical of the current regime) who should not be invited to speak on television programs. In June 2010, the state media-monitoring agency acquired the right to demand that online media sources remove or edit certain comments on their websites if in the agency's view they violated the law. Editors could be held criminally responsible for refusing to comply.

ATTACK ON THE RUNET

But when in August 2008 the financial crisis led to a sharp economic decline, the Kremlin had to reorient its agenda in the media sector to focus on economic issues. In 2010–11, President Medvedev attempted to implement a soft and inconsistent set of political reforms, which led to the creation of new public forums—such as Open Government and the Expert Council— that began to discuss openly the major challenges facing the country and sometimes included representatives of the liberal opposition in their work. Thus in the last year of Medvedev's presidency, the Kremlin's grip over the information space, including federal television channels, somewhat loosened.

In December 2011, Russia held parliamentary elections. Only seven political parties were allowed to participate, each of which had agreed not to criticize the regime during the campaign. Although United Russia had all the state's information resources behind it, the Kremlin-sponsored party failed to secure a majority. Observers identified numerous instances of flagrant vote-counting fraud, which provoked massive opposition protests in Moscow and the regions. Some 120,000 people took to the streets in Moscow, more than at any time since 1991. The Kremlin was taken by surprise. President Medvedev, having refused to meet with the leaders of the protests, did announce some liberalization measures related to federal and regional elections. Though the momentum of the protests had dissipated by the spring of 2012 and Putin was comfortably reelected as president without any significant competition, the fear of a Russian Orange Revolution reemerged in the Kremlin, causing the regime to tighten its grip once more and to launch a new series of attacks against free media.

The Kremlin's total control over Russian television news made it possible to restrict free speech and the dissemination of information; only topics approved by the Kremlin were allowed to be discussed, and only 100 percent loyalty to the Kremlin's politicians and experts was allowed to be shown on television screens. And as everyone knows, if it's not on television, then it didn't happen. But the television-viewing audience was ageing (see figure 3-3). The younger generation was looking for alternatives, which became available as a result of new technologies. More than half of television viewers in the age bracket eighteen to fifty-five years prefer to watch entertainment channels, while almost three-fourths of those older than fifty-five prefer to watch state-controlled television channels, which carry a lot of information and propaganda.[39]

From mid-2000 on, the rapid spread of internet access throughout Russia, which accelerated under Medvedev,[40] resulted in the emergence of multiple online media sources, which played an increasingly significant role. Though television still remained the leading news source in the country, in the largest cities, for those younger than twenty-five, and for the highly educated,

FIGURE 3-3. **Shares of Individual Age Categories in**
Total Television-Viewing Audience (Age 18+) and
Internet Penetration (Age 16+) in Russia

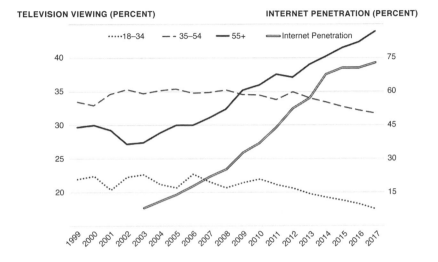

Source: Video International, "Internet v Rossii: Dynamika proniknobeniya. Vesna 2017 g."
[The internet in Russia: Penetration dynamics, spring 2017] (http://fom.ru/SMI-i-internet/13585).

Note: The sum of the various categories is not equal to 100 percent because the chart does not show the proportion of viewers under the age of eighteen.

online news sources were as important as television (see figure 3-2). Since the Kremlin had effectively cut off nonloyal politicians' access to television, the opposition turned to online media. The Kremlin was well aware that social media were a key tool for coordinating protests during the Arab Spring and in Russia in the winter of 2011–12. From 2012 on, the Runet (as the Russian-language internet is known) was regarded as a serious threat to the Kremlin's information control and became the primary target of the Kremlin's attacks against the media.

In the fight against the Runet, "rule by law" was the Kremlin's main approach: new laws and new penalties for violating old ones became so common from 2012 to 2014 that, by all appearances, regulating free speech was the top item on Russian legislators' agenda. On the Runet, traditional methods of restricting free speech were too slow and ineffective, as the Kremlin had learned. Thus its tools for suppressing free speech online were nonjudicial in nature: threats and administrative pressure on website owners and authors and a simplified mechanism for blocking information sources.

After the law restricting rallies and demonstrations was strengthened in 2012, legislators also introduced measures making editors personally responsible if their publications contained information about unauthorized public events.[41] Individuals posting information about such events on social media could also be held criminally liable. A year later, the prosecutor general's office acquired the power to request that the state media-monitoring agency block, without court order, access to news sources, websites, or social media accounts that included calls to participate in unauthorized mass demonstrations, or just posted information about such events.

Thus a law supposedly aimed at "protecting children from information harmful to their health and development" legalized censorship on the Runet: the state media-monitoring agency was granted the authority to draw up a blacklist of sites containing "harmful" information at its own discretion, and to block sites included on that list.

In its drive to control the flow of information, the Kremlin went so far as to push a "law on bloggers," which forced bloggers who had more than 3,000 daily visitors to comply with the kinds of regulations that normally applied only to larger news outlets. The state media-monitoring agency was instructed to keep an official registry of these bloggers, who were required to submit personal information about themselves to the agency. The law was passed in such a hurry that there were initially no penalties for violations, and the limit on readership—3,000 visitors per day—was so low that the registry would have had to include tens of thousands of bloggers. Furthermore, the vast majority of these bloggers had no connection to politics, and their posts posed no danger to the Kremlin. It was clear to everyone that the law was unworkable, but the Kremlin protested vigorously when lawmakers in the Duma began to call for its repeal, which finally occurred in 2017, after the second try.

An upsurge of public protests renewed Vladimir Putin's old fears of America's designs to change the Russian political regime, and he directly accused the U.S. secretary of state, Hillary Clinton, of giving a nudge to the Russian opposition.[42] This time the Kremlin saw the West's financing of the Russian opposition as the main threat. Since it failed to find any support for these al-legations, the Kremlin decided to act in a way that proved the truth of Václav Havel's adage, "If a country is governed by lies, the truth is the opposition."

In the middle of 2012, the Duma passed some amendments to the law on NGOs, conferring the pejorative label "foreign agent" on organizations that engaged in political activities while receiving foreign financing.[43] Apart from the insult that came with the term, the organizations subjected to the new law were obligated to hand over excessive amounts of reporting documents to the Justice Ministry. Just as with many other laws, the concept of "po-litical activities" was defined very vaguely, which made it possible to apply the term to any organization. In 2014 the Constitutional Court deemed the law on foreign agents constitutional and held that activities whose "aim is to influence the decisions of government bodies and their policies," includ-ing the influencing of public opinion, qualify as political. As a result, more than 100 organizations became subject to this law. Their ranks include the election monitor Golos Association; International Memorial, which collects and disseminates information on the Soviet political repressions of the 1920s to 1950s; and the Levada Center, a public opinion research center that also mostly collects and disseminates information.

The amendments to the law on personal data collection adopted in July 2014 required that all internet companies collecting such data must keep it on servers located on Russian territory. Of course, the main emphasis of this law was targeting global social networks, and the first of them, LinkedIn, was banned in Russia in August 2016 for refusing to comply with this require-ment. Russian authorities keep pressing other global companies—Facebook, Twitter, Amazon—to comply with that requirement, threatening to block them in Russia. In April 2018 another social network, Telegram, was banned in Russia for refusing to provide its comprehensive security codes to the Rus-sian secret police.

In December 2013 another law, dubbed "Lugovoy's law" after the person who poisoned Aleksandr Litvinenko with polonium in London in 2006, gave the prosecutor general's office the right to request extrajudicial blocking of websites that "contain appeals" to engage in extremist activity or public dem-onstrations organized in violation of established rules. The same day another law was passed imposing criminal penalties for "appeals to the effectuation of the activities violating the territorial integrity of the Russian Federation."

TABLE 3-1. Methods of Restricting Free Speech in Russia, 2011–17

NUMBER OF CASES

Type of restriction	2011	2012	2013	2014	2015	2016	2017
Administrative pressure, threats	173	208	514	1,448	5,073	53,004	22,523
Restriction of access	231	609	236	947	1,721	35,019	88,832
Court order	—	124	624	72	7,300	24,000	2,196
Criminal prosecution	38	103	226	132	202	298	411
Imprisonment	—	—	—	—	18	32	48

Source: AGORA, "Internet Freedom 2017: Creeping Criminalization" (http://en.agora .legal/fs/a_delo2doc/16_file_AGORA_Internet_Freedom_2017_ENG.pdf).

Those indistinct norms allowed almost unlimited application of the new laws. As a result, restrictive measures have been employed more and more frequently over the past six years, and especially after the annexation of Crimea and the start of the war in eastern Ukraine (see table 3-1). Websites that had become popular platforms for opposition politicians and critical journalists, with tens of thousands or even hundreds of thousands of visitors per day, were placed under government lock and key. In March 2014, at the request of the prosecutor general's office, the government media-monitoring agency blocked access to three popular opposition online media sources, Grani.ru, Kasparov.ru, and Ej.ru, though none of these media received any written notice explaining what the precise complaints were and what they should do to be unblocked.[44] But the website pages of ordinary social media users with subscribers in the single digits felt the heat as well. Government authorities formulated "standard" allegations against online sources, streamlining the process of implementing restrictive court rulings; there were forty times as many court decisions in 2016 as in 2013.

In May 2015 the new law gave the government the extrajudicial right to recognize "undesirable" foreign and international organization, force their liquidation, and expel foreign staff from the country. In 2015–18 George

Soros's Open Society, the National Endowment for Democracy, the National Democratic Institute, the International Republican Institute, and ten other organizations were declared undesirable by the minister of justice.[45]

In November 2017, Lugovoy's law was extended to allow the blocking of websites containing materials of undesirable organizations, as well as "information allowing obtaining access to all mentioned." According to this stipulation, any citation or reposting, even of very old information, could fall afoul of the law. Though the law on undesirable organizations covers only international and foreign entities, in December 2017 the network of Russian web resources linked to Mikhail Khodorkovsky (such as Open Russia, Open University, and Open Law) were declared linked to undesirable organizations and were blocked.[46]

A TRIED AND TRUE TOOL

Once, when asked about the loss of free speech in Russia as it had existed in the 1990s, Putin answered that the idea was to eliminate full freedom but not to create fear.[47] For a while, it seemed as though he might be able to maintain this balance. But it soon became clear that the methods that had been used to constrain traditional media were not getting the job done in the case of online sources of information: the owners of blocked sites were creating mirror websites located outside Russian jurisdiction, and social media users were sharing techniques for getting around bans. The Kremlin faced a choice: either it could admit it could not effectively control online media or it could try more heavy-handed measures. The first option would have signaled a decisive change in Kremlin policy with respect to free speech and would undoubtedly have required a substantial liberalization of the entire political regime, which was unacceptable to Putin. So the repression of political opposition figures and their supporters was the logical next step in strengthening an authoritarian regime in Russia. Before 2012, repression in Russia was applied mainly to those participating in demonstrations, and the primary form of punishment was a short administrative detention of five to fifteen days. Afterward this practice changed: ordinary Russians began to face criminal prosecution for the expression of personal opinions.

Political repression in modern Russia, though on a much smaller scale than that seen in Stalin's Great Purge, plays a similar role and has been no less effective. Like the Great Purge, modern political repression is system-based and represents essential institutional components of the political system. The goals of modern political oppression similarly resemble those of the Great Purge: obstructing free speech, eliminating political opposition, and keeping the political regime stable. Both forms of repression combine persecution of individual leaders with wide-scale pressure on ordinary people. The tools of repression are different today, but the nature of the activity remains the same.

In Stalin's era, large populations were concentrated in the cities and near major enterprises, but the state did not have the ability to track citizens electronically or reach them using tools of mass propaganda, particularly in rural areas, where most of the population still lived. To restrict freedom of speech and prevent potential actions against his regime, Stalin used mass repression to warn all Russians about the consequences of dissidence, not to mention being in opposition. The lists of victims were drawn up based more on quantity than on precision and comprised often randomly selected representatives of different social, professional, or ethnic groups.

In today's Russia, the Kremlin views mass political protests as a threat arising from participants in certain types of civil and political activity: from those Russians who actively participate in protests and demonstrations, from those distributing information about events taking place domestically and abroad that do not fit the image presented on state television, and from those actively criticizing the actions of the government. As these people don't work together, Stalin's methods of intimidation would be ineffective in Russia today. The Kremlin instead instrumentalizes the law to combat this threat: numerous changes to existing laws and vaguely worded new laws enable the Kremlin to dispense administrative and criminal penalties for specific types of political action. Ordinary citizens account for the majority of those hit by these repressions, but that is actually the point of such measures: the state chooses to make examples of a small number of ordinary Russians to sow fear among those who do not share the Kremlin's narratives. The idea is that the persecution of a select group will intimidate the rest.

The Kremlin's decision to use more repressive tactics was inspired by the turbulent events of the first half of 2014. At the end of February, Ukraine's president Viktor Yanukovych was removed from power after large-scale street protests. Putin had no doubt that the protests in the Ukrainian capital had been instigated by Western governments in the hope that the protests would spread to Russia. Discussion in the Kremlin focused on the new wave of pressure on Russia, the geopolitical conflict with the United States, and the use by Western forces of tactics of "hybrid warfare," including economic sanctions and "information aggression."

"Certain Western politicians are already threatening us, not just with sanctions, but with the prospect of worsening internal problems. I'd like to know what they mean: the actions of some kind of fifth column, national traitors?[48] Or do they think they can negatively affect socioeconomic conditions in Russia and thereby provoke discontent in the populace? We see such statements as irresponsible and unquestionably aggressive," said Putin in a speech at the Kremlin announcing the annexation of Crimea.[49] The notion that America was engaging in information warfare subsequently became a running theme in presidential addresses. "We see that certain countries are trying to use their dominant positions in the global information space to achieve military and political aims, as well as economic ones. They are actively employing information systems as instruments of so-called 'soft power' to serve their interests,"[50] he said in October 2014 while discussing Russia's Information Security Strategy. That document directly stated that one of the main threats to Russia was "the use of information and communication technologies . . . as 'information weapons' in military and political conflicts . . . aimed at discrediting the sovereignty [and] . . . interfering in the internal affairs of sovereign states, and inciting disorder."[51]

Soon after Putin spoke of "national traitors" and a "fifth column" in Russia, parliament and state-owned television stations began to host discussions about creating lists of Russian politicians and media figures who held undesirable (to the Kremlin) views,[52] and placards began to appear on the streets of Moscow and other Russian cities demanding reprisals against them. With the rise of this Kremlin-instigated hysteria, it was a simple enough matter to set the engine of repression in motion; many Russian laws were written so vaguely that a person could be sentenced not only for publishing his own writing but also for reposting someone else's material, including photographs or scenes from films.[53] As a rule, those who criticized Russian politics or Putin personally received criminal sentences; those who opposed the annexation of Crimea or supported the Ukrainian authorities in the military conflict in eastern Ukraine were treated with particular severity. But sometimes even supporters of the Russian government found themselves caught up in the engine of repression.[54]

Figure 3-4 shows a marked increase in repressive activity after 2014, and on a scale unprecedented in post–Soviet Russia. Against the general backdrop the number of persecutions on political grounds may seem insignificant (about 100 per year), but this number is comparable to the level of repression in the Soviet Union from the mid-1970s on.[55] By mid-2018, fifty-three people were in prison as a result of politically motivated prosecutions, another 269 were in temporary detention, and forty were under house arrest or restricted in their movements. The number of people sentenced for different types of social network activity exceeds 200 annually.

FIGURE 3-4. Number of Prosecutions (Criminal Cases and Convictions) on Political Grounds in Russia, 2011–August 2018

NUMBER

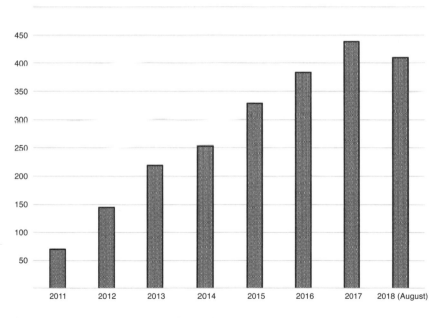

Source: PolitPressing.org (www.politpressing.org).

Note: The figure shows the number of people prosecuted in a given year. If a prosecution lasted several years, it is registered in each of those years.

JUST BUSINESS

In its struggle against political opponents and free speech, the Kremlin hadn't forgotten that the media not only were useful tools for influencing public opinion but could also be financially profitable as well. Thus much of the state's effort was directed not toward eliminating independent media resources but toward convincing them to adopt a different agenda, which could be done quite easily by putting pressure on their owners. In March 2014, for example, the Kremlin demanded that Aleksandr Mamut, owner of Lenta.ru, a leading information portal at the time, fire his editor in chief and senior journalists for their harsh criticism of the Crimean annexation.

At the end of 2013, the FSB demanded that Russia's most popular social networking site, VKontakte (In Contact), hand over personal data for the authors and administrators of two dozen groups of Ukrainian users. The CEO and founder of VKontakte, Pavel Durov, refused to do so, saying that Russian jurisdiction didn't extend to Ukrainian users. Durov publicly spoke about the pressure the FSB had put on him personally and decided to sell his shares in the company. "But I don't regret anything," he said. "Protecting people's personal data was worth that, and a lot more."[56]

Soon after that, the prosecutor's office requested that Durov ban hundreds of user groups on his social network, including Alexey Navalny's group. The businessman categorically refused to carry out this demand. "Neither I nor my team are going to participate in political censorship. . . . The free dissemination of information is an inalienable right in a postindustrial society. Without this right, there's no point for VKontakte to even exist," he said, after which he resigned and left Russia.[57] "I'm out of Russia and have no plans to go back. . . . Unfortunately, the country is incompatible with Internet business at the moment. . . . I'm afraid there is no going back . . . not after I publicly refused to cooperate with the authorities. They can't stand me."[58]

Six months later, Mail.ru, a company belonging to billionaire Alisher Usmanov, a close associate of Prime Minister Dmitry Medvedev, acquired sole ownership of VKontakte. Russian *siloviki* had no further trouble blocking groups or accessing the personal data of site users after that. Most cases of criminal prosecution for publications on social networks involved defendants who were registered on VKontakte. Mail.ru, which owns VKontakte, created a special position in the company, deputy CEO, who is in charge of supplying users' personal data, their activity, location, and connections to *siloviki* upon request, even if those requests are not supported by a court decision.[59]

At the end of 2015, Mikhail Prokhorov, one of the country's wealthiest businessmen and then owner of RBC Media Holding, admitted, "I read RBC every morning and think, 'What angry calls am I going to get today?'" RBC published several investigative pieces related to Putin and his inner circle, including members of his family. Several weeks after Prokhorov made those comments, the FSB conducted searches of Prokhorov's headquarters and the offices of companies he owned. The businessman decided not to wait for any "angry calls," and fired the editor in chief of his holding. Prokhorov sold RBC a year later to a Russian businessman who had never been involved in any political intrigues and was described by state officials as "understanding the rules. If he has to break one, he goes and gets permission from the right person first."[60]

In October 2014, Putin signed a law limiting foreign ownership in Russian media companies to 20 percent (effective January 1, 2017). This was one of the Kremlin's responses to the Western countries' sanctions and sharp criticism of Russian aggression in Ukraine. The Kremlin thought that foreign owners of Russian media outlets could be forced by their governments to criticize Putin or his policy, as he himself had done by transforming RIA Novosti and RT (Russia Today) into propaganda machines.

The law covered almost a thousand Russian media outlets, according to information from the government media-monitoring agency. Only a vanishingly small number of them could be suspected of disseminating political information. Many of them were, however, quite attractive from a commercial point of view, which was the reason for this mass redistribution of media properties. Foreign media owners tried but failed to find ways to comply with the law without selling off their assets. One after another, they pulled up stakes and left Russia.

The tastiest morsels in the industry went to businessmen who were not only loyal to the Kremlin but also personally close to Putin and Medvedev. The shareholders of the NASDAQ-listed broadcaster STS-Media, specializing in entertainment, were forced to sell their shares in December 2015 to Usmanov for 5 percent of the share price in mid-2013.[61] President Putin's crony Kovalchuk bought the television network Discovery, combining eleven satellite channels, including the Discovery Channel, Animal Planet, and Eurosport.

The Kremlin believed that the buyers of financially less promising media assets focused on politics or investigative reporting shouldn't need any special instructions to understand the Kremlin's requirements for their editorial agenda. Some buyers were quick on the uptake. Aleksandr Fedotov, who purchased *Forbes* magazine and Forbes.ru, together with OK!, GEO, and Gala Biography, from Axel Springer, immediately announced, "[W]e will soon be . . . making the journal less political. . . . I'm certain that they [readers] are less interested in politics. . . . We will simply try not to go into political territory. . . . I sincerely believe that the people who read *Forbes* don't care about government salaries. . . . I don't think it's necessary to write about that."[62]

But it seemed that some buyers didn't realize they had stepped onto a minefield. The family of Demyan Kudryavtsev[63] acquired the leading Russian business journal *Vedomosti*, owned in equal shares by Sanoma,[64] the *Financial Times*, and the *Wall Street Journal*, and which was known for its incisive, in-depth investigative reporting. The publication of investigative pieces didn't come to an end with the change of ownership: the paper's journalists targeted the son of Igor Sechin, Russia's minister of interior affairs and the highly influential owner of Rosneft. A year and a half after Kudryavtsev bought *Vedomosti*, in the summer of 2017, a court revoked his Russian citizenship; the migration service claimed that Kudryavtsev had provided false information about himself when submitting his application for citizenship.

SOVEREIGN INTERNET

Advances in information technology significantly complicated the use of traditional methods for suppressing free speech—a lesson the Russian state learned all too well. Online media sources today aren't tied to a single physical location that the secret police can raid or shut down by seizing computers and data storage devices. Opposition politicians and journalists critical of the state can address their supporters through YouTube, which has replaced traditional television broadcasting for many. All you need to access the latest news and discuss it with your friends is a smart phone in your pocket. Attempts by the Kremlin to quickly block online media and social media pages met with little success, since information could so easily be shared online. This targeted repression created a PR problem for the Kremlin without achieving the desired result; the number of publications criticizing the government wasn't going down.

Understanding its own limitations, the Kremlin began to discuss harsher methods: isolating the Runet from the World Wide Web. In 2014 the Russian Security Council instructed the government to "ensure internet security," and the Ministry of Communications soon thereafter lifted the veil of secrecy over what was being said in the Kremlin. Draft legislation had been introduced in the Duma that would forbid the use of a communication channel belonging to a foreign company when transferring data internationally. This would mean that all internet traffic going into or out of Russia would go through communication channels belonging to Russian companies, which would never refuse to give the security services access to information passing through their networks. In addition, the Kremlin wanted to ensure that, by 2020, 99 percent of Russian internet traffic would be transferred to information channels operating within the country and belonging to Russian telecommunications operators. Another target was to "duplicate 99 percent of critical internet infrastructure in Russia." That figure was at 0 percent in 2014; it was expected to reach 40 percent in 2017.

Although government officials insisted that these initiatives had been taken to increase the resilience of the Runet in case of "aggressive actions against Russia" to cut the country off from the World Wide Web, many experts characterized the measures as the construction of a system of state control over the Runet. This system could alter the architecture of Russia's entire telecommunications network and lead to all internet traffic passing through government filters. The resulting mechanism would not only act like a Russian version of the Great Chinese Firewall; it would allow Russian authorities to substitute content whenever they wished.

Putin was quick to grasp the role of the media in modern society. He experienced it personally in the fall of 1999: an unknown official who had in no way distinguished himself in life up to that point and who was unable to explain his objectives or principles became the most popular politician in Russia and was elected president of his country by a wide margin. Putin observed his administration as it learned to use the principle of the "tail wagging the dog," when television anchors both decimated his opponents' public image and exaggerated and embellished his achievements. He saw that the Russian media had become a powerful weapon in political conflicts, and he resolved right from the start of his presidency to block his opponents' access to the most popular media source, television.

Political scientists say that control over the media is the norm rather than the exception for authoritarian leaders. It allows them to protect themselves by complicating collective action and preventing coordination among regime opponents (whether elite or otherwise). In this sense, bringing the media under control was indispensable for Vladimir Putin's efforts to retain personal power. Whether he counted his greatest threat at any given moment to be a politician or a protest movement, for him the defensive mechanism remained the same: a crackdown on free media.

While there were historically unprecedented levels of media freedom in the 1990s, Russia's media landscape at the time was nonetheless restricted by the subordination of the largest media outlets to a few competing private financial groups that largely determined the media's agenda. This made Russian media uniquely vulnerable: when Putin sought to consolidate power, it was easier for him to gain control over a few individuals than over a plethora of institutions. By using state security resources to nationalize Vladimir Gusinsky's media holding, the Kremlin simultaneously removed another dangerous player from the Russian media scene, Boris Berezovsky. These two decisive actions radically altered the Russian media landscape. Attempts to create independent television news channels were swiftly suppressed by the Kremlin. President Putin had no interest in any critical analysis of his actions, seeing it as a threat to his retention of power. There was now a de facto ban on any televised criticism of Vladimir Putin or his policies.

Entering his second presidential term, Vladimir Putin gradually moved toward comprehensive control over information and suppressing free speech in Russia; the Kremlin began to regularly ban opposition politicians from appearing on air, and executives at leading media outlets began to receive lists of people that they weren't to touch. The repression of individual journalists and media outlets for violations of vaguely worded legal provisions led to widespread self-censorship; fearing the loss of their licenses, media executives established internal systems of control over their journalists.

As internet access widened and the role of online media and social networks in the dissemination of information grew, the battle against free speech intensified. Nonjudicial bans and restrictions grew more common. After the surge of street protests in Russia in the winter of 2011–12, and radical changes to Russian foreign policy, this practice evolved in the spring of 2014 into mechanisms of repression that became an institutionalized part of the Russian political system.

State dominance of the news media led, predictably, to the creation of a propaganda machine, which first made itself felt after the color revolutions of 2003–05. The biased coverage of events in neighboring countries caused a radical shift in Russian public opinion over the course of a few months: yesterday's friends became enemy nations overnight. The state redoubled its propaganda efforts in 2014; the Kremlin intensified its depictions of Russia as a country surrounded by external enemies who supported "traitors" hiding inside the country. One tragic consequence of the hostility emanating from state television networks was the murder of political opposition leader Boris Nemtsov in February 2015.

The Kremlin became fairly open about its intention to continue to repress free speech and the free dissemination of information in Russia. In May 2017, Putin approved the Strategy for Developing the Information Society in Russia, which included the statement that the authorities planned to "improve mechanisms of restricting access to and deleting information, the distribution of which is prohibited in Russia by federal law." The Kremlin also plans to "improve mechanisms for the legislative regulation of the actions of sources of mass information, as well as means of ensuring access to information, which are equivalent in many respects to media sources, but are not defined as such (internet television, news aggregators, social networks, internet websites, messenger programs)." That is, Putin's plan to carry out the same agenda: to restrict the right of Russian citizens to receive information and to speak freely.

The implementation of this plan has already begun: in September 2017 courts in occupied Crimea convicted two journalists.[65] Their sentences include a three-year ban on engaging in any public speaking activities, including making public speeches, publishing blogs or articles in print or on online media, and speaking on the radio or television—a ban that clearly violates the right to free speech guaranteed by the Russian constitution.

Notes to Chapter 3

1. President of Russia, "Vystupleniye i otvety na voprosy na vstreche s prepoda-vatelyami i studentami Kolumbiyskogo universiteta" [Speech and answers to questions at a meeting with teachers and students at Columbia University], transcript, Moscow, September 26, 2003 (http://kremlin.ru/events/president/transcripts/22129).

2. I. D. Laptev, "Russian Print Media: Issues and History," *Current Issues in Journalism: Materials from the Professional Conference "Journalism in 1996: Media in Post-Soviet Society," Moscow, February 4–7, 1997* (1997), pp. 7–11.

3. The growth of television was also slowed by technical issues: the number of VHF television channels was limited, and television stations had a limited number of set programs.

4. See the website https://rsf.org/en/russia (accessed May 25, 2018).

5. Moreover, Gazprom also owned a 30 percent stake in NTV. While the loans to Media-Most were made at the request of then prime minister Chernomyrdin, Gazprom made the decision to buy a stake in NTV on its own, in the hope that this would prevent NTV from publicly criticizing the company or its top managers.

6. Aleksandr Voloshin, interview by the author, Moscow, January 12, 2016.

7. Vladimir Gusinsky, interview by the author, White Plains, New York, May 26, 2016.

8. In his interview with Oliver Stone, Putin said he had informed President George W. Bush about the CIA's support of Chechen rebels, citing names and evidence. President Bush, according to Putin, promised to sort it out, but three weeks later the CIA responded, saying, "We supported all political forces in Russia, and will continue to do so." Oliver Stone, *The Putin Interviews* (Visit 1, day 2, July 3, 2015) (Moscow: Alpina, 2017).

9. Vladimir Gusinsky, interview by the author.

10. Evgeniy Petrov, "Primakov ne stal osuzhdat' voynu v Chechne" [Primakov did not condemn the war in Chechnya], *Nezavisimaya Gazeta*, November 2, 1999.

11. It is worth noting that, with the exception of Mikhail Kasyanov, Putin publicly respected former prime ministers, and co-opted all of them into government structures. Viktor Chernomyrdin was the Russian ambassador to Ukraine for nine years, Sergey Stepashin spent fourteen years as head of the Audit Chamber and is now chairman of the board of directors of a state-owned corporation; Mikhail Fradkov was head of Russian intelligence for nine years and is now chairman of the board of directors of Almaz-Antei (one of Russia's largest military suppliers); and Victor Zubkov is still chairman of Gazprom's board of directors.

12. Vladimir Gusinsky, interview by the author.

13. The European Court of Human Rights later qualified this agreement as a

transaction under duress and acknowledged the political nature of Gusinsky's persecution. *Gusinskiy v. Russia*, no. 70276/01, ECHR 2004-IV.

14. Tatyana Yumasheva, "Berezovsky (chast' vtoraya)" [Berezovsky (part two)], LiveJournal.ru, January 9, 2010.

15. Tatyana Yumasheva, "Berezovsky. Chast' tret'ya, poslednyaya" [Berezovsky. Part three, the last], LiveJournal.ru, February 6, 2010.

16. Ibid.

17. Ibid.

18. "Federal'nyye vybory v tsentral'nykh SMI" [Federal elections in the federal media], *What the Papers Say,* March 15, 2000 (http://wps.ru/arhiv/elections/elections-2000-03-15/).

19. If that happened, new elections would be called, in which the candidates from the elections declared invalid would not be able to participate.

20. President of Russia, "Interv'yu radiostantsii 'Mayak' [Interview with the radio station Mayak], transcript, Moscow, March 18, 2000 (http://kremlin.ru/events/president/transcripts/24186).

21. On May 31, 2000, Berezovsky published an open letter to President Putin sharply criticizing the president's proposed federal reform laws, calling them unconstitutional and antidemocratic. See also Boris Berezovsky, "Lichnyye svobody — glavnyy zakon demokraticheskogo obshchestva. Otkrytoye pis'mo prezidentu Rossiyskoy Federatsii Vladimiru Putinu" [Personal liberties are the main law of a democratic society. Open letter to the President of the Russian Federation Vladimir Putin], *Kommersant* 96, May 31, 2000, front page; and "Prilozheniye: Predvaritel'nyy yuridicheskiy analiz" [Annex: Preliminary legal analysis], *Kommersant* 96, May 31, 2000, p. 2.

22. Lesin died in a Washington, D.C., hotel room under unusual circumstances in November 2015.

23. Vera Chelishcheva, "Aleksandr Voloshin: 'K presledovaniyu Gusinskogo imeyet neposredstvennoye otnosheniye Genprokuratura'" [Alexander Voloshin: "The prosecution of Gusinsky is directly related to the prosecutor general's office"], *Novaya Gazeta,* November 16, 2011.

24. Marina Litvinovich, a political consultant working for the Kremlin at the time, claims it was a result of her personal initiative that Putin canceled his vacation: "When the *Kursk* [tragedy] happened, the whole country was in mourning. . . . And the president . . . was sitting in Sochi. . . . And if I . . . hadn't suggested it . . . he probably wouldn't have gone anywhere. . . . Voloshin and I had a heated, angry conversation at that meeting. And my idea was only successful thanks to Dobrodeyev's [CEO of the second state-owned TV channel, *Rossiya*] support. . . . We insisted, Voloshin made the call, and persuaded him (persuaded!), and he [Putin] traveled there [to the city where the naval base that housed the families of the *Kursk* crew was located]." See also Marina Litvinovich, "Kogda poyavilsya Putin, komanda El'tsina vospryala dukhom:

Mozhno delat' vse" [When Putin appeared, Yeltsin's team cheered up: We could do anything], Slon.ru, May 31, 2011.

25. Tatyana Yumasheva, "Zdes' ya budu borot'sya s lozh'yu. I nemnogo o Berezovskom" [Here I will fight with lies. And a little bit about Berezovsky], LiveJournal. ru, January 6, 2010.

26. This testimony was given during the *Berezovsky v. Abramovich* case in the London High Court in 2011. See also Chelishcheva, "Aleksandr Voloshin: 'K presledovaniyu Gusinskogo imeyet neposredstvennoye otnosheniye Genprokuratura'" [Aleksandr Voloshin: "The prosecution of Gusinsky is directly related to the prosecutor general's office"].

27. Vera Chelishcheva, "Snachala kryshey Abramovicha rabotal Berezovskiy, a teper', ochevidno, Putin" [At first Berezovsky was working as Abramovich's "roof," and now, obviously, it is Putin], *Novaya Gazeta*, November 14, 2011. (*Krysha*, or "roof," refers to protection afforded by politicians or criminals.)

28. The lawsuit was filed based on a law requiring the liquidation of a company if its net assets fell below the minimum amount of charter capital over the course of several years. This provision was removed from the law two days after the liquidation of TV-6.

29. Those charges had a more solid basis than in Gusinsky's case and were related to embezzlement from the state-owned company Aeroflot, which was under Berezovsky's managerial control. In 2007 a Russian court sentenced Berezovsky in absentia to six years in prison. A Swiss court subsequently ordered the return to Aeroflot of $52 million that had been seized from a Berezovsky company bank account.

30. Litvinovich, "Kogda poyavilsya Putin, komanda El'tsina vospryala dukhom: Mozhno delat' vse" [When Putin appeared, Yeltsin's team cheered up: We could do anything].

31. "For us this [the color revolutions] is a lesson and a warning, and we will do everything we can to ensure that this never happens in Russia," said Vladimir Putin in November 2014. "Putin: 'Tsvetnyye revolyutsii' v ryade stran — eto urok dlya Rossii'" [Putin: "Color revolutions" in a number of countries—this is a lesson for Russia], RIA Novosti, November 20, 2014.

32. And this was one of the most important reasons for the downturn in Russian-American relations, that the Bush administration chose this moment to increase pressure on Russia to comply with human rights and democratic freedoms, which was clearly contrary to Putin's plans.

33. A few years after the revolutions in Tunisia and Egypt, the mass protests in Russia in 2011–12, and the Euromaidan in 2013–14 in Ukraine, the Kremlin was forced to relive its old fears. This period is discussed later in the chapter.

34. In August 2005, Gazprom-Media Holding was sold to Gazprombank, whose 47 percent stake belonged to the Gazfond pension fund, which was in turn controlled by

Kovalchuk's management company. The small stake was owned by one of Kovalchuk's companies directly. The Kremlin continued to maintain a tight grip on NTV's information policy, but Kovalchuk was in control of the financial resources of the media holding. It seems that this change of control came as a surprise to Vladimir Putin: several years later the government took back shareholder control over Gazprombank and his media holding.

35. Chubais was appointed to RAO UES by Boris Yeltsin in April 1998. After Putin came to power, he kept Chubais—who had opposed Putin's promotion as Yeltsin's successor—in that position, following the principle of "keep your friends close and your enemies closer."

36. A 30 percent stake in the channel went to the German company RTL Group, and two parcels of 35 percent each went to Russian companies Severstal and Surgutneftegaz.

37. Another Putin crony, Gennady Timchenko, has a minority stake in NMG.

38. Quoted in Andrey Kolesnikov, "'Eto ochen' khoroshiy chelovek.' Prezident i preyemnik" ["This is a very good person." President and successor], *Kommersant* 247, December 30, 2005, p. 13.

39. Mediascope, "Rezul'taty issledovaniy auditorii SMI" [Results of analysis of media audiences], survey conducted July 9–15, 2018, in Russian cities with a population of more than 100,000 (http://mediascope.net/services/media/media-audience/tv/national-and-regional/audience/).

40. Under President Medvedev, a state program for the development of broadband internet contributed to internet penetration outside major urban areas.

41. According to Russian legislation, the organization of any public event with two or more participants should be authorized by local authorities.

42. Government of Russia, "Predsedatel' Pravitel'stva Rossiyskoy Federatsii V.V Putin provël zasedaniye Koordinatsionnogo soveta Obshcherossiyskogo narodnogo fronta" [Prime Minister of the Russian Federation V. V. Putin held a meeting of the Coordinating Council of the All-Russian People's Front], news release, Moscow, December 8, 2011 (http://archive.premier.gov.ru/events/news/17330/). In his interview with Oliver Stone, Putin reemphasized his viewpoint: "[In 2012, the U.S.] diplomatic staff in their assigned countries, in this case Russia, became aggressively involved in our election campaign: they gathered opposition forces at their places, financed them, rushed to opposition meetings." Stone, *The Putin Interviews* (Visit 4, day 1, February 10, 2017).

43. The term "foreign agents" was actively used in the Soviet Union at the time of Stalin's purges and has a clearly negative connotation in Russian.

44. Access to those media in Russia is still denied at the time of this writing.

45. Ministry of Justice, "Perechen' inostrannyh i mezhdunarodnyh nepravitel'-stvennyh organizatsii, eyatel'nost' ktoryh priznana nexhelatel'noi na territorii Rossiiskoi Federatsii" [The list of foreign and international nongovernmental organizations

whose activity is recognized as undesirable on the territory of the Russian Federation] (http://minjust.ru/ru/activity/nko/unwanted).

46. Roskomnadzor (the government media-monitoring agency), "V Roskomnadzor iz Genprokuratury postupili trebovaniya ob ogranichenii dostupa k saytam s informatsionnymi materialami nezhelatel'nykh organizatsiy" [Roskomnadzor received from the prosecutor general's office requests to block access to websites with materials of undesirable organizations], news release, Moscow, December 12, 2017 (https://rkn.gov.ru/news/rsoc/news53170.htm).

47. Kolesnikov, "'Eto ochen' khoroshiy chelovek.' Prezident i preyemnik" ["This is a very good person." President and successor], p. 13.

48. There is no adequate translation for this term, *natsional-predateli.*" It comes from the German *Nationalverräter,* which was applied during Weimar Germany to the politicians who had signed the country's capitulation in World War I. Later this word was used in Adolf Hitler's *Mein Kampf,* and in the English version of that book it was translated as "persons who have enriched themselves from the public soil and betrayed the nation."

49. President of Russia, "Obrashcheniye Prezidenta Rossiyskoy Federatsii" [Appeal of the President of the Russian Federation], news release, Moscow, March 18, 2014 (http://kremlin.ru/events/president/news/20603).

50. Security Council of Russian Federation, "O protivodeystvii ugrozam natsional'noy bezopasnosti v informatsionnoy sfere" [On countering threats to national security in the information sphere], Moscow, October 1, 2014 (www.scrf.gov.ru/council/session/2059/).

51. Security Council of Russian Federation, "Osnovy gosudarstvennoy politiki Rossiyskoy Federatsii v oblasti mezhdunarodnoy informatsionnoy bezopasnosti na period do 2020 goda" [Fundamentals of the state policy of the Russian Federation in the field of international information security for the period until 2020 (approved by V. Putin on July 24, 2013)], Moscow, 2015 (www.scrf.gov.ru/security/information/document114/).

52. Dmitriy Petrov, "'Pyataya kolonna' v SMI: Takiye resursy mogut registrirovat' kak inostrannyye" [The "Fifth Column" in the media: These outlets can be registered as foreign], Vesti.ru, May 20, 2014.

53. Punishments were most often handed down to social media users for posting historical photos containing swastikas, who were thereby accused of "justifying Nazism."

54. In April 2016, for example, authorities criminally prosecuted the well-known internet entrepreneur and blogger Anton Nosik, who supported Russian military operations in Syria and had called for Syria to be "wiped from the face of the Earth." The state probably targeted Nosik because he was an uncompromising supporter of free speech online. He had strongly opposed Russian government policies on internet regulation for years and criticized government efforts to block websites.

55. According to the Supreme Court and the Prosecutor's Office of the USSR, in 1956–87, 8,145 people were convicted for such crimes. During 1956–60, 935 people were convicted on average every year; in 1961–65 the number was 214; in 1966–70, 136; in 1971–75, 161; in 1976–80, 69; in 1981–85, 108; in 1986–87, 14. See also Aleksandr Vdovin, "Dissidentstvo v SSSR" [Dissidence in the USSR], *Sovetskaya Rossiya*, August 19, 2000.

56. Elena Mukhametshina, "Durov ne v kontakte s FSB" [Durov is not in contact with the FSB], Gazeta.ru, April 17, 2014.

57. Pavel Durov, "13 marta 2014 goda Prokuratura potrebovala ot menya zakryt' antikorruptsionnuyu gruppu Alekseya Naval'nogo pod ugrozoy blokirovki VKontakte . . ." ["On March 13, 2014, the Prosecutor's Office demanded that I shut down the anticorruption group of Alexei Navalny under the threat of blocking VKontakte . . ."], Vk.com, April 16, 2014.

58. Ingrid Lunden, "Durov, Out for Good from VK.com, Plans a Mobile Social Network Outside Russia," TechCrunch.com, April 22, 2014.

59. "Kak MRG svidetel'stvuyet protiv vas" [How MRG (Mail.ru Group) bears witness against you], Telegram-channel@zalaykbot, August 17, 2018 (https://tlinks.run/zalayk/49), and Yaromir Romanov, "VKontakte otpravlalo Tsentru 'E' dannye o pol'zovatelyakh po elektronke bez ugolovnogo dela." [VKontakte sent users' data to E center without a criminal case], Znak.com, August 18, 2018 (www.znak.com/amp/137416).

60. Elena Vinogradova, Ivan Vasil'yev, and Irina Gruzinova, "Kak ustroyen biznes Grigoriya Berezkina i zachem emu media" [How is Grigory Berezkin's business organized and why does he need media], *Vedomosti*, June 19, 2017.

61. Vladimir Todorov, Karina Romanova, and Erik Khachatryan, "'STS Media' mozhet otoyti Usmanovu" [STS Media may be soon owned by Usmanov], Gazeta.ru, July 10, 2015.

62. Sergey Sobolev and Mariya Istomina, "Novyy vladelets Forbes — RBK: 'My budem starat'sya ne zakhodit' v politiku'" [The new owner of *Forbes*—RBC: "We will try not to go into politics"], RBK, October 16, 2015.

63. Demyan Kudryavtsev was quite a colorful person in the Russian media world. He was a trusted colleague of Boris Berezovsky in many endeavors, as exemplified by his lengthy tenure as director of Kommersant Publishing House. After Berezovsky sold Kommersant to Usmanov, he had to get special permission from then deputy prime minister Dmitry Medvedev for Kudryavtsev to remain in his position as director of Kommersant. The Russian security services were well aware of his collaboration with Berezovsky, including his role as Berezovsky's representative in Kyiv during the Orange Revolution. After the protests in the winter of 2011–12, during which *Kommersant*'s coverage was sympathetic to the protesters, the Kremlin demanded that Usmanov fire Kudryavtsev, and also banned other media companies from hiring him.

See also "Il'ya Zhegulev rasskazyvayet istoriyu Dem'yana Kudryavtseva, kotoryy kupil gazetu 'Vedomosti'" [Ilya Zhegulyov tells the story of Demyan Kudryavtsev, who bought the newspaper *Vedomosti*], *Meduza*, December 4, 2015.

64. Sanoma was also forced to sell its assets in other popular magazines published in Russia: *Men's Health, Women's Health, National Geographic, Esquire, Cosmopolitan, Harper's Bazaar, Good Housekeeping, Popular Mechanics*, and the *Robb Report*.

65. One of them, Mykola Semena, in his article wrote about the blockade of goods and energy supply from mainland Ukraine to Crimea that was launched by Ukrainian activists, saying that it was the first and necessary step toward the liberation of the peninsula. The indictment quotes from his text: *"Kyiv should not allow Crimea to remain under Russian occupation longer than under the German one"* (the reference is to the time of Nazi rule over Crimea in 1942–44). Semena was officially charged with encroaching on Russia's territorial integrity under the legal norm that provided for a punishment of up to five years in prison. That provision was introduced into the Russian Criminal Code in May 2014, shortly after annexation of the Crimea. And see "Nikolay Semena: Uslovnyy srok i zapret na professiyu" [Nikolay Semyena: Conditional term and prohibition from the profession], *Krym.Realii*, September 22, 2017. The second one, Ilmi Umerov, was tried for comments made to a Crimean Tatar television station in Kyiv in which he decried the 2014 annexation of Crimea. The court claimed the words contained a call to change Russia's borders by force, though during the hearing it became evident that his words had been incorrectly translated from the Crimean Tatar language into Russian. The total number of views of his YouTube video with this speech was 711. See also Shaun Walker, "Crimean Tatar Leader Convicted of 'Separatism' Will Not Seek Clemency," *The Guardian*, September 29, 2017.

Four

A UNIFYING SYSTEM OF POWER

Our country is unique and needs an appropriate system of governance.
                                        —Vladislav Surkov

Russia is officially known as the Russian Federation. The word "federation" is not just a legacy from the Soviet era but the result of a conscious choice by the authors of the 1993 constitution.

Russia was also known as the Russian Federation within the USSR, but no one treated the second half of that name seriously.[1] All regions, territories, and republics that were part of the Russian Federation (or RSFSR) had equal rights—which is to say, no rights at all. The Soviet Union itself was governed as a unitary state, with some external signs of a federative structure present. Its constituent republics had their own parliaments, governments, and occasionally even their own laws. Nevertheless, the entire country was managed by the all-encompassing Communist Party structures, the power vertical of the time. In the Soviet Union, there was no legislative separation of rights and responsibilities between the center and the republics, let alone between Russia and its constituent regions. There was also no system of budgetary federalism, which implies a statutory distribution of budget revenues and expenditures between different levels of government.[2]

However, this situation began to change rapidly on the eve of the Soviet Union's collapse. On April 26, 1990, the law on the sharing of powers between the Soviet Union and the subjects of the federation was adopted. On the one hand, this act recognized the sharing of powers between the center and the republics; on the other hand, it confused the situation even further. The law established general principles for relations between the constituent republics that were part of the USSR and the autonomous units that were a part of some of them, but it left the status of the territories and regions that were not autonomous units completely undefined.[3]

BUILDING FROM SCRATCH

From August 1990 on, Russia—still part of the Soviet Union—witnessed the "parade of sovereignties" of the autonomous republics unleashed by Boris Yeltsin's famous injunction, "Take as much sovereignty as you can swallow." Yeltsin, who became chairman of the Russian parliament (Supreme Council of the RSFSR) in late May 1990, had already embarked on his struggle to claim more authority for Russia from the Soviet Union's central government. The Russian leadership perceived the new Soviet law on power sharing as an attempt to undermine Russia's territorial integrity since its sixteen autonomous republics could potentially obtain powers equal to Russia's within the Soviet Union. Therefore, Yeltsin's desire to keep the national regions within Russia's orbit was understandable. But the consequences of his injunction were much more serious than one might have expected at the time.

National regions, which were part of the RSFSR, one after another began to issue declarations of sovereignty, though they did not go so far as to demand full state sovereignty—with an important exception. The Republic of Tatarstan's declaration, adopted in late August, described the republic as subject to international law while omitting any mention that it was still part of the Russian Federation.[4] In late October Irkutsk oblast, located in the middle of Siberia, one of many such areas without autonomous status, adopted a similar declaration. This grasping for sovereignty highlighted the asymmetry built into Russia's federal system: the subjects of the Russian Federation did not have equal rights.

After the collapse of the USSR, the political leadership of both the Russian Federation and the regions recognized the need to resolve the issue of federal relations. The Federation Treaty, which delineated the separation of powers between the federation and the regions, was signed in Moscow on March 31, 1992.[5] The new Russian constitution, adopted in December 1993, established the constitutional nature of the federation and contained a separate chapter on the federal structure of the country. Unlike the U.S. Constitution, which enumerates the powers belonging to the federal government and, through the Tenth Amendment, specifically reserves all other rights to the states (or citizens), the Russian 1993 constitution defines the powers of the federal government and the joint powers of the federal and regional (oblast or republic) governments while leaving all the rest to the regional level. The Russian constitution accords no specific powers directly to the local, municipal level beyond mentioning that government at the municipal level has all rights except those attributed to federal or regional levels and the powers shared by the federal and regional levels of government.

CHECKS AND BALANCES

The transition from a unitary to a federal state did not happen overnight. The center and the regions had frequently to adjust their relations through a process of trial and error. The upper chamber of the Russian parliament, the Federation Council, which consisted of representatives from the regions, had gradually become the learning-by-doing place where many building blocks of the new federal state were designed. As part of Yeltsin's reforms, beginning in 1995, seats on the Federation Council were assigned to regional governors and heads of regional legislatures, who understood the interests of their regions very well. As a result, the views of the Federation Council on many laws often differed sharply from those held by the lower chamber of the Russian parliament, the Duma, or the executive branch. These differences frequently required the creation of reconciliation task forces at various stages of the legislative process. The Federation Council consistently voted against bills supported by the State Duma or, alternatively, joined forces with the Duma to override presidential vetoes on certain legislation.[6] Both tactics were accepted as a normal part of political life, though controversial laws sometimes did spark serious struggles.

Russia inherited very little legislation from the Soviet Union, which necessitated the adoption of an enormous number of new laws at both the federal and the regional level. But since the constitution allowed "conjoint authority" on many issues, the federation and the regions increasingly adopted legislation on the same subjects as each strived to gain the most power. As a result, numerous contradictory legal norms surfaced, a situation that was not beneficial for the state-building process. Although the Russian constitution clearly stated that a law adopted at a higher level would take precedence in the event of a conflict, implementing this principle proved difficult in practice. A perennial budget crisis meant that federal authorities frequently were unable to meet their obligations to finance regional law enforcement and the regional court systems, a situation that allowed regional authorities to purchase prosecutors' and judges' loyalty out of regional budgets.

A MAJOR THREAT

This situation began to change after Vladimir Putin became acting president on the last day of 1999 and announced the principles undergirding the policies with which he would transform the whole country in the coming years. A month after moving into the Kremlin, Putin met with the heads of the police and secret police, as well as top members of the judiciary. He told these officials that they should join forces with him in establishing a "dictatorship of law" in the country—"the only form of dictatorship we must obey."[7] At the same time, Putin directed the thrust of his speech at regional legislative voluntarism, saying that "at the moment, the mechanism of state power is really neglected, loose, and disordered. . . . According to the Ministry of Justice itself, about 20 percent of legislative acts and other regulatory documents adopted in the regions contradict [federal] legislation, and sometimes even grossly violate human rights. . . . The gradual accumulation of such normative and legal acts can reach a critical mass that can blow up the country's legal framework."[8]

This goal—to eliminate legislative conflicts—seemed to be a rational one, but in reality, the Kremlin had already begun actively working on a set of laws that would, as the Kremlin's chief strategist on domestic policy issues, First Deputy Chief of the presidential administration Vladislav Surkov, later said, "seriously change the political balance in the country."[9] Putin and his inner circle believed that it was time to "instill order." "The regions are too independent, . . . laws are not being enforced locally. . . . We must somehow shift the balance toward the center. After all, the center actually came into existence only thanks to certain informal agreements of our eighty-eight respected regional leaders." In keeping with the popular practice of blaming one's predecessors for all current woes, members of the presidential team managed to convince Putin that the situation was "certainly a consequence of the policy that has been carried out in recent years. In fact, this policy was progressive at some point. But any technology becomes obsolete and counterproductive after a while. It's now time to modernize our technology of governing the country." In public, the Kremlin declared that "it's certainly not a question of going back, creating a unitary state, and trying to take charge of all local issues. . . . It's just a neat, delicate attempt to slightly change the balance." But in private conversations, the administration openly stated that Russia was not a federation at all, had never been one, and should be constructed as a unitary state.[10]

By the time Vladimir Putin entered the Kremlin, the wheel of politics in Russia had begun to turn. In December 1999 the political movement Fatherland–All Russia (Otechestvo–Vsya Rossiya, or OVR), which brought together many regional leaders into a "governors' bloc," suffered a serious setback in proportional voting in the elections to the State Duma, receiving just 13 percent of the votes rather than an anticipated 25 percent or more.[11] Moreover, its presidential candidate, Yevgeny Primakov, had decided not to run for president, thus eliminating Vladimir Putin's only real opponent. Nevertheless, the governors' bloc retained a strong position. The OVR established the third-largest faction in the State Duma. Its candidate in the Moscow mayoral election, Yury Luzhkov, scored a convincing victory with 69.2 percent of votes in the first round, while the OVR candidate in the Moscow oblast gubernatorial election, General Boris Gromov, won a hard-fought second-round election victory, 46 to 44 percent, over the Communist Party candidate, who was openly supported by Putin. The Kremlin and

Putin himself failed to get then deputy prime minister Valentina Matviyenko elected as St. Petersburg's governor; her support in the city was much lower than the support for the incumbent governor, one of OVR's leaders, Vladimir Yakovlev, who directly warned Putin in private conversation that selecting Matviyenko as a candidate would be "a big mistake that can get in the way of the main goal—achieving maximum voter turnout in the March 26 presidential election."[12] Describing Yakovlev's behavior as an act of political bargaining, Putin stepped back.

The tension between the federal center and the governors persisted, though by the spring of 2000 it was no longer as sharp as it had been a year earlier. Putin's convincing victory in the presidential election left no opportunity for the governors to manage the political agenda. As a result of the pro-Kremlin Unity party's success in the December Duma elections and its unexpected alliance with the communists in the Duma, the lower chamber of the Russian parliament began to support the president on many issues, which broke up the alliance between the left-leaning Duma factions and the governors-led Federation Council. Moreover, a large number of Duma members openly endorsed limiting the powers of the Federation Council and of the governors, who effectively controlled the upper chamber of parliament. Apparently the Duma members had different motives—they did not like the fact that the Federation Council often took opposing positions on new legislation in an effort to get its share of the lobbying pie. Some, like the right-wing liberal Union of Right Forces (SPS) party, wanted to become a junior but full-fledged participant in the ruling coalition.[13] As a result, the Duma began generating bills that, surprisingly, rehashed Putin's ideas.[14]

GETTING OFF THE POLITICAL STAGE

The master plan to crush the governors' bloc had already taken shape by the day of Vladimir Putin's inauguration, May 7, 2000. In his autobiography, *First Person*, published two months earlier, even before the elections, he wrote: "If we keep the gubernatorial elections . . . we need to discuss perhaps applying some sanctions. Maybe fire them."[15] The day before the inauguration, Putin briefly mentioned that "various proposals concerning the improvement of the structure and work of the Federation Council are currently being considered." He also stated that "the power vertical has to be strengthened and can be structured somewhat differently, but it would be wrong to deprive people of the right to elect their leaders. Gubernatorial elections stand for governors' accountability to the people who elected them."[16]

This statement contains two important points. First, when alluding to the "power vertical," which would eliminate the regions' autonomy, Putin drew on a poorly worded article of the Russian constitution, which reads: "Federal executive bodies and executive authorities of the constituent entities of the Russian Federation form a unified system of executive power in the Russian Federation within the jurisdiction of the Russian Federation and the powers of the Russian Federation in the subjects of joint jurisdiction of the Russian Federation and the constituent entities of the Russian Federation." Here is how the Kremlin interpreted this passage: a large portion of the powers within the Russian Federation was attributed to the "conjoint jurisdiction" of the federation and regions. Therefore, in all these matters it was necessary to build a "power vertical," a system in which the governors would be completely obedient to Moscow. To be sure, Putin would say something different three weeks later: "All the actions undertaken by the central authorities and my actions as the president of the country are not aimed at weakening such an essential link in state administration as the regional government. I mean both at the gubernatorial level and at the level of the representative body of local government."[17] Nevertheless, everything that the federal government would do from that time on with respect to reforming federal relations would lead to curtailing the power of regional and local authorities. Essentially, it would contribute to the building of a de facto unitary state in Russia—not a federation.

Second, as Putin was speaking of the need to preserve the gubernatorial elections, he knew full well that a bill asserting the president's right to recall governors was about to make its way to the Duma. According to Voloshin, Putin was quickly convinced that he needed the right to recall governors to be able to govern a country that had never been run as a federation and needed to maintain the administrative power vertical. Moreover, during discussions in the Kremlin, Putin suggested several times dropping the gubernatorial elections altogether. But his aides were able to persuade him that such a step would be unconstitutional and antidemocratic, and so the president withdrew his suggestion.[18] But he did not forget about it.

———————

A few days after his inauguration, Vladimir Putin demonstrated that his words about establishing a "dictatorship of law" and "destroying regional legislative voluntarism" were not accidental. His decrees invalidated several decisions made by the heads of Ingushetia,[19] Amur,[20] and Smolensk[21] oblasts. He also urged the Bashkortostan State Assembly "to take the steps necessary to bring . . . the provisions of the Constitution of the Republic of Bashkortostan into accordance with the Constitution of the Russian Federation."[22]

A week after his inauguration, Putin signed a decree establishing federal districts and introducing the position of presidential plenipotentiary envoy, who would be responsible for coordinating the activity of federal agencies in the regions. Aside from this role, presidential envoys were also granted the power to analyze the "efficiency and staffing of law enforcement agencies in regions," which essentially allowed them to supervise the activity of the police and prosecutor's office. Since the constitution assigned a significant number of questions to conjoint federal and regional jurisdiction, the regions had the right to veto appointments to the heads of regional branches of federal agencies. Most important was the fact that the heads of the regional police and prosecutor general's offices, as well as judges in the regional and local courts, couldn't be appointed without the preapproval of governors or regional legislatures. This practice led to the appointment of people who were more loyal to the regional authorities than to Moscow and who in many cases refused to abide by federal laws when they conflicted. The constitution didn't spell out a rule for coordinating the appointments of regional heads of federal agencies: it emerged from the agreements reached in preparation for the Treaty of Federation in 1992. The Kremlin's decision to allow presidential envoys in federal districts to participate in "appointing candidates to federal service positions" effectively did away with earlier agreements and demonstrated that the Kremlin did not intend to discuss new federal principles with the regions. Immediately after the presidential decree was signed, the prosecutor general's office established his divisions in the newly established federal districts and subordinated regional prosecutors general to those divisions.

Presidential envoys were also granted the right "to coordinate the proposed decisions of federal agencies that affect the interests of a federal district or a subject of the Russian Federation situated within this district," which de facto diminished the status of the governors. Before that point, the governors, being members of the upper chamber of parliament, were able to solve many issues by visiting the headquarters of federal agencies in Moscow. But from that time on they were forced to pay homage to the envoys to their districts and obtain their preapproval for any proposal before going to Moscow. Step by step, the presidential envoys didn't just control the governors' activities but also stood in for them on many issues.

The Kremlin's offensive against the governors was so impetuous that few of them were able to take in the full scope of the changes. The governors still believed they had some leverage, and made an offer to Putin to create a joint committee on legislative reform.[23] But such a move made no sense: the Kremlin had already swung its sword, and nothing could stop it. Ten days after his inauguration, Putin addressed the nation on television, stating that the main goal of his reform was "to imbue the constitutional principles of separation of powers and the unity of the executive vertical with absolutely real content." While explaining the essence of these impending changes a few days later, Putin began characterizing opponents of the reform as adversaries who were standing in the way of normal life in the country. "This is being deliberately done by those who are trying to disrupt our joint efforts. These—in my view—provocative elements are aimed at driving a wedge into our common position and undermining the unity that has been observed thus far and is helping us move forward along the path of strengthening our statehood," the president said.[24]

In his bills introduced in parliament, Vladimir Putin proposed radical changes in the balance of power in the country. According to his plan, the powers of regional leaders would be significantly undermined: governors and the heads of regional legislative bodies would lose their right to be members of the upper chamber of parliament and would be replaced by governors' and regional legislatures' representatives. At the same time, the president would acquire the right to remove governors and disband regional legislatures, even as governors would be granted the right to remove local executives and disband local legislatures.

On the one hand, the Kremlin's position appeared quite logical. Here was how Putin explained the new rules for constituting the Federation Council: "Today governors and heads of republics are institutions of executive power in and of themselves, but as members of the Federation Council, they are also parliamentarians, in other words, co-authors of the laws that they themselves have to comply with. This effectively violates the principle of the separation of powers." It was also hard to argue against the precept that the constitutional principle of supremacy of federal laws over regional ones (and regional over local) should be enforced. On the other hand, removing governors from the Federation Council deprived them of their parliamentary immunity, which was in truth the central motive behind the decision. By that time the Kremlin had accepted the use of either force or criminal prosecution against anyone who had fallen out of favor with the authorities, as was aptly demonstrated by the charges brought against Prosecutor General Yury Skuratov and media mogul Vladimir Gusinsky. During debates on the presidential draft in parliament, the president's representative in the Duma plainly described the menace of the new rules: "At least sixteen governors will be put on trial right after the bills are passed, and many [other governors] will be a bit later."[25] Four out of seven presidential envoys in the newly established federal districts came from the police or secret police and evidently were empowered to use their contacts to prosecute governors in the event of their disobedience to the Kremlin.

But for enforcing the supremacy of federal laws, the presidential decrees suspending decisions by regional authorities were an adequate instrument at the time. Moreover, in June 2000, on reviewing petitions from the Altai Republic and a group of Duma members, the Constitutional Court made two decisions that upheld the constitutional principle of the supremacy of federal laws and invalidated a number of provisions contained in the constitutions of national regions.[26,] As the Constitutional Court justice Mikhail Mityukov bluntly put it after the decisions were announced, the judges had done away with "flimsy federalism."[27] That meant the federal authorities had plenty of opportunities within the existing framework to ensure the supremacy of federal laws. It seems the court concluded that the main goal of the new laws was to reduce the power of Russia's regions. As Vladimir Putin himself forthrightly said, the governors needed to "start getting off the country's political stage."[28] It was not a slip of the tongue; the new Russian president wanted governors to be bureaucrats, not public politicians. In *First Person*, he launched this idea: "When the regional leader sets for himself such a task [the realization of personal political ambitions], to my mind, this destroys the country."[29]

The regional leaders put up a fierce resistance to prevent the president's bills from being passed. The Federation Council vetoed the bill after it was approved by the State Duma, but the Duma was able to override the veto with a two-thirds constitutional majority. The Federation Council as a whole, or even one-fifth of its members, could appeal to the Constitutional Court, but, faced with this prisoner's dilemma, decided not to take any chances and abandoned the idea of verifying the constitutionality of the president's new powers.[30] Better a bad peace than a good war, as the Russian saying goes. The federal electoral campaigns were over, and the governors' bloc saw no viable chances to gain power. The governors also reasoned that agreeing with the president would help their political survival. Most of the regional budgets depended on transfers from the federal coffers, and it would be difficult to receive federal funding in timely fashion while opposing the president's plan.

Aside from fiscal dependency, the human factor also played a role in the governors' efforts to seek a compromise with the Kremlin. In 1999 a law was adopted in Russia limiting the elected regional governors to two consecutive terms in office. Had this law been implemented, most of them would have had to leave their offices within the next two or three years, an eventuality they were not looking forward to. Under the circumstances, the Kremlin suggested amending the law so that it would not affect governors who had begun their terms before the law went into effect. As a result, sixty-nine of eighty-nine governors received the right to run for a third term and seventeen for a fourth one.[31] It is no surprise that many governors saw this as a well-deserved reward for renouncing their oppositional attitudes.

Three months after his inauguration, Vladimir Putin signed into law the changes he had initiated in May and decisively trounced his main political rival, the governors' bloc. The country's federal structure was fatally undermined; it became collateral damage in the struggle. The Kremlin didn't worry about the loss all that much; after all, those who had waged the war against the governors' bloc didn't even consider Russia a real federation. Why grieve over something that didn't exist?

Sixteen months later, on December 1, 2001, the governors' political movement Fatherland–All Russia merged with the pro-Kremlin Unity movement, giving birth to the United Russia party, the new force representing the ruling regime.

THE COURT SAYS "STOP!"

One of the eighty-nine Russian governors, however, did ask the Constitutional Court to verify the constitutionality of the changes initiated by the president. Nikolai Fedorov, the former Russian minister of justice and member of the first post-Soviet cabinet (Yeltsin-Gaidar), who was then the forty-two-year-old president of the Chuvash Republic, questioned the president's right to remove governors and disband regional legislatures, as well as the governors' right to disband local legislatures. Three months after the president's law went into effect, Fedorov sent his request to the Constitutional Court, but it wasn't reviewed for more than a year. On December 27, 2001, Fedorov withdrew his claim, saying that "since the president has not yet used this law to fire anyone, there is nothing to review."[32] However, during this time, the MPs of Adygea and Yakutia Republics had addressed the Constitutional Court with similar questions.

The decision of the Constitutional Court in April 2002 was twofold.[33] On the one hand, the court had no choice but to confirm the supremacy of federal laws and make sure that the court did not contradict its earlier decision in which the president gained the right to remove the prosecutor general without the consent of the Federation Council. For this reason, the court confirmed the president's right to remove governors who did not comply with federal laws and the right of the federal parliament to disband regional legislatures on the same grounds. On the other hand, the Constitutional Court justices fully understood that the new legal norms imposed at the Kremlin's behest were destroying the independence of regional and local governmental institutions and making them dependent on higher authorities. To over-come this threat, the court significantly complicated legislative procedures by ruling that the presidential decree on removing governors from office should be preceded by at least three decisions of courts at different levels that confirmed a violation of the law. "The dismissal procedure is complex, and the rights of the subjects [of the federation] are protected," commented the chief justice of the Constitutional Court, Marat Baglay, on the decision.[34] But Vladimir Putin would not forgive the disloyalty of the Constitutional Court and would not accept its authority to thwart his plans.

Apparently, the Kremlin itself recognized that its legal position on the right to dismiss acting governors was not strong enough, and so it never tried to use this right—either before or after the Constitutional Court's decision. But this did not mean that Vladimir Putin had abandoned the idea. A true judo practitioner, he waited for a convenient moment to score a clean victory that would leave his opponent with no chance to win.

DOTTING THE I'S

That moment came for Putin in September 2004, although few anticipated it. On September 1, the first day of the school year in Russia, Chechen terrorists took over a school in the North Ossetian city of Beslan, holding more than 1,100 hostages, mostly children, for three days. Three hundred thirty-three people, among them both hostages and rescuers, died when security forces stormed the building three days later.

The terrorist attack itself, as well as the large number of casualties that came about during the effort to free the hostages, resulted from mistakes made by the security services. In his September 4 televised address, Putin rightly pointed out this fact: "We stopped paying due attention to the ques-tions of defense and security and allowed corruption to strike at the judicial and law enforcement spheres."[35] However, corporate solidarity—the FSB was leading the operation to free the hostages—prevented Putin from as-signing any responsibility for the failures to the security forces. Putin prom-ised to respond to the incident and prepared "a set of measures aimed at strengthening the unity of the country." He added, "I especially stress that all these measures will be carried out in full accordance with the constitution of the country."

Ten days after the Beslan tragedy, Putin held an extended government meeting to which all Russian regional governors were invited. Counterterrorism measures topped the agenda. However, at this meeting there was no analysis of the causes of the tragedy, no talk of the failures of law enforcement bodies or the secret police, and no discussion of the causes of the failed rescue operation. Instead, the country learned of the president's desire to drastically change Russia's political system. Putin began by describing once again his idea of the vertical of power "I consider the unity of the executive power system to be the key factor of strengthening the state. . . . The executive bodies in the federal center and in the constituent entities of the Federation form a unified system of power and hence should work as an integral, coordinated single organism." The Kremlin's already four-year effort to change Russian laws to this end notwithstanding, Putin continued: "We must recognize that such a system of government has not yet been created." Finally, he announced his proposal: "The highest officials of the subjects of the Russian Federation should be elected by the legislative assemblies of the territories after being nominated by the head of state"—that is, by the president himself.[36] Aleksandr Voloshin, then chief of the presidential administration, was caught off guard by the proposal, as Putin had not discussed it with him since 2000. A few years later Putin emphasized that the "current system of bringing governors into power was suggested by me personally. It was not someone from the administration who suggested the idea, or some specialists—I was the one who came up with it personally, based on the conditions in the country at the time."[37]

The fall of 2004 was one of the key turning points in the history of Putin's transformation of Russia, which ultimately led to the demolition of the system of checks and balances. The timing was surprising. United Russia had won half the seats in the State Duma elections in December 2003, and Putin had won the March 2004 presidential election with more than 70 percent of the vote, facing no serious rivals. Thus nothing threatened the stability of the political regime inside Russia, and the Kremlin had plenty of mechanisms to govern the country.

But by the fall the Russian president had become caught up in fears about what might happen at the end of his presidential term. The possibility of political instability, inspired by both domestic and external factors, was of special concern. In a televised address after the Beslan attack, Putin said:

> We have not shown understanding of the complexity and danger of the processes taking place . . . in the world as a whole. . . . In any case, we could not adequately react to them. We've shown weakness. And the weak get beaten up. Some want to tear a bigger and better piece off us, while others help them. They help, believing that Russia—as one of the world's largest nuclear powers—is still a threat to someone. Therefore, this threat must be eliminated. . . . This is an attack on our country.[38]

The Kremlin's chief strategist in domestic policy, Surkov, was more outspoken in describing the events: "Among the decision makers in America, Europe, and the East, there is a group comprised of public figures who see our country as a potential opponent. . . . Their objective is to destroy Russia and fill its enormous territory with numerous nonviable quasi-state entities." Surkov went on to explain Putin's decision: "The unity of government is a necessary condition for the unity of the nation. . . . Of course, [the rules of gubernatorial appointment] in themselves . . . cannot guarantee a victory over the enemy. However, they would considerably increase the integrity of our political system and adapt the mechanism of government to the extreme conditions of an undeclared war."[39]

This marked the first time Putin articulated the idea of external enemies as an important if not decisive factor in his desire to eliminate political pluralism in Russia. This point he would return to continually from that time on. What had happened to raise his concern level?

In November 2003, Georgia witnessed the bloodless Rose Revolution, the first in a series of color revolutions on former Soviet territory. As a result of the demonstrations, the incumbent Georgian president, Eduard Shevardnadze, was removed from power and Mikheil Saakashvili, who did not hide his pro-Western sentiments and was actively supported by the West, primarily the United States, was elected Georgian president. These events triggered changes in the George W. Bush administration's policy toward Russia, and a "democracy promotion" policy soon replaced pragmatic cooperation. The Bush administration began to publicly criticize the situation in Russia, noting restrictions on freedom of speech and political competition.

These events lay behind the marked turn in Vladimir Putin's political views. Before then he had continued to pursue the foreign policy approach inherited from Boris Yeltsin, which was aimed at deepening relations with the West, strengthening cooperation with major Western powers within the G-8, and introducing Russia into the community of Western states.[40] However, as a result of the Bush administration's criticism of Russia and its open support for the pro-Western political transformation in Georgia, Putin came to believe that the ultimate goal of U.S. policies was to oust him from power. And since it was the Georgian parliament that had removed then president Eduard Shevardnadze from office, the Russian regime started to see any hint of electoral success on the part of the opposition as a threat to its stability.

Putin's assessment of the domestic political landscape was uncomfortable for him. His phrasing—the "unified system of power . . . has not yet been created"—was not just empty words but revealed his deep anxiety and fears. He was concerned that the Kremlin had to compromise during gubernatorial elections and "share" central power with the opposition or with the independent governors who still held power in many oblasts.

The latter problem was compounded by the holdover of many of the political heavyweights of Yeltsin's era in key gubernatorial positions. To induce them to leave, the Kremlin was occasionally willing to pay huge compensation packages for their early departure. Putin himself called the governor of Primorsky krai, Yevgeny Nazdratenko, and asked him to resign; the ex-governor was soon appointed head of the federal State Fishery Committee in exchange for agreeing to leave the region.[41] In exchange for his resignation in 2003, Putin's old acquaintance, St. Petersburg's governor Vladimir Yakovlev, received the government post of deputy prime minister for eight months and then the post of presidential envoy to the Southern Federal District for another six months. He then became a minister for three years before retiring from public service.[42]

New politicians too could see their careers short-circuited if the Kremlin did not approve of them. From time to time, regional legislatures delegated to the Federation Council politicians who were totally unacceptable to the Kremlin: former prosecutor general Yury Skuratov got his mandate from the Buryatiya Republic's legislature soon after his dismissal from office, and one of Yukos's top executives, Vasily Shakhnovsky, became a member of the upper chamber of parliament by decision of the Evenkiya Autonomous District's legislature two days after the arrest of the company's CEO and main shareholder, Mikhail Khodorkovsky. Although a reprimand from Moscow was usually sufficient to get regional legislators to revise their decisions, the Kremlin could clearly see that the regions were not necessarily loyal. And he was concerned about the governors' ability to exact revenge.

Independent politicians continued to win regional elections. Forty out of sixty-nine gubernatorial elections held in Russia in 2001–04 were won by incumbents, with all-out supporters of United Russia winning in only nine cases. In some regions, business leaders, frequently associated with oligarchic clans, became regional leaders. This development alarmed the Kremlin and frightened Putin, who believed that "oligarchic rebellion" in Russia was a real possibility. "Recently I've been anxiously watching the process of increasing influence of economic groups and economic clans, as well as their increasing influence on the regional level of government," he said.[43] The Kremlin recognized it couldn't really control the regional governments, that the governors commanded considerable resources, and that the Kremlin's nominees didn't stand much chance of winning gubernatorial elections. It seemed that the much-desired power vertical wouldn't be constructed any time soon.

Presidential chief of staff Aleksandr Voloshin addressed these fears honestly: "The genetics of power pushes us toward using administrative tools more than is required." "The center doesn't always help elect the most effective manager. . . . Besides, Moscow can't always cite sufficient arguments that the person that we're curating is better than the one we forced to leave." The Kremlin saw it as unacceptable that "a great many externalities still influence elections, including the personal interests of different groups that can gain access to the federal level," and suggested it might be better not to hold elections at all if they continued to allow "even an ape [to be] elected without being shown to the people."[44]

EVERYBODY IS UNDER CONTROL

The September 2004 bills that embodied Putin's fears about internal or external actors destabilizing the country put the governors directly and openly under the control of the Kremlin. The president was effectively granted the right to appoint governors. Though the law described a procedure for voting within the regional legislature, only the president had the right to nominate a candidate. As president, neither Putin nor, later, Medvedev ever proposed more than a single candidate. Moreover, the president was granted authority to disband a regional legislature by decree if his candidate was rejected three times.[45] Unsurprisingly, not a single one of the proposed presidential candidates was vetoed by regional legislatures in the eight years this law was in force. Despite the Constitutional Court ruling that necessitated court decisions before the president could dismiss a governor, the new law gave the president unconstrained authority to remove any of them from their post. The law did specify that the president had to officially explain his decision to lay off a governor, but vague reasons, such as loss of the president's trust or poor job performance, were considered sufficient.

The Kremlin's dominance of the Duma was more than strong; the bill received 80 percent of the vote. By that time the Russian governors had learned the new rules of the game and understood that they stood no chance of winning a war against the Kremlin. Only one of them, Vladimir Butov, the head of Nenets Autonomous District, opposed the presidential initiatives. He told journalists that "people of the regions should independently choose who will lead them. This is the right granted to them by the Russian Constitution. Electing heads of regions through legislatures will be ineffective."[46] Soon Butov faced criminal charges, and the court handed him a suspended sentence of three years, although the complainant eventually withdrew his testimony.[47]

Moreover, the governors quickly found something to like about the new law. They had previously been limited to two consecutive terms in office, but the new law did away with this constraint, so any governor could be reappointed as long as he pledged allegiance to the president. The governors wasted no time in doing that: half of them submitted their resignations to the president immediately after the law came into force regardless of when their terms were set to expire, in the hope that Putin would reappoint them. Most of them got what they hoped for: only seven of forty-four governors who voluntarily resigned were not reappointed.[48]

Since 2004, new rules for the election of regional parliaments have been adopted. According to these new rules, half of the regional parliaments are to be elected by proportional voting, but only federal parties are allowed to nominate candidates. Before 2004, parties had played an insignificant role in the regions, since the central leadership did not have enough financial or organizational resources to maintain regional branches and strong politicians knew that belonging to a party would not bring them additional votes. Moreover, the role of the parties had been declining over time. During the first wave of gubernatorial elections, from the summer of 1995 to the spring of 1997, one in five candidates had been affiliated with a party; during the second wave, from the summer of 1997 to the end of 1999, one in seven candidates had party affiliation; and from 2000 to 2002, only one out of fifteen did. Regional legislative elections, as well as gubernatorial ones, had been of a person-specific nature.

The amended legislation gave parties that did not enjoy considerable influence at the regional level a monopoly on putting forward party lists during regional elections. Now even those governors who positioned themselves as independent politicians were forced to make arrangements with party structures. Otherwise they risked ending up with an opposition-minded parliament, which could complicate their lives considerably.

The introduction in early 2005 of the practice of appointing governors presented regional leaders with a cynical choice, either to support the Kremlin—that is, United Russia—or to lose their positions. Most of them agreed to assimilate into the new system of government without complaint. It became virtually compulsory for the governors to participate in regional legislative elections. They began to take top positions on United Russia's party lists and consequently became personally responsible to the Kremlin for election results.

The Kremlin began regularly informing regional leaders about election forecasts, which many governors recognized as orders to be carried out. And what else could they do when Vladimir Putin publicly voiced his position in the following manner: "Could the election result [of United Russia] . . . affect the official position [of governors and mayors] or serve as one criterion for assessing their work? . . . In those places where governors run in direct elections without achieving a positive result, this points to the level of support—or a lack thereof—of citizens living in a specific territory. In some cases, if I were a leader of a region, I would consider handing in my resignation to the president."[49]

Russia's federal structure had been effectively drawn and quartered. Russian citizens lost their right to elect governors, as the Kremlin assigned to itself a monopoly to appoint them and converted governors into its subalterns much more interested in following the Kremlin's orders than the people's will. At the same time, Russian citizens lost their right to elect their representatives to the regional legislatures; the candidates whose names appeared on ballots were those preapproved by the Kremlin. Putin insisted that this power vertical, growing through incremental changes to election and other laws, was the only possible method of governing Russia.

DECEPTIVE CONCESSION

In December 2011 mass political protests broke out in Moscow, inspired by the outsized electoral fraud in the just-concluded Duma elections. Among other political demands heard in the streets of Moscow, restoration of the direct election of governors was at the top of the list. In an attempt to reduce political pressure, President Medvedev, who had entered the office in 2008, after the end of Putin's first two terms as president, yielded to the protesters' demands and announced the return of direct election of governors. But Putin, who by that time had announced his intent to return to the Kremlin in May 2012, in no way wanted to diminish his power to control gubernatorial nominations. Speaking in a live broadcast on Russian state television, he tried to come up with a new concept to defend the practice: "I have thought about this [the mayoral and gubernatorial elections], and . . . this filter at the presidential level has to be preserved to prevent the people who are backed by half-criminal or, God forbid, separatist elements from coming to power. . . . For example—this is an option to consider—all the parties that entered the regional legislature through direct elections by secret ballot could suggest their gubernatorial candidates to the president. . . . He has the right to reject any candidate. Then the party puts forward a different candidate until the right one is found, and then all these candidates run in direct elections by secret ballot." Not only did Putin oppose direct gubernatorial elections, he also categorically declared that the president's right to dismiss governors should be preserved: "And, of course, the president should have the negative control, that is, the right to dismiss governors for committing certain acts while in their official gubernatorial capacity."[50]

Medvedev's bill was introduced to the Duma in January 2012 with none of the filters mentioned by Putin. This was not the result of any ideological conflict between the two men but of the Kremlin's inability to invent the proper mechanism, being short on time. A month later, Putin reemphasized his intention to retain control "in matters relating to governors' elections. Yes, society has come close to this . . . [but] we have passed through the period of direct elections, and what was the outcome? Behind the candidates local oligarchic structures arose immediately, and sometimes criminals. . . . [We] need some type of a filter; we need elements of checks and balances."[51]

In early April 2012, following Putin's victory in the presidential election and the law's approval by the Duma on the first reading, President Dmitry Medvedev announced an amendment introducing a "municipal filter" for gubernatorial candidates. This filter required candidates to collect the signatures of 5 to 10 percent of municipal lawmakers (depending on regional legislation). Moreover, those lawmakers were required to represent three-fourths of municipalities in the region.[52] Although this scheme excluded the president from the decision-making process regarding gubernatorial candidates, in reality it turned out to be much tougher than it initially appeared. For many years the Kremlin had been consistently depriving local authorities of their power, transferring it (along with budget resources) to the regional level. As a result, municipal lawmakers could not influence the decision-making process; politicians were not interested in elections to local legislatures, and the majority of seats in the local legislatures were occupied by public employees paid out of the budget, who were nominated by local executives representing United Russia. Apart from United Russia, not a single party had enough municipal lawmakers to nominate its candidates in the Russian regions. The filter proved to be much tougher than Vladimir Putin could have dreamed. Should one be surprised, then, that the Constitutional Court once again recognized such a change as legitimate?[53]

The newly styled gubernatorial elections did not differ a lot from the presidential nominations. Before gubernatorial elections were abolished, they had been rather competitive. In 2000–04, only one out of every three elections had a gap between the winner (usually the incumbent governor) and the loser that exceeded fifty percentage points; in more than half the cases, no candidate was able to win the election on the first round. In twenty-four out of eighty-three cases in which the incumbent governor ran for reelection, he or she lost. But after gubernatorial elections were reintroduced in 2012 their results became easily predictable—figure 4-1 shows that in 2012–17 there was only one case (in eighty-seven elections) in which a second round was needed, and only one of the incumbent governors lost an election. To make the electoral choice easier, the Kremlin introduced yet another informal rule that applied to gubernatorial elections: when the Kremlin wanted to replace an incumbent governor, he was dismissed many months prior to the election and an acting governor, the Kremlin's candidate of choice, was appointed in the dismissed governor's place. The Kremlin's candidate then had time to secure the full support of the federal and regional bureaucracy and was able to dominate the elections.

FIGURE 4-1. Competition in the Gubernatorial
Elections in Russia, 2000–04 and 2013–17

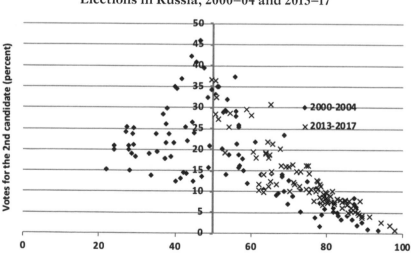

Votes for the 1st candidate (percent)

Source: Central Electoral Commission of the Russian Federation database, "Vybory, referendumy i inyye formy pryamogo voleizyavleniya" [Elections, referendums and other forms of direct declaration of will], Moscow (http://www.izbirkom.ru/region/izbirkom).

FINANCIAL LEASH

The ability to manage public finances is one of the key elements of governmental authority. Any federal state provides for a system of fiscal federalism that establishes rules for distributing budget revenues and expenditures between different levels of government, as well as rules (or principles) of financial assistance that the higher level of government offers to the lower. The Soviet Union had no system of fiscal federalism, so Russia inherited none after the Soviet collapse. Even the framework for such a system was lacking; there was no tax system in the Soviet economy until shortly before its demise, one being introduced only in the first half of 1992.

Fiscal relations between the federal center and the regions were chaotic in the early years after the Soviet collapse. The federal government did not have a cohesive approach to building fiscal relations with the regions, and regional leaders sought to secure advantages over their rivals based on their political weight. As a result, many of the more developed and fiscally sustainable regions signed individual tax-sharing agreements with the federal government, making the overall fiscal system in the country chaotic.

Beginning in 1994, the government gradually created a uniform system of fiscal relations with the regions. Regions received certain tax freedoms, such as the right to determine independently of the federal government the profit tax rate that would go to the regional budgets (though the maximum rate was limited). Regional and local authorities also received the right to introduce regional and local taxes.[54] In addition, the Duma passed formula-based regulations for tax revenue sharing between budgets at different levels. Regions received funds through a special Fund for Financial Support of the Regions that was established within the federal budget. Of course, this process was neither peaceful nor smooth: many of the requirements came into existence as a result of lengthy and repetitive budget negotiations in both the Duma and the Federation Council. Nevertheless, a clear shift away from individual agreements with the regions to uniform regulatory mechanisms occurred. An increasingly large share of federal budget funds for regional support was being redistributed through the established fund; by 1998 it had reached 80 percent, up from only 10 percent in 1994 and 49 percent in 1997.[55]

This system of fiscal federalism continued to be refined after the 1998 financial crisis. The adoption of the Tax Code established an exhaustive list of taxes, and their assignment to federal, regional, or local budgets established the right to set tax rates at different levels of government. Meanwhile, federal laws in the sphere of budget expenditures were revamped as well. The government tried to improve the mechanisms of revenue sharing with the regions and, looking for more flexibility, decided to establish three more dedicated funds to support the regional budgets. (In 2000, the per capita gross regional product for the top five wealthiest regions was ten times higher than that of the bottom five.)[56]

It soon became clear, however, that after the reform of the Federation Council in 2000 the federal center lost its negotiating partner. The governors, who had previously represented their regions' interests in the upper chamber of parliament, were replaced by regional lobbyists, whose goal was to get money out of federal agencies; businesspeople, who quickly appreciated the opportunities that a senator's seat provided; or retired federal officials, whom the Kremlin awarded with golden parachutes for one reason or another. This formed a one-way street of sorts: whatever the Ministry of Finance proposed was immediately accepted by both the federal parliament and the regions.[57]

Facing no constraints, the Ministry of Finance under Aleksey Kudrin established a new budgetary framework in which the regions completely lost their fiscal independence. On the one hand, the federal budget began to absorb a growing share of budgetary revenues; whereas in 1998 the share of regional budgets in the consolidated revenues exceeded 55 percent, by 2005 it had fallen below 37 percent (see figure 4-2). This redistribution to a large extent was promoted by economic growth and an increase in global oil prices, which boosted revenues concentrated in the federal budget. But at the same time, the Ministry of Finance insisted on concentrating all VAT and a significant portion of profit tax revenues in the federal treasury and prohibited the regions from imposing their own taxes.

On the other hand, the Ministry of Finance gradually began to impose tough regulations on the spending authority of the regions, prescribing standards and limitations for different types of expenditure. The Finance Ministry abandoned the idea of four funds that took shape in 2001, as well as the concept of developing budget federalism.[58] In 2005, the funds-based system was replaced with eighteen types of subsidies (subventions, grants, and a variety of other transfers) to be divided among the regional budgets.[59] By 2012, their number had increased to thirty-six, and it increased further, to 100, by 2016.[60] The federal Ministry of Finance did not conceal its intention to control the regions, defending this policy by stating that, when the regions had freedom to spend, their expenditures were not rational, and that many of them preferred to spend money on rebuilding offices and purchasing luxury cars rather than on schools and hospitals. Federal functionaries openly declared they knew better what items should be financed in a given region, and the share of regions in consolidated expenditures gradually declined from 50 percent in 1999–2000 to 37–38 percent (see figure 4-2).

The overall situation was aggravated in 2012, when Putin returned to the Kremlin as president and signed a set of decrees that forced the governors to significantly increase wages in health care and education. Though the governors had no choice but to follow these orders, the regions didn't have enough revenue to finance the plans and so began to cut investments as well as to borrow from banks. Fearing a repeat of the past, in which several regions defaulted on their debts, the Ministry of Finance made its control comprehensive: 97 percent of all regional expenditures became regulated by Moscow, and governors accepted full budgetary dependency as the new normal. Did it make any sense to promote business activity in the region and to boost the tax base if the next year's federal budget would reduce subsidies to the region? Seventy-three of eighty-five Russian regions could not balance their budgets without federal subsidies, and those that could were required to claim federal co-funding for many investment plans.

At the end of his presidential term, Dmitry Medvedev announced a plan to shift revenue collection and spending authority to the regional level, promising to boost revenues of regional budgets by 15 percent within the next presidential cycle. But that was not Vladimir Putin's intention; he recognized that financial independence would strengthen regional politicians. During his presidential terms, regional revenues declined from 13.7 percent of GDP to 12 percent, while the overall amount of federal subsidies to the regions declined from 3 percent to less than 1 percent of GDP.

By imposing this system, the Ministry of Finance helped the Kremlin deprive the regional authorities of any desire to claim more rights or free-

FIGURE 4-2. Share of Regional Budgets in the Russian Federation's Consolidated Budget Revenues and Expenditures

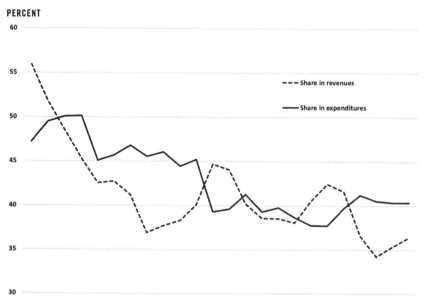

PERCENT

- - - Share in revenues

—— Share in expenditures

1998 1999 2000 2001 2002 2003 2004 2005 2006 2007 2008 2009 2010 2011 2012 2013 2014 2015 2016 2017 2018 2019 2020 2021

Sources: For 1998–2017, Russian Federal Treasury, "Ispolneniye byudzhetov. Konsolidirovannyy byudzhet Rossiyskoy Federatsii i byudzhetov gosudarstvennykh vnebyudzhetnykh fondov" [Execution of Budgets: Consolidated Budget of the Russian Federation and of the Budgets of Extra-Budgetary Funds] (http://www.roskazna.ru/ ispolnenie-byudzhetov/konsolidirovannyj-byudzhet/). For 2018–21, Ministry of Finance of the Russian Federation, "Proyect Osnovnyh napravlenii byudzhetnoy, nalogovoy i tamozhenno-tarifnoy politiki na 2019 god i na planovyy period 2020 i 2021 godov" [Draft of the main guidelines of the budgetary, tax, and custom tariff policies for 2019 and the planned period of 2020 and 2021], Moscow, July 11, 2018 (http://minfin.ru/ru/ document/?id_4=123006&area_id=4&page_id=2104).

Note: The regions' increasing share in revenues in 2009–10 and 2015–16 was the result of lower oil prices, which reduced the revenues to the federal budget. The sharp decline in the regions' expenditures in 2009–10 was the result of the fiscal stimulus plan implemented by the federal government, which used previously accumulated reserves.

doms. The lack of financial sustainability required all governors to be loyal to the Kremlin.

———————

When Vladimir Putin became Russian prime minister in 1999, as well as a candidate for the presidential elections, his main political opponent was the governors' bloc. Because they controlled the upper house of the Russian parliament, the regional governors had the ability to veto many legislative initiatives of the federal government and many important political nominations. Disagreements between the federal center and the regions are normal in a federal country; they force both sides to better understand each other's needs. The experience of the Russian Federation in the 1990s demonstrated that through negotiations, the federal government was able to build consensus with respect to the main principles of the transformation while also promoting a flexible federative policy in a country with a complex composition.

Fearful of the possibility that the governors' bloc would prevail in the parliamentary and presidential elections, Putin and his team opted not to negotiate with but to fight their political opponents, and in doing so they began to dismantle the federation. But Putin could not forget the threat that the independent governors posed to him in the early 2000s. In the following years he undermined, step by step, the regions' capacity to be present and heard on the federal political scene.

When introducing Sergey Kiriyenko as presidential envoy to the Volga Federal District in May 2000, Putin said, "I want to underscore and remind once again that the constitutional principles of federalism are an absolute priority. Our actions will not and should not be carried out in a way that violates these principles. In my view, this will bring nothing but problems." It might seem from this statement that the president understood quite clearly that the constitutional principles of federalism shouldn't be undermined, but then he went on to say "Our goal does not consist just in building the power vertical (the vertical is not a goal in and of itself). We have to create the conditions for preserving the unity of our state while also making this state more effectively manageable."[61] Apparently, two conflicting approaches—federalism and vertical subordination of different levels of government—could coexist in the president's mind, but not in practice. Either federalism or the power vertical was going to disappear.

Before his second presidential term expired in 2008, Putin had transformed Russia into a de facto unitary state in which citizens had no voice to
express their needs and no means to defend their interests, and in which governors and members of regional legislatures felt and behaved like functionaries, not politicians. Vladimir Putin had constructed the vertical of power he
had dreamed of since his earliest days in the Kremlin but was unable to make
this system function efficiently: citizens cannot communicate their needs to
governors and regional legislatures during elections because the concentra-
tion of all decision-making power in Moscow gives gubernatorial and regional functionaries no interest in receiving those signals.

Notes to Chapter 4

1. The Soviet Union itself was constructed as a federation with fifteen union republics, Russia being one of them. The standard regional subunits within republics were oblasts (regions). Russia and some other republics also had so-called autonomous (ethnic) republics or autonomous regions within their borders as well. Moreover, within some Russian regions autonomous districts existed, and in these cases the regions were called kray.

2. The Soviet Union had no tax system as such. Individual decisions on profit sharing regulated fiscal relations between enterprises and budgets.

3. The legal norm that gave autonomous republics and the USSR's constituent republics equal rights in certain respects further complicated the situation. According to the norm, "in the area of economic and sociocultural development on its territory, an autonomous republic has the same rights as the USSR constituent republic, with the exception of those rights that are in the jurisdiction of the constituent republic as per mutual agreement." See also Zakon SSSR ot 26.04.1990, "O razgranichenii polnomochiy mezhdu Soyuzom SSR I sub'yektami federatsii" [The law of the USSR of April 26, 1990, "On the division of powers between the USSR and the subjects of the federation"], *ConsultantPlus*, April 26, 1990 (http://www.consultant.ru/cons/cgi/online.cgi?req=doc&base=ESU&n=17#0).

4. On this basis, Tatarstan claimed its right to independently join the renewed Soviet Union throughout 1991.

5. All subjects of the Russian Federation except Tatarstan and Chechnya signed the Treaty of Federation. Bashkortostan signed the treaty under special conditions that granted the republic greater rights to manage state property and receive budget revenues than the other regions.

6. The Federation Council overrode a presidential veto at least thirty-eight times in 1996–99. "Sovet Federatsii 'gubernatorsko-spikerskogo' sozyva i Prezident" [Council of the Federation "governor-speaker" convocation and the president], *Politika*, September 8, 2000.

7. Irina Nagornykh, "I.o. prezidenta vvedet v strane diktaturu" [Acting president will introduce dictatorship in the country], *Kommersant* 14, February 1, 2000, p. 2.

8. President of Russia, "Ispolnyayushchiy obyazannosti Prezidenta, Predsedatel' Pravitel'stva Vladimir Putin prinyal uchastiye v rasshirennom zasedanii kollegii Ministerstva yustitsii" [Acting president Prime Minister Vladimir Putin took part in an expanded meeting of the collegium of the Ministry of Justice], news release, Moscow, January 31, 2000 (http://kremlin.ru/events/president/news/38065).

9. Ibid.

10. Aleksandr Voloshin, interview by the author, Moscow, January 12, 2016.

11. Evgeniy Petrov, "Primakov ne stalosuzhdat' voynu v Chechne" [Primakov did not condemn the war in Chechnya], *Nezavisimaya Gazeta*, November 2, 1999.

12. "V chem obvinyali gubernatora Yakovleva" [What were Governor Yakovlev's acquisitions], *Kommersant* 100, June 10, 2003, p. 1.

13. The SPS initially supported Putin during the presidential election and came out with the slogan "Kiriyenko for Duma, Putin for President," during the December Duma election. However, the Kremlin opted for an alliance with a more numerous communist faction in January 2000, leaving the SPS with no significant seats on Duma committees.

14. One of the SPS's leaders, Boris Nadezhdin, prepared a bill calling for the removal of governors by decision of the Supreme Court for violating the constitution and for a series of other violations—for instance, interfering with the work of the prosecutor general's office. Yelena Mizulina, who represented the Yabloko faction in the Duma at that time, proposed stripping governors and speakers of regional legislatures of their seats on the Federation Council.

15. Vladimir Putin, *Ot pervogolitsa* (*First Person*) (Moscow: Vagrius. 2000; New York: PublicAffairs, 2000), p. 165.

16. President of Russia, "Vladimir Putin prinyal uchastiye v soveshchanii rukovoditeley izbiratel'nykh komissiy sub'yektov Federatsii" [Vladimir Putin took part in a meeting of heads of election commissions of the subjects of the federation], news release, Moscow, May 6, 2000 (http://kremlin.ru/events/president/news/38126).

17. President of Russia, "Vystupleniye vo vremya predstavleniya polnomochnogo predstavitelya Prezidenta v Dal'nevostochnom federal'nom okruge" [Speech during the presentation of the Plenipotentiary Representative of the President in the Far Eastern Federal District], news release, Moscow, May 26, 2000 (http://kremlin.ru/events/president/transcripts/24113).

18. Aleksandr Voloshin, interview by the author, Moscow, January 12, 2016. Putin admitted he had discussed the idea of direct presidential appointments of governors when presenting his envoy to the Far Eastern Federal District on May 26, 2000: "There were also some radical suggestions—all the way to appointing the head of the region." See also President of Russia, "Vystupleniye vo vremya predstavleniya polnomochnogo predstavitelya Prezidenta v Dal'nevostochnom federal'nom okruge" [Speech during the presentation of the Plenipotentiary Representative of the President in the Far Eastern Federal District].

19. President of Russia, "Vladimir Putin podpisal Ukaz 'O postanovlenii Pravitel'stva Respubliki Ingushetiya ot 3 avgusta 1998 g. No. 204, O merakh po ispolneniyu Ukaza No. 72 ot 28 fevralya 1997 g. Prezidenta Respubliki Ingushetiya, Postanovleniya Soveta Bezopasnosti Respubliki Ingushetiya No. 4 ot 27 maya 1998 g.'" [Vladimir Putin signed the decree "On the Resolution of the Government of the Republic of Ingushetia dated August 3, 1998, No. 202, 'On Measures to Implement

Decree No. 72 of February 28, 1997, of the President of the Republic of Ingushetia,' Resolution of the Security Council of the Republic of Ingushetia No. 4 of May 27, 1998"], news release, Moscow, May 11, 2000 (http://kremlin.ru/events/president/ news/38142). See also President of Russia, "Vladimir Putin podpisal Ukaz 'Ob Ukaze Prezidenta Respubliki Ingushetiya ot 16 sentyabrya 1997 g. No. 229, O merakh po uluchsheniyu sbora platezhey za potreblennyye gaz i elektroenergiyu'" [Vladimir Putin signed the decree "On the Decree of the President of the Republic of Ingushetia from September 16, 1997, No. 229, 'On Measures to Improve the Collection of Payments for Consumed Gas and Electricity'"], news release, Moscow, May 11, 2000 (http://kremlin.ru/events/president/news/38144).

20. President of Russia, "Vladimir Putin podpisal Ukaz 'O postanovlenii glavy administratsii Amurskoy oblasti ot 23 iyunya 1999 g. No. 365, Ob organizatsii propuska grazhdan Rossiyskoy Federatsii v torgovyy kompleks g. Kheykhe (KNR)'" [Vladimir Putin signed the decree "On the Resolution of the Head of the Administration of the Amur Region dated June 23, 1999, No. 365, 'On the Organization of the Pass of Russian Citizens to the Kheikhe Shopping Center (KNR)'"], news release, Moscow, May 11, 2000 (http://kremlin.ru/events/president/news/38141).

21. President of Russia, "Prezident podpisal Ukaz 'O postanovlenii glavy administratsii Smolenskoy oblasti ot 26 iyunya 1998 g. No. 271, O vzimanii platezhey za zagryazneniye okruzhayushchey prirodnoy sredy s inostrannykh yuridicheskikh lits i grazhdan, ekspluatiruyushchikh avtotransportnyye sredstva na avtodorogakh Smolenskoy oblasti'" [The President signed the decree "On the Resolution of the Head of the Administration of Smolensk Region of June 26, 1998, No. 271, 'On Collecting Payments for Environmental Pollution from Foreign Legal Entities and Citizens Who Operate Vehicles on the Roads of Smolensk Region'"], news release, Moscow, May 16, 2000 (http://kremlin.ru/events/president/news/38163).

22. President of Russia, "Vladimir Putin napravil Predsedatelyu Gosudarstvennogo Sobraniya Bashkirii Konstantinu Tolkachevu pis'mo, v kotorom obratilsya k respublikanskomu Gosudarstvennomu Sobraniyu s predstavleniyem o privedenii v sootvetstviye s Konstitutsiyey Rossiyskoy Federatsii i federal'nymi zakonami Konstitutsii Bashkirii" [Vladimir Putin sent a letter to the chairman of the State Assembly of Bashkortostan, Konstantin Tolkachev, in which he addressed the Republican State Assembly on the idea of bringing the constitution of Bashkiria in line with the constitution of the Russian Federation and federal laws], news release, Moscow, May 11, 2000 (http://kremlin.ru/events/president/news/38143).

23. "Gubernatory prizvali Putina k sovmestnoy rabote" [The governors called Putin to work together], *Kommersant* 86, May 17, 2000, p. 2.

24. President of Russia, "Televizionnoye obrashcheniye k grazhdanam Rossii" [Television address to the citizens of Russia], news release, Moscow, May 17, 2000 (http://kremlin.ru/events/president/transcripts/21440).

25. Irina Nagornykh, "Gubernatoram prigrozili skam'yey podsudimykh" [The governors were threatened with the dock], *Kommersant* 94, May 27, 2000, p. 2.

26. Opredeleniye Konstitutsionnogo suda Rossiyskoy Federatsii [Definition of the Constitutional Court of the Russian Federation], June 27, 2000 (http://doc.ksrf.ru/decision/KSRFDecision32184.pdf). Postanovleniye Konstitutsionnogo Suda Rossiyskoy Federatsii [Regulation of the Constitutional Court of the Russian Federation], June 7, 2000 (http://doc.ksrf.ru/decision/KSRFDecision30359.pdf).

27. Vladimir Nikolayev, "Konstitutsionnyy sud razvyazal ruki Kremlyu" [The Constitutional Court untied the Kremlin's hands], *Kommersant* 102, June 8, 2000, p. 2. .

28. President of Russia, "Otvety na voprosy zhurnalistov posle vstrechi s rukovodstvom administratsii i predpriyatiy Yaroslavskoy oblasti" [Answers to questions from journalists after a meeting with the leadership of the administration and enterprises of the Yaroslavl region], news release, Moscow, May 31, 2000 (http://kremlin.ru/events/president/transcripts/24131).

29. Putin, *Ot pervogolitsa* (*First Person*), p. 171.

30. Alla Barakhova, "Sub'yektov federatsii razob'yut po odinochke" [Subjects of the federation will be split one by one], *Kommersant* 200, October 25, 2000, p. 2.

31. In the summer of 2002 the Russian Constitutional Court recognized this amendment as conforming to the Russian Constitution.

32. Vladimir Putin respects strong opponents who have views of their own and are prepared to defend them up to a certain point. So Putin finds it expedient to keep his potential opponents in close proximity to the ruling regime by offering them a worthwhile "compensation" for refusing to publicly advocate their position. Anatoly Chubais is one beneficiary of such an approach; Nikolai Fedorov, whose political career proceeded successfully, is another. Fedorov remained president of Chuvashia until 2010 and subsequently became a member of the Federation Council for three years. In November 2011, Fedorov became chair of the influential Federation Council Committee on Constitutional Law, Legal Issues, and Civil Society. After Putin returned to the Kremlin in May 2012, it became clear that Fedorov could prove an obstacle to the Kremlin's new initiatives, and he was nominated for agricultural minister. After he resigned his ministerial post in 2015, he returned to the Federation Council as its first deputy chairman.

33. Postanovleniye Konstitutsionnogo Suda Rossiyskoy Federatsii [Regulation of the Constitutional Court of the Russian Federation], April 4, 2000 (http://doc.ksrf.ru/decision/KSRFDecision30339.pdf).

34. Vladimir Nikolayev, "Eto postanovleniye lishit nekotorykh vozmozhnosti shalit'" [This regulation will deprive someone of the opportunity to play games], *Kommersant*, April 5, 2002.

35. President of Russia, "Obrashcheniye Prezidenta Rossii Vladimira Putina" [Ad-

dress of the President of Russia Vladimir Putin], news release, Moscow, September 4, 2004 (http://www.kremlin.ru/events/president/transcripts/22589).

36. President of Russia, "Po zavershenii programmy 'Razgovor s Vladimirom Putinym. Prodolzheniye': Predsedatel' Pravitel'stva Rossiyskoy Federatsii otvetil na voprosy zhurnalistov" [After the program "Conversation with Vladimir Putin. Continuation." The chairman of the Government of the Russian Federation answered journalists' questions], news release, Moscow, December 15, 2011 (http://archive. government.ru/docs/17411/). Although the law included a formal provision stipulating that gubernatorial candidates nominated by the president had to be approved by regional legislatures, not once was the president's candidate rejected by any regional parliament.

37. Government of Russia, "Stenogramma programmy 'Razgovor s Vladimirom Putinym. Prodolzheniye'" [Transcript of the program "Conversation with Vladimir Putin. Continuation"], Moscow, December 15, 2011 (http://archive.premier.gov.ru/ events/news/17409/).

38. President of Russia, "Obrashcheniye Prezidenta Rossii Vladimira Putina" [Appeal of the President of Russia Vladimir Putin], news release, Moscow, September 4, 2004 (http://kremlin.ru/events/president/transcripts/22589).

39. Larisa Kaftan, "Zamestitel' glavy administratsii Prezidenta RF Vladislav Surkov: Putin ukreplyayet gosudarstvo, a ne sebya" [Vladislav Surkov, deputy head of the administration of the President of the Russian Federation: Putin strengthens the state, not himself], *Komsomol'skaya Pravda*, September 28, 2004.

40. As acting president, Putin allowed for the possibility of Russia's joining NATO in March 2000.

41. Aleksey Chernyshev and Il'ya Bulavinov, "Sud'ba gubernatora Nazdratenko reshena" [The fate of the governor Nazdratenko is sealed], *Kommersant* 20, February 6, 2001, front page.

42. Yakovlev's resignation paved the way for the promotion of Valentina Matviyenko as St. Petersburg's governor, something Putin had dreamed about back in 2000. Since September 2011 Matviyenko has headed the Federation Council.

43. President of Russia, "Interv'yu direktoru direktsii informatsionnykh programm 'Pervogo' kanala Kirillu Kleymenovu, glavnomu redaktoru sluzhby informatsii telekanala NTV Tat'yane Mitkovoy i politicheskomu obozrevatelyu telekanala 'Rossiya' Nikolayu Svanidze" [Interview with the head of the direction of information programs of Channel One Kirill Kleimenov, editor in chief of NTV television channel Tatyana Mitkova, and political observer of the Rossiya television channel Nikolai Svanidze], news release, Moscow, November 18, 2004 (http://kremlin.ru/events/president/transcripts/22690).

44. Natal'ya Gorodetskaya, "'Vertikal' ot Dmitriya Kozaka" ['Vertical' from Dmitry Kozak], *Vremya Novostey*, June 3, 2002.

45. According to the 2000 law, the president could disband a regional legislature by submitting a bill to the Duma.

46. "Gubernatorskaya gorizontal' protiv prezidentskoy vertikali" [The gubernatorial horizontal line against the presidential vertical], *Kommersant* 200, October 26, 2004, p. 3.

47. Elena Rotkevich and Viktor Filippov, "Vladimiru Butovu dali srok" [Vladimir Butov was sentenced], *Izvestiya,* January 11, 2005..

48. "Gubernatory, naznachenie po novoy scheme" [Governors who were appointed under the new scheme], Scilla.ru, 2005 (http://www.scilla.ru/works/raznoe/gub .html).

49. Government of Russia, "V pryamom efire telekanalov 'Rossiya 1,' 'Rossiya 24' i 'RTR-Planeta,' radiostantsiy 'Mayak,' 'Vesti FM' i 'Radio Rossii' vyshla spetsial'naya programma 'Razgovor s Vladimirom Putinym. Prodolzheniye'" [Airing on the television channels Russia 1, Russia 24 and RTR-Planet, the radio stations Mayak, Vesti FM and Radio of Russia a special program, "Talking with Vladimir Putin. Continuation"], news release, Moscow, December 15, 2011 (http://archive.government.ru/ docs/17409/).

50. Ibid.

51. Government of Russia, "Predsedatel' Pravitel'stva Rossiyskoy Federatsii V.V. Putin vstretilsya s politologami" [Prime Minister Vladimir Putin met with political scientists], news release, Moscow, February 6, 2012 (http://archive.government.ru/ docs/18008/).

52. Irina Granik, Maksim Ivanov, Natal'ya Korchenkova, and Natal'ya Gorodetskaya, "Gubernatorskim vyboram udvoili fil'tr" [The gubernatorial election doubled the filter], *Kommersant,* June 6, 2012.

53. Postanovleniye Konstitutsionnogo Suda Rossiyskoy Federatsii [Regulation of the Constitutional Court of the Russian Federation], December 24, 2012 (http://doc. ksrf.ru/decision/KSRFDecision118883.pdf).

54. However, this decision had serious negative consequences—in many regions dozens of minor taxes were introduced—and in early 1997 this opportunity was removed.

55. At the same time, a significant part of federal budget investment spending (the so-called special-purpose federal programs) took place in certain regions, and the federal government continued to discuss how to redistribute these funds between the regions. Besides, the government (specifically the Finance Ministry) had control over budgetary loans and the funds transferred to regional budgets in the process of accounts reconciliation, when the regions received compensation for financing part of the federal spending on their territory. Technically, neither means of funding could be considered financial aid, but the federal government actively used both mechanisms to affect regional budgets.

56. Rosstat, *Valovyy regional'nyy product po regionam Rossiyskoy Federatsii 1998–2012* [Gross regional product by regions of the Russian Federation in 1998–2012], Federal State Statistics Service of the Russian Federation (www.gks.ru/free_doc/new_site/vvp/vrp98-12.xls).

57. For instance, during the 2001 budget vote, after very little deliberation, both houses of parliament approved the transfer of 15 percent of VAT to the federal budget, although these funds had previously been received by regional budgets, making up 8 percent of their total tax revenues.

58. Government of Russia, "Postanovleniye Pravitel'stva Rossiyskoy Federatsii ot 15.08.2001 g. No. 584, 'O Programme razvitiya byudzhetnogo fcdcralizma v Russiys-koy Federatsii na period do 2005 goda'" [Decree of the Government of the Russian Federation of August 15, 2001, No. 584, "On the Program for the Development of Budgetary Federalism in the Russian Federation for the Period to 2005"] (http://government.ru/docs/all/39732/).

59. Federal'nyy zakon ot 23.12.2004 N 173-FZ (red. ot 04.11.2005) "O federal'nom byudzhete na 2005 god" [Federal Law No. 173-FZ of December 23, 2004 (as amended November 4, 2005), "On the Federal Budget for 2005"] (http://www.consultant.ru/document/cons_doc_LAW_50877/).

60. Federal'nyy zakon ot 14.12.2015 N 359-FZ (red. ot 22.11.2016) "O federal'nom byudzhete na 2016 god" [Federal Law No. 359-FZ of December 14, 2015 (as amended November 22, 2016), "On the Federal Budget for 2016"] (http://www.consultant.ru/document/cons_doc_LAW_190535/). The figure of 100 comes from Kudrin's speech at the Sochi Forum in February 2017.

61. President of Russia, "Vystupleniye vo vremya predstavleniya polnomochnogo predstavitelya Prezidenta v Privolzhskom federal'nom okruge" [Speech during the presentation of the President's Plenipotentiary in the Volga Federal District], transcripts, Moscow, June 2, 2000 (http://kremlin.ru/events/president/transcripts/24207).

Five

JUST A DREAM

Obedient Court

To us, the people, independence [of the courts] guarantees nothing.
                    —Dmitry Kozak

The third branch of government, the independent judiciary, plays an extremely important, perhaps even decisive, role in protecting the people's rights. These include political, economic, constitutional, and other fundamental rights. The rule of law affords the judiciary a unique opportunity to review any government decision or any citizen's action for legality. The independence of the judiciary from the executive and legislative branches of government is meant to guarantee the rule of law. Easy to say . . .

THERE WAS NO NEED

By the time Russia gained independence, it could not claim to have, among other things, an independent judiciary. Moreover, the judiciary wasn't even recognized as a separate branch of government. As with all other institutions

of the totalitarian state, the Soviet judiciary was part of the consolidated executive branch and was completely controlled by the Communist Party. The
jurisdiction of Soviet courts was extremely narrow. For instance, an ordinary
citizen couldn't sue the state. The state owned all property, and disputes
between state-owned companies were subject to government-run arbitration
structures whose decisions were more often based on pragmatic considerations than on the law. Reviewing government decisions for constitutionality
was completely out of the question. The court's day-to-day activities were
overseen by the prosecutor's office, which de facto played the role of the judiciary: prosecutors received the results of an investigation from the militia
(police), arrived at a decision based on their evaluation of that evidence, and
drafted an indictment, which was later rubber-stamped by the court in sen-
tencing. There was no jury trial, and the defense played only a symbolic role.
In half of all court hearings during the Soviet era, prosecutors didn't show up
in court at all, so the judges assumed their role.[1]

So it should come as no surprise that, after the collapse of the Soviet
Union, the judicial system Russia inherited from the Soviet Union had to
be rebuilt from scratch. Moreover, the judiciary had to become an independent branch of government that could disagree with and oppose the decisions
made by the legislative and executive branches. As long as the judiciary was
unable to reverse the decisions of the executive, it could not be considered an
independent real power.

The *Concept of Judicial Reform* was approved by the Supreme Council of
the RSFSR in October 1991, before the disintegration of the USSR. That was
the starting point for the establishment of the judicial branch in modern-day
Russia. In June 1992, parliament passed the law "On the Status of Judges,"
which codified the principles of judicial independence, immunity, and lifetime judicial appointments.[2] In 1993 the law "On Appealing the Actions and
Decisions of Government Agencies" established the courts as the arbiter in
disputes between the government and individual citizens.[3] The constitution
of the Russian Federation adopted in 1993 confirmed the fundamental principle of separation of powers into co-equal legislative, executive, and judicial
branches. In late 1996, after lengthy deliberation, parliament passed the law
"On Judicial Reform," which set forth the structure and organizational principles of the judiciary in Russia.[4]

FIRST ROLLBACKS

But implementation of the 1991 *Concept of Judicial Reform* eventually got bogged down: many of its provisions had not been implemented and others were being revised, whether de facto or de jure. For example, the introduction of a system of jury trials had been postponed for a long time, and the idea of creating judicial districts for general jurisdiction courts had not been implemented at all.[5] (These districts would not have correlated with the country's administrative divisions and would therefore have interfered with the ability of local and regional authorities to put pressure on judges.)

The principle of judicial independence did not last long either. In the spring of 1993, lifetime judges' appointments were replaced with term limits: an initial five-year term for lower-level court (municipal, city district, garrison) judges was introduced, and only after serving for this period could they be reappointed for life. In 1995 the five-year term became a three-year term and was extended to regional court judges. The Constitutional Court reviewed the constitutionality of this legal norm in 1999 and accepted it on condition that the first three-year term be regarded as a probationary period, after which a judge had to be automatically reappointed for life if he had not previously been removed for cause. This decision later led to the creation of a loophole that allowed unwanted judges to be removed "upon the expiration of the term" even if no grounds were cited. The courts have never granted appeals by judges removed in this fashion.

Additional legislation adopted in 1995 stipulated that judges in lower and regional courts would be appointed by the president after "consultation" with regional legislatures,[6] a process that gave regional bureaucracies substantial leverage. Meanwhile, judges became much more vulnerable to removal for cause: now they could be dismissed if they were found to be "acting in a way that diminishes the authority of the judiciary." In practice, this meant that any critical statement a judge made about the judicial system could be interpreted as diminishing its authority, thus triggering the judge's dismissal.

What happened to judicial reform after the new constitution was adopted in late 1993? Why did it slow down? The experts who drafted judicial reform in 1991 cited three reasons why it fell off the Kremlin's radar as an important issue.[7] First, the slow and painful pace of the economic transition made the economic agenda more important than state building. Second, Russia inherited the Soviet Union's extremely paltry financing system for the judiciary; judges were among the lowest-paid state officials. Court facilities and infrastructure were also in terrible shape, and judges had an incredibly heavy workload (on average, each of them had to review 45.4 cases a month).[8] The federal budget was unable to fully finance the judicial system, forcing courts to plead for additional financing with local and regional authorities and even private sponsors, all of which chipped away at the courts' independence. Third, no one seriously lobbied for the interests of the judiciary; the general citizenry, for its part, was too preoccupied with day-to-day problems to keep tabs on the reform process in this area. From 1991 to 1993 the Kremlin co-opted a number of qualified and respected legal scholars to work on judicial reform; many of them retained their positions on the parliamentary committee and were sponsors of the reforms. During the 1993 parliamentary elections, none of them was reelected, and the committee became dominated by the day-to-day interests of the chief justices of the two Russian higher courts, who were mostly focused on financial issues.

JUDICIAL HIERARCHY

The federal system of general jurisdiction courts put together by the Supreme Court was intended to create a uniform legal framework in the country and to prevent atomization of the judiciary. After the "parade of sovereignties" in the early 1990s, the Supreme Court wanted to avoid weakening the federation, which had only recently been consolidated on the basis of the new constitution. But everything has its price. While it supported the unity of the legal space in Russia and aimed at unifying the law, the Supreme Court failed to establish the principle that its decisions superseded all others. It stopped short of insisting that its decisions were binding on the regional and local courts.[9] The Supreme Court recognized that a proactive stand on this issue would encounter fierce resistance from the judicial community at lower levels, which was backed by local and regional authorities. Instead, the Supreme Court settled on an ostensibly easier way to reach its target: it built a hierarchy of courts within courts.

The key feature of this hierarchy, a "chief justice" that existed in all courts, was inherited from the Soviet era but was significantly strengthened in the mid-1990s. Not only was a court's chief justice put in charge of all of a given court's administrative resources (budget appropriation, office space, personnel, bonus payments, and apartment distribution) and decisions about case assignment among judges, he or she also had enormous capacity to influence the subordinates' careers. A court's chief justice was also empowered to initiate decisions on a new judge's lifetime reappointment after the initial five-year (and then three-year) term; he or she had the right to disregard the recommendation of the Qualification Collegium of judges, or Judges Qualification Board (JQB), and to recommend promotion of a judge or award a higher qualification grade. All this made the court's chief justice not just another judge but the boss of all the judges in his or her office, one who could bring a great deal of pressure to bear on colleagues to see things his or her way. If a particular judge refused to follow the court's chief justice's view as to the interpretation of a case, he could be saddled with a heavy caseload or be given cases that he didn't feel comfortable handling, which could then lead to judicial errors.[10] It seems clear that very few judges would resist their court's chief justice.

This system of hierarchical subordination within the courts was supplemented by a hierarchy of courts' chief justices. According to the law, the Russian president nominated all judges (except those of the three higher courts) in the country and all courts' chief justices. But the president appointed a court's chief justice based on the recommendation of the chief justices of the upper-level courts. And it was obvious that anyone who kept (or was looking for) the position of chief justice would have to accept the rules of the game and not contradict the opinion of his or her superiors.

As a result, the power vertical within the Russian judiciary emerged even before Vladimir Putin started talking about it. But this vertical was counterbalanced by the law requiring consultations (de facto—preapproval) of the regional legislatures of all candidates for judgeships and chief justice positions. On the one hand, this led to the judiciary's dependence on the regional authorities, but on the other hand, it also meant that nomination power was not concentrated in a single person's hands. After Vladimir Putin announced his intent to build the power vertical, the only thing left for him to do was to subordinate the judicial power vertical to himself only. This he began to do in 2001.

A FURTIVE PLAN

The Russian judicial system was far from ideal when Vladimir Putin came to power. But in Boris Yeltsin's era the Constitutional Court was not afraid to reject laws signed by the president. The justices of the Supreme Court could dispute presidential decrees. The judge of the Moscow City Court could block decisions of the regional parliament extending its authority. The authors of the 1991 *Concept of Judicial Reform* hoped that "as soon as the judicial branch becomes institutionally independent and the judicial community will become an autonomous system, the frog will become the Frog Prince." But these hopes were short-lived. Equipped with new social status and legal guarantees, Russian judges "[fell] into the same temptations as the rest of the Russian post-Soviet society," they pointed out several years later.[11] Without doubt, rooting out corruption in the courts was the right goal, but the tool selected during the course of the 2001 judicial reform—comprehensive presidential control over judges—was ill-suited for the job.

The first deputy chief of the presidential staff, Dmitry Kozak, having been tasked with preparing the judicial reform, refused to cooperate with the judicial community and legal scholars and made every effort to conceal his discussions and ideas from the public. During the Congress of Russian Judges in November 2000, with President Putin on the stage, the chairman of the Council of Judges said: "The issues of improving judges' status is now again on the agenda and is being actively discussed. . . . We can easily see that most proposals are aimed at curtailing judges' independence. . . . Whom do these proposals originate from? We don't know. Ghostwriters with made-up names publish various proposals without citing any documents. . . . We have invited [them] . . . to the Council of Judges and to the regional councils' seminars, but they refused to engage in a dialogue with judges."[12] While the preparations for the reform were in full swing, Vladimir Putin tried to camouflage his intentions: "An independent judiciary in Russia . . . actually emerged. . . . In its fundamental details, the *Concept of Judicial Reform* has been implemented. I agree . . . the judicial reform needs to be accelerated.

Moreover, we finally have to complete it. But only in the details that have been specified earlier. I think it would be incorrect to say that we have to start another fundamental reform now."[13] Nevertheless he disclosed one of the vectors for future changes: "Today any judge is accountable only to the Judges Qualification Board. These bodies were created to ensure judges' independence. But they are elected by judges themselves, and they consist only of judges. Maybe this corporate isolation can be expanded a bit. Members of the legal community and parliamentarians could be added to the boards."[14] During his speech at the Congress, Putin employed his favorite co-optation technique: he announced a 20 percent pay raise for judges but expected to receive their loyalty in return.[15]

It soon became clear that the judicial community's fears had been justified. In late January 2001, Kozak's group began to disclose its intentions. The main slogan, "Let us reform the judiciary through its key figure—the judge," was so appealing in and of itself and received such good press coverage that even many judges failed to see the glaring flaw immediately.[16] "Just like the other branches of government, the courts have to guarantee citizens' political, economic, and social rights and freedoms; they have to be an instrument that ensures equality before the law. . . . It is very important to preserve the judges' independence from the other branches of government. . . . [It is proposed] introducing into law a clear and understandable list of legal grounds on which a judge's term can be ended prematurely . . . to protect the judge from arbitrary decisions."[17]

At the same time, some statements by the Kremlin demonstrated that the authors of the reform did not see the judiciary as an independent branch of government power and did not recognize its main purpose in providing justice: "Courts and law enforcement agencies are the main links in the mechanism of state coercion. . . . This mechanism—the state's repressive machine—provides protection for most citizens." Moreover, Kozak openly announced the Kremlin's plans to significantly limit judges' independence by "lifting the current ban on operative investigative activities directed against judges [monitoring, surveillance, the interception of phone calls], as well as allowing investigation of judges without the consent of the JQBs."[18] Actually, not everyone saw the threat. The liberal politician and SPS party leader Boris Nemtsov supported the proposed reform at the time, saying that its implementation "will encounter fierce resistance on the part of judicial bureaucracy" and that the president needed to demonstrate political will to ensure its success.[19]

THE OTHER SIDE OF THE COIN

Indeed, the Kozak reform wasn't entirely negative; it incorporated many good ideas. For instance, the budgetary outlay for the judicial system from 2002 to 2006 increased significantly, allowing new judges to be hired, their caseloads to be reduced,[20] higher salaries, and enhanced facilities for the courts. These changes demonstrated the Kremlin's concern for judges' problems and were appreciated by the judicial community.

But the extra budgetary financing was a Trojan horse that ultimately posed a threat to the independence of the judiciary. Those funds were not distributed at the discretion of the highest courts but were structured as a government target-oriented program with performance criteria. Based on the criteria, courts' chief justices could be promoted up the hierarchical ladder, and courts could receive better financing and more apartments for judges and court employees. There is nothing wrong with performance targets in budget planning per se; they can be a useful instrument for managing government expenditures, provided they are commensurate with the goals that the recipients of the funds set for themselves. But that clearly did not happen in the case of the Russian judicial system. The chosen targets were formal (for instance, the number of cases reviewed in a timely fashion), and some of them clearly contradicted the principle of judicial independence. The number of reversals on appeal became one of the most important performance indicators for individual judges and the courts at the primary level. In practice, this performance target led to situations in which a judge from an upper court could call the lower court's chief justices and tell them how a particular case should be decided. The lower court's chief justices would then transmit this message to the judge hearing the case, who knew full well that a reversal of his ruling would result in a deterioration in his or his office's performance criteria and would create problems both for him and for his colleagues in the court.

DEMOLISHING THE PILLARS

Many of the legislative changes submitted by President Putin to the Russian parliament undermined the rule of law in Russia. Judges' independence from the executive branch, their immunity from prosecution, and lifetime appointments all helped guarantee the rule of law. The 2001 judicial reform assailed all three of these components.

The Kremlin's first move was to purge the judges: lifetime appointments were replaced with forced retirement by age sixty-five. (As soon as this consideration was passed, the law was revised once again: three months after the sixty-five-year age limit went into force, it was extended to seventy years.) The ruling allowed the Kremlin to squeeze out of the Supreme Court, the Supreme Arbitration Court, and the regional courts many experienced judges who had played an important role in the transformation of the judiciary in the 1990s. Additionally, many of the various courts' chief justices were replaced by persons selected by the Kremlin. According to the Kremlin's plan, however, the powers of the court's chief justices were not diminished but strengthened: they became responsible for the judicial selection process in their offices and gained the right to veto the recommendations of the JQBs on appointments.

Evidently the Kremlin's goal was to make them all "obedient" and loyal to the Kremlin, not to regional authorities. It wasn't particularly difficult to accomplish this, given the chief justices' propensity to keep their position as long as possible. Since the courts' chief justices were appointed by the president on the recommendation of the chief justices of the Supreme Court or Supreme Arbitration Court, with preapproval by regional legislatures, the solution consisted of two parts. First, regional preapproval was eliminated. The regions sought to challenge this decision in the Constitutional Court, but to no avail. Second, the term for the courts' chief justices was limited to six years, with the possibility of reappointment for one more term.[21] This meant that any court's chief justice who wanted to retain his position had to obey his superiors and cater to their wishes. Under this system, his superiors would be both the chief justices of the Supreme Court and Supreme Arbitration Court and the presidential administration. On this ground, courts' chief justices received additional powers, which strengthened the hierarchical system of the courts. Before the 2001 reform a simple majority vote of the JQB could override a court's chief justice's veto of a judge's appointment; after the 2001 reform, a two-thirds majority vote was required.

The combination of the initial three-year term for judges, the removal of lifetime judiciary appointments, and an increase in the number of judges in the country allowed the Kremlin effectively to purge the judicial community. By 2012 almost 60 percent of Russian judges had received their authorities after 2002—that is, after undergoing the new selection process. Court chief justices began to play a key role in the judicial selection process: they set up the application process and submitted the candidate to the JQB and higher court for approval. Under the new system, timely case resolution and the number of times a judge was reversed by a superior court became key criteria for evaluating a judge's job performance. This prompted the lower-court judges to take the recommendations of superior court judges more seriously. After all, a judicial decision that contravenes the recommended one is more likely to be reversed, which would negatively affect both the judge's and his court's job performance evaluations. As a result, chief justices prefer promoting to judges' positions clerks who have worked in their court for five to seven years, learned the ropes, and demonstrated their complete loyalty to them.

The process of selection and promotion of judges was put under close supervision by the *siloviki*, who assigned themselves the decision-makers' powers. It became the new norm for candidates for judicial positions to receive an informal approval from the secret police (FSB),[22] both at the initial appointment stage and on reappointment. FSB operatives researched the candidates and the judge's political views, personal connections, and preferences. Apart from being responsible for submitting their official documents, the candidates had to acquire a number of certificates from the prosecutor's office, the police, and other agencies. These certificates became the prerequisite for the formal procedure: lacking any of them prevented the candidate from submitting his documents for consideration.

UNDER THE KREMLIN'S CONTROL

As it built the power vertical, the Kremlin could not allow anyone to dispute or, worse yet, block its decisions. A new law gave the key voice in the judges' nominating procedure to the presidential administration. According to Putin's previously announced view, the rules governing the composition of the JQBs had been changed: before that only judges could be members of the JQBs; after that one-third of the seats were dedicated to the "general public" (usually meaning clerks from the regional administration), and one seat on each JQB was given to a presidential representative. The later decision not only put the presidential administration in control of all decisions of the JQB but also allowed it to influence any decision if necessary: all judges in Russia knew that their careers depended on the Kremlin, and few of them were ready to dispute the recommendations of presidential appointees.

In 2004 the Kremlin wanted to go even further: at the suggestion of the chairman of the Federation Council, all judges in the highest JQB should be replaced with people nominated by the Federation Council. As the Federation Council chairman said, "None of the branches of power should remain out of control. . . . We [the Federation Council] want more control over the Highest JQB." But this idea was strongly opposed by the chief justices of the Supreme Court and Supreme Arbitration Court, who appealed to Putin, who nixed the idea.

Under the old version of the law, the president had the power to appoint judges after they were recommended by the chief justices of the higher court. But if the president refused to appoint the recommended candidate for a position, he had to explain his decision, and the JQB had the right to recommend the same candidate again. Under the amended law, the president's refusal was final, and he didn't have to explain his decision.[23] In other words, the president, or rather his administration,[24] acquired complete and unrestricted control over judicial appointments. There were no specific norms or criteria or time limitations for deciding on a candidate, so a particular candidate could wait a long time indeed to be considered.

NO ONE IS IMMUNE

The proposals also sought to introduce significant changes concerning judicial immunity. Of course, a judge's immunity from prosecution is not synonymous with impunity; judges all over the world are subject to prosecution for breaking laws, but there is a special procedure to prove their guilt. The 1992 law "On the Status of Judges" allowed only the prosecutor general to bring a criminal case against a judge after receiving approval from the JQB, which consisted solely of judges. The JQBs decided whether the prosecutor general had enough legal grounds to bring charges against a judge. However, this legal norm never worked well in practice; the judicial community showed strong solidarity in refusing to prosecute members even in cases where guilt was evident.

As retired deputy chief justice of the Constitutional Court Tamara Morshchakova acknowledged, "The JQBs had only one task—to answer the question whether the initiated prosecution was a means of influencing a judge or his future decisions or of punishing a judge for a past decision. In the absence of these circumstances, and given the presence of elements of a crime, JQBs had no right to block the prosecution. But . . . [judges] did not conduct themselves in the best possible manner. They decided that it is their goal to protect their members."[25] Retired deputy chief justice of the Supreme Court Viktor Zhuykov shared the same view.[26]

The Kremlin's amendments deprived the JQBs of the right to evaluate the legality of a judge's conduct and transferred this function to a panel of three Supreme Court justices. As a result, the Supreme Court justices would decide the legality of a judge's conduct, and the JQB would then decide whether or not criminal charges should be brought against the judge. It should be obvious that the members of the JQB were essentially reduced to rubber-stamping the Supreme Court justices' decisions on the legality of judges' conduct. After that, the review of the veracity of the charges brought against a judge, and the obligation to investigate the possibility of retribution against a judge, melted away.

Another serious threat to judges that came out of the president's bill was the possibility of disciplinary charges being brought against a judge on vague grounds such as "violating the norms of judicial ethics." Although such a charge would not automatically result in a judge being stripped of his status, a few of them could allow the court's chief justice to initiate termination proceedings against the judge. Besides, disciplinary charges would provide grounds for depriving a judge of his bonus, deprioritizing him on the housing waiting list, and transferring a judge to a lower court or a remote region.

Here is how Zhuykov shed light on these changes: "[These] proposals will allow the early termination of a judge's status if he has been brought up on numerous disciplinary charges. As a result, we have this chain: the court's chief justices become very dependent on those who will eventually be deciding whether to reappoint them [with guidance from the Kremlin and superiors]; and [they] are provided the authority to initiate the process of bringing disciplinary charges against judges [who are not loyal enough or want to be really independent], while the JQB [which includes a presidential representative] has the right to remove them. In other words, a mechanism for influencing judges and punishing them will be created."[27]

In addition, the bill introduced administrative sanctions against judges. According to another retired deputy chief justice of the Supreme Court, Vladimir Radchenko, at that time eighty agencies in Russia were allowed to bring administrative charges against individuals, so the new legal norm put judges on the same level as regular citizens. While the Duma made the procedure for bringing such charges against judges extremely complicated, it didn't remove this threat entirely.

RELYING ON PARLIAMENT

The Duma became the main battlefield over presidential bills. The judicial community tried actively to oppose measures that would clearly deprive judges of their independence and lifetime tenure. The chief justices of the Supreme Court and Supreme Arbitration Court spent days in Duma committee meetings explaining the essence of the proposed changes and why they were unacceptable to judges. Their main argument was that the proposed amendments afforded the executive branch ample opportunity to influence the judiciary. Their efforts paid off. The Duma committee, chaired by the former chairman of the Soviet parliament Anatoly Lukyanov, a lawyer by education, took the judges' side and discarded or amended some of the Kremlin's proposals.

Supreme Court and Supreme Arbitration Court justices engaged in public debate on the proposed bills, openly calling out their opponents: those bent on restricting judges' independence. Deputy Chief Justice of the Supreme Court Zhuykov directly attacked them: "We did not try to join forces with the prosecutor general's office, since their problems have nothing to do with the status of judges. I think that they will be happy to support all the proposals directed at reducing our immunity. After all, will it be bad for a prosecutor if a judge becomes more manageable?" Moreover, he essentially accused the presidential administration of wishing to obtain control of the judicial system. "I believe that in this respect, judicial reform is equivalent to counterreform. Its authors either don't understand it or are intentionally trying to make judges dependent. Of course, I can't claim that the presidential administration has an interest in creating a dependent judiciary, but I'm sure that's what the end result will be."[28]

Angered by the accusation,[29] the Kremlin immediately responded, in Kozak's voice: "Judges are saying that infringements on their rights are unacceptable. . . . The country is facing a very dangerous situation: we now have a caste of 20,000 untouchables who are working for themselves. . . . The judicial system turned into an employment service; it's stable and comfortable there. . . . We have the most untouchable judges in the world. For ten years, they've been building themselves a house, and now someone has come along and is trying to destroy it. We want to make judges maximally independent. But calls to leave them alone and just give them money are unacceptable."[30] In a fit of rage, Kozak also said at a Duma committee meeting: "Independence has become an end in itself for judges. To us, the people, independence guarantees nothing. The people need judges' 'impartiality,' which in fact is the goal of the judicial reform."[31]

Deputy Chief Justice of the Constitutional Court Morshchakova also publicly opposed the presidential proposals. "The court's chief justices initiate disciplinary proceedings against a judge. In fact, the law doesn't clearly define the infringements that can trigger disciplinary charges. In other words, if a judge in a lower-level court issues a ruling that a higher court disagrees with, not only will this ruling be reversed but the judge can also be punished as a result. Should the judge be afraid? He should."[32] Another Constitutional Court justice, Vladimir Yaroslavtsev, echoed Morshchakova's sentiments. "If the amendments to the law proposed by the Kozak group will pass, the judicial corps may lose its autonomy and independence."[33]

None of this dissuaded the Kremlin from its course. While the president's team lost a battle in committee, it won during the Duma session, receiving the support of the leaders of the main Duma factions, who made a joint statement urging a vote for the president's amendments despite the committee's position.

When presenting the bill, Kozak said that it had been agreed upon with the Council of Judges, although he knew full well that there was no such agreement. On the contrary, the judicial community vehemently opposed the proposed amendments.[34] The Duma vote violated a number of procedural and legal norms, which Morshchakova pointed out: "The amendments [to the Criminal Procedure Code, whose first reading was four years earlier], which blatantly contradict the current laws on the status of judges, the judicial system, and the Constitutional Court, should not have been introduced. It can be seen as a kind of tactical move: the section on restricting judges' immunity was introduced as a supplement and was passed on the second reading, along with many other amendments. . . . The next stage after adopting the Criminal Procedure Code was passing the law "On the Status of Judges" on first reading. During their deliberations of the law, to remove all doubts, parliamentarians were being convinced that, since they had passed the second reading of the Criminal Procedure Code, which simplifies the criminal prosecution of judges, they should also approve similar provisions in the law "On the Status of Judges." After all, the Duma can't contradict itself. In the same fashion, the Duma automatically passed basic amendments to the federal constitutional laws on the judicial system and on the Constitutional Court. Meanwhile, more than 300 votes are required to amend constitutional laws [and they were not there]."[35]

By the end of November 2001, the judges' opposition had been broken, and the law, including the presidential amendments, passed both chambers of parliament and was signed by the president. The judicial community was astonished by the lack of political support: not one party or group of parliamentarians said a word in its defense or petitioned the Constitutional Court. Both higher courts also refused to question the constitutionality of the amendments: all judges recognized that the Kremlin could easily once again change the legal norms regulating their terms and dismiss some if not all of them, as had happened in the early 2000s with the justices of the Constitutional Court.

RULE BY TELEPHONE

What was the outcome of this judicial reform?

Three years after Putin's reform was implemented, its author, Dmitry Kozak, acknowledged that it had failed, calling the situation "catastrophic and menacing." "Just like other [systems], this system is rife with corruption, and it's impossible to find truth there."[36] Of course, just as with any other reforms in situations in which the human factor plays an important role, three years is too short a time to draw final conclusions. But it is sufficient time to confirm the main fear that the independence of the judiciary would be seriously undermined, and that it would again become subservient to the executive branch.

In the spring of 2003, Eduard Rebgun, a practicing lawyer who would become Yukos's court-appointed bankruptcy manager three years later, said: "Not enough steps were taken, even theoretically, on the path of the judicial system's modernization to protect it from corruption. In practice, I believe, the judicial system suffers from this terrible malady, which is like a cancerous tumor that metastasizes. . . . Many businessmen don't want to take risks anymore now, so they pay the court even for a legitimate decision. . . . All this is disgusting, but it's become virtually universal because many judges are being attacked by administrative agencies and receive award packages for the 'right,' or rather the 'necessary,' decision. The majority of—let me emphasize, the majority, rather than just some—judges are ready to make the 'necessary' decision."[37] His views were echoed by Vasily Vitryansky, deputy chief justice of the Supreme Arbitration Court, who publicly confirmed that not only did ordinary judges have no independence, but those from the higher courts lacked it as well: "There is great pressure on us. There are plenty of meetings in executive offices where they want us to change our decision."[38]

At the Congress of Judges in late 2007, there was a pointed exchange between the chief justices of the country's highest courts. Supreme Arbitration Court chief justice Anton Ivanov then said, "Frankly speaking, judges' independence has not increased lately. And that's putting it very diplomatically." Chief Justice of the Supreme Court Vyacheslav Lebedev reacted immediately: "Judges' independence is a perennial theme. . . . Guarantees [of independence] are already in place; one just has to abide by them. And if some judge lacks a 'pivot' and starts adjusting himself to someone else, it has nothing to do with guarantees. Such a judge should quit the judicial system; he has no place in it."[39] What happened to judges who lacked a pivot came to light six months later.

A seemingly ordinary trial was wending its way through the courts in Moscow in May 2008. A government official had sued a journalist for defamation. The defendant, talk-show host Vladimir Solovyev, said on one of his radio programs that the FSB general and administrative aide to the president's personnel department, Viktor Boyev, "is in charge of the Supreme Arbitration Court." The trial turned out to be anything but ordinary. One of the defense witnesses, Supreme Arbitration Court deputy chief justice Yelena Valyavina, testified that during one of her cases, Boyev came to her office, told her that she "doesn't completely understand state interests," and asked her to reverse her earlier decisions on the case. When Valyavina remarked that no one had the right to give her any instructions on a case she was reviewing, the Kremlin official told her directly, "You will need to be reappointed,"[40] and added that she would "have problems" when her candidacy was being considered for reappointment. Valyavina also stated that the official contacted another justice of the Supreme Arbitration Court on a different case with a similar request. Responding to a question about the role this official had in the judicial appointment process, Valyavina said, "As a representative of the president's administration, he is present at the Highest Judges Qualification Board meetings, where he can publicize certain materials [expressing his objections to the judge's appointment]. He also has a say in how soon judges are appointed."[41] Following this testimony and the defense attorney's request to call three more high-ranking justices as witnesses, the plaintiff withdrew his claim. Despite its legal obligation to file criminal charges for obstruction of justice, the prosecutor general's office failed to do so in this case—which, of course, surprised no one.

In 2009, Supreme Arbitration Court chief justice Ivanov spoke about the continued pressure on judges and the reluctance of *siloviki* to stop this practice. He also proposed an original remedy, which, of course, wasn't even put up for discussion: "When we file complaints citing the pressure that we are subjected to, we get rejection responses. As a result, judges don't know whom to turn to. I believe it would be advisable to allow courts to file criminal cases on the grounds of obstruction of justice."[42] We don't know whether Ivanov was alluding to Valyavina's case or not, but we can assume he came under pressure from the Kremlin after that: three years later, when Valyavina's term as Supreme Arbitration Court deputy chief justice expired, Ivanov didn't offer her candidacy for reappointment. Justice Valyavina also failed to make it to the Supreme Court when the Supreme Arbitration Court and the Supreme Court merged three years later.

In 2011, the Constitutional Court had an opportunity to somewhat strengthen judicial independence as it was reviewing the appeal of a judge who had been disqualified. The justice who presented the issue to the court stated that "the norms in question should be deemed unconstitutional because their excessive vagueness allows [the state] to punish or not punish a judge for the same act." The court, however, couldn't bring itself to weaken the system of fear that all Russian judges work under. The court's decision preserved the status quo, in which JQBs, whose members are totally dependent on courts' chief justices and the president's representatives, have discretion to punish or pardon judges on the basis of unclear and often contradictory legal norms.

Although basic principles of judicial reform were passed into law at the end of 2001, the readjustment of legislation that regulated the work of the courts continued in the coming years (see figure 5-1). Since 2002, the basic laws regulating the judicial system have been changed every single year. Unwittingly or otherwise, the Kremlin signaled to the Russian judiciary that its status could be changed at any time and in any direction.

Of all these changes, two were perhaps the most significant. First, there were numerous amendments to the law on the Constitutional Court, the institution that the Kremlin saw as posing the greatest obstacle to its reforms at the start of the Putin presidency.[43] The second significant change was the liquidation of the Supreme Arbitration Court.

AN OVERACTIVE JUSTICE

The Constitutional Court of the Russian Federation appeared in late October 1991, one and a half months before the Soviet Union's collapse. It was chaired by the ambitious forty-eight-year-old lawyer Valery Zorkin. Right from the start, the Constitutional Court established itself as an independent government body by confronting head-on both Boris Yeltsin and public opinion. After President Yeltsin issued a decree that eliminated the Soviet secret police, the KGB, as an independent institution and incorporated it into the newly established Ministry of the Interior and Security, in mid-January 1992 the Constitutional Court declared the decree unconstitutional because exceeding presidential authority. Ten months later, the Constitutional Court

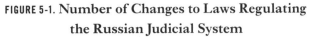

FIGURE 5-1. **Number of Changes to Laws Regulating the Russian Judicial System**

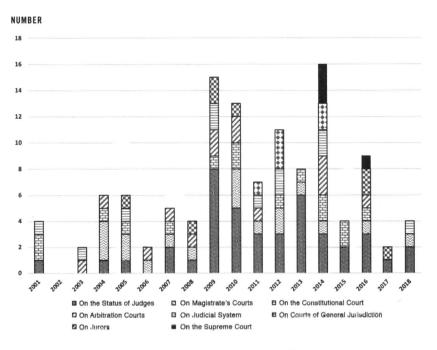

NUMBER

On the Status of Judges · On Magistrate's Courts · On the Constitutional Court
On Arbitration Courts · On Judicial System · On Courts of General Jurisdiction
On Jurors · On the Supreme Court

Source: Information and Legal Portal Consultant.ru (http://www.consultant.ru/).

Note: Data cover the period after the adoption of the 1993 Russian constitution through July 10, 2018, and include amendments to laws established earlier and drafts regulating the establishment of cassation courts and courts of appeal in common jurisdiction courts submitted by the Supreme Court of the Russian Federation to the State. A few laws shown were adopted much later than the 1993 constitution: the law *On Juries* was adopted in 2004, the law *On the Courts of General Jurisdiction* appeared in 2011, and the law *On the Supreme Court* was adopted in 2014.

invalidated Yeltsin's decree outlawing the Communist Party, allowing the Communists to reestablish their party organizations across the country. These decisions ran counter to the general spirit of change prevalent at the time. They prevented Russia from breaking with its Soviet past by dismantling the two organizations that had propped up the regime for seventy-five years. Nevertheless, the judges showed no fear in following the law wherever they believed it led them.

Tensions between the Constitutional Court and President Yeltsin escalated sharply during the 1993 political crisis. The Russian Constitution, adopted during the Soviet era, caused serious conflicts in relations between the legislative and executive branches that couldn't be resolved through negotiations and compromise. The Constitutional Court and its chief justice decided to play an unexpectedly active role in this stand-off. In fact, they assigned themselves the power to review certain controversial issues. For instance, on Zorkin's initiative, the Constitutional Court declared the president's announcement in a television address of a referendum on the constitutional reform and on confidence in the president to be unconstitutional. In April, the court blocked Yeltsin's attempt to resolve the conflict by means of a referendum. In response, Yeltsin stated that "the authority of the Constitutional Court has really declined" in his eyes and that he no longer intended to petition the court, which by now had firmly aligned itself with parliament.

On September 21, 1993, President Yeltsin decided to break the impasse by signing a decree disbanding the parliament and called for new elections and a constitutional referendum. The very next day, with some members missing, the Constitutional Court initiated a review of this decree, ruling the president's actions unconstitutional and declaring there were grounds for removing him from office. A number of Constitutional Court justices unsuccessfully tried to deescalate the conflict, but most of their colleagues supported the chief justice's position and suspended the powers of several dissenting justices. Although a few days later Zorkin proposed to hold new presidential and parliamentary elections at the same time as a compromise, it was too late: the president and his associates believed that the chief justice of the Constitutional Court had exceeded his authority by trying to become a political player.

The political conflict morphed into an armed confrontation that the president won. The parliament's supporters took over the Moscow mayor's office and the television center, Ostankino, prompting Yeltsin to order the shelling and takeover of the parliament building. Having crushed the resistance, the Kremlin established full control of the situation, suspending the activity of the Constitutional Court. The president's chief of staff called the judges and offered them a simple choice: they could either pressure the chief justice to resign or lose their status. The Kremlin also threatened to have Zorkin charged with the "providing legal support to a coup d'état." Zorkin judiciously stepped down as chief justice.

After his resignation, Zorkin stayed on as a Constitutional Court justice and continued his work, but he never reconciled himself to the outcome of the dispute. He vented his frustration publicly, condemning Boris Yeltsin twenty years later: "Yeltsin made a real mess of things. [Because of him] . . . the country was plunged into the abyss of criminal infighting and ethnic strife, into the abyss of destruction and devastation; at some point, it literally found itself on the brink of nonexistence."[44]

THE SECOND ADVENT

In February 2003 the term of the Constitutional Court's chief justice, Marat Baglay, expired. Although three years earlier he had received eighteen out of nineteen votes in elections (that is, a unanimous decision), he failed to get reelected, despite overwhelming Kremlin support.[45] Baglay was convenient for the Kremlin—after all, the Constitutional Court didn't make any major decision opposing the Kremlin after Putin came to power. In 2001, when judicial reform was discussed in parliament, Baglay refused to support the judicial community, thus condoning the president's move to restrict judicial independence. But Baglay's loyalty to the Kremlin came at a cost: his relations with many judges deteriorated and he lost the support of the majority on the Constitutional Court. Baglay was succeeded by Zorkin, whose election was an obvious slap in the face to the Kremlin. Evidently, most of the justices hoped that the Constitutional Court would be more independent from the Kremlin under the new chief justice. But the justices weren't the only ones who remembered Zorkin's past. Zorkin himself had forgotten nothing, saying that "reasonable people must learn their lessons from those events."[46]

The new chief justice saw what was happening in Russia and wasn't afraid to talk about the problems the judicial community was facing. In the fall of 2004, he engaged in a heated debate in the media with the Supreme Court justices over the situation in the Russian courts. Zorkin criticized the judiciary, saying that "[judicial] reform hasn't changed the generally negative opinion most people have of the Russian judicial system. . . . People continue to believe that the Russian court is ineffective, unjust or, even worse, corrupt. . . . Bribery in the courts has become one of the most powerful corruption markets in Russia. Judicial corruption is incorporated in various corruption networks at different levels of government: for instance, in the networks that undermine criminal cases or take over someone else's business."

Zorkin's assessment of Russia's changed political landscape was realistic. He understood that the real power in the country had shifted to the president. Consequently, the chief justices of Russia's three highest courts approached the president in the fall of 2003 to tell him about the need for a legislative clarification of their overlapping powers. Although it is parliament's job to create legislation, the chief justices understood that parliament lacked politicians who were ready to discuss this issue, let alone act on it.[47] In fact, the president didn't just make legislative changes. His administration took care of the fiduciary aspects of the courts' operation and judges' lives, from the upkeep of court facilities to providing automobiles and housing for judges. Zorkin quickly realized how dependent he was on the Kremlin. "Can courts be independent . . . when I myself try to secure apartments for the new judges, some of whom can't receive housing in Moscow for two years?"[48]

HUMILIATION

In late 2006 the Kremlin publicly humiliated the Constitutional Court. The court accepted the humiliation, which firmly established its subservient position in the Russian political system.

Vladimir Putin was born and raised in St. Petersburg. After the Russian capital moved from St. Petersburg to Moscow in 1918, the city's dynamic development slowed down, and it was on its way to becoming just another large provincial center. After becoming president, Putin did a lot to restore St. Petersburg's status—so much so that the city soon acquired the moniker "Russia's second capital." The Kremlin instructed large state-owned companies and banks to transfer their headquarters to St. Petersburg to fill the city's treasury with tax revenues. On the eve of St. Petersburg's 300th anniversary celebrations in 2003, Putin directed the government to adopt a massive municipal infrastructure investment program that was financed out of the federal budget.

When campaigning to be St. Petersburg's governor in 2003, Putin's protégée Valentina Matviyenko promised to have Russia's three highest courts transferred to St. Petersburg. The judicial community vehemently opposed the idea when the government began discussing it in early 2004, so the move was postponed. But in December 2005, a day before the Constitutional Court was to rule on the elimination of gubernatorial elections, Matviyenko urged the Duma to pass legislation reallocating the court to St. Petersburg. Although the Constitutional Court completely supported the presidential initiatives, Putin forced Valery Zorkin to publicly support the court's transfer from Moscow.[49]

The Constitutional Court's justices opposed the decision. They would now have to change their lifestyle, and no one had asked their opinion or explained to them the reasons for the change. The judges maintained that moving the court would isolate it from other government agencies. They also argued that they would have to travel regularly to Moscow and would face a number of day-to-day challenges. The Kremlin rejected all these arguments, and the bill quickly made its way through parliament. After the lower house of parliament passed the bill, in mid-December 2006, Zorkin unexpectedly addressed the president and both chambers of parliament, accusing them of undermining the Constitutional Court's independence, autonomy, and prestige.[50] But the Constitutional Court's chief justice was outraged by certain changes made to the law rather than by its essence. In the final stages, the lawmakers stripped the bill of the language that allowed the court to hold visiting sessions and maintain an office in Moscow. Zorkin retracted his objections to the bill after a brief meeting with Putin during which the president promised to insert the deleted language into the bill in exchange for Zorkin's assurances that the Constitutional Court would fully move to St. Petersburg. A few days after that meeting, the upper chamber of parliament overwhelmingly rejected the Duma's bill, which was later amended.

A CREATIVE JUSTICE

Putin's interest in what the Constitutional Court's chief justice had to say, as well as his willingness to yield some ground on nonessential questions, wasn't accidental. By that time Zorkin had come to play an important role in the

Kremlin's power vertical: the Constitutional Court's chief justice enthusias-
tically endorsed the idea that state interests superseded individual interests
and freedoms and actively applied this approach to the court's rulings. The
Constitutional Court saw no contradictions between the Russian constitution
and the Kremlin's political reforms, arguing that the articles of the constitution could be interpreted in light of the "evolving sociohistorical context." It
maintained that "specific social and legal conditions for implementing [the
Constitutional Court's past rulings], which include changes in the regulatory
system," allowed the Constitutional Court to reconsider its past decisions.

Such a flexible approach to constitutional norms gave the Kremlin carte
blanche to change the existing legislation and precluded any objections to the
newly adopted laws. In the summer of 2003, the Constitutional Court sustained the ban for holding popular referenda in the same year as presidential
and parliamentary elections. In the winter of 2005, the court refused to strike
down a new law on political parties that dramatically increased the membership requirements for registering a political party and outlawed regional parties. In December 2005, it recognized the constitutionality of the president's
right to recommend gubernatorial appointments and refused to take up a
challenge to the constitutionality of the president's right to dismiss governors for "losing [the president's] trust" and to disband regional parliaments.
Unexpectedly for the Kremlin, opponents of the expansion of presidential
powers in the early 1990s had become supporters ten years later. Absent any
pressure, the Constitutional Court and its chief justice agreed to become a
part of the power vertical, apparently remembering full well what it meant to
fall from the heights of power.

THE PURGE

The composition of the Constitutional Court underwent rapid change after
Vladimir Putin became president in 2000. Russian law in no way restricts
the president's power to recommend candidates for the Constitutional Court.
Although the law allows many political entities and civil society to propose
candidates, the president doesn't have to review them or explain his choice.
Upon retirement, judges with federal-level judicial or legislative experience
were being replaced by individuals who lacked experience but were ready to

support the Kremlin in all its endeavors. The pool of nine justices appointed on Putin's and Medvedev's recommendations featured a regional prosecutor, two regional election commission chairmen, two Ural Law Academy professors, a professor and a docent from St. Petersburg University, the chief justice of a regional arbitration court, and a deputy chairman of St. Petersburg's committee on pardons. Being ill qualified to hold their positions, most of them unequivocally supported the chief justice's views. Meanwhile, judges who tried to formulate an independent position were subjected to pressure and persecution.

In April 2008 the FSB prohibited the journalist Natalia Morar from entering Russia, deeming her work to be a security threat. The appeals of this decision came to naught, since the courts claimed they had no jurisdiction over decisions made by the secret police. The Constitutional Court, which reviewed the case a year later, also failed to find constitutional violations in the case even though the secret police presented neither evidence of wrongdoing nor any statement about which regulations or laws had allegedly been violated. Two justices dissented from the ruling at the time. One of the dissenters, Justice Vladimir Yaroslavtsev, spoke out three months later, providing a candid description of the situation. "Strengthening authoritarianism leads to increasingly greater dependence for judges. . . . The Presidential Administration serves as a decision-making center. The authoritarian regime wants to stay in power as long as possible. . . . The security agencies may do what they please, while courts are left to just rubber-stamp their decisions. The security agencies, they are the ones in charge."[51]

Soon after, in an unprecedented incident at the Constitutional Court's closed plenary session, Zorkin accused Yaroslavtsev of violating the Code of Judicial Ethics and the law "On the Status of Judges" that directs judges "to avoid anything that may diminish the authority of the judicial branch." The same law also doesn't allow judges "to cast doubt on court rulings that are currently in effect and criticize the professional activities of their colleagues outside the realm of professional sphere." However, the majority of the judges refused to recognize the event as a disciplinary infraction, which would have triggered the justice's removal from the Constitutional Court. It was merely recommended to Yaroslavtsev that he remove himself from the Council of Judges, where he served as the Constitutional Court's representative.

The other dissenter in the Morar case, Justice Anatoly Kononov,[52] later said that "Yaroslavtsev was 'flogged' in our plenum in keeping with our best traditions." He also added that the law in Russia was being changed in a way "that allows the executive branch to manage the judicial system."[53] Colleagues didn't forgive Kononov for airing their dirty laundry in public. One Constitutional Court justice said, "Speaking critically from newspaper pages is unacceptable. . . . One can express his own view in dissenting opinions but not criticize the court's decisions that are currently in effect." It was suggested that Justice Kononov resign voluntarily to avoid being brought up on official disciplinary charges. "We didn't resort to repressive measures. . . . The Justices recommended . . . ," was how Zorkin described the situation.[54]

The decline in the professionalism of the Constitutional Court's judges and the court's removal to St. Petersburg exacted a heavy toll on the institution. The executive branch stopped taking it seriously. Federal ministers, chairs of parliamentary chambers, and even their deputies stopped showing up at the court's sessions. "High-ranking officials prefer not to travel here. The level of representation by all government bodies went down to the level of Northwestern Federal District officials. Fewer complainants come to court now, and that's bad," said the Constitutional Court's vice chief justice.[55]

But the Kremlin's disrespect for the Constitutional Court and the constitution goes much further. In the rare cases in which the Constitutional Court has no other choice but to declare a law unconstitutional, it never suspends the law if it's important to the Kremlin. Instead, the court issues its recommendations on how the law should be applied and suggests that the parliament amend it.[56] For instance, certain clauses in the laws on public protests, the prosecutorial review of NGOs, and mayoral elections were declared unconstitutional by the Constitutional Court, but Russian courts ignored the Constitutional Court's position, and the Russian parliament refrained from rescinding the laws that are now in effect. Moreover, the Duma for several years failed to act on thirty bills to bring them in line with the Constitutional Court's position.[57]

AN IRREMOVABLE JUSTICE

But the humbled status of the Constitutional Court had the opposite effect on Zorkin's future.

In 2009 the Constitutional Court's judges unexpectedly lost their right to elect the chief justice. Without advance notice to or consultation with the Constitutional Court's justices, the law was changed: the chief justice would be appointed by the Federation Council on the president's recommendation. One of the longest-sitting Constitutional Court justices immediately reacted: "This amendment contradicts the independence of the judiciary. . . . It is an attempt to influence the court."[58] During the debates in parliament, the Kremlin's representatives declared their intention to unify the rules for the nomination of all the highest courts in Russia, and not one deputy asked them why the chief justices of the other high courts could not also be elected by justices.

At the same time, the term of the chief justice of the Constitutional Court was extended from three to six years. The position was further strengthened in 2011, when the new law eliminated the age limit (seventy years), making nominations potentially for life. In addition, the Constitutional Court chief justice could no longer be removed for incompetence upon the recommendation of five Constitutional Court judges, followed by a secret vote by the full court. The chief justice also received greater powers: the court would no longer have two independent chambers, each with decision-making powers; instead, all the court's decisions were to be made in full sessions. The court's procedural rules were changed as well: previously all Constitutional Court judges chaired the court's sessions in a rotation by alphabetical order; now only the chief justice or his deputy was allowed to do it.

Zorkin once again deemed it necessary to publicly pledge his loyalty to the regime right before President Medvedev was due to submit his proposed nominee for chief justice of the Constitutional Court. In the midst of mass protests over voter fraud in late 2011, Zorkin said that the protests were "actively fueled from abroad." After such statements, it's no wonder that the Constitutional Court sustained the constitutionality of the laws enacted in the summer of 2012 that drastically curtailed the freedom to organize and participate in public political activities and imposed stiffer penalties for breaking the law, including possible imprisonment.

In February 2012, President Medvedev submitted Zorkin's candidacy for Constitutional Court chief justice to the Federation Council, which later confirmed his powers for another six years. The choice surprised no one: not only has Zorkin refused to make a single decision that was inconvenient to the Kremlin, but he has also openly stated that "it's odious and spiteful to claim that the judicial system is controlled by the Kremlin. . . . There has never been such meddling, and, I hope, will never be." So when Medvedev moments later proposed "just discussing the current situation and legal constructs that may indeed improve the work of the Constitutional Court," the president of the court heard nothing out of the ordinary.[59]

In the same way, the Constitutional Court declined to rule unconstitutional the "municipal filters" for gubernatorial elections in December 2012. It also had no issue with the 2015 law that declared that Russian authorities weren't bound by the decisions of the European Court of Human Rights (ECHR).[60] "Life forces us to make new decisions. . . . This is not calling black white. . . . It's just that life is changing, and we have to take that into account," said Zorkin, who readily grasped the political realities of modern Russia.

In January 2018, President Putin submitted Zorkin's candidacy for Constitutional Court chief justice to the Federation Council, which five days later confirmed his powers for another six years.

AN UNWANTED INSTITUTION

The second important legislative change relating to the Russian judicial system was the decision to abolish the Supreme Arbitration Court. Putin first suggested this in June 2013 without citing any specifics. In fact, one could even find some progressive intentions in the president's suggestion: "To ensure uniform approaches to resolving disputes involving both individuals and organizations, as well as disputes with federal and local government entities, I suggest consolidating the Supreme Court of the Russian Federation and the Supreme Arbitration Court."[61]

The Kremlin's designs weren't apparent right away. Some might have thought that the intent was to reconcile the conflict between the two highest courts by taking the best from both. "We are talking about consolidating the two highest courts. . . . Then there will be reconstitution, and I believe acting justices of the Supreme Court and the Supreme Arbitration Court have absolutely equal chances to become the justices of the [new] Supreme Court," said Putin's adviser, former Supreme Arbitration Court chief justice Vladimir Yakovlev.[62] He added that the main reasons for consolidating the two courts had to do with the need to delimit administrative control and ensure the application of a uniform legal standard. "Of course, it will be easier to solve these problems, but they'll remain. They're inevitable."[63] But when the new legislation package was introduced in the Duma in early October 2013,[64] it once again became clear that "the proposal wasn't discussed with judges"[65] and "doesn't mention consolidating the highest courts but rather essentially abolishes the Supreme Arbitration Court,"[66] as Tatyana Andreyeva, deputy chief justice of the Supreme Arbitration Court, put it.

The proposed legislation was vehemently opposed by the Supreme Arbitration Court's justices. Perhaps catching a whiff of Putin's plan, Anton Ivanov, the court's chief justice, gave an extended interview the day before the presidential initiative was announced in which he talked about the work of arbitration courts and said, in passing, "A unified highest court will hardly be effective."[67] The Supreme Arbitration Court sent its extremely negative review of the bill to the Duma, pointing to the bill's legal and substantive flaws. The justices criticized both the bill's text and the general procedure for conducting the reform. "All the changes of the Russian judicial system should be comprehensive in nature, the corrections of law should be done at once," the document says.[68] Seven Supreme Arbitration Court justices resigned,[69] in large part because the bill undermined the judges' lifetime appointments: the law didn't guarantee that judges who weren't reappointed to the renewed Supreme Court would receive lifetime pensions. However, the judges' resistance wasn't supported by either the public or politicians—only the communist faction of the Duma voted against the president's proposals. All laws were signed and went into effect in early February 2014. The Supreme Arbitration Court ceased to exist on August 6, 2014.

It's not surprising that the Constitutional Court essentially refused to take up the Duma members' request to review the constitutionality of the president's proposals, citing its lack of jurisdiction. "A review of the amendments to the Constitution of the Russian Federation introduced by this legislative act, being in effect a review of the norms of the Constitution itself, is beyond the direct competence of the Constitutional Court of the Russian Federation."[70] Thus the Constitutional Court recognized, a priori, the constitutionality of any future amendments to the Russian Constitution.

WAS THERE A REASON?

What did the arbitration courts do to warrant such treatment? Why wasn't the Kremlin too afraid to virtually halt in its tracks a well-functioning mechanism, inevitably causing numerous problems? True, Chief Justice of the Supreme Arbitration Court Anton Ivanov, who was one of the most powerful members of Dmitry Medvedev's rather small team, was at times openly critical of the current regime's policies. For instance, in December 2012 he declared during his speech at the judges' congress: "The state in which citizens will have no right to judicial protection is no longer a civilized democratic state; it's a tyranny. And what has led to this situation, lack of budget funds, unwillingness to make any changes, or some other factors—it is not that important. . . . We are facing the most serious crisis—the crisis of faith in the judicial system."[71] It hardly comes as a surprise in this context that Ivanov wasn't selected for the new Supreme Court and received no further job offers.

Nevertheless, it seems the personality of the chief justice of the Supreme Arbitration Court was not the main reason for the Kremlin's assault on the arbitration court system. Most likely the regime was concerned by the courts' increased independence and focus on ensuring the rule of law. For instance, the arbitration courts' district borders didn't coincide with administrative ones, which significantly diminished the ability of local and regional authorities to exert pressure on judges. The arbitration courts also introduced the audio recording of court proceedings, preventing judges from distorting the parties' positions when preparing transcripts and issuing decisions.[72] The resolutions of the Supreme Arbitration Court's Presidium and Plenum were binding on the lower arbitration courts, which meant that the courts' decisions could be reviewed if they contradicted the higher court's resolutions, thus facilitating uniform court practice. Another instrument the Supreme Arbitration Court used was the nonbinding information letter, instances of which were nevertheless used by the lower courts, since they reflected the superior court's position. Neither of these norms work in general jurisdiction courts. As a result of all these practices, the business community and state agencies got more or less even odds in arbitration. The Supreme Arbitration Court also supported a system under which the losing party was responsible for the other party's legal costs. For instance, tax collection agencies had to fully compensate a taxpayer for legal costs in case the latter won the case. In courts of general jurisdiction, this kind of compensation would have been nearly impossible.

The Kremlin obviously could not rely on such "irresponsible" courts, as an independent judiciary posed too much of a threat. Being unable to change the system, the Kremlin had no other remedy but to destroy it.

PURGE AT THE TOP

Along with eliminating the "irresponsible" court, Putin implemented another purge at the top level of the judiciary. The presidential bill[73] did away with judges' lifetime tenure[74] and essentially implied the reconstitution of the full Supreme Court. The Kremlin, by accruing to itself the right to oversee and manage the transition, decided to purge the highest Russian court. Despite the existence of the Highest Judges Qualification Board, which had all rights to preselect candidates for the Supreme Court, a new temporary entity, known as the Special Qualification Board, was established for this purpose. Nobody explained why such an entity was needed, but, as became evident later, it allowed the Kremlin to veto the appointment of any candidate proposed to the Special Qualification Board. In other words, the actual purpose of the reform was to test candidates for loyalty.

The purge of the highest courts was meticulous and proceeded very slowly, which pointed to the seriousness with which the Kremlin was approaching the task. During its initial half-year term, the Special Qualification Board rejected more than half of the candidates, selecting only 91 candidates for the Supreme Court for 170 seats.[75] By the time the new Supreme Court opened for business, only half of the justices' seats were filled, which necessitated an amendment lowering the number of judges required to form a decision-making quorum.

The justices of the Supreme Arbitration Court became the main targets of the purge. Two-thirds of the court's members were not reappointed and lost their status as judges. All in all, by midsummer 2018, one-sixth of the thirty seats on the Supreme Court Collegium on Economic Disputes were vacant, which seriously diminished the effectiveness of this body. Even the experts who held a favorable view on the consolidation of the highest courts noted that the Supreme Court had effectively become inactive for the time being.

———————

Launching its judicial reforms in 2001, the Kremlin publicly professed that its goal was to increase public trust in the judiciary. Ten years later, in a speech to the Congress of Judges in December 2012, Putin emphasized the people's greater "trust in the judicial system and the judges' corps."[76] At first glance this statement appeared to be corroborated by polling data—from 2002 to 2010, the level of trust in Russian courts grew from 25 percent to 53 percent. Nevertheless, the share of people who distrusted the judicial system remained high and even increased: the government aimed to reduce the level of distrust to 6 percent, but this figure actually increased to 43 percent by late 2010. In the following years public trust in the Russian judiciary, despite some fluctuations, remained at the same level, but the judiciary had declined in influence relative to the presidential administration, prosecutors, and secret police. It is unsurprising, then, that trust in the courts was not selected as one of the performance criteria for the governmental program at the end of 2012.[77]

In 2010 the International Commission of Jurists conducted a comprehensive study of the Russian judicial system, publishing its report afterward. Although the report came out more than seven years ago, it still characterizes the current situation in Russian courts quite accurately:

Although there have been advances in reforming the judicial system, in particular in the early 1990s, and improvements to the salaries and material conditions of judges, there have also been counterreforms that have had a negative effect, and it is far from clear that the executive and legislative branches have wholeheartedly or consistently pursued the goal of an independent judiciary. Lack of political will or consensus is clearly a significant factor in the slow and uneven progress of judicial reform. . . . The poor state of judicial independence is clearly facilitated by a legislative and administrative framework that fails to protect judges from undue influence by state or private interests. . . . The system pressures judges to show loyalty to state bodies or certain officials and to take into account political considerations.[78]

The Kremlin's comprehensive control over judges' careers and its incessant pressure on courts and the legal system essentially created a distinction between "general" and "special" legal processes in Russia. In the "general" process, according to Vladimir Putin, "a decision made by a judge and the court is the pinnacle of the actions taken by the entire law enforcement system: the MVD, FSB, or any other law enforcement agencies and investigative bodies."[79]

That means that though judges are independent and may make decisions based on their judgments, in criminal cases it is better for them to accept the view of the prosecutor and investigative agency. Judges accept 97 percent of investigators' requests for phone interceptions and for the preliminary arrest of suspects; judges may refuse to accept evidence or expert witnesses from the defense and may reject the validity of video or audio evidence. That's why "not guilty" is heard in Russian courts in fewer than 1 percent of cases, and why in two-thirds of cases suspects accept a plea deal in order to secure a lighter sentence.[80]

In the "special" legal process, judges have to recognize and accept the existence of "state interest." Those cases are reviewed under informal instructions, often by specially selected judges. But "state interest" is treated broadly: in one case, it may be asserted by the Kremlin, in another by the local head of police. In one case the opposition leader may plead guilty and be forbidden to present any proof of his innocence during the court hearing and be placed in jail. In another a businessman may lose his company because the court accepts at face value the request of the police to freeze his bank accounts. The judge's decisions in such cases are always motivated by someone higher up who has made the judge an offer he can't refuse.

Having implemented its judicial reforms, the Kremlin achieved the desired results: full subordination of all judges individually, and of the judicial system as a whole. Though the Russian judicial system cannot protect the interests of Russians, it is very effective when it comes to protecting the interests of Vladimir Putin, his lieutenants, and his cronies.

At the beginning of 2018, the Kremlin proposed several technocratic changes to the legislation; the recommendations had been prepared by a think tank headed by former deputy prime minister Alexey Kudrin.[81] Though the ideas underlying the recommendations were comprehensive and aimed to increase judicial independence, the Kremlin limited these initiatives. Its principal goal is to increase the pace of the judicial process. According to new rules, the courts' chief justices lose part of their powers (managing administrative issues, the distribution of benefits, assignment of judges to individual cases) and audio recording will be used in all court trials. Meanwhile, the core element of the Kremlin's control over judges—the authority to determine all promotions and reassignments—remains untouched, though Kudrin's experts say that is one of the most important elements of their proposals.

Notes to Chapter 5

1. Vladimir Radchenko, "Sudebnaya reforma prodolzhayetsya" [Judicial reform continues], *Otechestvennye Zapiski* 2 (11), 2003.

2. The judges themselves were divided on whether lifetime judicial appointments were a good idea. For example, Chief Justice of the Supreme Arbitration Court Vladimir Yakovlev said, "I actively opposed lifetime appointments for judges at their inception . . . believing that we still lacked the appropriate judicial corps, but now I'm a supporter. . . . Repealing lifetime appointments runs counter to the principle of independence." Congress of Judges, *V Vserossiyskiy S'yezd Sudey* [V All-Russian Congress of Judges], November 27–29, 2000 (www.ssrf.ru/page/845/detail/).

3. According to the retired deputy chief justice of the Supreme Court Vladimir Radchenko, up to 87 percent of appeals were granted in the first few years after the law went into effect. By 2001 the share of appeals granted had declined to 66 percent, but citizens' chances of winning an appeal remained very high. See also Radchenko, "Sudebnaya reforma prodolzhayetsya" [Judicial reform continues].

4. This law had been circulating in draft form in the Russian parliament for almost two years, since the deputies in both chambers couldn't agree on the general principles on which the Russian judicial system should be constituted. Minister of Justice Kalmykov advocated for the "American model" of the judicial system in which only the Supreme Court and Military Court should be federal, while regional and municipal courts should be under the jurisdiction of the federation's subjects. For its part, the Supreme Court supported the position that all courts, including regional and municipal ones, should come under federal jurisdiction, arguing that such a system would offer the people the best protection from the arbitrary decisions of local officials. Ultimately the Supreme Court prevailed, which had the negative consequences discussed later in the chapter. See also Radchenko, "Sudebnaya reforma prodolzhayetsya" [Judicial reform continues].

5. From 1992 to 2014 there were two independent court systems in Russia: the general jurisdiction courts, with the Supreme Court at the top, which were in charge of criminal and civilian cases, and the arbitration courts, with the Supreme Arbitration Court at the top, which were in charge of economic disputes. There is also the Constitutional Court, which rules on disputes regarding the constitutionality of legislation. The arbitration courts were established in 1992 and the principle of extraterritorial districts was incorporated from the start, while the general jurisdiction courts inherited their structure from the Soviet era and their offices were located in the centers of the administrative units. In 2018 the draft legislation establishing extraterritorial cassation courts and courts of appeal in the Russian general jurisdiction courts was submitted to the State Duma. By mid-2018 one of the drafts had passed the first hearings.

6. This norm was repealed in late 2001.

7. *Sudebnaya reforma: Ot kontseptsii 1991 goda do segodnyashnego dnya* [Judicial reform: From the 1991 concept to today] (Moscow: Centr sodeistviya pravosudiyu, INDEM Foundation, 2001).

8. Nikolai Il'yasov, "Ne v sud'yakh sut'" [The judges are not the essence], *Otechestvennye Zapiski* 2 (11), 2003.

9. This practice was implemented for the newly established arbitration courts, where the decisions of the Supreme Arbitration Court had gradually become uniform (courts no longer issued different rulings in similar situations).

10. Additionally, if a judge's decision was revised by the upper court, that could be interpreted as a mistake on the part of the judge, resulting in a smaller bonus or slower promotion. Such a recalcitrant judge could also lose his or her position on the housing waiting list.

11. A. K. Gorbuz, M. A. Krasnov, E. A. Mishina, and G. A. Satarov, *Transformation of the Russian Judicial Branch: The Complex Analysis* (Moscow–St. Petersburg: Norma, 2010), p. 57.

12. Congress of Judges, *V Vserossiyskiy S'yezd Sudey* [Fifth All-Russian Congress of Judges], p. 845.

13. Ibid.

14. President of Russia, "Vystupleniye na V Vserossiyskom s'yezde sudey" [Speech at the Fifth All-Russian Congress of Judges], Moscow, November 27, 2000 (http://kremlin.ru/events/president/transcripts/21125).

15. Going forward, Putin was more generous when it came to "gifts" for the judges. The president laid out his ideas in this regard at the next Council of Judges in December 2004, when rising oil prices injected funds into the country's budget: "I just want to say that the increases in monetary compensations to judges will be significant. Significant means that it may increase two or perhaps even three times in the first stage, and in the near future, there will be another similar increase." See also Congress of Judges, *VI Vserossiyskiy S'yezd Sudey* [Sixth All-Russian Congress of Judges], Moscow, November 30–December 2, 2004 (www.ssrf.ru/page/846/detail/).

At the same time, right before the Constitutional Court reviewed the constitutionality of the president's decision to eliminate gubernatorial elections, Putin signed an executive order that bestowed a pay raise 6.5 times the previous rate on the chair of the Constitutional Court and a pay raise 5.5 times the old rate on the court's justices.

16. Il'yasov, "Ne v sud'yakh sut'" [The judges are not the essence].

17. Ekaterina Zapodinskaya and Il'ya Bulavin, "Sud'i otvetyat perednovym zakonom" [The judges will meet the requirements of the new law] (interview with Dmitry Kozak), *Kommersant* 24, February 12, 2001, front page.

18. Il'yasov, "Ne v sud'yakh sut'" [The judges are not the essence].

19. Svetlana Mikhailova and Victor Khamraev, "Dve stupeni sudebnoy reformy" [Two steps of the judicial reform], *Vremya Novostey* 53, March 27, 2001.

20. The average caseload of a general jurisdiction judge dropped from 45.4 to 23.2 cases a month. See also Ministry of Economic Development of the Russian Federation, "Doklad o khode realizatsii federal'nykh tselevykh programm v 2005 godu" [Report on the realization of the federal target programs in 2005] (http://fcp.economy.gov.ru/npd/doklad2005.htm). But in 2009, the chair of the Supreme Arbitration Court stated that "the research-backed norm for a judge's caseload is 15 cases a month. Our judges review 45 cases on average, and some up to 100." See also Ekaterina Butorina, "Sudebnaya arifmetika" [Judicial arithmetic], *Vremya Novostey* 222, December 2, 2009.

21. In 2012 the chairs' two-term limit was removed. By that time the Kremlin was able to renominate all chairmen of all courts in the country and needed to keep loyal persons in their seats instead of looking for other ones.

22. Valentin Kuznetsov, "Kandidatov v sud'i proveryayut militsiya i FSB" [Candidates for judges are checked by the police and the FSB]. This interview has been removed from the Supreme Court's website but its text is available at www.index.org.ru/turma/ic/2003/132/658-1.htm. This quotation is incorporated as well into the report by the International Commission of Jurists, "Appointing the Judges: Procedures for Selection of Judges in the Russian Federation" (2014), p. 41. The text is available at www.icj.org/wp-content/uploads/2014/11/RUSSIA-Selecting-the-judges-Publications-Reports-2014-Eng.pdf.

23. In truth, the previous norm that required the president to explain his negative decisions had never been followed.

24. There are about 30,000 judges in Russia, and all of them are to be nominated by the president. On average, every year the president must make 2,000 nominations (new judges and new appointments), or forty nominations per week. Obviously, the president cannot dedicate his time to the bulk of nominations, and so in practice this power is delegated to his staff.

25. Tamara Morshchakova, "Na polputi k pravosudiyu" [Halfway to justice], *Otechestvennye Zapiski* 2 (11), 2003 (www.strana-oz.ru/2003/2/na-polputi-k-pravosudiyu).

26. Viktor Zhuykov, interview with the author, Moscow, March 2, 2016.

27. Vladimir Nikolayev, "Sudebnaya reforma prevrashchayetsya v kontrreformu" [Judicial reform is transforming into counterreform], *Kommersant* 96, June 5, 2001, front page.

28. Ibid.

29. The Kremlin won't forget Zhuykov's position. He was not reappointed when his Supreme Court term expired in 2007, though he was still ten years short of the required retirement age. But Zhuykov would definitely make it into the annals of the Russian justice system since it was his protest that made the Moscow City Court annul President Boris Yeltsin's decree dismissing the governor of Lipetsk region in 1994.

30. Vladimir Nikolayev, "U naspoyavilas' kastaiz 20 tysyach neprikasayemykh" [We have a cast of 20,000 untouchables], *Kommersant* 97, June 6, 2001, p. 3.

31. Svetlana Mikhaylova and Viktor Khamrayev, "Sudeyskaya oborona" [Judicial defense], *Vremya Novostey* 195, October 23, 2001.

32. Vladimir Nikolayev, "Ot nezavisimogo statusa sud'i nichego ne ostayetsya" [There is nothing left of the judge's independent status], *Kommersant* 122, July 13, 2001, p. 3.

33. Vladimir Nikolayev, "Sud'i ot prazdnovali pobedu nad Kremlem" [The judges celebrated the victory over the Kremlin], *Kommersant* 208, November 14, 2001, p. 2.

34. Later Kozak admitted his "tactical trick": "We talked about plans to organize the institutional system of the judicial community at the meeting with the executive committee of the Council of Judges. When the discussion was over I asked, as I usually do, whether there were questions on other topics. No one in the audience reacted, although the topic of the judge's status came up at any similar meeting. Apparently, based on this, it was mistakenly concluded that the version of the bill introduced to the Duma no longer elicits the objections it did in the past." See also Nikolaev, "Ot nezavisimogo statusa sud'i nichego ne ostayetsya" [There is nothing left of the judge's independent status].

35. Nikolaev, "Ot nezavisimogo statusa sud'i nichego ne ostayetsya" [There is nothing left of the judge's independent status].

36. However, Kozak's solution lay in giving even greater powers to the Kremlin's officials. He suggested that presidential envoys on JQBs be granted the right to petition prosecutors to bring charges against a particular judge for an improper decision he or she made. See also Diana Dadasheva, "Dmitriy Kozak vzyalsya za staroye" [Dmitry Kozak returned to the old], *Kommersant* 14, January 28, 2005, p. 4.

37. Eduard Rebgun, "Khotelos' by uvazhat' sud" [I would like to respect the court], *Otechestvennye zapiski* 2 (11), 2003.

38. "Ot napisaniya do ispolneniya" [From writing to execution]. *Russian Federation Today* 15 (2007), p. 25.

39. Ekaterina Butorina, "Femida prositsya v parliament" [Themis asks to enter parliament], *Vremya Novostey* 223, December 5, 2007.

40. The deputy chair of the Supreme Arbitration Court was appointed for six years, and the judge could serve two consecutive terms in this capacity.

41. Even after the JQB approved a particular candidate, the appointment documents could languish for months on the desks of presidential administration officials before being signed by the president.

42. Butorina, "Sudebnaya arifmetika" [Judicial arithmetic].

43. For instance, the Constitutional Court essentially blocked the 2000 legislative change that allowed the president to disband regional parliaments, supplementing the change with conditions that virtually made it dysfunctional.

44. Valeriy Zor'kin, "Dukh zakona" [The spirit of the law], *Rossiiskaya Gazeta* 5655 (279), December 12, 2011.

45. In 2001, two months before Baglay was to resign in accordance with the law, the Kremlin had the law changed, allowing him to remain chair for another nine years. This legal change didn't apply to Baglay's deputy Morshchakova, who had often publicly opposed the Kremlin's initiatives.

46. Valeriy Zor'kin, "Istoriya nikogda ne povtoryayetsya" [History never repeats itself], *Kommersant*, February 22, 2003.

47. Yuriy Kolesov, "Tret'ya vlast' na troikh" [The third power for three], *Vremya Novostey*, November 5, 2003.

48. Yuriy Kolesov, "Valeriy Zor'kin: V kazhdom iz zven'yev sudebnoy sistemy est' defekty" [Valery Zorkin: In each part of the judicial system there are defects], *Vremya Novostey*, June 16, 2005 (http://vremya.ru/2005/105/13/127672.html).

49. Andrey Kolesnikov, "Vladimir Putin brosil deputatam KS" [Vladimir Putin threw the Constitutional Court to the deputies], *Kommersant* 243, December 26, 2005, p. 1.

50. "Chto vozmutilo Valeriya Zor'kina" [What outraged Valery Zorkin], *Kommersant* 239, December 21, 2006, p. 1.

51. "En Rusia Mandan losórganos de seguridad, comoen la épocasoviética" [In Russia, the security organs are in command, as in the Soviet era], *El Pais*, August 31, 2009.

52. Kononov issued dissenting opinions in over fifty court rulings, much more frequently than his colleagues did.

53. "Sud'ya Kononov: Nezavisimykh sudey v Rossii net" [Justice Kononov: There are no independent judges in Russia], *Sobesednik*, October 27, 2009.

54. "Sud'ya KS RF Kononov ushel v otstavku po sostoyaniyu zdorov'ya—Zor'kin" [Justice of the Constitutional Court of the Russian Federation Kononov has resigned for health reasons—Zorkin], RIA Novosti, December 2, 2009.

55. Anna Pushkarskaya, "Valery Zorkin prishel na chetvertuyy srok" [Valery Zorkin got in for a fourth term], *Kommersant* 32, February 21, 2009, p. 1.

56. In such cases the Constitutional Court uses specially crafted language, labeling the law to be "in agreement with the Constitution taking into account the constitutional and legal meaning discovered by the justices."

57. Anna Pushkarskaya, "Osoboye mneniye o KS" [Special opinion on the Constitutional Court], *Kommersant*, October 28, 2016.

58. Anna Pushkarskaya, "Valeriyu Zor'kinu ne do biblioteki" [Valery Zorkin won't be going to the library], *Kommersant*, February 11, 2012.

59. President of Russia, "Vstrecha s sud'yami Konstitutsionnogo Suda" Meeting with judges of the Constitutional Court], news release, Moscow, December 12, 2011 (http://kremlin.ru/events/president/news/13965).

60. In 2010, Zorkin published an extensive article in which he claimed that the decisions made by the ECHR often contradicted Russia's interests and were aimed at de-

stabilizing the situation in the country. "Let's imagine that the European Court grants the complaint of the 'united opposition' [regarding the 2003 electoral fraud]. Won't this decision be used to destabilize Russian society as was done during 'orange,' 'tulip,' and other engineered 'revolutions'? Every decision made by the European Court is not only a legal but a political act. . . . When the [ECHR] rulings directly affect national sovereignty, fundamental constitutional principles, Russia has a right to develop a defensive mechanism against such rulings. . . . If they impose the external 'choreography' of the legal situation in the country on us, while ignoring the historical, cultural, and social situation, these 'choreographers' must be corrected. Sometimes in a very forceful way." In Valeriy Zor'kin, "Predel ustupchivosti" [Limits of compliance], *Rossiiskaya Gazeta* 5325 (246), October 29, 2010.

61. President of Russia, "Plenarnoye zasedaniye Peterburgskogo mezhdunarodnogo ekonomicheskogo foruma" [Plenary session of the St. Petersburg International Economic Forum], news release, Moscow, June 21, 2013 (http://kremlin.ru/events/president/news/18383).

62. "Yakovlev: Proyekt govorit o bob"yedinenii vysshikh sudov, a ne o pogloshchenii [Yakovlev: The project speaks about the merger of higher courts, and not about the takeover], RIA Novosti, October 16, 2013.

63. "Ekspert: Vopros edinstva pravo primeneniya posle sliyaniya sudov ostanetsya" [Expert: The question of the uniform application of law will remain after the merger of the courts], RIA Novosti, November 26, 2013.

64. Judging by this delay in introducing the bills, one may assume that Putin's proposal came as a complete surprise to the Kremlin's attorneys.

65. "Problema ne v sliyanii sudov, a v tom, kak ono idet" [The problem is not in the merger of courts, but in how it's done], RIA Novosti, October 10, 2013.

66. "VKKS rassmotrit zayavleniya semi sudey VAS RF o slozhenii polnomochiy" [VKKS will consider the resignations of seven judges of the Supreme Arbitration Court of the Russian Federation], RIA Novosti, October 22, 2013.

67. Ibid.

68. Maksim Ivanov and Anna Pushkarskaya, "Vyssheye arbitrazhnoye osuzhdeniye" [The highest arbitration deprecation], *Kommersant*, November 12, 2013.

69. "Vysshiy arbitrazhnyy sud podtverdil, chto sem' sudey ukhodyat v otstavku" [The Supreme Arbitration Court confirmed that seven judges are resigning], RIA Novosti, October 10, 2013.

70. Anna Pushkarskaya, "Konstitutsionnyy sud otkazalsya rassmatrivat' 'unikal'nyy sluchay' " [The Constitutional Court refused to consider the "unique case"], *Kommersant*, July 27, 2014.

71. Council of Judges, "Vystupleniye Predsedatelya Vysshego Arbitrazhnogo Suda Rossiyskoy Federatsii A.A. Ivanova na VIII Vserossiyskom s'yezde sudey" [Speech of the Chairman of the Supreme Arbitration Court of the Russian Federation A. A.

Ivanov at the All-Russian Congress of Judges], news release, Moscow, December 18, 2012 (www.ssrf.ru/page/9099/detail/).

72. This practice still hasn't been introduced in general jurisdiction courts, nor is it supported by the Russian authorities.

73. The bill was passed by the Duma with virtually no changes.

74. The lifetime appointment of a judge in Russia can be terminated only pursuant to the procedure and on the grounds set forth by federal law, while the elimination of a court cannot serve as one of these grounds. In such a case the judges are to be appointed to another court without going through any additional checks, exams, or other selection procedure. The implementation of Putin's proposals resulted in the termination of all judges of both highest courts—the Supreme Court and the Supreme Arbitration Court. Even the Supreme Court judges were not automatically reappointed to the newly constituted Supreme Court, although the court itself wasn't eliminated.

75. Anastasia Mikhailova, "Novyy Verkhovnyy sud nachnet rabotat' bez poloviny sudey" [The new Supreme Court starts working without half of judges], RBC, August 5, 2014.

76. President of Russia, "Vladimir Putin prinyal uchastiye v rabote VIII Vserossiyskogo s'yezda sudey" [Vladimir Putin took part in the work of the VIII All-Russian Congress of Judges], news release, Moscow, December 18, 2012 (http://kremlin.ru/events/president/news/17158).

77. Anastasiya Kornya, "Sudy obnovili, a doveriya net" [The courts are updated, but there is no trust], *Vedomosti*, December 16, 2013.

78. *The State of the Judiciary in Russia*. IJC Report, 2010, pp. 5–6, 7, and 7, seriatim (www.icj.org/wp-content/uploads/2012/05/Russia-indepjudiciary-report-2010.pdf).

79. President of Russia, "Seminar-soveshchaniye predsedateley sudov" [Seminar meeting of courts chairmen], news release, Moscow, February 16, 2016.

80. In Russia, signing a plea deal does not determine punishment. It is up to a judge to determine punishment, which is limited to no more than two-thirds of the maximum prison term. Statistical research shows that in plea deals on average the sentence does not differ from similar cases without one.

81. Anastasiya Kornya, "Experty Kudrina raskryli plan uzhe nachavsheisya reform" [Kudrin's experts disclosed the plan of the reform has already begun]. *Vedomosti*, February 8, 2018.

Six

PREVENTING COMPETITION

Our party's program is simple: We want to rule Italy.
—Benito Mussolini

Only ten days after his inauguration in May 2000, Vladimir Putin announced his intention to build a "vertical of power" and proposed a drastic change in the relationship between the federal center and the regions in Russia. Amid the heated political battles of the summer of 2000, regional elites came to terms with considerable restrictions on their rights and authority but nevertheless managed to assert their independence. With the support of the Constitutional Court, the regional elites torpedoed Putin's effort to assert the right to dismiss them, but the ambitions of the governors' bloc had been crushed. The regional leaders had been pushed out of the Federation Council, and they never again challenged the president's dominance. Putin seemed to have achieved his goal.

However, it soon became clear that his understanding of the vertical of power was much more encompassing than most had perceived. Without warning, the Kremlin set in motion a long-term process of transforming the Russian electoral system, which soon led to the elimination of all political competition in the country. The opposition was split into a "system" faction, which agreed to cooperate with the Kremlin's scheme, and a "nonsystem" faction, which soon was pushed out of political life for disloyalty to Putin. The presidential administration obtained full control over the federal parliament, and Putin gained the right to use the legislature's full resources to rule the country in his way.

COHABITATION WAS POSSIBLE

Boris Yeltsin became a leader of Russia in a tense fight. In late May 1990, one year before he became president of Russia, Yeltsin was elected speaker of the Supreme Council of the Russian Soviet Federative Socialist Republic (RSFSR) in the third round. Although Yeltsin won more than 57 percent of the vote in the first round of the June 1991 presidential elections he never enjoyed the solid support of the Russian parliament and often had to build situational coalitions. The Russian parliament supported many of Yeltsin's reform initiatives at the time, but the president and parliament frequently clashed.

These clashes intensified after the collapse of the Soviet Union at the end of 1991, when Russia's Supreme Council transformed into a full-fledged legislative body of an independent country. An inauspicious beginning for the economic reform agenda seriously undermined the situation in the country, and parliament became the key place to criticize the government. Meanwhile, the ambitious parliamentary speaker Ruslan Khasbulatov wanted to dominate the political arena. He sought to place the parliament over the president, often undermining any chance for compromise and taking political differences personally. The conflict between the president and parliament continued to intensify until it finally exploded into an armed confrontation in October 1993—out of which President Yeltsin emerged victorious.

During the State Duma elections that took place two months later, Yeltsin refrained from supporting any political party out of a desire to remain the "president of all Russians." The Liberal Democratic Party of Russia (LDPR), with its nationalist and populist leader Vladimir Zhirinovsky, won the election with 22.5 percent of the proportional vote. Although Yegor Gaidar's reformist party only came in second, with 15.5 percent of the vote, it could create a caucus equal in size to that of the LDPR, thanks to its good performance in majoritarian districts.[1] The presence of eight parties that had reached the 5 percent threshold to obtain seats in the lower chamber of the Russian parliament, as well as the presence of 130 independent lawmakers (out of 450), allowed Yeltsin to achieve situational majorities when needed. However, this convocation of the State Duma lasted only two years. The situation changed drastically after the December 1995 election.

Whereas thirteen parties had run in the 1993 Duma elections—of which eight had won a combined 80 percent of the vote and obtained seats—a total of forty-three parties and electoral blocs participated in the 1995 legislative elections. Such a high number of participants on the ballot dispersed the vote, and thirty-nine parties and blocs failed to reach the established 5 percent threshold. The four parties that were able do so were unexpectedly rewarded with a much higher number of seats in parliament than they could have hoped for. The Communist Party won a decisive victory by obtaining, together with its allies, almost half the seats in the State Duma. In the 1995 legislative elections, President Yeltsin once again elected to remain "above the fray," even refusing to support the party created by his closest associate, Prime Minister Viktor Chernomyrdin. As a result, this party performed extremely poorly, taking just slightly more than 10 percent of the national vote.

All told, the 1993 and 1995 legislative elections showed that Boris Yeltsin feared neither free elections nor an opposition minded parliament. Moreover, both he and his administration did not possess the "administrative resources," as they later would be called, to influence the results of the vote. Regional governors and legislatures nominated the regional election commissions, and the Kremlin had no influence on their actions (to say nothing of opportunities for election fraud). The fact that in the 1995 Duma elections, the prime minister's party won more than 15 percent of the vote in only ten out of eighty-nine Russian regions—whereas Zhirinovsky's party crossed this threshold in twenty-three regions, and the Communist Party reached it in sixty regions—proves this point.[2]

FROM HATRED TO FRIENDSHIP

The 1999 Duma elections posed a serious challenge to the Kremlin, forcing it to fight several battles simultaneously. On the one hand, Boris Yeltsin effectively had anointed Vladimir Putin as his political successor, nominating him prime minister. In the late summer of 1999, Putin's political standing was extremely weak, and the Kremlin wanted to improve it before the 2000 presidential elections. Strategists working with the prime minister had no room for error. On the other hand, the State Duma had a left-wing majority, and the Kremlin—aware that one leg of mutton helps lower the other, as the saying goes—was worried about the prospect of the communists winning yet another parliamentary election. If the communists succeeded in maintaining their 40 percent representation in the lower house of the Russian parliament, their candidate would become an obvious presidential front-runner.

Moreover, one could not disregard the fact that many governors had consolidated around former prime minister Yevgeny Primakov and Moscow mayor Yury Luzhkov, causing dissent within the political elite. If bureaucrats across the country supported this alliance, and if a strong majority based on the union of communists and governors were to form in the State Duma, this could pose a real challenge to the Kremlin. As presidential chief of staff Aleksandr Voloshin said, "I try to imagine elections in 2000, sterile and fair, with no use of administrative resources. . . . There was a high probability of a rollback, i.e., a victory of the communists . . . I would say 50/50 chances."[3] This threat grabbed the Kremlin's full attention, and the presidential administration was ready to use all instruments of influence to obtain an election victory.

The Kremlin's team fought like a wounded bear; the desire to win helped it overcome many barriers. Having settled on the Luzhkov-Primakov alliance as its main opponent, the Kremlin brought the full might of state-controlled television to bear on the problem, breaching moral norms to humiliate both politicians. At the same time, the Kremlin began limiting the activity of the NTV channel, which supported the Kremlin's opponents.

Although the communists won the Duma elections, their result (24.3 percent of the proportional vote) was virtually identical to their previous one.[4] This suggested that the communist forces' presidential candidate lacked serious impetus. Moreover, the communists lost a third of the seats they had won in single-member districts in the previous election. Although the party still formed the largest caucus in the State Duma, it controlled fewer than 30 percent of seats.

The communists' weak showing once again deprived them of the chance to become a dominant force in parliament. When the Kremlin made them the unexpected offer to build a majority coalition, they gladly accepted it. The Kremlin's logic was clear. On the one hand, it wanted to avoid an opposition-minded parliament. The communists accepted this desire by joining the majority coalition, since they saw their participation as burnishing their image with a victory. On the other hand, the Kremlin's main opponent was still the party of the governors' bloc, Fatherland–All Russia (OVR), and attempts to reach an agreement with it had failed. The OVR was prepared to enter a coalition with the Unity bloc established by the Kremlin at the end of the summer of 1999, but would do so only if former prime minister Primakov became speaker of the Duma, which would have significantly raised his chances in the presidential campaign. Out of two bad options, the Kremlin chose the devil it knew best: compared to Primakov, the communist presidential candidate was a minor threat. Supported by three small parliamentary groups, the pro-presidential Unity bloc built a coalition and shared almost all top positions in the State Duma with the communists, even handing them the speakership of the lower chamber. The OVR obtained the irrelevant chairmanship of the Committee for the Commonwealth of Independent States and rapidly began losing its influence in the country.

However, this was not a stable structure. From the point of view of its public image, the Kremlin hardly rejoiced at its union with the communists. Moreover, from time to time the communist factions in the Duma refused to support the Kremlin's legislative initiatives, compelling the Kremlin to look for support from other factions. Yet when Putin became president, the confrontation between the federal center and the governors soon faded. Because most Russian regions were financially dependent on the federal budget and the governors were unable to influence political life through representation on the Federation Council, one governor after another pledged loyalty to the Kremlin. By the end of the summer of 2001, no substantial differences remained between Unity and OVR, and thus it seemed only natural that they should merge to form the United Russia party later in the year. After that, the top positions in the State Duma were redistributed, the communists lost their seats "at the holiday table," and the commanding heights of power were assigned to United Russia's representatives.

BUREAUCRACY SUBDUES POLITICIANS

The Kremlin began to prepare for the 2003 parliamentary elections two years in advance, when the law on political parties was adopted in mid-2001. It remembered well the 1995 elections, when half the vote went to parties that had failed to cross the 5 percent threshold, so it concentrated its initial efforts on fighting smaller parties. The first step was to introduce state control over the establishment and operation of political parties. The 2001 law gave the executive branch instruments of administrative pressure on parties at every stage of their existence. Under this law, only parties were allowed to put forward proportional voting lists for the State Duma—previously, national political associations and movements, as well as electoral blocs, had had the right to do so as well. Moreover, a new provision stipulated that to create an electoral bloc, at least one political party had to participate.

The law established an authorization-based procedure to replace the declaratory principle of party creation and registration, giving the executive branch the right to dissolve parties on relatively vague grounds. Parties now had to jump through numerous bureaucratic hoops at both federal and regional levels to establish themselves; at any point, their registration could be denied because of minor mistakes or irregularities in their legal paperwork. The law also established a minimum party membership of 10,000 people and demanded that parties have regional branches in at least half of all Russian regions; at the same time, it banned the creation of regional or interregional parties.[5] The regulations on party size and regional branches applied to existing parties, which were required to submit proof to state authorities that they had met these criteria.[6]

The new law immediately demonstrated the Kremlin's resolution to clean up the political scene by liquidating parties it found unmanageable or undesirable and preventing new ones from registering. Before the 1999 Duma elections, 139 political and public associations in Russia had the right to field candidates in federal elections, and two-thirds of them exercised this right. By the time of the 2003 Duma elections, only forty-four registered parties were left. "After the reregistration . . . there will be no more than ten parties left," forecasted Deputy Justice Minister Evgeny Sidorenko. "Chiefly, these will be the parties that are represented in the State Duma."[7]

Having seen how the regional election commissions were able to affect vote tabulation results, the Kremlin decided it should have a personal monopoly on this method of political control, and drafted legislation establishing a vertical system of election commissions. From then on, all electoral commissions were part of a hierarchical structure, with the Central Election Commission (CEC) at the top. The CEC had sole authority to appoint the chairs of the regional election commissions, and most members of lower-level election commissions were appointed by the higher-level commissions. In March 2003, the Federal Protective Service (FSO) took control of the Vybory (Elections) state automated system, which kept the lists of voters and absorbed information from almost 2,800 local election commissions.[8] Consequently, all information about eligible voters and flows of election results was now managed by the secret service that was closest to the president and was not under civilian control. Election commissions, including the CEC, now received the results of the vote counting directly from the Kremlin.

CONTROL OVER THE DUMA

Unlike Boris Yeltsin, who never showed support for any political party, the newly elected Vladimir Putin and his administration did not try to hide the fact that United Russia was their party. "We have been supporting and will continue to support United Russia," Kremlin strategist Vladislav Surkov declared publicly.[9] Surkov was well aware he did not need to worry about violating the law prohibiting government officials from using their position to advance the interests of political parties.

This change in perspective immediately affected the results of the 2003 election campaign. United Russia representatives, who occupied official positions in both the legislative and executive branches, had virtually unlimited access to federal television channels, because their appearances were said not to be part of their election campaigns. Most of the twenty-three parties registered for the election received access to state-controlled television channels—and yet their combined coverage equaled that enjoyed by United Russia alone. The Kremlin-created vertical structure of election commissions worked without a hitch. Approximately two-thirds of the members of these commissions turned out to be representatives of the executive branch or employees of budget-funded organizations, and United Russia representatives obtained the majority of commission seats allocated to political parties. As a result, during the registration, many politicians whom the government saw as undesirable were not allowed to participate in the election, including former vice president Aleksandr Rutskoy, former prosecutor general Yury Skuratov, and several State Duma members.

The arrest of Mikhail Khodorkovsky—the major sponsor of the liberal parties SPS and Yabloko—in October 2003, eight weeks before the election, had a crucial impact on the campaign. It led to a sharp decrease in these parties' finances, and also spurred talk in Moscow that Khodorkovsky had been arrested for funding above all the Communist Party's election campaign.[10] Despite the lack of youth and vitality in the communists' campaign, the Kremlin still saw the communists as its main opponents and directed its main efforts against them. According to Gleb Pavlovsky, then adviser to the presidential administration, "The crushing of [the communists] was part of our election strategy."[11]

As part of its fight against the communists, the Kremlin approved the registration of several parties and electoral blocs that shared the Communist Party's positions on numerous issues in order to erode its voter base. This tactic worked. The Motherland (Rodina) bloc, which had emerged only fourteen weeks before the election, won 9 percent of the vote with nationalistic and leftist rhetoric, while the communists finished with only two-thirds of the vote they had expected. Insofar as the communists lost as well three-fourths of the seats in the majoritarian districts they had won in 1999, the party suffered a crushing defeat. At that moment, the Communist Party lost any serious claim to a position of leadership and influence in Russia's decision-making process. The communists' ambitions faded as they realized that the only way they could maintain their position in the political arena was by being loyal to Putin and allowing themselves to be co-opted into the Kremlin-arranged system.

The 2003 State Duma elections were the first in Russian history in which the Kremlin was accused of rigging the results. Three parties—the Communist Party, Yabloko, and SPS—organized observation teams for all 95,000 polling locations. Based on copies of the counting protocols, they declared that the ballots of 3.5 million people who had not voted had been added to the result, a figure that amounted to 5.5 percent of the official turnout. International observers also identified many violations of election procedures. Figure 6-1 presents data from elections analyst Sergey Shpilkin's assessment of the election fraud that improved United Russia's result by an additional 4.5 million votes.[12] For comparison, figure 6-2 shows the relatively modest nature of the fraud in the 2000 presidential elections, when many regional election commissions were controlled by governors, many of whom did not support Putin.[13]

United Russia won 37.57 percent of the vote by the proportional system, but thanks to the success of its candidates in majoritarian districts, the party obtained half of all seats in the State Duma. The Kremlin, however, decided to go further. Dozens of independent legislators and smaller parliamentary groups soon joined the Kremlin's party, and consequently the United Russia caucus reached a total of 304 members (out of 450). It now had enough votes to adopt any laws it wished—including constitutional amendments—without the support of other parties, and to override the Federation Council's vetoes.

United Russia representatives occupied top leadership positions in the new Duma, including the positions of speaker, both of his first deputies, and five out of eight deputies, as well as all twenty-nine committee chairs and twenty-three first deputy chairs. The vertical of command and control in the federal legislature had been created. Because all appointments to top leadership positions in the Duma were made by the leaders of the United Russia caucus, who in turn were nominated by the Kremlin, the slightest failure to carry out the Kremlin's instructions was punishable by dismissal. There were no such men of courage in the Duma.

The 2004 presidential election was probably the most comfortable one for Vladimir Putin himself and for his administration. The main parliamentary opposition parties, the Communist Party and the LDPR, nominated little-known candidates. The liberal parties, SPS and Yabloko, refused to put forward any candidates at all. But even under such conditions the Kremlin hampered free and fair elections. The CEC categorically refused to register

FIGURE 6-1. Evaluation of Fraud during the Vote Tabulation in the December 2003 State Duma Elections

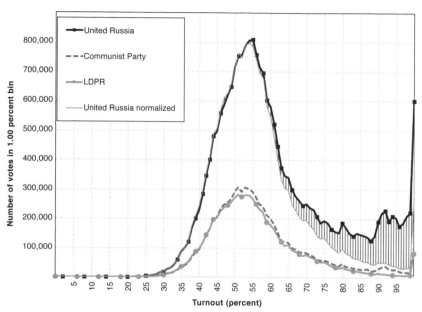

Sources: Russia's Central Electoral Commission and Sergey Shpilkin's calculations.

Notes: CPRF, Communist Party of the Russian Federation; United Russia; LDPR, Liberal Democratic Party of Russia. "Number of votes in 1.00 percent bin" refers to the number of votes received by each party or candidate in the elections that can be attributed to polling stations with turnout in each percentile (from example, from 0.0 to 0.99999, from 43.000 to 43.9999).

Sergey Shpilkin's hypothesis is the following: in a situation of free and fair elections, the voting results of different candidates are dispersed among polling stations in the same manner (the "normal distribution"). This hypothesis works rather well in Russia with respect to the results of all candidates and parties except the Kremlin's candidates (United Russia, Vladimir Putin, Dmitry Medvedev) in the polling stations with a turnout well above the national average. In the latter the results for the Kremlin's candidates exhibit an unusual distribution known by Russian political scientists as the "dinosaur's spine," with spikes at the rounded turnout numbers (65 percent, 70 percent, 75 percent, and so on). To assess the number of votes added for the Kremlin's candidates, Shpilkin builds distributions of their results ("normalized") similarly to distribution of results of other candidates. The difference between official and the normalized results is shown by the hatched area. Shpilkin's methodology is described in Sergey Spilkin, "Statisticheskoye issledovaniye rezul'tatov rossiyskikh vyborov 2007–2009 gg." [Statistical analysis of the results of Russian elections in 2007–2009], Moscow region, Troitskiy variant, October 27, 2009 (http://trv-science.ru/2009/10/27/statisticheskoe-issledovanie-rezultatov-ros-sijskix-vyborov-2007-2009-gg/). It is also available at Dmitry Kobak, Sergey Shpilkin, and Maxim S. Pshenichnikov, "Statistical Anomalies in 2011–2012 Russian Elections Revealed by 2D Correlation Analysis" (arXiv:1205.0741v2 [physics.soc-ph]).

FIGURE 6-2. Evaluation of Fraud during the Vote Tabulation
in the March 2000 Presidential Election

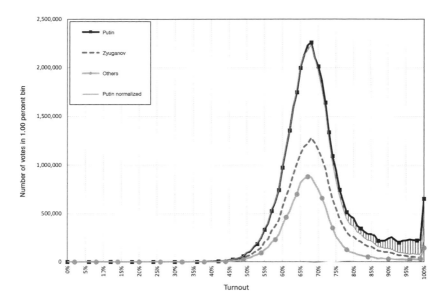

Sources: Russia's Central Election Commission and Sergey Shpilkin's calculations (see note to figure 6-1).

Viktor Gerashchenko, the former head of the Russian Central Bank and a charismatic candidate from the Motherland bloc. Though Gerashchenko had no chance of winning, the Kremlin evidently worried that he could siphon off enough votes to make Putin's victory look less impressive. During the election campaign, the main state-controlled television channels spent hours covering the activity of the incumbent president, even as they completely ignored the other candidates. All other candidates combined received only 22 percent of Putin's airtime on Russian television.[14] The unofficial goal consisted in Putin winning the votes of half of all Russian citizens.[15] Although this goal was never achieved, the 2004 election, based on its results, turned out to be a landslide. Vladimir Putin won 71 percent of the vote, whereas the next candidate, backed by the communists, received less than 14 percent.

Although no one doubted that the incumbent president would win the vote, the results were rigged in many Russian regions. According to estimates, Vladimir Putin received approximately 9 million additional votes.

THE OLIGARCHS' REVENGE: FEAR OF THE PAST

The 2003 and 2004 elections brought the results the Kremlin had been seeking. They demonstrated that there was no real threat of Putin losing his hold on power and no real opposition capable of challenging him. However, the ink was barely dry on the ballots when the Kremlin launched a sustained assault on the electoral rights of Russian citizens, gradually limiting their ability to participate in political life—their right both to elect and to be elected. As often happens with politicians trying to hold on to power, the Kremlin uncovered both domestic and external enemies. "We all have to realize that the enemy is at the gates," said Surkov. "The front line passes through every city, every street, every house."[16]

Five months before Mikhail Khodorkovsky's arrest, an expert report appeared in many Kremlin offices that offered a colorful description of the potential threats to political stability in Russia. Although the report was emotional in nature and lacked facts or evidence, some of its statements must have rattled Putin and his inner circle. "The country is on the verge of a creeping oligarchic takeover," it claimed, stating that "[the oligarchs] came to the conclusion that a personal union between government authorities and the largest businesses had to be secured to provide oligarchs with direct access to top government positions." Therefore, these oligarchs decided to "limit the authority of the president of the Russian Federation and to transform Russia from a presidential republic into a presidential-parliamentary one." Although the report stated that the "main ideologist of such transformation is . . . Mikhail Khodorkovsky, [who] can pursue rather ambitious long-term [political] goals," the report's authors repeatedly noted that other oligarchs also supported Khodorkovsky.[17]

Only four months after Vladimir Putin's second inauguration, the Kremlin launched a new wave of legislative changes regulating the country's political life. Although the drama of the Beslan school hostage crisis in September 2004 served as a formal pretext to initiate this process, the real reason had nothing to do with terrorism. The Kremlin was afflicted with an array of phobias, seeing threats to its power everywhere. That was not so strange in itself: by early 2004, the power balance in Putin's closest circle had changed considerably. Voloshin resigned as presidential chief of staff in protest at

Khodorkovsky's arrest, and four months later Putin dismissed Prime Minister Mikhail Kasyanov, who also had publicly criticized the oligarch's arrest. As a result, the influence of the *siloviki* in both the Kremlin and the government strengthened. *Siloviki* knew nothing about political competition, but they knew very well how to wield power against enemies.

The *siloviki* used this fear of an oligarchic comeback to gradually mold the president's worldview into one in which he was surrounded by enemies. Putin adopted this paradigm, which would come to define his policy in subsequent years. Pavlovsky confessed that "in the late summer of 2003 the Group [consisting of Sergey Pugachyov, Igor Sechin, and Viktor Ivanov[18]] turned into a key player in Russian politics . . . [and its] main objective was . . . to fundamentally adjust the country's political and economic development policy implemented by the president and the government. . . . In fact, the destroyed oligarchic system was being replaced by a new oligarchy of the *siloviki* . . . directed at achieving its goals by using state instruments and administrative resources."[19]

After Khodorkovsky's arrest, Putin appeared to fear an "oligarchic comeback." He was not entirely certain that the oligarchs would not seek revenge for Khodorkovsky, although after the initial emotional response, top Russian business owners seemingly forgot about corporate solidarity and allowed the Kremlin to tear Khodorkovsky and his company to pieces. Even though Putin believed that his 2004 victory had been convincing, he was still concerned about a potential countermove by business owners, especially because by mid-2004 the plans for nationalizing Yukos had been finalized and were gradually being implemented. A few years later, Surkov described the fears haunting the Kremlin at the time: "We have a political force that would like us to take a step backward. I would call it the party of the oligarchic comeback. This political philosophy has its potential political leaders too, as well as its foreign sponsors. There is no doubt that we cannot allow the restoration of an oligarchic regime. . . . There is a potential threat of their comeback, which we cannot ignore."[20]

But besides these domestic enemies, an external one emerged.

NO SPACE FOR OPPOSITION TO HIS MAJESTY

The Rose Revolution in Georgia in November 2003 immediately provoked talks in the Kremlin about "U.S. interference" in the post-Soviet space—and the alleged ultimate target of such measures, Vladimir Putin—intended to bring Russia under Western control. To reach this lofty goal, the external enemy allegedly was building up support within Russia. "A fifth column of leftist and rightist radicals emerged in our virtually besieged country," Surkov proclaimed. "Lemons and certain apples are now growing on the same branch. Fake liberals and real Nazis increasingly have more in common. They have common foreign sponsors."[21]

The Orange Revolution in Ukraine in November–December 2004 and the Tulip Revolution in Kyrgyzstan in the spring of 2005 proved to the Kremlin that its fears of external enemies were not theoretical.[22] "What threatens [Russia's] sovereignty? . . . A soft absorption using modern 'orange' technologies," Surkov stated in February 2006. "I cannot say that this issue has been removed from the agenda because if they succeeded in four countries, why not try it in a fifth? I believe that these attempts will not be limited to 2007 and 2008. Our foreign friends can try to do it again in the future."[23] The Kremlin certainly noticed that parliamentary opposition had played a decisive role in the ousting of the Georgian president Eduard Shevardnadze, which led to an obvious conclusion: the Russian parliament could only be allowed to be the opposition *of* His Majesty—not opposition *to* His Majesty.[24]

In the same September 2004 speech in which Vladimir Putin proposed eliminating gubernatorial elections in Russia, he announced new steps significantly restricting political competition: "National parties must become a mechanism for ensuring a real dialogue and cooperation between society and government authorities in the fight against terror. In the interests of strengthening the country's political system, I consider it necessary to introduce a proportional system of electing the State Duma."[25] Putin never explained how the election of Duma members in majoritarian districts hampered the fight against terror, so Surkov did it for him: "How will this help in the fight against terror? [It will help] because it will not be as in the 1990s, when there were a trillion so-called couch parties, complete chaos, the particularization and atomization of society. And, naturally, all possible germs and all diseases wriggled into this mixture, this decomposing organism. . . . Elections from party lists . . . will cut down the corrupt practices of lawmakers."[26] What could be clearer?

Having identified the threat—too many disloyal political actors—Putin decided to do as much as he could to limit his enemies' participation in political life. Even as it professed to be strengthening the role of parties in the electoral process, the Kremlin was eliminating Russia's genuine multiparty system. Quantitative requirements were raised sharply: a party had to have at least 50,000 members, as opposed to the previously required 10,000. The existing parties had to submit to a reregistration process that included all the procedures for initial registration. The threshold for entering the State Duma was raised to 7 percent, and —in a move that affected voters' interests most of all—the formation of electoral blocs was prohibited.

The use of electoral blocs had been an important component of political life in Russia. The emerging political parties did not enjoy stable public support, and they differed not so much in ideology as in the names of their ambitious leaders. It was hard for politicians to make long-term agreements when most alliances and unions were situational, so many parties, realizing they had a slim chance of passing the threshold, chose to form electoral blocs before the elections. The newly increased 7 percent threshold for the Duma further reduced the chances for many parties to win seats, though it seemed that electoral blocs could help consolidate party life. However, this did not suit the interests of the Kremlin, which sought to allow only a loyal system of opposition in the Duma. An attempt at getting around this restriction by nominating candidates from several parties on one party list was immediately curbed by a new law passed in the summer of 2006, which banned parties from nominating members of other parties on their lists. To pass this law in the State Duma, the Kremlin rewarded the system opposition for its loyalty. A provision was added to increase by a factor of ten the state financing of parties represented in parliament.

Besides guaranteed financial support, the parliamentary parties received one more gift from the Kremlin: their activities would be covered by one of the federal news channels. Unsurprisingly, parties that were not represented in the Duma received no such right to media coverage. Although from a legal standpoint, all parties were equal and as such should have received equal airtime, in real life this was not the case. So long as a politician's party affiliation was not specified in an identifying caption during a broadcast, he or she could appear on the news without having the appearance count against the airtime allotted to a particular party. The politicians who typically enjoyed this benefit were representatives of United Russia who held various federal and regional government positions. As a result of this practice, United Russia received on average twice as much airtime as other parties.

The seriousness of the Kremlin's intentions to assume complete control over the Russian political system soon became obvious. By the 2007 elections, only fifteen of the forty-four parties that had existed in late 2004 remained. Parties whose leaders were seen as undesirable by the Kremlin were dissolved under made-up pretexts. Not one of them succeeded in defending its rights in the Russian courts.[27] All these factors made a State Duma seat an unattainable goal for politicians who were unwilling to cooperate with the Kremlin and assimilate into the political structure created by Putin.

Politicians who did not cooperate were classified as "nonsystem opposition," and the only remaining form of political activity open to them was public rallies, which the Kremlin did not welcome. According to Voloshin, Putin himself believed that street protests were an absolutely unacceptable method of carrying out political activity.[28] The Kremlin saw that post-Soviet color revolutions stemmed from the combined pressure of parliamentary opposition and street protests, so it imposed tough restrictions on rallies and demonstrations. The law on public rallies adopted in the summer of 2004 established a procedure for securing local authorities' approval for rallies and demonstrations—thus essentially amending the Russian constitution's guaranteed freedom of assembly. The authorities began using this law to regularly reject opposition politicians' requests to hold rallies, or to grant permits to hold them only in remote districts. This practice led to many Russian opposition rallies and demonstrations being held without permits, which the Kremlin considered illegal. The Kremlin responded by repressing protest leaders, whom police regularly detained and the courts later sentenced to administrative arrest.[29]

THE UPPER CHAMBER HAS NOT BEEN FORGOTTEN

The removal of regional governors and speakers of regional legislatures from the Federation Council turned the upper chamber of the Russian parliament from a body representing and protecting the interests of the regions into an assembly of lobbyists. In the previous decade, all Russian governors had run in direct elections, and some had even run twice. Now, these public political figures were being replaced by people whose strength consisted in securing access to the relevant offices and making deals with government officials. Although the Federation Council no longer posed a threat to the Kremlin, it did not fit into the vertical of power that was being built—and this was unacceptable.

Although the Kremlin had abandoned the idea of once again changing the rules forming the Federation Council, it addressed this issue in a comprehensive way. The composition of the Federation Council was just the tip of the iceberg; the real problem was the Kremlin's lack of control over political life in the regions. Many governors and most members of the regional legislatures were elected as independent candidates backed by various interest groups. It was impossible to sort out the intricacies of local politics from the Kremlin's offices. Moreover, presidential envoys to federal districts were not particularly good at conducting dialogues or building coalitions. Political pliancy was not their strongest point; instead, they preferred more forceful methods of solving problems. Consequently, the Kremlin had to figure out how to drastically weaken the independence of the regional elites by depriving them of opportunities to defend their interests. The first part of this equation—the cancellation of the governors' elections—was relatively easy to solve. The second part—taking control of regional legislatures—was more challenging.

The underlying framework for this decision was built into the package of radical changes to the elections legislation approved in 2002 and 2003, which enforced the introduction of proportional elections for Russian regional legislatures.[30] Although the regions had the right to determine the ratio of lawmakers elected by proportional vote versus those elected in majoritarian districts, the number of the former could not amount to fewer than half of the seats. In 2005 and 2006, the legal electoral thresholds for parties to gain seats in regional legislatures was toughened considerably—from 3 percent to 10 percent, to be defined for each region by the regional legislature—and this arrangement cleared the way for the Kremlin to establish control over regional lawmakers.

Because regional elections occurred at different times, it took several years to fit regional lawmakers into the vertical of power. But it soon became evident that the new rules worked—for the Kremlin, that is. United Russia was the only beneficiary of the changes. From 2003 to 2005, the Kremlin's party came in second only three times in thirty-two regional election campaigns, winning the rest on the party-list ballot. And that was just the beginning. As gubernatorial elections were replaced with presidential nominations, United Russia's election results began to improve even more. Out of twenty-five election campaigns from the fall of 2005 to the spring of 2007, the Kremlin's party came in second only once, and won an absolute majority in twelve regional legislatures. Since the fall of 2009, United Russia has reliably placed first in the proportional elections throughout all Russian regions. And since half of the members of the Federation Council were nominated by the regional legislatures, the Kremlin thereby guaranteed that no undesirable persons would make it into the upper chamber of parliament.

A drop in United Russia's electoral support from 2009 to 2011 prompted the Kremlin to give the governors more flexibility (see figure 6-3). A law was amended to allow the regions to increase the share of lawmakers elected in majoritarian districts, and many regions took advantage of this change. Although this measure seemed to benefit United Russia's opponents, in reality it resulted in increased administrative pressure on undesirable candidates. Instances of independent candidates or representatives of parties other than United Russia winning in single-member districts became few and far between.

By mid-2018 there was not a single Russian regional legislature in which United Russia held fewer than 60 percent of the seats. In fifty out of eighty-five regions, it controlled more than 75 percent of the seats. There is no one region in Russia where any other party had more than 20 percent of the seats in the regional legislature. After the 2017 election campaign, out of 3,994 regional legislators, 3,099 were members of United Russia. Because United Russia itself reflects a strict vertical structure in which the center supervises

FIGURE 6-3. Electoral Ratings of United Russia Party, 2006–11

PERCENT

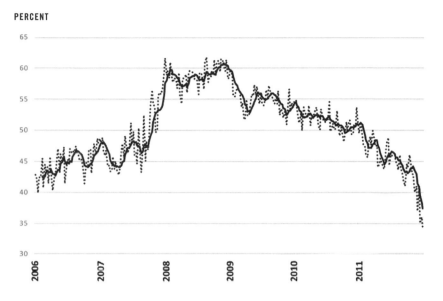

Source: WCIOM (Russian Public Opinion Research Center), "Reyting politicheskikh partiy" [Rating of political parties] (https://wciom.ru/news/ratings/elektoralnyj_re jting_politicheskix_partij/).

Note: Figure shows weekly data plus six-weekly floating average.

all regional branch decisions, there is no doubt that only people entirely loyal to the Kremlin can become regional lawmakers for the party. Naturally, this allows the Kremlin to determine who will represent regional legislatures in the Federation Council.

Insofar as the other half of the Federation Council was nominated by governors who were nominated by the president, it was evident that the upper chamber of the Russian parliament had fallen fully under the control of the Kremlin and had lost its role in Russian political life.

INDISCREET DESIRE

After his reelection as president in 2004, Vladimir Putin tasked his administration with maintaining the established political structure. He declared he would not violate or amend the constitution to run for a third term in a row, but already he was considering his options for staying in power after the end of his presidential term in 2008. The only question was which post he should occupy. In early 2006, Surkov described Putin's objective: "We need to win more votes than all the other party lists combined. . . . United Russia's goal is not just to win in 2007, but to think of everything and do everything to ensure the party's dominance in the next ten to fifteen years."[31]

The transition to a proportional system of elections to the State Duma reduced opportunities for vertical mobility in Russian politics. Now, political careers were possible only within seven registered political parties, of which only four were represented at the federal level. A few months before the 2007 Duma elections, the Kremlin initiated a reconciliation procedure for approving the candidates' lists of parliamentary parties and stated its requirements: candidates were not to participate in street rallies and could not be involved with the nonsystem opposition. Moreover, the Kremlin had its own list of undesirable politicians—ones it saw as difficult to handle or unwilling to be co-opted into the established system. Among the people rejected from party lists at the Kremlin's demand were well-known State Duma members with different political positions—Vladimir Ryzhkov, Dmitry Rogozin, Aleksandr Lebedev, Sergey Glazyev, and Yevgheny Roizman—each of whom could have improved his party's results in the election.[32] As usual, each of them had to choose his future, and their choices were different. Ryzhkov moved to the nonsystem opposition and lost in the Duma elections in 2016. Rogozin allied with the Kremlin and became deputy prime minister in 2012–18, then became the CEO of Roskosmos. Lebedev financed the opposition until his business came under attack from the government and he was ruined. Glazyev became an adviser to President Putin and one of the most radical Kremlin proponents of invading Ukraine. Roizman was elected mayor of Yekaterinburg and lost this post in 2018 when mayoral elections were eliminated by the decision of the regional parliament.

The Kremlin not only restricted its opponents' ability to communicate with the public by imposing a full blackout on state-controlled television, it also banned opposition candidates from reaching voters with their viewpoints. Shortly before the election, the rules on campaigning were changed. The law prohibited the use of television to disseminate negative information about opponents or to discuss the possible consequences or implementation of their ideas. At the same time, the part of the law that demanded that top government officials (ministers and governors) go on vacation during their election campaigns was annulled. After that, all campaign activities of government officials were covered by the state-controlled media as part of their official duties, and neither the courts nor the CEC saw this as a violation of the law.

The Kremlin's behavior in this matter was understandable. In 2008, Vladimir Putin's second presidential term was coming to an end, and Russia was entering a period of potentially increased political volatility. In Putin's opinion, this uncertainty could serve as a breeding ground for an Orange Revolution in Russia. Thus it was imperative for the Kremlin that the election results not produce any surprises. Putin's pledge not to run in 2008 notwithstanding, he clearly had resolved to maintain his hold on power. His decision to head United Russia's list in the Duma elections sent a signal to the political elite that there were no politicians in the country who were Putin's equal, and United Russia's electoral victory was needed to keep him in power.

Putin himself publicly voiced this idea ten days before the election: "The United Russia party . . . has to win a majority in the State Duma . . . [so that] the Duma does not turn into a gathering of populists paralyzed by corruption and inane talk." As he put it, "The only thing we need is victory . . . the main objective [consists in] ensuring the continuity of the policy directed at a stable and steady development of the country, as well as in protecting our motherland's welfare and security from political risks." Yet the risks that bothered Putin were not new. He was frightened of "those who oppose us and want to see our plan fail. Because their goals and plans for Russia are entirely different. They want a weak, ailing state. They want a disorganized and disoriented society, a divided society, so that they can do their deeds behind its back and eat cake on our tab." Underscoring the domestic threat, he added, "These people have not left the political arena. You will find their names among the candidates and sponsors of certain parties. They want to get even, to return to power, to the spheres of influence. And to gradually restore the oligarchic regime."[33]

Government officials saw this objective, so bluntly expressed by Putin, as an order to be carried out, not discussed. The regional authorities became the most fervent supporters of United Russia—and its leader. During a meeting with the heads of municipalities, Volgograd governor Nikolai Maksyuta openly stated whom it was proper to vote for: "I don't want to beat around the bush—I work in a state's structure. My direct superior is President Vladimir Putin. How can I vote for anyone else?! How can you vote for anyone else while you are working under me?"[34] Krasnodar governor Aleksandr Tkachyov's message was just as direct: "There has not been a time in Russian history when the head of state called for a vote of confidence in him and in what he does in such an open way. . . . December 2 will be a real referendum in support of Vladimir Putin."[35] Those who missed Tkachyov's point paid dearly. Two weeks after the election, fourteen heads of municipalities and their deputies were fired for "poor organization of work during the election," and seventeen more received reprimands.

The election results were impressive: United Russia won 64.3 percent of the vote and 70 percent of the seats in the State Duma (315 out of 450). The regime-built mechanism for keeping the Russian parliament subordinated to the Kremlin passed this test without a hitch. During the 2007 State Duma election, the Kremlin-built system for controlling elections ran smoothly. Russian television allocated three-fifths of airtime to United Russia.[36] The CEC and the courts disregarded all election law violations. The scale of election fraud exceeded 13 million votes, setting a new record.

One week after the elections, Putin unveiled his secret plan to stay in power. First of all, he chose Dmitry Medvedev, a weak person who enjoyed hardly any support among the elites, as his successor.[37] In the first half of the 1990s, Medvedev had worked as Putin's assistant in St. Petersburg, and he owed his career to the Russian president. Medvedev then announced that, if elected, he would appoint Putin prime minister. Since Russia's law enforcement authorities answer directly to the president, the government is responsible for economic and social policy, as well as for budget planning and execution. It obviously was more important for Putin to control financial resources than to control the State Duma;[38] nothing could threaten United Russia's dominant position there. By 2008, parliament's real role in the Russian political system had become so insignificant that the prospect of working in the State Duma did not appeal to the outgoing president. The dominance of one party had resulted in the Russian parliament's becoming "not a place for discussions," in the words of then Duma speaker Boris Gryzlov. Key decisions concerning bills being considered by parliament were made in the Kremlin.

A political structure with Dmitry Medvedev as president and Vladimir Putin as prime minister was a necessary but undesirable solution that posed huge risks to Putin. He had become hostage to his promise not to run for a third term. Under Russian law, the president has the right to dismiss the prime minister at his discretion at any time without parliamentary approval. (Such approval is required for the prime minister's appointment.) Though Putin announced that he would work "without altering the balance of power between the office of presidency and the government itself," in practice he created the mechanism of the "tandem," in which both politicians, seen by the public as a duumvirate, exercised equal powers. The work of the tandem was based on strict observation of the legally established principle of separation of powers between the government and the president. However, both the president and the prime minister had an informal veto over one another's decisions. Thus, one could act only if the other did not object.[39] Naturally, this mechanism could work only if the president was the weaker figure. In fact, this was why Putin hand-picked Dmitry Medvedev as his successor.

Though the Kremlin easily obtained the desired results during the December 2007 parliamentary elections, it did not see any reason to loosen its steel grip on voters' throats during the 2008 presidential election. The price of a potential mistake was too high, and the Kremlin did not intend to take any risks.

The liberal SPS party nominated former deputy prime minister Boris Nemtsov as its presidential candidate. Because SPS was not represented in the State Duma, Nemtsov had to collect 2 million signatures to get on the ballot. When it became clear a few days later that he could not procure funding for his campaign office, Nemtsov withdrew his candidacy. Although former prime minister Mikhail Kasyanov, running from his own party, did manage to achieve the impossible by collecting the required 2 million signatures in four weeks, he nevertheless failed to be registered as a presidential candidate. The CEC declared almost 14 percent of his signatures void, exceeding the 5 percent limit for invalid signatures. Yet according to handwriting experts, only 231 of the 380,000 signatures declared void were invalid; the CEC had rejected the rest over claims of improper figuration (such as ink color and font size problems, typing errors, and abbreviations). Kasyanov's attempt to challenge this decision in the Supreme Court proved unsuccessful. Moreover, during the hearings, a CEC representative declared that "criminal cases are being initiated in a number of regions in connection with the forging of signatures in Kasyanov's support."[40]

The election results were predictable: Dmitry Medvedev won over 70 percent of the vote, and Communist Party leader Gennady Zyuganov came second with less than 18 percent of the vote. According to Shpilkin's estimates, Medvedev received more than 14.5 million fraudulent votes (see figure 6-4). The first important decision of the new president was to invade Georgia in August 2008. The second was to initiate a constitutional amendment extending the presidential term from four to six years, starting in 2012.

FIGURE 6-4. Evaluation of Fraud during the Vote Tabulation in the March 2008 Presidential Election

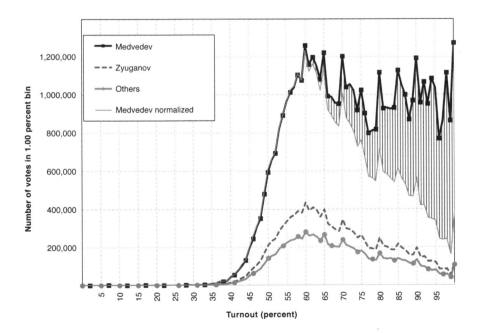

Sources: Russia's Central Election Commission and Sergey Shpilkin's calculations (see note to figure 6-1).

PROKHOROV'S COMET

The 2008 global financial crisis came as a complete surprise to the Kremlin. Even in October 2008, the Russian authorities were still denying that things had fundamentally changed. As the State Duma was considering the following year's budget bill, Finance Minister Alexey Kudrin claimed there was no reason to expect a crisis in Russia: the economy would maintain its high growth rate, and the ruble would remain stable. Life, however, had other plans for Russia. The demand for Russian commodities on the world market plummeted. A sharp decrease in oil prices led to a collapse of the ruble. The Russian economy experienced a 10 percent decline. A huge amount of resources was spent to overcome the crisis. The Russian Central Bank spent more than a third of its foreign exchange reserves to support the ruble's exchange rate. The fiscal stimulus exceeded 4.5 percent of Russia's GDP. The government and the central bank spent even more—5.4 percent of GDP—to rescue the banking system.

The slow postcrisis economic recovery followed the oil prices. Thus, in February 2011, world oil prices once again exceeded U.S. $100 per barrel, and by the end of 2011 the Russian economy returned to its precrisis maximum of the second quarter of 2008. The Russian authorities in general, and Prime Minister Vladimir Putin in particular, were preoccupied by economic issues, and as a result, Medvedev's more liberal rhetoric resulted in decreased censorship of state-controlled television. Opposition politicians now began to appear in the media once in a while. The new president's idea of modernization of the economy was seen as reflecting his desire to turn the country toward democratic values, at least slightly. "It's time to change the development paradigm. . . . We need to develop the whole society and the economy. . . . There is not any alternative to a big modernization of the economy and social sphere," declared Medvedev.[41]

In this context, the Kremlin refrained from tightening the election laws before the 2011 State Duma elections. The executive branch was comfortable with a parliament that had been brought entirely under its control, and there were no serious new threats. With the number of parties that had the right to nominate candidates reduced to seven, and with United Russia controlling the governors and legislatures in practically all the regions of Russia, the election at the end of the year did not appear to pose any problems.

However, at the beginning of 2011 a wave of mass political protests—the so-called Arab Spring—arose in the Middle East, bringing down Egyptian and Tunisian leaders who had ruled for more than thirty years. These events did not have a noticeable impact on the political situation in Russia, but the Kremlin, ever mindful of the "orange threat," chose to be proactive. In May 2011, at the Kremlin's invitation, the billionaire Mikhail Prokhorov became the leader of the Right Cause party and agreed to head its list in the Duma elections.[42] Having failed to fit the opposition leaders of Yeltsin's era into the new political system, but aware of the widespread public support for democratic ideas, the Kremlin decided to "let off some steam" by creating a controlled liberal party. Prokhorov, one of Russia's wealthiest men and a person who had never criticized Vladimir Putin or his policies, was expected to attract those who were willing to accept Putin's domination of Russian politics and to be co-opted into his political system.

However, this idea failed. Within months, Prokhorov got involved in a public conflict with Surkov, describing the latter's role in Russian political life in a markedly unflattering way: "I had firsthand experience of what a political monopoly looks like when you get calls with instructions on a daily basis. . . . There is a puppet master in the country who has long privatized the political system, has been misinforming the country's government, has been putting pressure on the media—his name is Vladislav Surkov."[43] The reason for the dispute did not appear to be serious. Prokhorov had refused to exclude his friend Yevgheny Roizman from the party list. The Kremlin had deemed Roizman—a charismatic politician—undesirable, and had removed him from Just Russia's party list in 2007. Yet one person, especially as a member of a small caucus, could hardly change anything in the 450-member State Duma. It seemed that the Kremlin might be willing to loosen its grip on politics somewhat to facilitate the creation of a democratically minded party loyal to the Kremlin.

Nonetheless, this did not happen. The key question for the Kremlin was whether Prokhorov's party would be as obedient as the other Russian parties, not whether Roizman himself would become a member of the State Duma. Having realized that Prokhorov was not prepared to be entirely loyal, the Kremlin decided it was a better option to cut its losses rather than take the chance that the project could slip from its control and go viral among other Russian politicians. In a matter of days, Prokhorov was thrown out of the party he led. This upheaval happened in September, splitting the party as it was trying to approve a list for the upcoming election. The majority of delegates abandoned Prokhorov on the Kremlin's recommendation and held the party's congress without him or his supporters. The party congress elected a new leader and finalized a Kremlin-approved list of candidates.

Following these events, an enraged Prokhorov lifted the veil on the methods the Kremlin used to control political parties and its mechanisms for approving candidates. He claimed that he had been explicitly told during meetings that "these people seem worthy" or that "we do not particularly care for this or that person, he has to be taken off the list." Prokhorov concluded that "the administration finds it surprising when a party does not follow its recommendations." He also revealed Surkov's role in managing parties, as shown in his involvement in creating a rift in the Right Cause party by meeting with delegates to the party congress and using the regional administrations to pressure them where they lived. "Surkov is used to having all the parties dance to his tune like puppets. The Right Cause party did not dance to his tune," Prokhorov explained.[44]

Prokhorov, an inexperienced politician, did not immediately realize that the decision to have him expelled from the party list had been made at the highest level. Leading a head-on attack against Surkov, he counted on support from Putin and Medvedev. He made one strong statement after another. "I will have a talk with the country's leaders," he declared in one interview.[45] Although he acknowledged the likely sources of Surkov's power—"I very much hope that Surkov is not backed by Putin and Medvedev"—he said candidly, "As long as such people [as Surkov] rule the political process, real politics is impossible in the country. I will do everything I can to have Surkov dismissed."[46] However, Prokhorov was soon informed who was in the right in this conflict. Putin's press secretary declared that the prime minister knew about the "rift" in the Right Cause party but "did not plan" to have a meeting with Prokhorov.

The Kremlin did not forgive Prokhorov for his disobedience. In 2013, when Prokhorov wanted to run for mayor of Moscow, a law was adopted that essentially prohibited him from participating in the election. This law was one in a series of restrictive measures directed at gradually limiting Russian citizens' rights.

NO RIGHT TO BE ELECTED

Beginning in 2006, an avalanche of restrictions was placed on the right to be elected in Russia. The first to be affected by the new laws were Russian citizens who held dual citizenship or residence permits in other countries. A year later, Russians convicted of serious or very serious crimes received a lifetime ban from public office.[47] Essentially, this amounted to the imposition of yet another (extrajudicial) criminal penalty; when this provision came into force, it was applied retroactively. The adoption of this law, however, was so little noticed that many election commissions continued to accept documents submitted by candidates affected by the restriction. The courts later had to annul their registration.

Although the Russian constitution says that only "citizens recognized by a court as legally unfit, as well as citizens kept in the places of confinement by a court sentence," can be deprived of the right to elect and be elected, all attempts at challenging the imposed restrictions in courts proved unsuccessful. In December 2007, the Russian Constitutional Court recognized as lawful the ban on the election of Russian citizens with dual citizenship, declaring that this ban was caused by "the need to defend the pillars of the constitutional order in Russia."[48] And in October 2013, the Constitutional Court confirmed the constitutional character of the voting restrictions aimed at Russian citizens who had served their sentence but still had convictions on their records, noting only that this could not be a lifelong ban.[49] The decision of the Constitutional Court was technically respected, but in reality the ban remained in place. It takes eight and ten years, respectively, for serious and very serious criminal convictions to be cleared from an individual's criminal record, and the ban on being elected remains in force for another ten years for serious criminal offenses and fifteen years for very serious ones.

The Kremlin explained that these restrictions were necessary to prevent criminal elements from infiltrating government structures. It was obvious that the law was directed at specific people. Thus it affected Mikhail

Khodorkovsky and his partners convicted in the context of the Yukos case, as well as Russian political émigrés who sought refuge in foreign countries. Not long after, Alexey Navalny was also affected by this restriction as he pled guilty to a spoof crime.

Additional targeted restrictions were introduced hastily in the spring of 2013. Russian citizens possessing foreign bank accounts or "using foreign financial instruments" lost the right to be elected.[50] Later, candidates were required to submit financial documents stating their ownership of foreign assets, including securities, real estate, and vehicles.[51] Mikhail Prokhorov, who had won more than 20 percent of the Moscow vote in the 2012 presidential election and was considering running for mayor of Moscow in September 2013, was one of the obvious targets of this law. Having asked the chair of the CEC about the requirements for registering the transfer of his assets to Russia in order to comply with the law, Prokhorov received the cynical answer that "we are going to elaborate the rules to use of this norm by applying it"—in other words, you'll know how we apply the law when we apply it.

AN UNEXPECTED OCCURRENCE

Prokhorov's expulsion from Right Cause deprived the party of any chance for electoral success, but thanks to its billionaire former leader the party owned the biggest campaign war chest in Russia. Yabloko and the Patriots of Russia, two other registered parties, also had no chance of crossing the 7 percent Duma threshold. Moreover, just before the election campaign the Kremlin deprived Sergey Mironov, leader of the Just Russia party, of his position as speaker of the Federation Council, an act intended to damage the party's image and diminish its recognizability. It seemed that the United Russia party had laid the groundwork for yet another triumph, and nothing could prevent the Kremlin from maintaining its control over the State Duma.

However, Vladimir Putin himself disrupted the smooth operation of the political process. Although the 2012 presidential election was seven months away and Dmitry Medvedev's term was to end in nine months, on September 24, 2011, when the United Russia congress was to approve the party's list of candidates for the parliamentary election, Vladimir Putin announced his intent to execute a political "castling"—that is, his intent to slide back into the presidency. To be precise, he made Medvedev announce it for him, and explain that Medvedev himself would return to the position of prime minister.

The Kremlin anticipated that Vladimir Putin's popularity would boost United Russia's poll standing. Because of the worsening economic situation, a poll boost was crucial; United Russia's approval rating had been decreasing gradually since 2009 (see figure 6-3). Indeed, the party faced the possibility that it would lose its majority in the State Duma. The Kremlin's plans, however, had precisely the opposite of their intended effect. The active part of the Russian population reacted extremely negatively to the tandem's behind-the-scenes power-sharing agreement. Voters believed that by castling, Putin and Medvedev were depriving them of choice. Navalny's label, the "party of crooks and thieves," stuck to United Russia. But the voters had almost no means of influencing the situation. The list of parties allowed to participate in the State Duma elections was extremely short and included no parties that offered an alternative to Kremlin policies. Although none of the politicians sought to consolidate the protest vote, a movement to vote for any party but United Russia soon emerged—despite several electoral options aimed at diluting it.

On election day, the scale of fraud was mind-blowing (see figure 6-5). Hundreds of observers recorded irregularities in polling places. In Shpilkin's opinion, the addition of more than 15 million fraudulent votes did not save United Russia from essentially losing the election; according to official data, the Kremlin's party won less than half the vote (49.32 percent). This resulted in a reduced number of State Duma members from the United Russia party. However, the Kremlin maintained control over a majority of the seats in the lower house of parliament (238 out of 450).

The scale of the election fraud was so phenomenal that mass protests rocked Moscow the evening of the election. For the next three weeks, political protests were the main feature of life in the Russian capital. During two protest rallies on December 10 and 24 that brought together between 100,000 and 120,000 people in Moscow, marchers made several demands for changes in election laws and democratization in Russia. The protesters demanded that the State Duma election results be annulled, that the registration proce-

FIGURE 6-5. **Evaluation of Fraud during the Vote Tabulation in the December 2011 State Duma Elections**

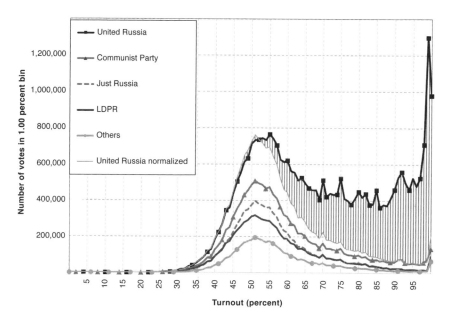

Sources: Russia's Central Election Commission and Sergey Shpilkin's calculations (see note to figure 6-1).

dure for political parties be liberalized, that the threshold for election to the State Duma be lowered, that gubernatorial elections be reinstated, and that the chair of the CEC be dismissed.

The protests caught the Kremlin off-guard and frightened it badly. The possibility of an alliance between street protesters and the parliamentary opposition seemed to be more unsettling than anything else. Two of the four parties that had been elected to the State Duma—the Communist Party and Just Russia—refrained from taking their seats for several days. The Kremlin nervously cast about for any solution to break the newly emerging alliance; the unified opposition was the biggest threat. As is often the case, a solution presented itself. Ten days after the election, President Medvedev met with the leaders of the parliamentary parties and promised to give them the chairmanship of several Duma committees. The leaders of the system opposition accepted this offer and withdrew their demand to review the election results nationwide, adding they would still reserve the right to challenge the results in specific regions. All the elected lawmakers took their seats in the State Duma. The menace of a united opposition had been overcome.

Putin was happy. "Our elections were objective and fair. . . . Beyond any doubt, the results of these elections reflect the actual lineup of forces in the country," he declared. "As to fraud, as to the opposition being unhappy with the election results, there is nothing new here; it has always been and will always be like this."[52] As the year drew to a close, he reiterated his approval of the results: "The election to the State Duma has ended. All the parliamentary caucuses have begun working; the speaker has been elected; the Duma is functioning. No discussions about any reviews are possible; there is only one way stipulated by law, which is bringing the matter before the court."[53]

Yet he did not try to hide the fact that he was more concerned about the upcoming March presidential election: "The attacks on the last election [results] are secondary; the primary goal is the next election, the Russian presidential election. [Our opponents want to have] an opportunity to point out that the last election was, or that the upcoming one will be, unfair; [they want] simply to delegitimize the country's power structure."[54]

The nervous Kremlin was looking for a way to appease the protesters. Ignoring their demands would exacerbate the situation. The Kremlin needed to avoid this at virtually any cost in the run-up to the presidential election, but obviously it could not afford to annul the Duma election results. The least dangerous option was to concede the demand for direct gubernatorial elections. The governors' terms were limited to five years, and even if all Kremlin candidates lost these elections—a highly unlikely worst-case scenario—it would take five years to replace all the governors.

Less than three weeks after the elections, in his address to the Federal Assembly, President Medvedev announced his intention to carry out a "complex reform . . . of the political system."[55] The bill introduced in the State Duma soon after provided for direct gubernatorial elections and liberalization of the rules for registering political parties. It reduced the minimum number of members required for a party to be registered to 500 people. Moreover, parties represented in the State Duma or in at least one regional legislature were exempt from the need to collect signatures to run in Duma elections,[56] and parties that were not represented in the State Duma now only had to collect

100,000 signatures in order to nominate presidential candidates.[57] However, only the parties represented in the State Duma or in the legislature of the region where the election was being held were exempt from collecting signatures to participate in regional legislative elections.

There was talk of a "thaw" in Russia, an echo of the period of liberalization in the Soviet Union in the late 1950s to early 1960s, after Stalin's death. But this was merely an illusion.

FORGET IT—THE THAW HAS ENDED!

The long holiday season and the parliamentary opposition's unwillingness to form an alliance with the street protesters gradually weakened the protest pressure. Although the protests continued and many opposition politicians participated in street rallies, none of them could come up with a plan of action. Moreover, because of the legislative restrictions, opposition forces could not nominate candidates for the presidency. Meanwhile, Mikhail Prokhorov, who suddenly declared his intention to run for presidency, refused to publicly criticize Vladimir Putin and refrained from supporting the opposition movement.

According to the official data, Vladimir Putin won 63.6 percent of the vote in the 2012 presidential election, having faced no serious challenger. Although the election was yet again marred by widespread fraud—according to Shpilkin, Putin's result was inflated by 11 million votes—the vote difference between the incumbent prime minister and the communists' Gennady Zyuganov, who came in second with 17.2 percent, was so wide that none of the participants wanted to challenge the results.

On May 6, 2012, the eve of Putin's third presidential inauguration, clashes erupted between the police and participants of an authorized protest rally near the Kremlin as a result of provocations staged by the authorities. The clashes led to mass arrests of the participants, and excessive use of force by the police escalated into atrocious violence. More than thirty participants in the rally who had attempted to resist the police or to contain their aggression later became defendants in the Bolotnaya criminal case. Fourteen of them received prison sentences of varying lengths.

It is hard to tell whether Putin knew that the clashes with the police had come as a result of a provocation or whether the events were presented to him as evidence of an "orange threat" in Russia,[58] but the May 6 protests triggered a sustained crackdown on the opposition. Aside from the criminal prosecution of ordinary participants in the rally, the Kremlin initiated criminal proceedings against two leaders of the protest movement, Alexey Navalny and Sergey Udaltsov. Several criminal cases were initiated against Navalny; under two of them, he received suspended sentences for "organizing embezzlement," even though the documentation submitted by the prosecution pointed only to regular commercial activity.[59] Udaltsov was charged with inciting disorder during the May 6 protests and was sentenced to four and a half years in prison. In the summer of 2013, recently elected Yaroslavl mayor Yevgeny Urlashov, an active member of Mikhail Prokhorov's party, was arrested on charges of corruption and sentenced to a long prison term, though no evidence of him having been involved in corrupt practices had been offered in court.

Ten days after the clashes near the Kremlin, the State Duma passed a law on the first reading that severely tightened the rules surrounding rallies and demonstrations in Russia. The vague character of the newly introduced regulations allowed authorities to treat a gathering of two or more people as a public event—thus placing it within the scope of the law—and to hold the organizers of public events liable for the behavior and actions of participants. The law also sharply toughened the existing types of administrative penalties, including fines, community service, and short-term incarceration, and incorporated criminal penalties.[60] Three weeks later, the law was adopted by both chambers of the parliament and signed by Vladimir Putin, and the next day it went into force. In April 2014 the new law imposed criminal penalties (up to five years in jail) for the organizers of nonsanctioned rallies and demonstrations, including picketing.

ABSOLUTE DOMINANCE

The liberalization of the law regulating party activity resulted in the emergence of dozens of new parties.[61] In combination with United Russia's poor performance in the 2011 election, the profusion of new parties prompted the

Kremlin to yet again change the rules for State Duma elections. In mid-2013, a new law restored the old system of forming the lower chamber of the Russian parliament. Half of all lawmakers would be elected by proportional representation, and the other half would be elected in majoritarian districts.[62]

The Kremlin's logic was straightforward: Putin's return to the Kremlin improved United Russia's poll standings, but it was obvious that all the new parties would dilute its voter base. Meanwhile, because political life had been harshly restricted in previous years, political newcomers were not able to sustain careers under the conditions of the Kremlin's total control over the regional legislatures. Thus, no capable independent politicians emerged as challengers. At the same time, the Kremlin had no problem co-opting plenty of well-known persons who were happy to take seats in the parliament. These handpicked candidates were granted free access to the voters through the state-controlled television channels; moreover, as they were under fewer financial constraints, they had much better electoral chances than unknown candidates from other parties.

Tight controls over the funding of political parties created obstacles for politicians who were not in the Kremlin's favor. Business owners could not afford to openly finance Putin's opponents, since this would inevitably lead to administrative inspections of their businesses. Those who attempted to defend their political opinions ended up with closed bank accounts and a ban on further business activity.

The maximum size of a party's electoral fund was set at 700 million rubles (U.S. $11 million at that time's exchange rate) at the federal level and anywhere from 15 million to 100 million rubles at the regional level, depending on the size of the region's population. These restrictions allowed United Russia to form electoral funds amounting to 2.4 billion rubles (U.S. $38 million) in the 2016 election, whereas the other three parliamentary parties combined managed to collect only 80 percent of this total. Nonparliamentary parties faced even more limitations on procuring financing. Yabloko, which had been receiving budget financing based on its 2011 election results, and Russian business ombudsman Boris Titov's Party of Growth managed to raise 40 percent and 30 percent, respectively, of the established maximum for the electoral fund at the federal level. No other party managed to raise more than 5 percent of the established maximum to finance its campaign.

Along with financing elections for the proportional vote, parties also were supposed to help finance the campaigns of their candidates in majoritarian districts. According to experts, on average a candidate's election campaign could cost from 40 million to 50 million rubles, which obviously was something only a few parties could afford.

The first half of 2014 marked a turning point in Russian history. The annexation of Crimea radically altered both Russia's position in the world and its domestic political situation. The ensuing wave of patriotic frenzy came as no surprise: short, victorious wars have always helped strengthen the position of authoritarian leaders. Vladimir Putin, who assumed full responsibility for the decision, reaped obvious political dividends. His personal popularity grew, and politicians who opposed the Russian aggression were publicly labeled "traitors and enemies of Russia." Not a single major political party dared oppose the Kremlin's Crimea stunt.

The so-called "Crimean consensus" in Russian politics rallied around Putin's narratives: Russia is the only country in the world that has dared to challenge U.S. hegemony. In this context, the Euromaidan movement in Ukraine in the winter of 2013–14 was a thinly veiled U.S. aggression against Russia, and all the subsequent events—the annexation of Crimea and the war in the Donbas—were Russia's attempts to protect itself. Both state-controlled television propaganda and the system opposition actively supported this position.[63] The assassination of antiwar movement leader Boris Nemtsov in late February 2015 not only deprived the opposition of a strong leader but also served as an obvious warning to politicians opposing the Crimean consensus. Putin, as the author of this concept, became the center of consolidation for such sentiments. With his backing, United Russia, which positioned itself as "Putin's party" in the 2016 election, was attracting the votes of his supporters.

This momentum created an insurmountable barrier for politicians who lacked the Kremlin's support to enter parliament. Even the completely loyal system opposition had only a slim chance of performing decently in the election; on top of financial restrictions, they had trouble finding prominent public figures who were willing to run as opposition candidates. Having noticed this long before the election, the Kremlin decided to "reward" its satellites by offering thirty majoritarian districts to the parliamentary parties to divide among themselves. Each party would receive ten districts in which the other parties would not put forward their candidates. Although officially the agreement was not concluded, United Russia did not nominate any candidates in seventeen districts, thus allowing the system opposition to compete for a "consolation prize."

The Kremlin also was forced to more carefully use the traditional instruments of fraud during the vote count. In regions where the protests in the winter of 2011–12 had been especially active, the practice of inflating United Russia's votes was implemented either very moderately or not at all (see figure 6-6). However, in the end the scale of fraud was only slightly lower than in the record-setting 2011 election (12.1 million additional votes).

In regions where the population did not protest against vote theft, regional authorities did not try to restrain themselves. Figure 6-7 shows the two–part division between Russian electoral districts. In 80 percent of them, where the turnout fluctuated between 30 percent and 55 percent, United Russia won

FIGURE 6-6. Evaluation of Vote Fraud during the Vote Tabulation in the December 2016 State Duma Elections

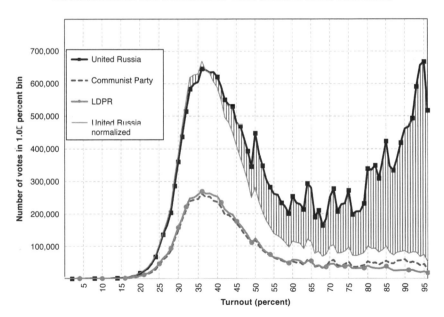

Sources: Russia's Central Electoral Commission and Sergey Shpilkin's calculations (see note to figure 6-1).

between 30 percent and 50 percent of the vote. Meanwhile, in this group the election results did not demonstrate a clear correlation between the turnout and the level of support for United Russia. In the remaining 20 percent of the electoral districts, where the turnout exceeded 55 percent, United Russia's election result clearly correlates with voter turnout figures in a way that is suggestive of fraud.

United Russia obtained 54.2 percent of the proportional vote, and its representatives won in 203 out of 207 single-member districts where United Russia nominated its candidates. As a result, the Kremlin won a considerable majority—75 percent—of the seats in the lower chamber of parliament.

FIGURE 6-7. **Distribution of Electoral Districts in the 2016 State Duma Elections Based on the Turnout and United Russia's Official Election Results**

PERCENT

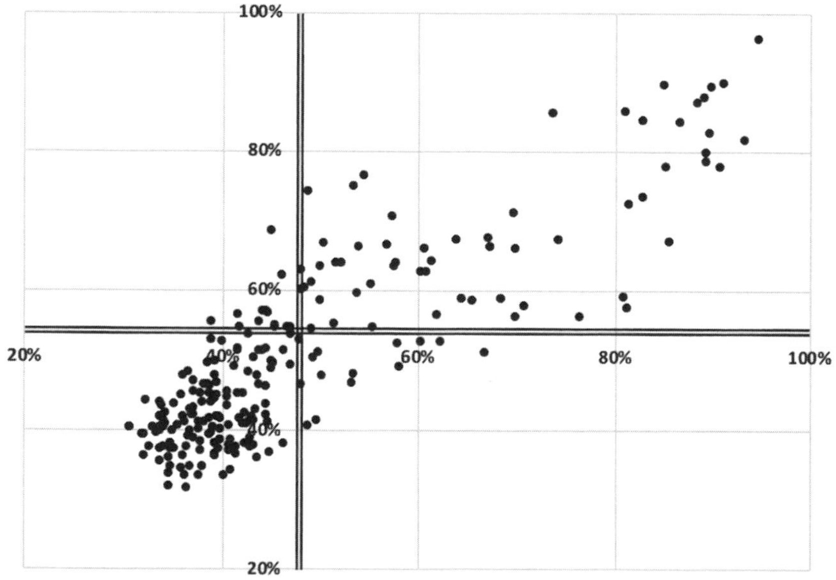

Source: Russia's Central Election Commission database, "Vybory, referendumy i inyye formy pryamogo voleiz yavleniya" [Elections, referendums and other forms of direct declaration of will], Moscow.

Note: Crossing lines are average levels for Russia.

THERE IS NO ROOM FOR COINCIDENCE

In the summer of 1999, Vladimir Putin accepted Boris Yeltsin's offer to become Russia's prime minister and Yeltsin's successor. However, he did not feel up to the task. In pursuit of this objective, he would have to go through two election campaigns, first for the State Duma and then for the presidency. Although by that time Putin had already climbed to the top of the Russian political pyramid, he had no experience in public political activity. He was afraid of elections, as he openly admitted to Yeltsin in response to the offer. Putin has never overcome this fear of elections and losing that he experienced in 1996. Russian society knew practically nothing about Vladimir Putin when he became their prime minister. He was not famous for any accomplishments or victories; feeling very insecure in open debates, he had not proven himself in any way in public politics. (For the entire eighteen years of his rule, he has avoided any debates with his political opponents, even during election campaigns, always saying that he has more important things to do as part of his official duties.)

In the fall of 1999, Putin realized, based on his own experience, how quickly a man whom no one knew could be turned into a popular politician. The Unity party demonstrated to him how a party created a few weeks before an election could win. But if he and the Unity party managed to do this, then in just a few years' time, someone else could do it as well. Putin may have found himself at the zenith, on Mount Olympus, but this was not his achievement; it did not come as a result of his focused efforts. From Putin's point of view, his position was the result of a series of coincidences, supported by his strategists' skillful use of the opportunities created by liberal election laws and free media.

Putin's victory in the 2000 presidential election appeared to be an easy one, but Putin himself did not see things this way. A hostile Federation Council; the forced coalition with the communists in the State Duma; the Luzhkov-Primakov alliance, backed by many influential governors; harsh media criticism—all these things forced Putin to fight on many fronts simultaneously in his first months in power. He did not find victory easy, and possibly did not even believe he had deserved it. Later, after a few years as Russia's president, he openly admitted the unusual nature of his position. "I am not a politician," he said. "I am a citizen of Russia who—bam!—became president. I had not been preparing for this."[64]

When Putin became prime minister in 1999, little was known about his political views. Boris Yeltsin and his close circle honestly believed that Yeltsin's successor would continue his political course, which was supposed to lead Russia toward becoming a stable democracy. Yeltsin's opinion of Putin was based on their personal interactions, but in those moments Putin was unlikely to let his patron know what he really thought and how he perceived the Russian system of government. Thanks to his work experience in the intelligence services, where his time was mostly devoted to recruiting potential agents, Putin had learned to make conversation in such a way as to convince his interlocutor that he was dealing with an ally and a like-minded person. Besides, in his regular meetings with Yeltsin during the president's last months in power, Putin saw that the fading Yeltsin was not interested in long philosophical talks but rather was looking for support from his interlocutors; by that time, the once-powerful president had few political allies left.

It is worth noting that, at the time, most democratically minded politicians supported Putin. SPS, then a leading pro-democracy party, ran in the 1999 State Duma elections with the slogan "Putin for president, [party leader Sergey] Kiriyenko for the State Duma." As Alexey Ulyukaev, Yegor Gaidar's closest aide, expressed it, "In this act [Putin's arrival in the Kremlin] I saw the realization of the slogan 'A free market and strong police.' That is precisely what we need!"[65] Ulyukaev made a good career in Putin's time, being first deputy minister of finance, then first deputy governor of the central bank. In November 2016, as minister of economics, he was indicted on the ground of corruption and arrested. The charges against Ulyukaev were dubious, and the trial went ahead with many procedural violations. Nevertheless, thirteen months later he was convicted and sentenced to eight years in prison. According to experts, the underlying reason for such punishment was a conflict with Putin's closest ally, Igor Sechin.

As acting president, and even after winning the March 2000 election, Putin remained tight-lipped about his plans. Perhaps he was just beginning to form his plans during his discussions with members of his inner circle. Or perhaps, before the inauguration, Putin did not yet feel like a full-fledged president and was concerned about possible contingencies that could prevent him from occupying his office in the Kremlin. But as soon as the waiting was over, he immediately announced his plans to reconstruct Russia. Instead of adjusting and fine-tuning the system of checks and balances provided by the Russian constitution, he began building the vertical of power that gradually would destroy all the checks and balances fostered by Boris Yeltsin.

To do so, Putin relied on the use of force and coercion rather than discussion and compromise. He began to get rid of his opponents with the help of the secret police, which he had under his sole control. He ousted some of his opponents from Russia under the threat of criminal prosecution. Using a carrot-and-stick approach, he co-opted others into his system. The communists happily accepted the proposal to share leadership positions in the Duma in January 2000, after which the degree of their criticism decreased considerably. Stripped of parliamentary immunity after the reform of the Federation Council, and dependent on budget transfers from Moscow, the regional governors decided to merge their party with the pro-Kremlin one. The budgetary financing of political parties established by a 2001 law[66] became an important instrument for co-opting many politicians, especially after such financing increased tenfold in 2006. After this, not a single parliamentary party dared strive seriously for power, choosing to be content with playing the role of a decorative opposition. In general, by 2015 the real (inflation-adjusted) budgetary financing of parties had increased by eighty times its original 2003 levels.

In tandem with these more brutal tactics, since the first months of his presidency Putin has consistently used legislative means to weaken his opponents' chances of challenging his hold on power, let alone winning control. Bureaucratic filters were set up to prevent "undesirable" politicians from participating in elections. The election laws were amended to give massive federal and regional electoral advantages to parties co-opted by the Kremlin. The Kremlin-controlled judicial system recognized all these changes as constitutional. The state-controlled media gave the Kremlin's candidates in the Duma and presidential elections more airtime than the candidates of all other parties combined. The Kremlin-controlled election commissions manipulated the vote tallies, inflating support for preferred candidates by millions of votes. Law enforcement practices certified a series of unjust and unfair elections as lawful regardless of whatever proof of fraud was presented.

The 2006 election reform thus was an important step toward the annihilation of political competition at the federal level. The transition toward the proportional-only vote, combined with a "purge" of political parties, a ban on forming electoral blocs, and the introduction of a 7 percent threshold, restricted Russian citizens' rights to political representation in the lower chamber of parliament. These measures, alongside the phenomenon of mass fraud during the vote tabulation—which by then was considered normal—allowed the Kremlin to maintain total control over the State Duma and to amend legislation any way it saw fit. By degrees, the executive branch subdued the legislative branch. From 2001 the upper house of the Russian parliament (the Federation Council) was formed by appointments only. From 2005 the regional governors became presidential appointees. In this fashion, the Kremlin proceeded to destroy the most important aspects of the system of checks and balances.

Table 6-1 illustrates the gradual disappearance of political competition in Russia. It shows not only how the Kremlin successfully limited voters' choice from 2003 onward by reducing the number of parties allowed to participate in elections but also how comparatively stable and dominant United Russia's parliamentary representation has been. Over more than a decade, the Kremlin effectively turned Russia into a one-party country.

Free elections had essentially vanished at the federal level by the time that such restrictions became necessary to maintain the stability of Putin's system—namely, when he decided not to run for a third presidential term. By then the Kremlin had co-opted the parliamentary opposition. In the 2007 and 2011 parliamentary elections, system opposition parties secured the Kremlin's approval for their lists, and Russian voters could vote only for these preapproved candidates.

The methods of election fraud adopted by the Kremlin were increasingly used in Russian parliamentary elections after 2003 to guarantee stable majorities for United Russia in the State Duma. The Kremlin left no room for the contingencies that worried Vladimir Putin. Only those who had pledged loyalty to the Kremlin were able to assume seats in the State Duma and the Federation Council. A parliament formed under such conditions had no problem extending the presidential term to six years at the end of 2008 and did not question Putin's right to be elected in 2012 for a third time. Yet Putin was

TABLE 6-1. Indicators of Political Competition in Russia Based on the Results of State Duma Elections, 1995–2016

| | Number of political parties in Russia[a] | | | Effective number of parties (Golosov's index)[b] | | Number of seats in the State Duma held by United Russia (out of 450 total) |
	Parties with the right to participate in elections	Parties that submitted documents for participating in elections	Parties registered for the ballot	Electoral (distribution of the proportional votes)	Parliamentary (distribution of seats in the State Duma[c])	
1995	273	51	43	9.76	4.56	—
1999[d]	139	32	28	6.90	5.93→4.52→2.22	73→139→237
2003	64	26	23	4.11	1.36	304
2007	15	14	11	1.74	1.52	315
2011	7	7	7	2.44	2.14	238
2016	75	22	14	2.25	1.36	343

Source: Russia's Central Election Commission.

Notes: a. Before the 2003 election, including electoral blocs and public associations. b. The "effective number of parties" is an adjusted number of political parties in a country's party system. Parties are counted on a weighted basis that reflects their relative strength. The relative strength refers to their vote share ("effective number of electoral parties") or seat share in parliament ("effective number of parliamentary parties"). The methodology is described in Grigorii V. Golosov, "The Effective Number of Parties: A New Approach," *Party Politics* 16 (2010): 171–92. c. Parliamentary caucuses, parliamentary groups, and independent State Duma members as separate entities were factored in. d. In the 1999 elections the Unity bloc won seventy-three seats and the OVR bloc won sixty-nine seats. They created the United Russia party in the fall of 2001. Starting in 2002 two deputies' group—Regions of Russia and People's Deputy—de facto joined United Russia, adding an additional ninety-eight seats.

never able to vanquish the fear of a color revolution in Russia like Georgia's Rose Revolution, and his inner circle did everything it could to stoke those fears as parliament backed him in his fight against politicians who opted for public opposition methods such as demonstrations and rallies.

The parliamentary opposition's willingness to be co-opted by the Kremlin likewise reduced its role to that of a mere decoration: the opposition parties, which share 25–35 percent of the seats in the lower chamber of parliament, have no way of blocking the Kremlin's legislative initiatives. The restrictions on and persecution of the nonsystem opposition and the sustained deformation of the electoral process in Russia have deprived Russian citizens of the right to free and fair elections. A significant part of the electorate, especially voters in the big cities, have lost confidence in elections to such an extent that they have stopped voting altogether, recognizing that they are unable to elect politicians who will make changes. Even official CEC data show a significant decline in propensity to vote among Russian citizens (see table 6-2). This has led to a situation in which the decisive role in determining election results belongs to the regions, where the authorities can most easily falsify vote tallies. In the 2016 State Duma elections, the thirty-three (out of 225) electoral districts with the lowest turnout (less than 35 percent) and the thirty-six districts with the highest turnout (more than 61 percent) had approximately equal numbers of voters registered, totaling 15 percent of all Russian voters. In the first group of electoral districts, United Russia received a little more than 40 percent of the vote; in the second, it received a little less than 75 percent. That said, in the first group of districts United Russia received only 7.6 percent of the total number of its voters; in the second group, it received 34.4 percent.

Through its abuses during elections and its use of administrative resources, the Kremlin has secured United Russia's dominance in the State Duma and in regional legislatures. This has allowed the Kremlin to change laws at any time and in any way it wishes to make it more difficult for the opposition to operate, thus making free and fair elections impossible.[67] But these limitations, whether through legal, financial, or media propaganda constraints, deprive the Kremlin of fair, accurate measures of the public mood in the form of election results. As table 6-2 suggests, election fraud has become routine in Russian elections to an astonishing degree. The pro-Kremlin

TABLE 6-2. Election Fraud in Russia, 1999–2018

Year	General turnout		Performance of United Russia / Putin / Medvedev		Calculation of added votes (as percentage of total)	
	Official results (millions)	Shpilkin's estimate (millions)	Official results (millions)	Shpilkin's estimate (millions)	Total official turnout (percent)	United Russia's official result (percent)
2000	75.1	72.0	38.4	35.3	4.1	+ 8.8
2003	60.7	56.2	22.8	18.3	7.4	+24.6
2004	69.5	60.7	50.0	41.2	12.7	+21.4
2007	69.6	56.5	44.7	31.6	18.8	+41.5
2008	69.1	54.5	52.5	37.9	21.1	+38.5
2011	65.7	50.5	32.4	17.2	23.1	+88.4
2012	71.7	60.3	45.6	34.2	15.9	+33.3
2016	52.6	40.5	28.5	16.4	23.0	+73.8
2018	72.8	62.9	56.4	46.5	13.7	+17.7

Sources: Russia's Central Election Commission and Sergey Shpilkin's assessment (see note to figure 6-1).

party, United Russia, has achieved election results close to double what it needs to keep the Russian legislative branch under its full control.

Vladimir Putin would take issue with being named an opponent of political competition. But his closest lieutenant, Vladislav Surkov, being more straightforward, declared openly that the Russian political system did not need actors who were not under the Kremlin's control: "Four parliamentarian parties express, represent all spectrum of important opinions of the society."[68] When asked about the possibility of a change in power, Putin answered, "As for the change of government, of course, it should be happening. Of course, there should be healthy competition during these processes, but it should be between nationally oriented individuals, those oriented toward the interests of the Russian people."[69] But in today's Russia, Putin and his lieutenants alone determine which politicians are "nationally oriented" and which are not. And all political competition takes place in the Kremlin's offices, while a significant part of the Russian population lacks effective representation in legislative bodies, and thus lacks opportunities to defend its rights and interests.

––––––––––

The outcome of the regional elections in September 2018 may create the illusion that the situation is starting to change: a second round of voting will take place in four of the twenty-two gubernatorial elections. In two out of these four regions the incumbent governor, representing United Russia, took second place on the first round. In three of the sixteen regional legislative elections United Russia took second place in party voting, with the Communist Party taking first place. But those numbers must be interpreted cautiously: in June 2018 the government proposed amendments to the pension legislation that would increase the pension age from sixty to sixty-five years for men and from fifty-five to sixty-three years for women effective January 1, 2019. This proposal earned a negative reception from more than 90 percent of Russians and was supported in the first hearing in the Duma by the votes of United Russia only. The result was a significant fall in the approval rating of President Putin and Prime Minister Medvedev and a surge in protest activity among Russian voters, who, having no real choice, voted for any party except United Russia. It is uncertain whether the animus for the protests will continue and possibly grow in the coming months or will die out.

Notes to Chapter 6

1. From 1993 to 2007, the State Duma had 450 members, half of whom were elected by proportional representation within single federal districts and half were elected in majoritarian electoral districts. This system was reestablished in 2106.

2. Six months later, in the June 1996 presidential election, Yeltsin's team's use of administrative resources was already apparent. State-controlled Russian television channels covered Yeltsin's campaign more actively than they did the campaign of his main opponent, Gennady Zyuganov, the leader of the Communist Party. The Kremlin successfully secured the support of all prominent Russian business owners, who were generously financing Yeltsin's election campaign (with state support). However, the incumbent president's second-round victory was so obvious that it is more useful to talk about more *efficient* electoral technologies.

3. Vladimir Fedorin, "Aleksandr Voloshin o ministrakh-biznesmenakh i dorogikh chasakh" [Alexander Voloshin on business ministers and expensive watches], *Forbes*, November 16, 2009.

4. The 1999 election was the last one not to be rigged in favor of the pro-Kremlin party. On the contrary, ballots were falsified in favor of the governors' bloc party, the OVR, which was openly opposing the Kremlin. There was nothing strange about this: at the time, the governors were in charge of forming local election commissions.

5. This norm was challenged in the Constitutional Court, which in February 2005 approved the Kremlin's decision by declaring that the "creation of regional political parties . . . could compromise national unity and the unified system of government as the foundation of Russia's federal form of government" and that the imposed ban was necessary to "protect constitutional values, and principally to ensure the country's unity in the current context characterized by the development of democracy and the rule of law in the Russian Federation." At the same time, the Constitutional Court ruled that the "said ban is temporary and should be lifted when the circumstances that had caused it cease to exist." But, as the saying goes, there is nothing more permanent than a temporary measure; no one ever brought up this aspect of the decision again.

6. Moreover, the law stipulated that parties that crossed the 3 percent threshold in the Duma elections or that had at least twelve MPs elected in single-member districts would be financed from the federal budget. This norm created a rift between parties. Parties that were represented in the State Duma had an interest in reducing the level of political competition and became the Kremlin's allies in preventing newcomers from getting into parliament. Even the democratically minded Union of Right Forces (SPS) and Yabloko both adopted this position.

7. Yuriy Chernega, "Partiy dolzhno byt' nemnogo" [There should not be many parties], *Kommersant*, July 20, 2001.

8. Until that moment, the automated system had been under the control of the Federal Agency of Government Communications and Information (FAPSI), a Russian security agency created in December 1991 when Boris Yeltsin split the Soviet KGB into several parts. It was assumed that such a division would reduce the political influence of the secret police in Russia and help create a system of checks and balances within the Russian secret services. This was probably the reason why Putin revisited Yeltsin's decision in May 2003 and reunited many independent secret service agencies within the FSB.

9. "Surkov ne isklyuchayet, chto vskore prezident RF smozhet vstupat' v partiyu" [Surkov does not rule out that soon the Russian president will be able to join the party], RIA Novosti, June 28, 2006.

10. Khodorkovsky himself denied that he had financed the communists, though he admitted that some of Yukos's top managers ran as Communist Party candidates in that election and were free to finance the communists' election campaign using their own money. But it is hardly believable that this suspicion was the main reason for Khodorkovsky's arrest. In fact, the ensuing destruction of Yukos underscored that the real motive was to nationalize the oil company. However, at the time of Khodorkovsky's arrest, presidential chief of staff Aleksandr Voloshin said that in the summer and fall of 2003, Putin repeatedly had been misinformed about the businessman's activity, and that most of the false information pertained to alleged contacts between Khodorkovsky and the leader of the communist factions, Gennady Zyuganov.

11. "Gleb Pavlovskiy: V porazhenii pravykh sil — zalog pobedy liberalizma" [Gleb Pavlovsky: The defeat of right forces is a guarantee of victory of liberalism], Manekin .narod.ru (www.manekin.narod.ru/pavl2.htm).

12. Sergey Shpilkin is a Russian scientist who uses statistical methods to analyze election results in Russia. This kind of analysis became possible in 2003, when the CEC began publishing the results of vote counting at each polling place. Shpilkin's approach consists of describing the turnout by normal distribution, an approach that has been validated on election results in different countries and for all Russian parties except United Russia. Analysis of the results of United Russia (and of Vladimir Putin and Dmitry Medvedev in presidential elections) shows an unusually large number of polling places where the percentage of voters considerably exceeds both Russia's average participation level and the percentage of voters in neighboring polling places. In these polling places, according to official data, United Russia wins considerably more votes. Moreover, the analysis shows an unusually large number of polling places where the percentage of voters reaches a whole number divisible by five (sixty, sixty-five, seventy, and so on). This phenomenon was labeled the "dinosaur's spine" for its stacked appearance. Since 2003, this practice of inflating United Russia's votes has been observed in all federal elections.

13. To evaluate the scope of fraud during the vote count, Shpilkin sets up an alter-

native distribution of polling places with a high turnout and a high level of support for United Russia that corresponds to the distribution of election results for other parties (candidates). Thus the difference between the official election results and the alternative evaluation (hatched areas in figures 6-1 and 6-2) represents the estimated number of added votes.

14. Medialogia data provided by the company (www.mlg.ru).

15. A number of Russian governors publicly admitted that the Kremlin had given them the task of guaranteeing a 75–80 percent turnout, assuming that 70 percent of voters would support the incumbent president.

16. Larisa Kaftan, interview with Vladislav Surkov, "Putin ukreplyayet gosudarstvo, a ne sebya" [Putin strengthens the state, not himself], *Komsomol'skaya Pravda*, September 28, 2004.

17. Ten years later, Stanislav Belkovsky, one of the authors of the report, virtually admitted the artificial and provocative character of the described threats: "In 2003, knowing so very little, [we] expected a different Putin, expected him to transform into a leader who would take Russia on a new path in history. . . . Now, ten years later, it is time to finally admit: we were naive and wrong back then." Stanislav Belkovsky, "Gosudarstvo i oligarkhiya: 10 let spustya" [Government and the oligarchy: 10 years later], *Slon*, June 4, 2013.

18. Sergey Pugachyov is a Russian businessman who was close to the Kremlin in the late 1990s and early 2000s and was involved in several business projects in partnership with the Presidential Property Management Department. Igor Sechin, then deputy chief of the presidential administration, was responsible for the president's working schedule and controlled what documents reached Putin's office. Viktor Ivanov, another deputy chief of the presidential administration at the time, was in charge of appointments to executive bodies and law enforcement agencies, and of judicial nominations.

19. Gleb Pavlovskiy, "O negativnykh posledstviyakh 'letnego nastupleniya' oppozitsionnogo kursu prezidenta RF men'shinstva" [On the negative consequences of the "summer offensive" of the minority opposing the course of the president of the Russian Federation], *Novaya Gazeta*, September 2, 2003.

20. "Suverenitet — eto politicheskiy sinonim konkurentosposobnosti" [Sovereignty is a political synonym for competitiveness], *Rosbalt*, March 9, 2006.

21. Kaftan, interview with Vladislav Surkov, "Putin ukreplyayet gosudarstvo, a ne sebya" [Putin strengthens the state, not himself]. "Lemons and apples" is wordplay referring to Eduard Limonov, the leader of the leftist National Bolshevik Party, and the moderate liberal Yabloko (Russian for "apple") party.

22. Pavlovsky admitted that "the idea [of an orange threat] belonged to the team of ideologists in the 2005 administration. . . . This was a concept of threat. At first it was used as defensive counterpropaganda against [U.S. president George W.] Bush and his idea of the expansion of democracy, including on our doorstep." See also Gleb Pav-

lovskiy, "Privychka k obozhaniyu u Putina voznikla ran'she" [Putin's habit of adoring appeared earlier], *New Times*, March 26, 2012.

23. Vladislav Surkov, "Suverenitet — eto politicheskiy sinonim konkurentospo-sobnosti" [Sovereignty is a political synonym for competitiveness], PolitNauka.org, February 7, 2006 (www.politnauka.org/library/public/surkov.php). This text is in a "restricted access" zone of United Russia's website (http://www.edinros.ru/news.html?id=111148).

24. This formula was introduced into Russian politics in 1909, when, during a visit of the Russian parliamentary delegation to London, the Constitutional Democratic Party leader Pavel Milyukov said, "As long as there is a legislative branch in Russia to control the budget, the Russian opposition will remain an opposition of His Majesty—not to His Majesty."

25. President of Russia, "Vstupitel'noye slovo na rasshirennom zasedanii Pravitel'stva s uchastiyem glav sub'yektov Rossiyskoy Federatsii" [Opening remarks at the enlarged meeting of the Government with the participation of the heads of subjects of the Russian Federation], transcript, Moscow, September 13, 2004 (http://kremlin.ru/events/president/transcripts/22592).

26. Surkov, "Suverenitet — eto politicheskiy sinonim konkurentosposobnosti" [Sovereignty is a political synonym for competitiveness].

27. In 2011, the European Court of Human Rights (ECHR) ruled in favor of the Republican Party of Russia in a case concerning its unlawful dissolution by the state. The party reclaimed its registration certificate, which had been annulled by Russia's Supreme Court in 2007. The ECHR noted that Russian legislation regulating the size of political parties had been repeatedly amended, which gave the ECHR sufficient cause to conclude, based on international legal practice, that this was an attempt to manipulate election law in favor of the ruling party.

28. Apart from the fact that street protests were an important element of the color revolutions that Putin always called an unconstitutional change of government, the Russian president had personal reasons to be afraid of public protests. In December 1989, Putin witnessed a crowd storming the Dresden headquarters of the Stasi (the Ministry for State Security, the East German equivalent of the KGB); a short time later, he had to singlehandedly block demonstrators at the entrance to the KGB build-ing where he worked. Putin described these events: "The crowd had just ransacked the district office of the Ministry for State Security, taking the arms from there that ended up in who knows whose hands. Nothing good could come out of this. . . . That night, I was in charge of our site . . . which was guarded by a small group of border patrol agents whom I alerted. As is appropriate in such cases, they unloaded arms, grenades, ammunition, opened the windows and held the barrels of their machine guns pointed out of the windows. And I went to the fence to talk to the crowd. . . . [Putin told the demonstrators that this was a Soviet military site, and he was an interpreter.] And

then I and an armed soldier, whom I quietly ordered to deliberately reload his weapon, turned away and slowly went inside. People did not disperse for a while. However, they abandoned their intention to storm the building." Putin seems to have held on to the memory of these events. (Extract from R. Medvedev's book, *Vladimir Putin* [Moscow: Molodaya gvardiya, 2007].)

29. A punitive measure that provides for a short (up to fifteen days) jail term. In 2014, the maximum jail term for violating the regulations on organizing and holding rallies was increased from fifteen to thirty days.

30. In the spring of 2011, a similar norm affected municipal representative bodies with twenty or more members.

31. Surkov, "Suverenitet — eto politicheskiy sinonim konkurentosposobnosti."

32. Elena Ivanova and Maksim Glikin, "Soglasovannaya Rossiya" [Conformist Russia], *Vedomosti*, July 26, 2007.

33. President of Russia, "Vystupleniye na forume storonnikov Prezidenta Rossii" [Speech at the Forum of Supporters of the President of Russia], news release, Moscow, November 21, 2007.

34. Elena Pashutinskaya, "Gubernator vybral nachal'nika" [The governor chose the chief], *Vysota* 102, November 20, 2007.

35. "Aleksandr Tkachev: 'Est' tol'ko odin put' — dvizheniye vpered'" [Alexander Tkachev: "There is only one way—moving forward"], *Nash Dom Sochi* 48 (254), November 29, 2007.

36. Medialogia data provided by the company (www.mlg.ru).

37. Some believed that Sergey Ivanov was an alternative choice to succeed Putin. However, this may have been one of Putin's typical false flag operations to shift the focus away from his first choice. Ivanov was a much stronger figure who had had a successful career in Soviet intelligence, rising to the rank of lieutenant general (significantly outranking Putin). He undoubtedly had the support of the Russian secret services and possibly a number of high-ranking military officers in Russia's armed forces (Ivanov served as defense minister from 2001 to 2007). It is hard to believe that Putin was prepared to surrender power in the Kremlin to such a strong figure.

38. As he evaluated his options for staying in power after leaving the presidency, Putin considered the post of Duma speaker, since technically the Russian constitution grants the State Duma ample opportunities to control the executive branch. However, an increased role for parliament inevitably would have led to a serious destabilization of Russia's entire political system—something Putin could hardly countenance.

39. Russia's de facto support for the March 2011 United Nations Security Council Resolution 1973 on Libya, which authorized NATO members to carry out military action against that country, is an example of a one-yes, one-abstain decision. Under Russian law, foreign policy belongs to the president's sphere of authority, and when Medvedev decided not to oppose this resolution, Putin for some reason chose not to

veto the decision but a few days later strongly criticized it, calling the Security Council resolution "flawed and inadequate" ("Predsedatel' Pravitel'stva Rossii V.V.Putin, nakhodyashchiysya s rabochey poyezdkoy v Udmurtii, v khode besedy s rabochimi 'Votkinskogo zavoda' prokommentiroval situatsiyu vokrug Livii" [Prime Minister of Russia V. V. Putin while on a business trip in Udmurtiya commented on the situation in Libya during his meeting with workers of "Votkinskii zavod"], March 21, 2011 (http://archive.government.ru/docs/14542/) and adding that he was "concerned by the ease with which decisions to use force are taken in international affairs" ("Predsedatel' Pravitel'stva Rossiyskoy Federatsii V.V. Putin provël v Votkinske soveshchaniye po voprosam vypolneniya gosudarstvennoy programmy vooruzheniya na 2011–2020 gody [Prime Minister of the Russian Federation V. V. Putin held a meeting in Votkinsk dedicated to issues of implementation of the state armament program for 2011–2020], news release, Government of Russia, March 21, 2011 [http://archive.government.ru/docs/14545/]). However, Putin also emphasized that the Russian government was not involved in foreign affairs, and his press secretary declared that Putin's statement was his "personal opinion."

40. Mariya-Luiza Tirmaste, "Mikhailu Kas'yanovu grozyat avtografy" [Mikhail Kasyanov is threatened with autographs], *Kommersant* 42, March 17, 2008, p. 3.

41. See the website at Kremlin.ru/events/president/transcripts/7896.

42. According to Prokhorov, he discussed this idea during his meeting with Vladimir Putin and gained his support. Prokhorov openly said: "I'm not an idiot to go there [into politics] without first obtaining his consent."

43. Mariya-Luiza Tirmaste and Natalya Bashlykova, "Mikhailu Prokhorovu pora zanyat'sya svoim delom" [It's time for Mikhail Prokhorov to deal with his business], *Kommersant*, September 16, 2011.

44. Svetlana Bocharova, "Mikhail Prokhorov: 'Po Royzmanu byl prosto predlog'" [Mikhail Prokhorov: "Roizman was simply an excuse"], Gazeta.ru, September 15, 2011.

45. "Prokhorov ushel iz 'Pravogo dela', chtoby otpravit' 'kuklovoda' Surkova v otstavku [Prokhorov left the Right Cause to push "puppeteer" Surkov to resign], *Forbes*, September 15, 2011.

46. "'Nikakaya nastoyashchaya politika v strane nevozmozhna'" ["No real policy is possible in the country"], *Kommersant*, September 15, 2011.

47. Crimes in Russia are grouped into four categories according to their severity and the longest possible sentence provided by the Criminal Code. The law stipulates a maximum penalty of up to ten years for serious crimes, and of more than ten years for very serious offenses.

48. "Opredeleniye konstitutsionnogo suda Rossiyskoy Federatsii" [Definition of the Constitutional Court of the Russian Federation], KSRF, December 4, 2007 (http://doc.ksrf.ru/decision/KSRFDecision16866.pdf).

49. Russian law provides for additional consequences for a convicted person that are lifted after an established period of time, thus clearing the individual's criminal record. The cancellation of an individual's criminal record—that is, the cancellation of those additional consequences—is carried out on the basis of a court decision.

50. The latter concept had not been legally specified in Russian legislation for a whole year, thus allowing election commissions to interpret it in an arbitrary way when registering candidates.

51. Candidates were required to submit information regarding their foreign assets, as well as the sources of funds used to purchase the said assets, including land plots and other real estate, transport vehicles, and securities.

52. Government of Russia, "Razgovor s Vladimirom Putinym. Prodolzheniye" [A conversation with Vladimir Putin. Continuation], news release, Moscow, December 15, 2011 (http://archive.government.ru/docs/17409/).

53. Government of Russia, "Predsedatel' Pravitel'stva Rossiyskoy Federatsii V.V. Putin provël zasedaniye Narodnogo shtaba i Federal'nogo koordinatsionnogo soveta ONF" [Prime Minister Vladimir Putin held a meeting of the People's Staff and the Federal Coordinating Council of the ONF], news release, Moscow, December 27, 2011 (http://archive.premier.gov.ru/events/news/17512/).

54. Putin did not doubt that the Moscow protests had been inspired by the West. He also was certain that the protesters were paid out of funds that Russian opposition forces were receiving from abroad. In a live broadcast on Russian state television, he stated, "In my opinion, everything is clear about 'color revolutions.' This is an established scheme of destabilizing society. I think this scheme did not appear on its own. We know about the events of the Orange Revolution in Ukraine. By the way, some of our opposition leaders were in Ukraine at the time and were officially employed as advisers to then-president Yushchenko. They naturally want to bring this practice to Russia. . . . The people who came into the square, and I know that they were paid to come." See Government of Russia, "Razgovor s Vladimirom Putinym. Prodolzheniye" [A conversation with Vladimir Putin. Continuation].

55. President of Russia, "Poslaniye Prezidenta Federal'nomu Sobraniyu" [President's address to the Federal Assembly], news release, Moscow, December 22, 2011 (http://kremlin.ru/events/president/news/14088).

56. Other parties had to collect 200,000 signatures to put forward their candidates to participate in Duma elections.

57. Independent candidates were required to collect 300,000 signatures.

58. Pavlovsky thus described the mechanism that scared Putin: "Later . . . when the substance has perished, the term [Orange Revolution] gets a life of its own. . . . As soon as the opposition mentioned a 'Snow Revolution' the previous concept of a menace—the 'orange revolution'—was brought back. . . . You [the opposition] call this a revolution? Wonderful. We can quote you on that then. This is how a chilling story

about a scary and ominous revolution is created. And the fewer participants in a rally, the more chilling the story. See Pavlovsky, "Privychka k obozhaniyu u Putina voznikla ran'she" [Putin's habit of adoring appeared earlier]. Meanwhile, strategists realized that there was no real threat of a revolution in Russia, "for a very simple reason: 'orange revolutions' point to a rift within the establishment, a split within the government system when one side leads the people out in the streets in order to put pressure on the other side. But we have no such split." See Valentin Baryshnikov, "Polittekhnolog Gleb Pavlovskiy — o tom, poterpit li Putin politicheskuyu katastrofu" [Political technologist Gleb Pavlovsky on whether Putin will endure a political catastrophe], Radio Svoboda, December 18, 2011.

59. In the first case—that of the Kirovles—Navalny initially received a real prison sentence. However, the day after the verdict the Prosecutor General's Office challenged the decision, and the court immediately changed it. In the second case—that of Yves Rocher—Navalny's brother was sentenced to three and a half years in prison. Navalny and the second person convicted in the Kirovles case, Pyotr Ofitserov, challenged their sentences at the ECHR. The ECHR ruled that they had been tried and found guilty of acts "indistinguishable from regular commercial activity." See "Case of Navalny and Ofitserov v. Russia," ECHR, February 23, 2016 (http://hudoc.echr.coe.int/eng?i=001-161060). Based on the ECHR decision, Russia's Supreme Court overturned the sentence and ordered the case reexamined. During a second round of court hearings, the Prosecutor General's Office came forward with the same charges and submitted the same evidence; the court's ruling was a word-for-word repetition of the conviction previously annulled by the Supreme Court.

60. In mid-2014, another law was adopted introducing criminal liability (with a possibility of a prison term of up to five years) for repeated violations (more than twice in six months) of the established order concerning the organizing or conduct of public events. The new law was soon put into effect. Although its regulations did not apply to single-person pickets, in January 2015 they were used to initiate a criminal case against Ildar Dadin, who had been detained repeatedly for holding one-man protests and was placed under administrative arrest for "disobeying a lawful order of a police officer." After spending ten months under house arrest, Dadin received a sentence of three years' imprisonment. Fifteen months later, Russia's Supreme Court annulled his sentence and recognized his right to rehabilitation, including compensation from the state.

61. Party registration liberalization was not comprehensive: the Kremlin's control over the judicial system allowed the registration of undesirable political parties to be avoided. Alexey Navalny's Progress Party, for instance, was denied registration twice despite having met the necessary requirements.

62. At the same time, electoral districts were formed in a "daisylike" pattern: districts were not formed in big cities anymore, as they had been before 2007, but were

cut into several districts to which rural areas were attached. In this way the Kremlin diluted the mostly urban protest electorate.

63. Only one of the 450 Duma members voted against the law on the annexation of Crimea. Three others did not participate in the vote.

64. N. Zlobin, "Sochi 2014 — eto 'korotkaya probezhka' v upravlencheskom stile V. Putina" [Sochi 2014—a "short run" in V. Putin's style of governance], *Journal "Upravlenie personalom"* 22, 2009 (www.top-personal.ru/issue.html?2243).

65. Natalya Kalashnikova, "Vos'midesyatniki" [The people of the eighties], *Itogi* 13, March 29, 2010.

66. Parties that win more than 3 percent of the vote in the Duma elections are entitled to budget financing. The amount of financing is calculated according to the votes for the party during the elections. Obviously, the additional votes given to United Russia during the vote count have an impressive monetary value.

67. Spain's Francisco Franco once declared the following principle: "To my friends, everything; to my enemies, the law." In November 2011, Vladimir Putin publicly stated: "I agree with this idea. Believe me, many of those present in this room know that I am trying to implement it in practice." And this was true. See "Putin byl by rad pomoch' rossiyskomu biznesu, no perezhivayet za potrebiteley" [Putin would be happy to help Russian business, but worries about consumers], Interfax, October 28, 2011.

68. "V politicheskoy sisteme dolzhno byt' bol'she stepeney svobody, no nestabil'nost' opasna — Surkov" [There should be more degrees of freedom in the political system, but instability is dangerous—Surkov], Interfax, June 18, 2009.

69. Oliver Stone, *The Putin Interviews* (Moscow: Alpina, 2017), Visit 3, day 3—May 11, 2016.

Seven

RISKY BUSINESS

Private property in Russia is not entirely private and not entirely property.

—Anatoly Chubais

Discussions of the relationship between power and business in Russia frequently wend their way to the "Yukos case." In that 2003–06 incident, the Kremlin brought the full force of the state's might down on Yukos, Russia's largest oil company, and its shareholders. The company itself was charged with tax evasion, although it had been paying considerably more taxes per barrel of oil produced than any other Russian oil company.[1] Russian tax authorities claimed that Yukos had been abusing the tax relief system, but none of Russia's other oil companies using similar schemes to reduce their tax burdens were punished as severely.

The amount the government claimed that Yukos owed in unpaid taxes was more than the company's annual revenues. The company could only settle such a large tax bill by selling off its assets. However, the Russian government did not allow the company's shareholders to carry out or control the asset sale. Nor did it initiate the process itself. First, in December 2004, in compliance with a court order, bailiffs sold off Yukos's major producing unit, making the company financially unstable. Sixteen months later, the Moscow court initiated bankruptcy proceedings against the company, during which Yukos shareholders were removed from the process and lost all opportunities to defend their interests in Russian courts.[2]

Even though Yukos had been destroyed as a company and all its assets had been turned over to the state-controlled Rosneft and Gazprom, the matter did not end there. Prosecutors also targeted the company's largest shareholders, Mikhail Khodorkovsky and Platon Lebedev, who were tried in criminal court and sentenced to lengthy prison terms. A few years later, before their sentences expired, the Russian state once again indicted Khodorkovsky and Lebedev—this time for the alleged crime of having stolen all the oil that Yukos's subsidiaries had produced over a span of several years. The manifest absurdity of this accusation did nothing to prevent the Russian court from pronouncing another guilty verdict. In late 2013, ten years after his initial arrest, Khodorkovsky was finally pardoned but was expelled from the country. A month later, Lebedev also was released by decision of the Russian Supreme Court but banned from leaving Russia. In addition to the prosecution of Khodorkovsky and Lebedev, the Russian state filed criminal charges against thirty Yukos employees, twelve of whom served prison terms of varying lengths and ten of whom emigrated from Russia and were convicted in absentia.

The Yukos case was neither the first nor the last of its kind—what we might call a "state takeover." But it was an important test case for the Kremlin in terms of both the size of the company that the state was bringing to heel and the scale and severity of the penalty imposed on the company's owners and managers. Many essentially similar "business cases" would soon follow, the highest profile of which are described below.

CARRYING OUT THE PRESIDENT'S ORDERS

The Soviet economy was based on central planning. Soviet ministries decided what to produce, where it should be made, who purchased what and from whom, how much a given product should cost, and how much its workers should be paid. The ministries also decided what factories to build and where to build them. Because there was no competition in the Soviet Union, it was often the case that there was a single producer of a specific product and a single consumer of said product. In a centrally planned economy, such supply-and-demand chains were taken for granted. However, after the collapse of the Soviet Union and the ensuing privatization of state-owned enterprises, the situation began to change. The heads of state enterprises became interested in turning a profit. Many cooperative business relationships collapsed because one or more of the participating enterprises lost money for every item produced and sold, which means that under market conditions the selling price of the manufactured goods was lower than the production cost. In these situations, it frequently was more profitable for many companies to sell their products to nontraditional customers. This practice became especially popular among enterprises that produced and preprocessed raw materials; export sales brought bigger profits than sales to the next link in the production chain.

Disruptions in cooperative ties intensified in the mid-1990s after privatization had been carried out in Russia, because enterprises were privatized separately and their mutual commitments concerning product supplies were not recorded in any way. One such production chain was connected with hydrocarbon processing by oil, gas, and chemical enterprises located in different regions of the country. In the mid-1990s, a group of businessmen led by Yakov Goldovsky decided to focus their efforts and began consolidating enterprises in this sector. It was not a secret that Goldovsky sought to recreate a vertically integrated group of companies incorporating the entire production path, from the deep processing of raw materials to the release of the finished product. This concept had been formulated in Soviet times by Gosplan, the State Planning Committee of the USSR, and the state had begun to develop and implement this proposed structure. However, even though the initial processing facilities had been built, the Soviet Union had not lasted long enough to create companies that were able to produce a finished product.

The key feature of this business model is that the value of a product increases considerably as it advances through each processing stage. However, the enterprises at the beginning of the production chain had been inherited from the Soviet Union, and consequently their profit-earning capacity was not very high. Moreover, dramatic cuts in the military budget in the early 1990s resulted in a sharp decline in demand for various products, and the vast distance between the centers of oil and gas processing and the raw materials along Russia's borders created enormous transportation charges that made export impossible. The stability of these businesses depended on the consolidation of scattered enterprises into one group—and on the relationship with Gazprom, one of the key suppliers of raw materials.

Goldovsky explained his business idea to the management of the gas monopoly, convincing them that, in the long run, cooperation would benefit both parties. Gazprom CEO Rem Vyakhirev initially rejected the idea of a joint business, but agreed to loan Goldovsky the money to purchase shares in associated gas-processing companies. In 1998, Goldovsky's company purchased from the state 71 percent of the shares of the holding company Sibur, which became the official name of the group. Sibur owned noncontrolling stakes in many gas-processing companies, and Gazprom helped Goldovsky acquire control over them, selling their debts to Sibur in exchange for Sibur's bonds.

After the 1998 Russian financial crisis, the consolidation process picked up speed. A sharp decrease in oil and gas prices meant that even the strongest companies were running short on funds to pay off their debts to Gazprom for supplied gas. Consequently, debts to the gas giant piled up. Also as a result of the crisis, many large Russian banks went bankrupt, and enterprises lost the money in their accounts. Both factors facilitated Sibur's negotiations with business owners.

By the end of 2000, the consolidation of the sector was nearly completed. It did not come cheap to Sibur: the company's balance sheet was riddled with debt amounting to 50 billion rubles (U.S. $2 billion at the exchange rate at the time), two-thirds of which was owed to Gazprom and the rest having been loaned to Sibur by Russian and foreign banks. The group's already complicated ownership structure became even more confusing. Because of conditions attached to the loans and the risk of counteraction by antitrust authorities, some of the assets were titled not in Sibur's name but in the name of companies owned or controlled by Goldovsky. However, Gazprom and Sibur had an agreement in place that all purchased assets were to be registered under Sibur's ownership within a limited time frame, and the company's debts to Gazprom were to be either restructured or swapped into Sibur shares. Negotiations between the companies were not suspended even when, in the summer of 2001, Vyakhirev was replaced as CEO of Gazprom by Aleksei Miller, Vladimir Putin's acquaintance from St. Petersburg. The partners eventually agreed on the profile of assets that were to be gathered within Sibur, the amount that Sibur owed to Gazprom, and a development path for the company's future.

To implement the approved consolidation scheme, Sibur had to carry out a new stock issue in which Gazprom was supposed to pay for its stake by converting Sibur's bond into equity and Goldovsky's group was supposed to pay for its stake with stock in gas-processing companies owned by his group outside Sibur's perimeter. The situation changed dramatically in November 2001. Goldovsky's group was the first to call in its assets, but at the same time it had decided to sell some companies. (Sharp increases in the government-regulated price of gas had made the gas-processing operations at these companies unprofitable, and so Goldovsky decided to sell these assets to partly pay Sibur's debts.) Under Russian law, Sibur's new stock issue had not yet been completed; in order for this to happen, either all shareholders had to make capital contributions or a certain amount of time had to pass. Several new managers that Miller had brought into Gazprom expressed concern that the consolidation of Sibur might drastically erode Gazprom's share in the company from 50.07 percent to 4 percent.[3] They wrote an alarmist letter to President Putin—who, while on a visit to a far-distant northern gas province soon after, remarked in passing to Miller, "Property questions should be treated seriously. Otherwise, while you are gawking, you will lose not only Sibur but other enterprises as well."[4]

After that, Gazprom's managers abandoned the previous agreements, which had fixed the composition of shareholders' stakes after Sibur's consolidation: 38 percent for Gazprom, 15 percent for Goldovsky's group; and the remaining 47 percent for the lending banks and new investors. Referring to the famous Russian maxim of that time—"51 percent is 100, while 49 percent is zero"—Gazprom insisted on receiving no less than 51 percent of Sibur's shares and an absolute majority on its board of directors. At the same time, Gazprom also demanded a change to a clause in Sibur's charter that stipulated that the general director could be appointed or dismissed only with the support of at least 75 percent of shareholders at a general meeting. Soon after that, Miller's deputy openly proposed that Goldovsky leave Sibur and transfer day-to-day management to Gazprom representatives.

Goldovsky rejected the proposal, and in doing so received unexpected support from Dmitry Medvedev, who at the time was first deputy Kremlin chief of staff and deputy chairman of Gazprom's board of directors. Medvedev held a meeting at which it was decided that Gazprom would be guaranteed to retain its shareholder control and that they would arrive at an alternative composition of Sibur's board of directors in which no shareholder had a majority. This decision was supported by Prime Minister Mikhail Kasyanov and Economic Minister German Gref, the latter of whom, like Medvedev, was close to Putin. Both Kasyanov and Gref knew Putin's position with regard to Sibur and were unlikely to make a decision that would directly contradict their boss's views. This decision was further secured by a government resolution from January 4, 2002. Putin undoubtedly received information about the decision but gave the green light to use force against Goldovsky.

Sibur's shareholder meeting was scheduled to be held on January 8, 2002. The day before, Goldovsky went to Aleksei Miller's office to discuss questions relating to the upcoming meeting and Sibur's future. Goldovsky brought a folder containing three possible proposals for Miller: (1) one partner would buy out the shares belonging the other one, (2) the partners would agree on shares in a joint business, or (3) the partners would sell off all assets and divide the profits after paying off debts. The time for the meeting came and went, but the head of Gazprom still did not invite Goldovsky into his office. Instead, representatives of the prosecutor general's office appeared and arrested Goldovsky. Sibur's legal counsel Evgeny Koshits and Gazprom's deputy CEO Vyacheslav Sheremet, who among other things had been supervising the financial aspects of the relationship with Sibur, were arrested on the same day.[5] Sibur's offices were searched and documents were confiscated. It turned out that, on the previous day, one of Miller's deputies had sent an official letter to the prosecutor general's office accusing Goldovsky of abusing his power at the expense of Sibur's interests when Goldovsky sold stakes in some companies, and requesting that the authorities launch a criminal investigation.

Sibur managers were held in pretrial detention for ten days without charge, during which time Goldovsky received an "offer he couldn't refuse": to transfer the voting rights attached to the shares belonging to his companies to Gazprom and sell the assets his group owned. Ten days later, both businessmen were officially charged with abuses of power, and the demand that Goldovsky sell the requested assets gained additional urgency. By the end of January, Goldovsky had agreed to the demands and hoped for a rapid release from detention. He signed all the required documents, turning over all voting rights at general meetings to Gazprom's representatives and pledging to transfer all the assets belonging to his companies to Gazprom.

However, as a proverb says, one shoulder of mutton drives down another—the more you have, the more you want. Goldovsky was asked to sell not only the assets that were supposed to be consolidated in Sibur but also his own real estate assets. Goldovsky refused, and the situation was frozen for two months. In May, the demand to sell the real estate assets was withdrawn, and the deal was signed.[6] However, the criminal case against Sibur's managers was not closed, and in late July the case went to trial. In August, both defendants were released on bail, which was made classified by the judge's decision. Although in July, Gazprom and Sibur had withdrawn their claims of having sustained material damages, in late September both businessmen were found guilty of abusing power and were sentenced to seven months' imprisonment, which amounted to time served. Goldovsky immediately left Russia and did not return for several years.

The fate of Sibur itself was not a gentle one. Initially, Gazprom's new managers did not see why they needed to maintain the consolidated company and were prepared to sell off the assets. However, they soon realized that Goldovsky's business ideas had merit, and continued to implement his development plan. But the processing of raw materials for competitive markets did not appeal to a monopoly like Gazprom: in 2007, it declared that oil, gas, and chemical industries were not within its sphere of interests. As part of an asset exchange, Gazprom gave Sibur shares to the affiliated Gazprombank, the management of which was in turn transferred to Rossiya Bank, owned by President Putin's crony Yury Kovalchuk. A year later, Gazprombank signed a contract to sell 50 percent plus one share in Sibur to the company's top managers. But in the midst of the global financial crisis, it was announced that the negotiations had been cut off owing to the "situation on the stock and bond market."

In July 2010, the state made an unexpected "gift" to Sibur; the Bank for Development (Vnesheconombank, VEB) loaned it U.S. $1.5 billion to construct a polypropylene manufacturing plant.[7] That September, Leonid Mikhelson, the principal shareholder of the fast-growing Russian gas company Novatek, showed his interest in Sibur by purchasing its shares from Gazprombank.[8] In October 2011, another Putin crony, Gennady Timchenko, bought a little more than a third of Sibur's shares from Mikhelson. In November 2014, Timchenko sold half of his stake to Kirill Shamalov—who, in addition to being the son of fellow Putin crony Nikolai Shamalov, was married to Putin's younger daughter, Katerina. It was announced that Gazprombank had loaned the young manager a little more than U.S. $1.7 billion to buy the stock.[9] In June 2015 the state made yet another "gift" to Sibur, when, on Putin's direct orders, a long-term loan for U.S. $1.75 billion was extended to the company from the National Welfare Fund for the construction of a pyrolysis plant—a major project with a cumulative investment amounting to slightly less than U.S. $20 billion.[10] In December of the same year, the Chinese company Sinopec bought 10 percent of Sibur's shares; one year later, the Silk Road Fund and the China Development Bank jointly purchased the same stake. Shamalov sold the bulk of his shares, securing a 30 percent profit in a year's time after the deal.

Today, Sibur is looking to offer its shares publicly, and investors value it at a little less than half of Gazprom. Such is the company that Yakov Goldovsky once intended to create.

GRAY WHALES ARE TO BE LOVED

In the 1980s, Soviet geologists discovered huge oil and gas fields in the Sakhalin Island area off Russia's Far Eastern coast, equivalent to about 45 billion barrels of oil. However, a lack of expertise prevented Soviet oilers from developing these reserves. In the late 1980s, the Soviet Union opened negotiations with major Western companies about possible reserve development projects based on a production-sharing agreement (PSA). In 1994, such an agreement was finally signed for reserves located in the Sakhalin-2 license area. Having become shareholders in Sakhalin Energy, the company created specifically for this project, Shell, Mitsui, and Mitsubishi began operations in 1996 after the adoption of a Russian law on PSAs.

In the 2000s, having decided to expand its business beyond the traditional European customers, Gazprom began sizing up the burgeoning Asian markets, zeroing in on liquefied natural gas (LNG). Naturally, Gazprom's first area of focus was on projects being implemented in Russia, and so it could not ignore Sakhalin Energy. Gazprom's desire to join the Sakhalin project was so strong that by July 2005 it agreed to an asset exchange with Shell: in return for 25 percent plus one share of Sakhalin Energy, Gazprom was prepared to give to Shell 50 percent of a huge project intended to develop gas deposits in Russia's Far North. Having announced the terms of their agreement, Gazprom and Shell also declared that the asset swap would be an unequal one and that, based on the results of a project evaluation, one of the parties would have to pay the difference.[11]

One can only guess at what motivated Shell's managers to choose the course they did, but just one week after the asset swap agreement had been signed, Shell declared that its assessment of the Sakhalin-2 project's expenditures had increased 70 percent, to U.S. $20 billion. This meant that Gazprom, as a project participant, would have to increase its own investment. Moreover, an increase in the project's expenses meant that the participants' first dividend date would be delayed, and that there was a risk that the state's future profits from the PSA would decrease sharply. The Kremlin and Gazprom's management saw in their partner's behavior an attempt to deceive them. Their attempts to arrange for a reduction in investment failed, and so the Kremlin decided that it would have to make an example of Sakhalin Energy—as it had with Yukos—so that other foreign companies in the oil and gas sector would be more pliable.

Sakhalin Energy was hit with a wave of state-instigated environmental inspections, which in short order found dozens of violations of environmental law, from unsanctioned clear-cutting to pollution of salmon-spawning waters to interruption of gray whales' migration routes. In July 2006 the Russian Ministry of Natural Resources and the Environment (MINREN) launched a complex environmental inspection of Sakhalin Energy. The official announcement of the environmental inspections made no effort to conceal the true motives: "Drilling dates, production levels, and hydrocarbon recovery rates are being altered. This has a negative impact on the interests of the Russian Federation because this puts off the moment of profit production sharing between the state and the investor to a later date, and leads to an increase in the cost of the project. From 2003 to 2005, the cost of the project, according to the company's estimates, had been constantly increasing and has doubled by now. Thus the receipt of profit product by the state is being delayed even more." Three days later, the Sakhalin regional court annulled a decision by the state's Environmental Expertise Agency, which had approved the construction of a temporary dock by Sakhalin Energy in Aniva Bay.[12] On August 30, a ministerial-level inspection team announced it had discovered evidence of pollution, and decided to open further investigations. In late August, Sakhalin Energy was forced to suspend indefinitely the construction of aboveground pipelines.

MINREN head Yury Trutnev called the working methods of Sakhalin Energy "barbaric." At the time, environmental fines under Russian law were modest and unlikely to frighten Western project participants. Thus the Russian authorities opted to use the "nuclear option" by announcing that it might withdraw the project's production license. First MINREN announced that it had discovered evidence of environmental pollution at Sakhalin Energy's offshore facilities and threatened to annul the company's water-use license. After that, Trutnev also annulled the Environmental Expertise Agency's approval for Sakhalin Energy's temporary dock but delayed any further action on the matter, thus putting the situation on ice.

To avoid accusations that they were selectively applying the law, Russian authorities pressured other Western companies as well. The state Ecological and Technical Inspection agency ordered Exxon Neftegas, the operator of the Sakhalin-1 project, to suspend loading oil into a pipeline feeding an export terminal, accusing the Western company of failing to carry out all necessary environmental protection measures. Then Russia's Audit Chamber completed its inspection of the Sakhalin-1 and Sakhalin-2 projects[13] and declared that the Sakhalin-2 project "was being implemented under conditions that are disadvantageous for Russia."

In late October, Trutnev declared that violations in the Sakhalin-2 project fell under at least five articles of the Criminal Code of the Russian Federation and ordered that materials relating to his probe be sent to the prosecutor general's office.[14] In mid-November, Trutnev's subordinate announced Russia's intention to file a lawsuit with the Arbitration Institute of the Stockholm Chamber of Commerce, seeking to collect up to U.S. $30 billion from the operator of the Sakhalin Energy project for causing environmental damage. At the same time, he signed a letter claiming that Sakhalin Energy had violated the terms of nineteen water-use licenses and asked that these licenses be revoked.[15] It was obvious that Sakhalin Energy could not continue its work on the project without the water-use licenses and so would not be able to complete the infrastructure part of the project by the end of 2008, as scheduled. Given that all future hydrocarbon production had already been contracted with customers, Sakhalin Energy was facing multibillion-dollar penalties for disruptions to the delivery schedule.[16] On December 5, twelve of nineteen water-use licenses were suspended.[17]

On December 8, while Vladimir Putin held a meeting of Russia's Security Council on the issue of shelf exploration, Shell CEO Jeroen van der Veer negotiated with Gazprom CEO Aleksei Miller, who clarified Russia's demands. Three days later, Shell had resigned itself to the fact that it stood no chance at all in a confrontation with the full might of the state machine, and declared that it was ready to cede a controlling stake (50 percent plus one share) in Sakhalin Energy to Gazprom.[18] The negotiations took less than a week. All foreign shareholders of Sakhalin Energy gave away half of their shares to Gazprom, worth a total of U.S. $7.45 billion,[19] which was much less than the U.S. $9–$10 billion predicted by analysts.[20]

One week later, during his meeting with Sakhalin Energy shareholders in the Kremlin, Putin demonstrated his generosity: "Russia's environmental agencies and our investors had agreed on the procedure of solving the existing questions," he said. "I know that you still have meetings at MINREN, but, as far as I am aware, the matter can essentially be considered closed, and problem-solving approaches can be considered agreed upon." At the same time, Putin brought to a close the question of the company's investment budget by declaring that a "solution to the risk issue relating to increasing expenses for the project implementation" had been found. "The Russian side was satisfied with a serious, insightful, and business-like approach of our partners, who are assuming responsibility for these risks," while an "increase in the (project's) cost will not have any impact on the Russian Federation's revenues."[21] And with that, Putin deprived Shell of control over Sakhalin Energy and revised the financial terms of Shell's participation in the project, while Gazprom canceled its promise to give Shell a stake in its northern gas project.

Three months later, Sakhalin Energy and MINREN agreed on a plan to address environmental concerns. The plan was "prepared with the participation of Gazprom specialists and members of the scientific community,"[22] and the largest part of it was scheduled to be implemented before the end of 2008. Meanwhile, it turned out that most of these measures were to be implemented in the project's context anyway, and consequently they would not require additional expenditures. The Sakhalin-2 project could move forward without any additional obstacles or delays. In December 2008, Sakhalin Energy won the Environmental Project of the Year award from MINREN and received a special diploma "For the Protection of the Gray Whale Population."[23]

PUSHED OUT IN A FRIENDLY WAY

Everybody knows that the oil and gas sector is a pillar of Russia's economy. Major reserves of Russian hydrocarbons and key extraction centers are located in western Siberia, where fields have been developed since the 1970s. Although in Soviet times, sufficient deposits had been discovered to guarantee uninterrupted operation of the oil and gas sector for twenty-five to thirty years, the centrally planned Soviet economy looked further ahead. Soviet geologists had been actively exploring eastern Siberia since the late 1980s. In 1987, in the hard-to-access and unpopulated taiga of the northern part of Irkutsk region, the massive Kovykta gas condensate field, with estimated reserves of 1.9 trillion cubic meters, was discovered. Aside from the field's location in an isolated area, 450 kilometers from Irkutsk, its potential development was further complicated by the absence of a gas distribution system in Irkutsk region. (The region received cheap electricity from hydropower stations on the Angara River.) Moreover, the gas itself was enriched with helium, for which there was no outlet whatsoever. For these reasons, the development of the Kovykta field was put off until a later date.

After the collapse of the Soviet Union, the Rusia Petroleum company, founded on the basis of the Kovykta field, began exploration drilling to measure the size and structure of gas deposits. The work progressed slowly since there seemed to be no market for the product. The neighboring regions within Russia did not have high needs, and gas export to China was considered impossible at the time (though a decade later, China's economy would become the world's largest consumer of natural resources). It also would be difficult to get the gas out of the area, as the closest gas pipeline owned by Gazprom was more than 1,000 kilometers away. Moreover, at the time, Gazprom was not experiencing a shortage of cheap gas for domestic use and for export—not least because one key gas exporter, Turkmenistan, could not sell the gas it was producing to anyone but Gazprom.

The operations of Rusia Petroleum in the 1990s were further complicated by a tough economic situation in the country. It proved impossible to secure long-term financing for such an uncertain project, and there was no single large investor capable of exerting control over the company, since its shares were divided between several players that disagreed with each other over the company's direction. By the end of the 1990s, the shareholder structure had consolidated somewhat, but three shareholders, each of which owned a blocking minority (Interros, TNK, and BP owned between 25 and 30 percent each, and the administration of Irkutsk region controlled a further 14 percent), arrived to make the new situation just as complicated as the old one.

The relationships between shareholders were tense. TNK and Interros were engaged in a corporate conflict around an oil company, Sidanko, in which BP owned a 10 percent stake purchased from Interros in 1997. Although Interros and its partners controlled 51 percent of Sidanko's shares, the lack of proper management, weak control over affiliated companies, and a decrease in oil prices made it impossible to keep the company solvent. In 1998, TNK initiated bankruptcy proceedings and later established control over Sidanko's key producing units. Not long after, Sidanko lost the Angara petrochemical plant and the Khabarovsk oil refinery. Although Sidanko's financial situation improved after that, it became obvious to Interros that the company had no prospects, and in 2001 Interros sold its stake to TNK.

The conflict between Interros and TNK continued within Rusia Petroleum. In the summer of 2001, based on claims filed by private individuals, courts in two Russian cities several thousand kilometers from Kovykta banned Interros from participating in the shareholders' meeting, during which Interros's stake became diluted when Rusia Petroleum issued new equity to TNK. Although Britain's BP was Interros's formal partner at the time, it did not block the decision made at the shareholders' meeting. Evidently, BP was already "building bridges" and establishing a relationship with TNK, a stronger player, which later resulted in the creation of the TNK-BP company.

At some point, the corporate conflict ran its course, and the relationship between its participants morphed into a state of tense neutrality. This was facilitated by the conclusion of the conflict over Sidanko, as well as by the fact that Chinese gas consumption had increased considerably to match strong economic growth. Numerous Russian and Chinese companies held talks about the supply of natural resources. Rusia Petroleum became an active participant in these negotiations, with its representatives taking part in all official visits by Russian leaders to China. This was the basis for the optimistic views of the company's business development prospects.

The emerging TNK-BP alliance gave representatives of these companies a majority on the board of directors, enough to facilitate many day-to-day decisions. Interros's blocking minority allowed it to play a decisive role in the selection of schemes, methods, and amounts of financing of the company's operations. Even though it was unable to participate in the management of the company, Interros blocked any decisions on raising new capital, forcing TNK and BP to finance Rusia Petroleum's expansion with their own loans.

At the beginning of the 2000s, eastern Siberia in general and China as a potential consumer of Russian gas in particular were not part of Gazprom's sphere of interests: the monopoly owned hardly any fields in this region, and its strategic planning documents openly stated that it did not see the Chinese market as an attractive option. Gazprom's main desire was to maintain its monopolistic control on gas exports from Russia. This was why Gazprom's representatives participated in all of Rusia Petroleum's meetings with Chinese delegations. Their key message was that Gazprom would continue to set prices and maintain monopoly control over exports.

By 2003, negotiations between Rusia Petroleum and Chinese consumers had advanced, and many commercial issues had been solved. It was already becoming evident that the key obstacles to Russia commencing exports to China in 2008 was the lack of clarity in construction of a gas pipeline, its future path, and its financing. In other words, Rusia Petroleum was ready to move from the stage of geological exploration to the initial stage of field development. This turn of events came as a surprise to Gazprom: the monopoly realized that it had been a big mistake to underestimate the potential of the Chinese market and swiftly toughened its position during its talks with Rusia Petroleum's shareholders regarding the terms and conditions for selling gas from the Kovykta field.

Gazprom based its position on a statutory provision according to which the monopoly was the only one allowed to build cross-country gas pipelines and to sell Russian gas to countries beyond the former boundaries of the Soviet Union. This position remained unchanged. Rusia Petroleum shareholders were forced to seek indirect options for selling gas. In mid-2003, with Russian energy minister Igor Yusufov acting as an intermediary, an agreement was reached under which Rusia Petroleum would sell all the gas it extracted "at the wells" to Gazprom, and in return the monopoly would build a gas pipeline from Kovykta to the Chinese border by the end of 2007 and finalize the gas supply negotiations with China. Such an agreement was not ideal for Rusia Petroleum's shareholders, but it allowed the company to ensure the stability of the business and to turn a profit.

During a meeting of Rusia Petroleum's board of directors, the question of signing an agreement with Gazprom was raised—and an unexpected thing happened. BP representatives declared they did not believe that all opportunities for improving Rusia Petroleum's negotiating position had been exhausted, and refused to support the agreement. This decision provoked an explosive negative reaction from Gazprom, whose management canceled all negotiations with Rusia Petroleum and declared that the monopoly would never sign any contract with this company.

The incident put Rusia Petroleum and its shareholders in an extremely difficult position. The government production license required the company to start field exploitation and commercial-scale gas production in 2006. After Gazprom severed relations with Rusia Petroleum, it became clear that even the sale of gas in Irkutsk region—let alone exporting gas to China—had been rendered impossible. Gazprom had refused not only to build any pipelines itself but also to authorize Rusia Petroleum's shareholders to construct a limited gas pipeline for their own use.

All attempts by the company's shareholders to change the terms and conditions of the license agreement failed. State authorities turned down all requests and pleas, making it clear that there would be no progress without Gazprom's approval. Gazprom itself had by that time entirely changed its tune with regard to the Chinese market: the political tensions between Russia and China had eased, and both countries' leaders began to support mutual trade and signed an agreement to supply China with Russian gas. It became obvious that the Kovykta reserves were critically important for ensuring a long-term supply of Russian gas to China; without them, there was no way to guarantee gas supplies for the next thirty years. That awareness pushed Gazprom to take possession of Kovykta.

The government therefore took an even harder line on compliance with the license agreement. It demanded that Rusia Petroleum achieve the impossible: that the company begin extraction without any means of transporting the gas! Moreover, at the same time, the government approved the Russian gas industry's development scheme, whereby gas extraction in the Kovykta field was scheduled to begin in 2017. By mid-June 2007, the situation was even more aggravated: MINREN head Yury Trutnev declared that his ministry had received an order to withdraw Rusia Petroleum's license.[24] The situation essentially replicated the Sakhalin-2 story right down to the outcome: a few days later, TNK-BP decided to call off the fight by signing a deal with Gazprom and selling its stake in Rusia Petroleum to the monopoly;[25] at the same time, TNK-BP received an option to buy out 25 percent of Rusia Petroleum's shares "as compensation."[26] Apparently, Gazprom was expected to come to an agreement with Interros regarding the purchase of the latter's stake in the company. Meanwhile, Gazprom also signed an agreement with TNK-BP to establish a joint gas-producing enterprise and promised to inject lucrative assets in that venture.

The negotiations had been proceeding at a leisurely pace, but the global financial crisis, which began a year later, almost brought them to a stop. Both Gazprom and TNK-BP faced serious problems following the drop in oil and gas prices, lower demand for hydrocarbons, and the collapse of the financial markets. In mid-December 2008, Gazprom openly stated that the "new market situation forced us to open our eyes to this deal"[27] and demanded that the price of Rusia Petroleum's stake be lowered considerably. In early February 2009, the negotiations stopped. BP's chief executive, Tony Hayward, declared that "this question has been put on ice rather than put off. We will see if we can reopen these negotiations, but I would not be too hopeful."[28]

By the end of 2009, oil prices had rebounded, but negotiations were not renewed. Meanwhile Gazprom's talks about gas supplies to China were moving forward: in April 2008, Gazprom obtained a development license for the Chayanda gas field, located even further east, in Yakutia, which the company decided to use as a primary source of gas for future supplies to China. From an economic perspective, this was a strange decision, because getting the Chayanda field ready for gas extraction demanded more time and a considerably larger investment than the Kovykta field. The cost of gas production turned out to be much higher than on the Kovykta field, but this decision hardly surprised anyone—after all, Gazprom's expenditures were always someone else's profits.

However, Gazprom did not forget about Kovykta, even though all public documents and speeches stated that the monopoly was not interested in it and that gas production from this field would not commence for another decade. In early 2010 the government resumed its pressure on Rusia Petroleum. The company was once again accused of breaching the terms of the license agreement. TNK-BP shareholders realized they had no chance of keeping Rusia Petroleum running and launched negotiations directly with the government about selling the company. Deputy Prime Minister Igor Sechin suggested Rosneftegas as a potential buyer;[29] Viktor Vekselberg, a TNK-BP shareholder, called the sale a done deal, claiming that it would be signed by the end of the year.[30]

Soon, Rusia Petroleum, citing its inability to comply with TNK-BP's demand to pay off the previously granted loans, began bankruptcy proceedings, choosing a plan intended to minimize acquisition costs. If the buyer purchased Rusia Petroleum's shares from TNK-BP, according to Russian law, it would have been required to offer to buy shares from all other shareholders at the same price. Meanwhile, during the bankruptcy proceedings, Rusia Petroleum's assets were subject to an auction sale, and the buyer had the right to relicense the development of the Kovykta field.

The auction to sell Rusia Petroleum's assets was scheduled for March 1, 2011, with the starting bid equal to the value of the loans that TNK-BP had granted to the company. Everyone was certain that Rosneftegas, backed by the mighty Sechin, would become the buyer. But this was not to be. Having unexpectedly declared its interest in Rusia Petroleum's assets in late February, Gazprom offered a price at auction that was 40 percent higher than Rosneftegas's bid. In early October 2011, the monopoly obtained the long-coveted license for the Kovykta field. Of course, all state-imposed requirements on Rusia Petroleum regarding gas production were withdrawn, and development of the Kovykta field stalled. The main reason behind Gazprom's "generosity" at the auction was its unwillingness to part with its monopoly on gas exports, which would have been threatened if Rosneftegas had purchased the Kovykta field.

Although TNK-BP did turn a profit from its investments in the project, it lost all prospects for the development of its gas business.[31] Other shareholders met with a different fate. Interros sold its stake in Rusia Petroleum for U.S. $576 million in 2008 to a Russian power-generating company, OGK-3, that it controlled via Norilsk Nickel. OGK-3 itself did not manage to get anything from Rusia Petroleum's bankruptcy and had to write off the amount paid to Interros as a loss. Thus the shareholders of both OGK-3 and Norilsk Nickel paid for Interros's exit from Rusia Petroleum. Irkutsk region, another Rusia Petroleum shareholder, received nothing after the company's bankruptcy.

A STORY WITH A HAPPY ENDING . . .

Russneft was a company very different from the giants of Russia's oil industry, which were created on the basis of major production companies inherited from the Soviet Union. Unlike these, Russneft had been built from scratch. From 2002 to 2005, its assets had been accumulated bit by bit by its owners, the principal one being Mikhail Gutseriyev. Having worked in the oil industry, he understood the business strategy of major Russian oil companies, which were interested in developing large deposits and lacked managers for small and medium-sized ones.

This strategy pays off elsewhere in the world. Most major oil players are not eager to buy small oil fields, leaving them to be developed by small and medium-sized businesses. The United States, for example, has more than 16,000 oil-producing companies, and about half the country's oil is produced by small businesses, with annual oil production volumes nearing 2.5 million tons. In Russia, however, this is an uncommon practice; major companies have been unwilling to give away small fields, believing that doing so would demonstrate to government authorities their inability to fulfill license agreements, and the government in turn would prevent them from obtaining licenses to develop new fields. As a result, Russia has fewer than 200 oil-producing companies, and the small ones—the annual production volumes of which do not exceed 2 million tons—account for only 3 percent of all oil produced in the country.

Gutseriyev decided to go down a "Western path" and began buying small oil fields. To some extent, he was lucky, because he had begun his project at a time when oil prices had pushed through the U.S. $30 per barrel level and were rising quickly. Moreover, he managed to obtain a U.S. $2.3 billion business startup loan from the Anglo-Swiss commodity trading company Glencore. By 2007, Russneft had grown considerably. Compared to 2002, its production had increased eightfold. However, on the scale of the Russian industrial sector as a whole, Russneft was still a small company, accounting for only 3.2 percent of Russian oil production.

All of this was under way when the state suddenly put Gutseriyev and his business in its crosshairs. It subjected the company to numerous tax inspections and closely examined the entire history of Russneft's business operations concerning the purchase of shares. The state then leveled a ridiculous accusation against the company, claiming it had violated the terms and conditions of its license agreements. Russneft was accused of having extracted 60,000 tons of oil (0.4 percent of the production volume) over the allowed limit.[32] In November 2006, criminal cases were initiated against several top managers of companies that had been acquired by Russneft, even though the events in question dated back to a time when these companies had not even been part of Russneft. In May 2007, a criminal case was initiated against Gutseriyev himself.[33] Although initially he pledged not to leave town, fearing the fate of Khodorkovsky he broke his promise and fled abroad. In June 2007, the Federal Tax Service filed eight lawsuits against Russneft companies, accusing them of making deals that "contradicted the fundamental principles of morality and ethics." Government officials demanded that the deals between these companies involving Russneft's shares be declared void and that the company's shares be confiscated. The Moscow Arbitration Court used the confiscation of Russneft's shares as an interlocutory measure.[34]

The reasons behind the attack on Gutseriyev were not entirely clear. One thing was obvious: Russneft was not Yukos. With its thirty-two operating companies and 170 oil fields, Russneft was extremely hard to manage,[35] and its assets did not represent any particular interest to the state. None of the state-owned companies—neither Rosneft nor Gazpromneft—showed any interest in absorbing Russneft assets.

The media formulated two theories about the Russneft case. In one possible scenario, it was said, Vladimir Putin might have noticed Gutseriyev as far back as 2002. At the time, the Kremlin had nominated FSB general Murat Zyazikov, deputy presidential envoy to the Southern Federal District, for president of the Republic of Ingushetia in the northern Caucasus region.[36] Gutseriyev, whose family was from Ingushetia and who was well established in Ingushetian political circles, did not get the message and backed his brother Khamzat in the election. At the same time, he implemented large-scale charitable projects in the republic, bankrolled by the state-owned company Slavneft (where he was the CEO). Khamzat Gutseriyev, who at the time was the interior minister of Ingushetia, was supported by the charismatic and very popular former Ingushetian president Ruslan Aoushev and was an obvious frontrunner in the election. Two days before the first ballot, Russia's Supreme Court requested the case in which Gutseriyev was accused of violations of electoral campaigning, even though it had not yet been considered by the Supreme Court of Ingushetia. Using vagaries of law, it removed Khamzat Gutseriyev from the election. This turn of events helped the Kremlin's candidate, General Zyazikov; though he won only 19 percent of the vote in the first round of the elections, Zyazikov made it to the second round, where he won the presidency with 53 percent of the vote, albeit under dubious circumstances.[37] This confrontation with the Kremlin resulted in Gutseriyev's dismissal as the CEO of Slavneft,[38] and there is no doubt that Vladimir Putin never forgot this conflict. He had already announced his vertical of power and could not condone something he believed to be unacceptable—namely, the coming to power of self-sufficient and independent representatives of big business.

The second episode that could have triggered an attack on Gutseriyev had to do with the fact that in 2005, Russneft bought some assets from Yukos:

a 50 percent stake in a small oil company that owned a license for a modest oil field with slightly more than 20 million tons of reserves and equally modest annual production volumes of 2–2.4 million tons of oil, and a 49 percent stake in a Slovakian oil pipeline.[39] Yukos was under Kremlin attack, and, according to a prearranged scenario, all its assets were to go to the state-controlled Rosneft and Gazprom. For Igor Sechin, who was supervising all processes related to Yukos, this impudent intrusion of an outside player who managed to score off him led him to seek revenge by persecuting his challenger.

Gutseriyev realized what the state-led persecution could result in, and decided to sell his assets. Oleg Deripaska, who had close ties to the Kremlin, was the only one who showed interest in buying Russneft. The negotiations moved on to a discussion of price. Gutseriyev publicly estimated the value of his company at U.S. $7–$8 billion; Deripaska offered U.S. $6 billion. At that moment, the tax authorities filed tax claims against Russneft in the amount of 20 billion rubles (approximately U.S. $900 million at the exchange rate at the time). Realizing that, as Lenin had put it, "delay is tantamount to death," Gutseriyev agreed to the offered price, sold the company, and left for London.[40]

There is no proof that Deripaska was on the Kremlin's "team" against Gutseriyev, or that he was the one who initiated the attack on Gutseriyev and benefited from it. Deripaska has always been loyal to the Kremlin; however, having signed a deal with Gutseriyev and having paid for Russneft, Deripaska could not finalize the acquisition. Having repeatedly reviewed the deal, a government commission chaired by then-prime minister Putin refused to give it a green light under the pretext that several offshore companies had acted as buyers for and on behalf of Deripaska. Then deputy prime minister Igor Sechin, who demanded that only a Russian-registered company should act as a buyer, was the strongest opponent of the deal.[41]

The purchase of Russneft did not bring Oleg Deripaska good fortune. In 2008, the global economic crisis erupted, leading to a collapse in oil prices. RUSAL and many other business projects of Deripaska's were under way, thanks to huge loans collateralized by stakes in his companies. With the stock market crash, creditors began issuing margin calls demanding loan repayments prior to maturity or increasing collateral requirements. To repay his debts, Deripaska decided to obtain additional loans that Russneft had been receiving from Russian banks, which led to a sharp drop in the company's value.

Moreover, low oil prices and the difficulties in managing Russneft prevented him from deriving any significant profits from the company's activities.

The 2008–09 crisis posed a big challenge to the Russian economy. No one wanted to waste energy and resources trying to catch the businessman who had fled abroad, especially given that Russneft had paid all of the tax claims. By May 2010, the criminal cases against Gutseriyev had been closed, and he returned to Russia. But even before that, in January of the same year, having lost all hope of obtaining government permission, Deripaska agreed to sell Russneft back to Gutseriyev for a minor consideration.[42]

. . . AND THEN PUTIN CALLED

The Soviet Union had a strong aircraft industry that manufactured 100 to 110 military and 70 to 80 civilian airplanes each year. Aircraft factories were located in different parts of the country: Komsomolsk-on-Amur in the Far East, Irkutsk in Siberia, Tashkent in Central Asia, Kazan on the Volga River, and even in Moscow. All aircraft require engines, obviously. Because of the closed and isolated nature of the Soviet economy, these engines were designed and produced without any intellectual or industrial cooperation with Western companies. No normal competition existed between Soviet enterprises; the decision to manufacture new types of any product was made based on the needs of the centrally planned economy.

In the late 1970s, the USSR State Planning Committee (Gosplan) was deciding what new types of passenger planes to develop. It was agreed that the engines for these aircraft would be developed and manufactured in Perm, 700 miles east of Moscow. The industrial enterprise located in that city had been manufacturing engines for the Tupolev Tu-134, a discontinued twin-engine narrow-body jet. Consequently, the enterprise needed new manufacturing orders.

The development of a new Perm engine, PS-90, had been badly delayed. When flight tests began in the late 1980s, the Soviet economy was already falling apart, and mass production lines for the new planes were never set up. Although the new engine was not very reliable and failed to meet efficiency and stability targets, during privatization the Perm company attracted the attention of the U.S. aerospace firm Pratt & Whitney, which acquired a blocking stake (25 percent). For Pratt & Whitney, the new Russian engine would fill a gap in its product line. Faced with a choice between investing in an upgrade of the Russian engine and developing its own, the U.S. company went with the former. A detailed diagnosis determined the weaknesses of the Russian engine. In the early 2000s, a plan to eliminate them was worked out, and a joint investment plan was prepared together with the Russian holding company Interros, which owned an approximately 30 percent stake in the Perm company. Just one thing was missing: an intellectual property agreement had to be reached with the Russian government. And here the project hit a snag.

First, instead of the traditional royalty agreement, the Russian government proposed that Pratt & Whitney buy up the intellectual property for about U.S. $1 billion, which rendered the whole project useless for the U.S. company. Soon after, the Kremlin categorically forbade Interros from continuing its cooperation with Pratt & Whitney. Interros later sold its shares to the state-owned VTB bank, while the Perm company went on vegetating without a reliable product in its arsenal.

In the city of Rybinsk, 160 miles northeast of Moscow on the banks of the Volga River, another producer of aircraft engines at the time of the collapse of the Soviet Union had a more fortunate fate. This factory manufactured engines for Ilyushin Il-76 cargo aircraft, Sukhoi fighter jets, and the most widely used Soviet passenger jets, the Tupolev Tu-154 and Ilyushin Il-62. By that time, the Tu-154 and Il-62 had already been discontinued, but an enormous fleet of previously built planes provided the enterprise with sufficient repair and maintenance work orders. This allowed the company to invest its resources in the development of new product lines. In one such instance, the company cooperated with Ukrainian companies in the design of a heavy-duty gas turbine for power plants that had never been manufactured in the Soviet Union. After the pilot model of the turbine had been completed, the Rybinsk company bought out the technical documentation, which turned out to be a smart move—in the early 2000s, economic recovery in Russia demanded next-generation capacities. The Rybinsk turbines had no domestic competitors, while the imported analogues were far too expensive.

In 1997, Yury Lastochkin, who became the director of the Rybinsk com-

pany, began accumulating his stake and soon became the company's controlling shareholder; however, the government retained a 37 percent stake. In
2001, following a merger with a design bureau that traditionally had helped
draft engines for the Rybinsk company, the company was renamed Saturn.[43]

Standing steadily on its feet, Saturn resolutely tackled the design of new
products. At the end of 2000, having visited the enterprise, newly elected
Russian president Vladimir Putin gave his blessing to the Russian Defense
Ministry to designate Saturn as the key company for the design, mass production, and repair of all naval gas turbine engines used by the Russian navy.
(Before, such engines had been developed and manufactured in Ukraine.)
Saturn began working on modifying the engines for Sukhoi jet fighters, a
process that led to the development of an engine for the fifth-generation
jet fighter. In 2001, Saturn signed a long-term agreement with Gazprom to
supply the latter with engines for pipeline compressors. In 2003, when the
Russian authorities decided to support the development and production of
a new passenger airplane called the Sukhoi Superjet 100 (SSJ100), Saturn,
together with French company Snecma (Safran Group), won the tender to
produce engines for the new aircraft. This cooperation with Snecma gave
Saturn access to modern technology solutions, helped it establish a cooperative relationship with Western producers, and gave it a chance to bring its
products to the international market. According to Lastochkin, it would have
been impossible to create a new engine without such cooperation, because the
Russian input into both development and production did not exceed 40 percent of the total amount of work.

Saturn was developing successfully; its production numbers and revenues
continued to rise. The company began to trade its shares on the stock market,
and its capitalization skyrocketed. However, this made the company attractive for a new state-created "predator," the United Engine-Building Corporation. In the mid-2000s, Vladimir Putin decided to adopt the South Korean
model of economic development based on chaebols, large operational and financial holdings closely linked to the state. Large state corporations emerged
in Russia with such an unusual status that it would not fit in the existing
legislation, and separate laws had to be adopted to create each of them.[44]

In September 1999, then prime minister Vladimir Putin appointed his
longtime associate from his work in East Germany, Sergey Chemezov, as

the CEO of a medium-sized state enterprise involved in the supply of dual-use goods.[45] After becoming president, Putin consolidated export of Russian arms within the company named Rosoboronexport and took it under his personal control by appointing Chemezov deputy CEO of the company. After Putin's reelection as president in 2004, Chemezov was promoted to CEO.[46]

Yet Chemezov soon became bored with mere arms sales and suggested that Putin create a state corporation to include all Russian defense enterprises. According to Chemezov, this would result in increased efficiency and growth in Russia's arms export business. Chemezov's initial list included 250 defense enterprises in which the state owned shares. But the further the idea advanced down the bureaucratic corridors, the longer the list became. Even a few manufacturers of exclusively civilian goods ended up on the list because of their profitability—under the pretext of "guaranteeing the state's biological security," dozens of leading pharmaceutical enterprises and research institutes were added to it. The number of enterprises on the list was nearing 600. Many members of the Russian government protested against such omnivorous behavior. Economic Development Minister Elvira Nabiullina demanded that they abandon the idea of giving the new corporate giant stakes in civilian enterprises that she proposed should be sold as part of the privatization process.[47] Deputy Prime Minister and Finance Minister Alexey Kudrin opposed the idea of providing the corporation with complete independence and the right to sell shares that were being transferred to it. "The implementation of this proposal represents a camouflaged privatization and implies both a lack of transparency of selling these assets, and the absence of control over the use of revenues by the corporation itself," Kudrin wrote to Putin, adding that such practice was "directed at drawing revenues from the sale of state assets away from the federal budget where these funds should be going."[48] Although these protests were futile, another of Putin's close associates, Sergey Ivanov, was more successful in curbing Chemezov's appetites. Ivanov had a group of defense enterprises—which he intended to transfer into the capital of another state corporation that was being built under his own auspices—removed from the list.[49]

Although the corporation was not established until November 2007, Chemezov began placing assets under his control long before that. In November 2004, President Putin transferred stakes in the producer of Mil helicopters, owned by the Russian government and the government of Tatarstan, to Rosoboronexport's subsidiary, Oboronprom. In August 2007, Putin ordered that the state-owned stake in the producer of Kamov helicopters be transferred to Oboronprom as well.

In 2006, Oboronprom CEO Denis Manturov, who was later promoted to become deputy minister of industry and technologies, had made an offer to Chemezov to consolidate aircraft engine manufacturers into one holding. In August 2007, Chemezov received Putin's approval to carry out this idea and to include Saturn in this holding.[50] The state corporation's interest in Saturn was understandable: this was the only stable company in its segment with a sound book of military and civilian orders, access to modern Western technologies, and, most important, steady profits. Numerous guests began visiting Lastochkin in Rybinsk. They all bore the same message: the president had decided that Saturn should be acquired by Oboronprom and that Lastochkin's stake should be given to the state "as a gift"—that is, for free. Lastochkin refused, saying that he did not see any point in a merger since other companies that Oboronprom wanted to unify had neither human nor technological nor industrial potential. Moreover, in December 2007, Lastochkin had launched a merger with an engine-building company located in Ufa (to which Oboronprom also laid a claim), bought an almost 20 percent stake, and signed a partnership agreement with the management of the Ufa company, which owned another 30 percent stake.

Oboronprom tried to sweeten the pill by offering Lastochkin the option to convert his Saturn stake into Oboronprom's shares. However, as Oboronprom CEO Andrei Reus put it, "the attitude of the head of Saturn to this offer was also detrimental."[51] Lastochkin's position was understandable: he was offered a minority stake in a company whose shares were not being traded on the stock market. However, under relentless pressure, Lastochkin finally agreed to sell his stake, but insisted on a market value for the position.[52]

Having met with unexpected opposition, Oboronprom used all its available administrative resources. President Putin's April 2008 decree directly ordered the government to "provide for the implementation of necessary measures" to increase the government's stake in Saturn's capital to "no less than 50 percent plus one share."[53] Three weeks after signing this decree, Prime Minister Putin—having moved to his new office by this time—personally addressed President Putin's order to nationalize Saturn. Six months later, in early October 2008, Putin had signed a special resolution to address the implementation of his April decree on increasing the government stake in Saturn. The following day, Oboronprom's Denis Manturov sent a letter to the Interior Ministry asking to initiate a criminal case based on the results of an inspection his ministry had conducted. A day later, the Interior Ministry sent ten top-ranking officers to Rybinsk to initiate four criminal cases and interrogate Saturn's managers and employees. These were followed by a team of forty-five tax officials, who immediately discovered about a billion rubles' worth of unpaid taxes.[54]

Just as the Rybinsk enterprise had been lucky at the time of the collapse of the Soviet Union, it was unlucky when the state decided to nationalize it. In the summer of 2008, the global economic crisis dealt a serious blow to the Russian financial system. Saturn needed loans to complete its investment plan and to finance its daily activities. However, state banks terminated Saturn's lines of credit, and the private banks with which Saturn had worked could not grant the company any loans because they were having troubles of their own. VEB, the state-owned bank that had received state funds to support enterprises during the crisis, laid down a stiff loan condition: Saturn had to transfer 13 percent of its shares to Oboronprom to give it a controlling ownership stake.[55] Despite the crisis, Saturn was prepared to issue new bonds, but the financial regulator's decision halted the placement. This happened two days before Saturn was supposed to make coupon payments on its previously issued bonds. Saturn defaulted, and private banks severed their negotiations with the company. Meanwhile, the Finance Ministry, led by Kudrin, declared that it was postponing the allocation of 5 billion rubles to Saturn provided by the law to complete the certification process for the engine for SSJ100 Sukhoi Superjet, and the Defense Ministry held off on signing a contract for new engines for the Russian air force. Lastochkin, recognizing that the enterprise was on the verge of bankruptcy, decided to fire 4,000 of its 19,000 employees.

On December 1, 2008, Vladimir Putin telephoned Lastochkin from Moscow, and, according to Lastochkin, the two men had a "frank conversation." Lastochkin realized that any further resistance was useless. The following day, Putin appeared in Rybinsk, surrounded by numerous ministers and heads of state-owned banks and companies. During a meeting covered by the media, the Russian prime minister firmly stated that he could not allow the enterprise to shut down, and that it would be difficult if not impossible to solve these problems without increasing the state's stake in the company's capital. To this end, an agreement with the owners had been reached, according to which Oboronprom would purchase virtually 100 percent ownership in Saturn. Stakes belonging to private owners would be purchased on an arm's-length basis and at market prices.[56] After that, Putin declared that the state-owned VTB bank would grant a loan to Saturn to refinance its debts, that the state corporation Rosnano would put in an order worth 1 billion rubles, and that 5 billion rubles would be immediately allocated from the federal budget to certify the engine for the SSJ100. Defense Ministry and Gazprom representatives spoke after the prime minister to express their willingness to sign new long-term contracts with Saturn, amounting to 10 billion rubles.

Putin left the meeting satisfied, and went to Oleg Deripaska's Autodiesel plant in Yaroslavl (not far from Rybinsk), which was experiencing similar financial problems. There he sang a very different tune: "State development institutions should of course help the plant by replacing the source of financing that the global economic crisis has made unavailable."[57] Only a few days later, VEB granted a 10 billion ruble loan to Autodiesel.

Although during the Rybinsk meeting, Vladimir Putin had declared that Lastochkin would remain Saturn's director, the latter could not embrace the change. Nine months later he left his post and was elected mayor of Rybinsk. In November 2013, however, Lastochkin was arrested on dubious charges, and in September 2015 he was sentenced to eight and a half years in prison. He is currently serving his sentence in the Bezhetsk penal colony in Tver region, 150 kilometers from his hometown. Once in a while, Lastochkin gives interviews, in which he retells the story of the state taking away his factory and of the huge funds that the state invested in Saturn after becoming its owner (according to him, about 50 billion rubles), which produced insignificant results. He also strongly criticizes the government's import substitution plans because, in his opinion, the Russian engine-building industry has no future without technological cooperation with the world's leading companies. He also openly accuses Sergey Chemezov and Denis Manturov (today a minister) of organizing his criminal prosecution.[58]

WHEN PARTNERS CAN'T AGREE

The Soviet economy was strongly militarized. The arms race demanded a continuous buildup of military potential, and the general inefficiency of the Soviet economic system forced the country to produce exhaustive amounts of primary resources to satisfy the appetite of the military-industrial complex. Among other materials necessary for the military production was titanium, heavily used in the construction of submarines, missiles, and aircraft. The USSR's largest titanium producer was VSMPO, an enterprise located in Verkhnyaya Salda in the Ural Mountains, 850 miles east of Moscow. Even though Mikhail Gorbachev admitted in the second half of the 1980s that it was impossible to further increase military spending, and so began intensive arms reduction talks with the United States, VSMPO implemented a large-scale investment program. Before long, VSMPO was producing more titanium alloy than the United States, Europe, and Japan combined.

In 1956, Vladislav Tetyukhin, a young engineer who had just graduated from Moscow Steel and Alloys Institute, came to VSMPO. The active development of the Soviet space and missile programs had caused an explosive growth in demand for VSMPO's products and scientific innovations related to the new alloys. Tetyukhin was maturing as a specialist. Four years after graduating from college, he, along with several other employees, was awarded the Lenin Prize, one of the most prestigious awards presented by the Soviet Union to individuals for accomplishments relating to science and technology. During his work at VSMPO, Tetyukhin pursued scientific research, earned a doctorate, and completed a postdoctoral thesis. By the first half of the 1970s, he had become the enterprise's deputy chief metallurgist for titanium alloys, but soon after he relocated to Moscow for family reasons, where he continued his research activity.

A sharp decrease in Soviet military spending in the late 1980s resulted in a slump in demand for titanium. The state essentially abandoned this enterprise and its employees to the tender mercies of fate. The law allowed the employees to directly elect the company's CEO, and later the state agreed to give away 80 percent of VSMPO's shares to the employees. Tetyukhin was remembered as a man associated with glorious chapters in the company's history, and so, when the question of the enterprise's survival arose, he was the one asked to head it.

Having accepted the proposal to return to VSMPO, Tetyukhin faced a new economic reality: a market economy and a thirtyfold decrease in the defense industry's demand for titanium, as well as corporate issues previously unknown to him. VSMPO became a joint-stock company, with its shares belonging to the firm's 20,000 employees, many of whom were prepared to sell them at any price since actual wages had fallen along with the Soviet economy. By a happy coincidence, Tetyukhin met lawyers who helped him to build a defense against a hostile takeover. He convinced the employees to swap VSMPO's shares for the shares of another company that would accumulate more than 50 percent plus one of VSMPO's shares, thus becoming a controlling shareholder.

In the late 1980s, Tetyukhin met Vyacheslav Brecht. Brecht, who was almost twenty years his junior, had worked in West Germany, where he had acquired practical knowledge of market economies. Eventually, a positive personal chemistry developed between the two men. Having returned to the Urals, Tetyukhin invited Brecht to work for him, and the latter soon became Tetyukhin's main adviser and later his business partner. Their discussions over the problems facing VSMPO convinced them that the only salvation for VSMPO was to be found in turning to Western markets. The enterprise began redeveloping. Efforts were made to obtain Western certificates of quality and to adjust the quality of their titanium alloys to the requirements of Western consumers.

Low energy prices in Russia and the low wages of its employees allowed VSMPO to actively engage in dumping practices, charging 15 to 20 percent below the prices offered by competitors. Export volume was gradually increasing. Soon, U.S. and European consumers were convinced of the quality of Russian titanium. In 1998, Boeing, followed by Airbus, Embraer, and other companies, signed direct contracts with VSMPO.

VSMPO had no debts, and so it weathered the 1998 Russian financial crisis without serious difficulty. The devaluation of the ruble made routine export supplies even more profitable. Moreover, before the financial crisis erupted, VSMPO had managed to solve a strategic issue: the company absorbed its main supplier, AVISMA, a producer of titanium sponge. Ironically, Mikhail Khodorkovsky's Menatep group was AVISMA's controlling shareholder at the time. The group was not interested in a long-term partnership with VSMPO, preferring to export its product. Brecht convinced three Western investment funds to purchase 60 percent of AVISMA's shares and later to exchange them for 17 percent of VSMPO's shares. Tetyukhin considered this deal strange: VSMPO obtained control over its supplier without paying a cent. The operating process, the volumes, and the quality of the manufactured metal products—this is what a typical Soviet manager considered important. Shares and corporate relationships were an unknown territory. Partners gradually began buying out shares of the company that owned a controlling stake in VSMPO from the enterprise's employees. However, they were soon joined by others. The enterprise had regained its footing and had successfully promoted its product in Western markets, attracting the attention of Russian oligarch Viktor Vekselberg, whose investment interests were concentrated in the Urals region.

One might think that, faced with a hostile takeover, the partnership between VSMPO's two top managers would grow even stronger, but instead the two men fell out. The reason behind the split was not obvious,[59] but Vekselberg cleverly exploited the opportunity to drive the wedge between Tetyukhin and Brecht even deeper, intensifying their mutual suspicions. As a result, with a mere 14 percent stake in VSMPO, he persuaded both managers, who owned more than 60 percent of the enterprise's shares, to play "Russian roulette" with him to settle the question of who would secure a controlling interest in the company. (In the 1990s, "Russian roulette" was a common way to solve corporate conflicts between major shareholders in situations in which none of them owned a controlling stake: If disputes could not be solved by negotiations, any party to the agreement could propose to buy out an opponent's shares for a posted price. The opponent could in turn agree to sell the shares or offer to buy out the shares belonging to the first partner for the same price.) In early April 2004, the three partners agreed to place their shares in a trust, promising not to increase their stakes and agreeing that any one of them could set in motion the Russian roulette maneuver, but not for at least a year. By that time, the relationship between Tetyukhin and Brecht had become so strained that their partnership had virtually ceased to exist, and the latter insisted on participating in the Russian roulette scheme separately without being bound by mutual obligations.

Vekselberg's hopes were motivated by the fact that neither Tetyukhin nor Brecht owned large wealth, and the trust agreement banned them from pledging the company's shares to obtain loans to buy up stock. Aware of that fact themselves, Tetyukhin and Brecht played another game and made colossal efforts to increase the company's capitalization: they simplified VSMPO's corporate structure and made announcements regarding new alloys and the signing of long-term contracts with major foreign customers. Managers began to discuss a potential IPO, with bankers meeting with potential investors. The price of VSMPO's shares soared from U.S. $35 per share at the moment the Russian roulette agreement was signed to more than U.S. $100 per share a year later. As a result, the value of the stake owned by Tetyukhin and Brecht exceeded U.S. $1 billion, which seemed to be a good defense against a hostile takeover.

However, in January 2005, the "market strategy" of their defense widened the rift between the two managers. During a meeting of the board of directors, Tetyukhin and Brecht had a serious clash while discussing the financial plan and budget for the following year. Although VSMPO's production schedule provided for a 40 percent increase in sales, Tetyukhin proposed lowering the financial forecast, canceling the dividend payments, and allocating the additional resources to research projects and investments. Brecht strongly criticized Tetyukhin's plan, doubting the economic feasibility of the investments, and insisted on the dividend payments that had been announced six months earlier. Tetyukhin received unexpected support from Vekselberg's representatives on the board of directors since Vekselberg saw the company's capitalization as disadvantageous to him because he was already preparing to buy out the managers' shares. Two independent members of the board sided with Brecht, which tipped the scales in the latter's favor. After a discussion lasting several hours, the board of directors supported Brecht.

In response, Tetyukhin made an unexpected announcement: he was thinking about giving away control of the company to the government and contemplating how it might be done. "This could be the 'golden share' mechanism [the right to cast the decisive vote while making critical decisions] or some other [mechanism], since we work with sectors that are strategically important to the state—space, aviation, submarine force," he said.[60] Nobody supported this idea, but Tetyukhin began sending letters to the Kremlin warning of a "takeover of a strategically important enterprise" by the oligarch Vekselberg, which would compromise the country's defense capacity. Initially, the state seemed to ignore these letters; however, as the saying goes, all would be revealed in good time.

An increase in VSMPO's capitalization encouraged Vekselberg to resolve the situation quickly; though his assets allowed him to attract considerable loans, at the time even he could not raise an amount exceeding U.S. $1 billion. In late April 2005, exactly one year after the agreement had been signed, Vekselberg launched the Russian roulette option—and lost.[61] Investor appetites for VSMPO had grown considerably, and the company had no difficulty finding friendly investors.[62] Renaissance Capital bank, which brought together a pool of investors and arranged a deal to buy out Vekselberg's shares, partnered with Tetyukhin and Brecht.[63] One might think that this was a happy ending for everybody. Tetyukhin and Brecht would maintain control over the company while at the same time acquiring friendly investors and thwarting Vekselberg, who had been planning a hostile takeover. And though his initial plan had failed, Vekselberg stood to make a 300 percent profit on the deal. However, the situation began to develop in unexpected ways.

Tetyukhin sent another letter to President Putin offering the golden share option to the state, as well as a seat on the board of directors for a state representative. The Russian parliament's official newspaper published a large article on VSMPO's plans to hold an IPO in Western stock markets that contained—on the face of it—some paranoid statements that nevertheless were seriously considered by attentive readers from the presidential administration. The article warned that "Russian titanium is sailing abroad," that "Western shareholders knew essentially everything about Russian titanium: how much of it the country was producing, who was buying this strategic metal, and at what price," and that "some New York–based speculative trader might appear as early as tomorrow and, as an owner of a blocking stake in the holding, might oppose the supplying of titanium to the Russian aircraft industry and might instead suggest selling it under contract with NATO. Incredible? Not a bit."[64]

Vekselberg refused to accept defeat, and waged a corporate war with the help of administrative resources. He accused Brecht and Tetyukhin of breaching the trust agreement; filed claims in Russian, British, and U.S. courts; and obtained a Regional Arbitration Court ruling ordering the sei-

zure of 73.4 percent of VSMPO's shares that had been involved in the Russian roulette scheme. This put in doubt the ability of the two partners to
maintain control over the company because the court banned them from
using the seized shares to vote during shareholders meetings. This meant
that the remaining 26 percent of shareholders could replace VSMPO's board
of directors and management. Tetyukhin once again wrote to the Kremlin
asking for state support—and received it.

On September 23, 2005, Prime Minister Mikhail Fradkov unexpectedly
appeared in the city of Berezniki, where AVISMA was located, and held a
closed meeting on the supply of titanium to domestic markets. "We have to
meet the needs of the developing high-tech manufacturing," he said during
a press conference. "Domestic titanium and magnesium consumption has to
increase." He also praised the company's managers for succeeding in "maintaining production." But the real reason behind Fradkov's visit was entirely
different. During a meeting with Tetyukhin and Brecht, he told them that
President Putin had made a decision: their stake in VSMPO should be sold
"at market price," and it was being decided which entity would be the one
to proceed with the purchase. According to Fradkov, this would likely be
some state-owned bank. Tetyukhin tried to object, saying that nationalization might jeopardize the company's contract with Boeing. Fradkov responded in a rather frank way: "The decision has been made, and we are not
going to discuss it. We do not care what Boeing will do." Fradkov added that
the Kremlin was not planning to replace the management and was asking
Tetyukhin and Brecht to remain in their posts. That calmed Tetyukhin, who
believed he would be able to retain real control over the company.

Tetyukhin and Brecht patiently waited for their fate to be decided.[65] One
month after Fradkov's visit, Brecht was invited to Moscow, where he met
with Rosoboronexport CEO Sergey Chemezov. Chemezov told Brecht that
the purchase of shares was "entrusted to him," and that the "decision had
been made at the highest level and had to be carried out." At the same time,
the state launched a bearish operation, trying to lower the price of VSMPO's
shares to a minimum to reduce the buyout cost. In mid-October 2005, the
state suspended trading of the company's shares on the stock exchange.
In November 2005, a team from the prosecutor general's office arrived on
VSMPO's premises and, backed up by heavily armed police, raided the com-

pany's administrative building. This action was followed by tax claims exceeding 2.6 billion rubles (approximately U.S. $85 million at contemporary exchange rates).[66]

The talks with Rosoboronexport proceeded without much enthusiasm, and were held separately with each shareholder. Renaissance Capital CEO Stephen Jennings, a New Zealand citizen, was made aware that VSMPO's shares belonging to his bank would be bought out at a market price, and that foreign investors participating in the consortium had nothing to worry about. Jennings expressed his gratitude and wisely kept quiet about his tag-along/drag-along agreement with Brecht. (Tag-along/drag-along is a type of agreement between shareholders in which they agree to provide each other co-sale rights; that is, if one of them receives an offer to sell his shares, he transfers this offer on a pro rata basis to the other.) Brecht was told that funds for the purchase of shares were limited, that Rosoboronexport only had U.S. $700 million, and that he should "show understanding" and agree to sell his shares at a considerable discount. Tetyukhin likewise was told not to worry, that the government would "make it worth his while," and that—most important—he would remain at the head of the company.[67]

On February 27, 2006, Brecht was asked to come to the Moscow headquarters of the FSB, where he and Chemezov met with FSB deputy director Aleksandr Bortnikov, the Russian Interior Ministry's Economic Security Department head Sergey Meshcheryakov, and an official from the presidential administration. Chemezov said with a smile, "Well, everyone is here now, so there is no one else left to complain to." Brecht was told that the time had come to transfer his shares to the government, and that this had to be done within two weeks. Brecht did not argue—which came as a surprise to the assembled officials—but immediately complied and offered to organize a meeting with lawyers to draft the necessary agreements.

The next day, Brecht went with his wife and children to Germany and categorically refused to return to Moscow. He declared that all negotiations regarding VSMPO would be held in either Israel or Germany. In mid-March, Rosoboronexport representatives arrived in Frankfurt to discuss the terms and conditions of the deal. They insisted that the shares be transferred virtually free of charge. The negotiations continued in a nervous atmosphere and were riddled with mutual threats; finally, exhausted, Brecht informed his opponents of his agreement with Renaissance Capital, to which he delegated the right to discuss the deal in further detail. Renaissance Capital immediately came under pressure, as authorities conducted searches at the bank's offices. But this did not help, and Rosoboronexport agreed to buy out the shares at market price. Attempting to protect himself, Brecht forced the VSMPO board of directors, Rosoboronexport, and Viktor Vekselberg to sign a special agreement freeing him from any potential claims for any actions performed during his work at the company. On September 1, 2006, the sale of VSMPO's shares was closed.

Tetyukhin did not show a similar tenacity. Saying that "human life is transient, while the state is eternal,"[68] and that he "believed that this would benefit the corporation,"[69] he agreed to sell his shares to Rosoboronexport for about a quarter of their value, securing his post as the company's CEO in the agreement. Two years later, VSMPO's board of directors broke the contract with him.

In April 2012, the state-owned conglomerate Rostec (which was created on the basis of Rosoboronexport and absorbed it) signed a deal that might appear strange to outsiders who do not understand the subtler aspects of Russian crony capitalism. Rostec sold 45.4 percent of VSMPO's shares (keeping a mere 25 percent stake) to a group of its own mid-rank managers, even though Chemezov had declared only a few months before that Rostec did not intend to part with VSMPO's shares. By that time, VSMPO had long-term contracts with the world's key aircraft producers. Boeing received more than a third of its titanium from VSMPO, Airbus received about 60 percent, and Embraer acquired all of its titanium from the company. These contracts are bringing in a fair profit to the company's shareholders to this day.

Brecht tried to obtain guarantees of personal safety from Rosoboronexport, but Chemezov, offended by Brecht's obstinacy during the negotiations, refused to have anything to do with him. Without these guarantees, Brecht has not been to Russia since 2006, in keeping with a well-known Russian proverb: "Here is no fence against ill fortune."

Having lost his post as the enterprise's director, Tetyukhin moved to a new project. He poured all his money from the VSMPO stock sale into a unique medical center in Nizhny Tagil, a large city not far from Verkhnyaya Salda.

WE ARE JUST RETURNING WHAT HAS BEEN PRIVATIZED

The Soviet economy was not consumer-oriented. Its main objective was to maintain and increase the country's military potential in the confrontation with the United States. Soviet citizens were used to shortages: there was not enough of anything, from meat and clothes to housing and furniture. In 1990 the population of the Soviet Union reached 290 million people, while that of the United States was 250 million. Meanwhile, from 1985 to 1990 the Soviet Union produced between 1.2 and 1.3 million passenger cars annually, while the United States annually produced 6 to 8 million passenger cars, or six times more per capita.

VAZ, designed and built by Fiat in Togliatti on the Volga River in the second half of the 1960s, produced half of all passenger cars in the Soviet Union. This plant was not only designed by the Italian company; the passenger car it manufactured was a clone of the Fiat 124, which was why its quality was considerably higher than that of other Soviet cars. Given the constant shortages, Soviet consumers were prepared to buy any car, but those manufactured in Togliatti were especially highly prized. Thus it was no surprise that, when CEOs of state companies were granted more freedom in the late 1980s, the CEO of VAZ found himself in possession of the proverbial goose that laid the golden eggs. His cars were being bought by everyone and were accepted without restriction in the barter schemes that were commonly used at the time. It is also no surprise that VAZ attracted the attention of numerous opportunistic businessmen who aspired to make money by reselling the cars.

Vladimir Kadannikov, who had been working with the plant since its opening, became the CEO of VAZ at the end of 1988. One of the businessmen with whom he built a relationship based on trust and partnership was Boris Berezovsky.[70] Kadannikov was a typical "red director" who was concerned about industrial matters and had a poor understanding of the workings of a market economy. Berezovsky, by contrast, was interested in profits, and all his business schemes were directed at maximizing revenue from car sales, even if doing so hurt the company. When VAZ was converted into a publicly listed company at the beginning of 1993, Berezovsky implemented a "looped" property control scheme: more than 60 percent of VAZ's shares belonged to its affiliated companies, and Kadannikov, as the company's CEO, used these shares to vote during shareholder meetings. This scheme satisfied the interests of both partners, allowing Kadannikov to keep his post as CEO and Berezovsky to make profits.

VAZ was one of Russia's largest enterprises, employing more than 120,000 people.[71] Several thousand enterprises scattered throughout the country also supplied the company with parts. According to some estimates, more than a million people worked in VAZ and companies connected with it. Automotive manufacturing is a complicated process that only people who have worked in this sector for many years can really understand. The transition to a market economy had rendered obsolete the system of industrial cooperation inherited from Soviet times. Kadannikov, however, was a man whose effort and experience allowed him to keep VAZ running even in the face of supply interruptions that could have seen the whole enterprise grind to a halt. Berezovsky, for his part, was the kind of person who got carried away easily, and for him the automobile giant was nothing but a cash cow. Berezovsky's interests soon switched to major-league politics, and he left the situation in VAZ largely unattended. Numerous criminal groups took advantage of the lack of oversight by establishing control over car sales, thus becoming a third partner in a very strange union.[72]

VAZ became riddled with debt. Its arrears in payments to suppliers and tax authorities were a matter of public discussion. Kadannikov, being incompetent in financial issues, could not restore order; Berezovsky and the criminal groups, for their part, were not interested in restoring order; and the government had no intention of getting involved. For a few months in 1996, Kadannikov was deputy prime minister, and used this position to protect the company against claims from the tax authorities. At the end of the same year, he returned to VAZ, and the government succeeded in forcing him to negotiate with the Korean company Daewoo to become controlling shareholder,[73] sign an agreement to pay off tax debts, and obtain VAZ's controlling block of shares as collateral. Nevertheless, none of these measures were enough to improve the automotive giant's financial position. Moreover, Russians' growing incomes and liberalization of passenger car import regulations meant that consumer preferences were shifting away from Russian cars. In the spring of 1998, VAZ's production was cut in half. With its warehouses filled with unsold cars, the factory was on the brink of shutting down.

Help came from an unexpected source. The August 1998 financial crisis led to a threefold devaluation of the Russian ruble, which immediately improved the competitiveness of VAZ cars compared to imported ones. The backlog of cars quickly sold out, and in November 1998 the enterprise was already back to working at full capacity. Influence from the ruble devaluation lasted for several years. VAZ stayed afloat even though it repeatedly sought government support to finance its investment program.

Boris Berezovsky's loss of influence in the Kremlin and his departure from Russia in 2000 deprived Kadannikov of his political support. Consequently, Kadannikov's control over VAZ was no longer seen as absolute. In 2000, the investment company Aton began buying out VAZ's shares on the market, thus increasing its stake to 4 percent. In 2005, Aton discerned that the state-owned bank VEB was also buying up VAZ shares. Assuming that "some state program existed with regard to VAZ," Aton decided to sell its shares to VEB, which ended up with nearly 9 percent of VAZ's shares.

However, as often happens, if one investment banker thinks of something, another one will think of it as well. Ruben Vardanyan, the founder and head of the Troika Dialog investment bank, was that other banker. But Vardanyan decided to work with the state instead of competing against it. He succeeded in convincing Rosoboronexport CEO Sergey Chemezov (whom we have already met twice in previous episodes) that VAZ was a diamond in the rough among Russian industrial firms. The automotive giant's sales volume was about U.S. $5.5 billion a year. It ranked first among all non-resource-based companies, and its poor financials could be explained by its managers' lack of skills and the fact that the company did not control the distribution of its own products.[74]

The offer Vardanyan made to Chemezov was simple: Troika Dialog would implement a scheme to destroy the looped ownership, as a result of which Troika Dialog and Rosoboronexport would each receive 25 percent of shares, and an additional 25 percent of shares initially would be transferred to Troika Dialog, to be later sold to other investors (or a strategic partner, or else would be publicly traded). Meanwhile, Rosoboronexport would obtain shares at no cost. The only thing Chemezov had to do was to arrange a telephone call to Vladimir Kadannikov from the Kremlin suggesting that, before resigning from his post, he vote for a slate of directors that would give representatives of Rosoboronexport and the state-owned VTB bank a majority on the board. This would allow the partners to appoint their representative as the company's CEO, thus establishing control over VAZ shares belonging to the affiliated companies.[75]

It would be unfair to accuse an investment banker, even if he promoted himself as a supporter of liberal reforms, of agreeing to sign a contract with Mephistopheles to make money—no matter how much was involved. Vardanyan's partner from Troika, Sergey Skvortsov, who currently works for Chemezov in Rostec (formerly known as Rostekhnologii, the state corporation built on the basis of Rosoboronexport), cynically described the essence of this deal. "We were just returning what had been privatized."[76]

Needless to say, the state-owned company accepted this tempting offer to put a major asset under its control. It did not really understand what to do with this prize, but the acquisition added tens, if not hundreds, of millions of dollars to its revenue. In the fall of 2005, Kadannikov was invited to the Kremlin, where he was openly asked to resign as head of the company. Kadannikov agreed without argument.[77] In December 2005, a general assault force of 200 high-ranking Interior Ministry officers forced out VAZ security personnel and blocked access to the company. There were no surprises during the shareholders meeting; Chemezov's corporation acquired control.

Immediately after that, Rosoboronexport informed the SOK Group—a Russian holding company that was VAZ's longtime partner and the largest single components supplier—of its wish to break previously signed agreements on components supplies without paying penalties. To make this offer one that the SOK leadership couldn't refuse, officials from the prosecutor general's office, the Interior Ministry, and the FSB searched SOK's offices and confiscated documents in connection with two criminal cases that had been opened the day before. The state also demanded that the SOK Group sell its enterprises that manufactured parts for VAZ. Although the SOK Group accepted all these demands, there were no big changes in the newly acquired VAZ. This was not a surprise, since neither Troika nor Rosoboronexport nor the government had a comprehensive plan for VAZ's development. VAZ saw three CEOs in quick succession over the next three years, further complicating the situation because none of them remained at the top long enough to draft a corporate plan. In the summer of 2007, Chemezov declared that the Russian steel producer Severstal could become VAZ's strategic investor.[78] In September of the same year, the new CEO of VAZ, Boris Aleshin, mentioned the necessity of a technological partnership with GAZ, a Russian manufacturer of light commercial vehicles, and KAMAZ, a truck manufacturer.[79] VAZ's relatively stable position was secured only by its continuing sales growth.

Meanwhile, the second—and the main—part of the investment bankers' plan was being implemented. It took Troika two and a half more years to destroy the looped ownership scheme. Despite rumors and expectations, bankers did not buy up VAZ's shares from companies affiliated with it—which could have cost them around U.S. $700–$800 million—but instead followed a cheaper path. They chose to buy up shares in affiliated companies from minority shareholders, who were only too happy to part with such an apparently unprofitable corporate structure. Estimates suggest that this transaction could have cost Troika U.S. $300–$350 million, plus no more than U.S. $150 million paid to VEB for its stake. As a result, by early 2008 Troika (along with Sergey Chemezov's close friend, the businessman Vitaly Mashchitsky) owned 50 percent of VAZ's shares, and Rosoboroncxport had 25 percent.[80] In February 2008, Troika and Mashchitsky sold 25 percent of VAZ's shares to the French company Renault for 1.3 billion euros.[81]

The 2008 crisis fatally undermined VAZ's stability. Car sales in Russia plummeted. VAZ could not sell the cars it was manufacturing, and the company immediately plunged into the red, declaring losses of U.S. $1,000 per produced car in 2008. In 2009, the devaluation of the ruble was followed by a sharp growth in imported parts prices, as well as in depreciation of imported equipment; consequently, the losses per each manufactured car increased fivefold. The enterprise went virtually bankrupt. Seeing no way to save it, many members of the Russian government were prepared to accept its collapse. However, following Prime Minister Putin's personal decision to allocate U.S. $2.5 billion from the national fiscal reserves to save VAZ, the company undertook a turnaround program similar to the one used by General Motors, while control over the company was given to Renault. The French group first obtained comprehensive management control, and then received shareholder control over VAZ in 2013 when it purchased the residual 20 percent stake from Troika and Mashchitsky. However, Rostec still owns a 25 percent stake in VAZ—and probably dreams of the day when it can sell this stake to Renault as well.

ABIDING BY THE LAW

"In this world, nothing can be said to be certain, except death and taxes"— this famous phrase was written by Benjamin Franklin in 1789. However, this rule did not always work in Russia in the 1990s and the early 2000s. Many small and medium-sized businesses operated in a gray zone, engaging in legal activities but settling accounts with cash in vaults or via offshore companies. The tax authorities were weak,[82] and their employees were not skilled enough to deal with these smaller cases; they concentrated their efforts on large companies, and their approach to small and medium-sized businesses often was built on a basis of "mutually beneficial" corruption. Companies would agree to make minimal payments to the state while paying some additional amounts to tax and law enforcement officials and sometimes even to thugs; in return, the latter groups guaranteed business owners a peaceful existence without the threat of tax inspections and claims. This corruption scheme was even more widely used to clear imported cargo at the customs offices. By vaguely outlining commodity groups and by establishing broad ranges of customs fees, the law provided customs officers with ample authority to calculate customs duties. To make the system even less transparent, customs authorities adopted specific regulations on clearing imported goods that demanded that importers use services provided by intermediaries; only those intermediaries who agreed to participate in corruption schemes were able to quickly clear cargo. Under such conditions, small and medium-sized businesses were doomed to complicity. Compared with official amounts, the use of corruption schemes to clear imports considerably reduced the amount of paid fees, even including the bribes paid to customs and law enforcement officials. As a result, those business owners who paid all taxes and official charges were at a disadvantage since their expenses were considerably higher. Those who refused to use services provided by customs intermediaries involved in corruption schemes faced clearance procedures that could take weeks or months, which undermined business activity.

When mobile phone service began developing in Russia in the late 1990s, recently emerged private providers paid special attention to establishing networks and searching for clients—but not to selling cell phones, a market segment that was filled by stand-alone companies. Evroset, which conducted a brazenly aggressive advertising campaign, was one such company; its cofounder and front-line player was Yevgeny Chichvarkin. Evroset was rapidly expanding its retail stores across the country. From 2000 to 2006, its annual growth rate exceeded 100 percent, and it was no surprise that by 2003–04 Evroset had become a market leader. And yet Evroset, like all other retailers, used corruption schemes to clear imported goods.

The Russian economy was growing fast and more Russians had become familiar with wireless communications, and as a result more cell phones were being imported. The scale of corruption proceeds attracted attention from opposite sides.[83] Some *siloviki* did not mind establishing control over these "revenues," but once in a while the Russian authorities went after the gray economy and illegal customs clearance schemes. Sometimes these two processes became intermingled in a most fantastic way.

Naturally, *siloviki* knew about the illegal schemes used to import cell phones into Russia, and from time to time they confiscated shipments of imported cell phones under the pretense of fighting violations of the law. Soon, however, the confiscated cell phones appeared on store shelves, for the law allowed police officers to release material evidence (cell phones) without a court decision and to sell it through specially organized auctions. Needless to say, only companies with a special relationship with law enforcement authorities were allowed to participate in these auctions. At the auction, the seized equipment was sold to these companies for 5 to 10 percent of the actual price, after which buyers resold these same cell phones for 25 to 30 percent of the actual price to the companies from which these cell phones had been seized at customs.[84] Since this scheme ran smoothly, law enforcement agencies began to fight among themselves to control this source of revenue.

In the spring of 2005, a man who introduced himself as a representative of the Interior Ministry's "K" division came to the customs office in Moscow's Sheremetyevo Airport, through which about a third of all the imported cell phones were passing. The K division was officially responsible for solving cybercrimes and setting up wiretapping. Unexpectedly for market players, this was the division that began actively and ostentatiously fighting against contraband household appliances, including cell phones. News reports about police raids regularly appeared on television channels and in newspapers. The representative of the K division demanded that customs intermediaries and companies involved in the importation of cell phones pay bribes on a simple scheme: U.S. $1 for each cell phone. One major importer refused to comply with the suggested scheme, which resulted in a full-fledged investigation by the prosecutor general's office, and in the end brought the customs corruption case to court.[85] In August 2005, shipments of imported cell phones (more than 1.2 million) in the total amount of around U.S. $100 million—about half the monthly sales on the Russian market—were seized at customs. At the same time, criminal cases were being initiated against managers of retail companies accused of shipping contraband.

This legal upheaval put the cell phone market on the verge of collapse, and President Putin ordered Economic Minister German Gref to address this problem. Besides being seen as a representative of the liberals in the Russian government, Gref was a close Putin acquaintance of long standing. Seeing him as the president's personal representative, the heads of retail companies agreed to the proposed deal, according to which they were to refuse all intermediaries' services and to honestly pay all the required customs fees and charges. In return, Gref personally guaranteed that their shipments would be cleared in a proper and expeditious manner. "If a shipment is delayed for even a couple of days, call my office immediately," the minister told them in parting.[86]

Evroset was one of the first companies to switch to a "fair" scheme. Although Gref's proposed deal would increase customs fees twofold,[87] retail companies soon realized that they benefited from it. Their business was becoming transparent, and banks were willing to grant cheaper loans, which allowed companies to grow even faster. Revenues became more easily predicted for investors and retail companies began contemplating offering their shares on the market. And, most important, the switch to transparent and fair business practices considerably increased the personal safety and removed risks of criminal prosecution for business owners.

About six months after the meeting with Gref, an incident took place. K division officials seized 167,500 cell phones imported into Russia by Evroset in accordance with a direct contract with the U.S. cell phone manufacturer Motorola. The purchase of these cell phones had been properly documented, all required customs charges had been paid, and the Sheremetyevo customs office had cleared the shipment. All the same, the police officers refused to provide Evroset with documents explaining the reason for confiscating the cell phones. Initially the Interior Ministry published a statement saying that the cell phones had been imported without clearing customs. Later it claimed that these cell phones "were not intended for use on the territory of Russia. The cell phones in this shipment were manufactured in Brazil, China, and Singapore and were intended for domestic use, that is, adapted for specific countries and providers of wireless service that do not meet Russian standards."[88] However, Motorola, which immediately rose up in defense of Evroset and its own reputation, said in an official statement that the "supplied cell phones were intended specifically for Russia" and that they had been delivered to Russia by an aircraft leased by Motorola that had secured insurance coverage for transportation risks. Cumulatively, "this proves the legal origin of the goods."[89] The Interior Ministry withdrew its statement but refused to admit the unlawful character of its actions,[90] and moved the confiscated cell phones to a warehouse. Evroset was worried that the shipment would be destroyed or sold at an auction for a fraction of its price, and launched a highly publicized public campaign against the police officers. It also published a statement with a detailed description of the incident, containing the names of the police officers involved in the confiscation of cell phones.[91]

In late April 2006, the Interior Ministry announced that, according to an analysis that had been conducted, the confiscated cell phones posed health risks. Based on this information, 30 percent of the cell phones (50,000) that had been confiscated from Evroset were crushed, even though no proof had been provided that, as officials claimed, these cell phones exceeded statutory limits of electromagnetic emission by 2.5 times, and no court ruling existed on this matter.[92] Although journalists were invited to witness the destruction of the purportedly dangerous cell phones, soon after the same "crushed" cell phones appeared in small retail stores.

Meanwhile, Evroset continued its fight with the police to have the confiscated goods returned, which was at the time a rather unusual thing for

Russia.[93] Evroset informed the international insurer under contract about the incurred damages, thus making an ally out of it. Evroset proved that the confiscated cell phones had been cleared through customs and that Evroset had nothing to do with cell phones from the confiscated shipment that were being sold in Moscow. Unexpected support came from the U.S. president George W. Bush, who raised this story while talking with Putin on the eve of the G–8 summit in St. Petersburg. An enraged Putin demanded an explanation from German Gref and the Interior Ministry. Having read their report, Putin sided with Evroset and ordered a full-scale investigation. It turned out that the results of the expertise claiming that the cell phones posed a health risk had been forged, and that no cell phones had been crushed. On these grounds, Boris Levin, Evroset's vice president and head of security, proved to the insurance company that the cell phones had been stolen. Evroset received the remaining 117,500 cell phones back from the police and the insurer compensated the company for its losses. Evroset then filed a claim with the prosecutor general's office, and a criminal case was opened against the K division officials. A top-ranking police officer who supervised the confiscation of cell phones in 2005 was accused of stealing them and was sentenced to a prison term.[94] Some of the police officials were ordered to pay a penalty; others were fired. The investigator from the prosecutor general's office who had given the order to crush the cell phones was sentenced in 2010.[95]

One would think it was a fairy tale with a happy ending! Many thought so, except for the police officers, who saw Evroset and Boris Levin personally as their worst enemies. The business owners found themselves subject to persecution, the only motive for which was vengeance for their wish to abide by the law.[96]

"I can account for every million I earned except for the first one," John Rockefeller said. Many Russian business owners would stand by these words; most have skeletons in the closet from the early days of their businesses, and the Russian state was so weak that it could not guarantee the protection of rights and the law even if it wanted to. Evroset had such a "skeleton" that dated back to 2003. At the time, when "gray" schemes were being used to import cell phones into Russia, retail companies had special employees, called "expediters," who were responsible for transporting goods out of warehouses after receiving customs clearance. One such expediter, Andrei

Vlaskin, stole U.S. $1 million worth of Evroset's cell phones. When Evroset's internal audit service discovered this theft, the company sought police assistance. A few months later the police located Vlaskin and arrested him. After questioning, he was officially released under pledge not to leave town, but was in fact handed over to Boris Levin, the head of Evroset's security. Vlaskin was handcuffed and subjected to physical coercive measures. Later, he promised to return the stolen goods, but managed to escape. Evroset made a statement to the police, and soon Vlaskin was located for the second time. This time, Vlaskin was made to cede the title of his house (then under construction) and several cars, all bought with the money from the sale of the stolen cell phones, to the name of an Evroset employee. The total value of the "compensation" covered more than half of the damages incurred by the company. Evroset withdrew its claim against the expediter, and the criminal case against Vlaskin was closed. "We had agreed then that he would return the stolen goods, and we would not initiate criminal prosecution, and both parties had been fulfilling these conditions until five years later Interior Ministry officials made Vlaskin file a police report against us," Boris Levin said later.[97]

This case reemerged in the fall of 2008, two years after the Motorola case, when the prosecutor general's office launched a criminal investigation of policemen who confiscated cell phones. By that time, Evroset had grown into a huge company, with annual revenues amounting to U.S. $5 billion. However, the company was riddled with debt; fast development required substantial financial resources, and the business was marginally profitable. In 2007, Evroset shareholders took notice of the mortgage crisis that had begun in the United States and decided to sell part of their shares. However, having received an offer to sell a 10 percent stake in their company to investment funds, they believed that the company was undervalued, and entered into negotiations with MTS, one of Russia's largest wireless providers, to sell the entire company. In June 2008, the parties agreed to the major terms of the deal, and MTS took a three-month break before making the final decision.

In early September 2008, a search of Evroset's offices found documents pertaining to the Vlaskin case in Boris Levin's office. Levin and his deputy were accused of "kidnapping, extortion, and vigilantism" and detained. On September 4, Moscow's Basmanny District Court authorized their arrest.

On September 8, Evroset's co-owner, Yevgeny Chichvarkin, was questioned in the context of this case. On September 27, another of Boris Levin's deputies was detained in the Domodedovo airport while trying to leave for the United Arab Emirates and was placed under arrest by a court order.

Meanwhile, MTS also realized the inevitability of a financial crisis and demanded that the price for Evroset be lowered considerably. Realizing that it would be extremely hard to maintain normal activity of a company under attack from *siloviki*, Chichvarkin and his partner decided to sell the company to Aleksandr Mamut,[98] who represented VimpelCom, Russia's second-largest wireless service provider, in the consortium. The expedited negotiations and the signing of all the documents took one day, right after the MTS exclusivity period expired. According to experts, the company was sold for a price that was 15 to 20 percent below its value.[99]

Meanwhile, the questioning of Chichvarkin and his partner continued. The arrested Evroset employees were forced to testify against Chichvarkin, whose status was soon changed from that of a witness to that of an accused. In mid-December, during an interrogation, he learned about the upcoming arrest. In late December 2008, Chichvarkin escaped from surveillance and left for London, where a few days later he was joined by his partner.[100] On January 28, 2009, Moscow's Basmanny District Court ruled in support of the claim of the prosecutor general's office to issue an arrest order for Chichvarkin in absentia.[101] Russian investigators followed Chichvarkin to London. In March 2009, he was placed on Interpol's international wanted list. In September, Britain's Supreme Court began considering his extradition case, which lasted for eighteen months.

Boris Levin and other Evroset employees remained under arrest until December 2010, when—unexpectedly for the police—a jury trial found them not guilty and released them from custody. In January 2011, when Russia's Supreme Court was considering the prosecutor general's appeal to review the jury trial's ruling, a representative of the prosecutor general's office withdrew the claim, and the Supreme Court confirmed the jury trial's decision. Two days later, investigators closed the criminal case against Chichvarkin,[102] and the arrest warrant issued by Interpol was annulled. In March 2011 the London court ceased consideration of the extradition case.[103] Yet Chichvarkin is still afraid to go back to Russia. "I would love to return to Russia because this is my motherland, but I fear persecution and I have reasons to believe that I would be persecuted since I am the designated guilty party," he said.[104]

General Boris Miroshnikov, the head of the Interior Ministry's K division, remained in his post until the end of January 2011, when he reached retirement age and was dismissed by President Medvedev.[105]

NO WAY BUT TO SELL

The emergence and growth of mobile communication in Russia aptly illustrated that the country went the way of the market economy. Although Russia had its first cell phone users as early as 1991, this service was accessible to only a limited number of people up until the early 2000s. At the end of 2000, there were only 2.2 SIM cards per 100 Russians. This figure is not surprising; the first cell phones were cumbersome and the service rates were out of ordinary people's reach. One domestic cell phone minute cost between 20 and 30 cents, at a time when the average Russian earned the equivalent of less than U.S. $100 per month.[106]

Many people believed that mobile service had no future in Russia, and that it made no sense to invest in it—or so the state-owned regional communication companies felt. These companies relied on the antiquated Soviet-era landline system, which needed major investments in maintenance and development. However, the rates in the sector were government-regulated, at an amount that did not allow for investment, and so it stood to reason that Russia's private businesses were not particularly eager to enter this sector. For its part, the state did not want to privatize these communication companies; with the exception of Moscow and St. Petersburg, the government had a controlling stake in the regional operators. In this context, private companies were attracted to new business opportunities, such as fiber optics, mobile communications, or the internet. There were no price controls there, and even though the risks were high, these sectors had plentiful profit and growth opportunities. By the early 2000s, Russia had two federal mobile phone operators, MTS and VimpelCom, and a host of regional and interregional operators. In 2002, the third-largest player, MegaFon, emerged following a consolidation of regional players.

Rapid economic growth in the aftermath of the 1998 crisis translated into rapid personal income growth. The average Russian's salary had increased by 25 to 30 percent annually between 2001 and 2005. The oil price increases dating back to mid-2002 had brought a flow of cash into the country. The ruble grew stronger: by the end of 2005, it had returned to its early 2000s levels and continued to grow, so that by mid-2008 it was 25 percent higher than it had been at the end of 2003. As a result, the average monthly salary in Russia approached U.S. $300 by 2003, a figure that doubled by mid-2008. The prices of mobile communication devices had dropped by more than half during that same period, and for the first time the average Russian could afford the technology. The number of cell phone users skyrocketed: by the end of 2005, there were 86 SIM cards per 100 Russians, and in the next year there were more than 100.[107]

Such a surge in standard of living and in the number of cell phone users generated enormous growth among mobile operators, whose capitalization dramatically exceeded that of the landline companies. The state-controlled Svyazinvest had tried unsuccessfully to enter this segment of the market. Even thought Svyazinvest was licensed to work in every region of Russia, its service was sluggish and uncompetitive, so it did not attract many consumers. Besides, its licenses and operating territory were limited by the borders of administrative regions,[108] and the simultaneous growth of several communication standards prevented the company from providing consumers with quality service all over the country.

In 2001, the Swedish telecommunications company Tele2 entered the Russian market. It first came to St. Petersburg, where it had license to operate, but soon expanded to other predominantly European Russian regions. Unlike the "Big Three" companies, whose major stakeholders were Russian, Tele2 was a 100 percent subsidiary of a Swedish holding company. This fact actually proved to be an insurmountable obstacle for the company: the Russian authorities thwarted its growth by all possible means, even though its rates were the lowest in the business. In the regions where it operated, Tele2 had more customers than the powerful federal competitors that had been operating in those areas much earlier.[109]

Tele2 had only 2G-standard licenses, so it could offer its customers voice calls and text messages but not mobile internet services. The company unsuccessfully tried to secure advanced-standard licenses by participating in auctions. Its attempts to lobby for technological neutrality—that is, providing more advanced standards while remaining in assigned frequencies—also failed, although other companies were able to receive such permits. For instance, the three biggest national mobile operators and Sky Link, which belonged to the state-owned Rostelecom, received permission to use frequencies previously assigned to 2G standards in Moscow and surrounding regions for building 3G-standard networks, while similar requests by Tele2 were denied by the government.[110] Tele2 also was effectively prohibited from entering the Moscow market and other lucrative regions. For instance, in March 2011, a week before the bidding results for the Primorsky region license were to be announced, the authorities changed the bidding rules, as it became clear that Tele2 would emerge as the winner.[111]

By the end of 2012, the Swedish parent company realized that its Russian subsidiary had no further room for growth. It had exhausted its potential in the 2G standard, failed to obtain licenses for 3G and 4G standards, and could not increase its customer base by expanding to other regions. It was clear that the lack of growth would lead to lost market share because consumers would look for a wider service spectrum. The parent company had no other option but to sell the Russian company, although almost half of its customers and over a third of its EBITDA came from Russia.

In late January 2013, Tele2 AB president Mats Granryd met Russian communication minister Nikolai Nikiforov in a last attempt to break down the barriers holding the company back. He believed that he could achieve the desired result, and he even appointed a new CEO for Tele2 Russia a week after.[112] But it soon became clear that the Kremlin not only intended to force an international investor out of a lucrative field but also had decided that the state should become Tele2's new owner. Granryd would shortly learn the name of the buyer—the state-owned VTB bank, which purchased Tele2 Russia for $3.55 billion. Tele2 AB was forced to reject more lucrative offers from competitors: Alfa Group was willing to pay $3.6–$4 billion,[113] and MTS and VimpelCom were offering even more: $4–$4.25 billion.[114]

The Swedish investor exited the stage at this point, but the Tele2 saga continued. As is often the case in Russia, Putin's cronies did not want to miss their chance. Six months later, VTB sold 50 percent of Tele2 Russia to

Putin's friend Yury Kovalchuk in partnership with Alexey Mordashov, Russia's second-wealthiest business owner.[115] Suddenly, Tele2's key problem—receiving licenses for more advanced communication standards—was resolved easily in a matter of weeks. Immediately after VTB bank CEO Kostin asked Putin to introduce the principle of technological neutrality in Russia, the president signed an unequivocal resolution directing the State Commission for Radio Frequencies to "review and support" the banker's proposal. In a matter of days, at its first meeting after the president's resolution was signed, the commission decided to introduce the principle of technological neutrality throughout the whole country.

But the alliance of the state-owned bank and one of Putin's cronies did not stop there. They were then drawn to the assets of Rostelecom, a state company that had licenses for communication services in seventy-one Russian regions.[116] (Tele2, by contrast, had had just forty-one licenses by that time.) In early February 2014, state assets were implicitly privatized—Tele2 and Rostelecom signed an agreement creating a joint venture to which the state holding contributed all its licenses and mobile communications companies in exchange for 45 percent of shares in the new venture. Fifty-five percent of shares remained in the hands of VTB bank and Putin's crony.[117]

Tele2 finally received a license to operate in the Moscow region, along with a low-interest loan issued by the government under the Investment Project Support Program, which would assist the company in building infrastructure in the Moscow region.[118] Government officials justified Tele2's entry into the Moscow market by the need to stimulate competition and develop communication and to remove infrastructure limitations, though competition in Moscow's mobile communications market had already been quite stiff and mobile operators, as well as their customers, had no issues with infrastructure limitations.[119]

WALKING A TIGHTROPE

Moscow is the capital of Russia and the country's largest city. It is no surprise, then, that Moscow is Russia's largest air hub. In Soviet times, Moscow was served by four airports, each of which had a geographic specialization. Two of Moscow's airports, Vnukovo and Bykovo, were in operation even before World War II, and the other two, Sheremetyevo and Domodedovo, were built in the late 1950s and early 1960s. The stories of the creation of the latter two are completely different. The first one was the result of an arbitrary decision by one man, while the second emerged as a focused effort in the context of the centrally planned economy.

Sheremetyevo was established in 1953 as the main airfield of the Soviet Air Force. In 1959, a plane returning from London with Soviet leader Nikita Khrushchev on board landed there. During his visit to the British capital, the Soviet leader was so impressed by Heathrow Airport that, as he exited his plane on the return home and contemplated the huge empty lot around him, Khrushchev said: "It's time we built such an airport [like Heathrow]." Only three weeks later, Sheremetyevo airport was turned over to the Ministry of Civil Aviation.

The Soviet government decided to build Domodedovo airport in November 1954, and the construction project was approved one year later. According to one document, the territory around the airport was being held in reserve, and any other construction projects in the area were prohibited because long-term plans included the construction of several additional runways. Airport construction was completed in the spring of 1962, when it began servicing inbound and outbound domestic civilian flights from Moscow eastward—from the Volga and Urals regions to Central Asia, Siberia, and Russia's Far East.

After the collapse of the Soviet Union, air passenger traffic decreased dramatically. The transition to a market economy immediately increased the cost of air transportation, making it inaccessible to most of the population. The Central Asian republics became independent states, and their connections with Moscow likewise decreased. Domodedovo began to fall into a decline. Sheremetyevo became a hub for passenger operations of Russia's main airline, Aeroflot, because it could handle international air traffic and allowed for connecting flights. Other airlines, particularly ones serving shorter-distance international flights, chose Vnukovo because of its proximity to Moscow.

As the owner of Domodedovo, the Russian government tried to keep it from falling into decay and allowed it to handle international flights. With its low tariffs and light airport traffic, Domodedovo gradually became a convenient logistical center for many Russian airlines involved in importing goods from China. In 1994, two young entrepreneurs became interested in airport-related business and established several companies providing aircraft servicing, airline catering, and cargo terminal servicing. However, their interests soon diverged. One of them went into politics and became a State Duma member, while the other remained as sole owner of the business. The latter's name was Dmitry Kamenshchik.

Kamenshchik invested all profits in business development, and soon Domodedovo opened a specialized cargo terminal providing services to importers. Before long, almost the entire volume of goods imported from China, worth billions of dollars, came through Domodedovo.[120] In 1996, Kamenshchik signed an agreement with the state-controlled company that owned the passenger terminal in Domodedovo to construct a new terminal,[121] and in 1998 his company signed an agreement with the government for a seventy-five-year lease of airfield facilities (including runways, taxiways, and aprons). A few years later, the state-owned company that owned a stake in the new passenger terminal went bankrupt, and Kamenshchik purchased its shares in the terminal at auction. This enhanced Kamenshchik's prospects for investing in the development of Domodedovo.

The fast-growing import transportation business became a source of investment funds. Kamenshchik established a cargo airline, East Line, that soon began running more than fifty planes. As a result, Russian business travel to China began to decline, because business owners' purchases could be loaded onto planes and brought to Moscow for them. East Line Airlines opened offices in Novosibirsk, St. Petersburg, Petropavlovsk-Kamchatsky, Saratov, Khabarovsk, and other large Russian cities. Around this time, however, the growing business attracted the attention of competitors and the *siloviki*, which joined forces to thwart the airline.

In September 2000, FSB operatives grounded three East Line cargo planes on their way from China on the grounds that the weight of the transported goods was higher than declared (which was not in itself a regulatory violation).[122] A criminal case was initiated, and the airline's offices were searched. East Line was banned from conducting any flights. A year later, freight from the grounded planes was confiscated,[123] but no violations of customs or aviation regulations were ever proven. Eight years later, several East

Line employees received suspended sentences; in Putin's Russia, this basically amounts to being declared not guilty.

Meanwhile, the liberalization of customs regulations and a growing economy made cargo transportation less attractive. From 2004 on, having sold East Line Airlines, Kamenshchik concentrated his activities on the airport.[124] In late 2000, Domodedovo had opened a modern passenger terminal that provided higher-quality services to passengers and airlines than Vnukovo or Sheremetyevo. Domodedovo's capacity utilization skyrocketed, and in 2005 it was ranked first among Moscow's airports in passenger traffic. However, the fast-growing business yet again attracted the attention of *siloviki*.

In 2004, the Federal Property Management Agency, with support from the FSB and the Kremlin's deputy chief of staff Victor Ivanov,[125] launched a series of criminal lawsuits challenging the results of the never-completed privatization of Domodedovo in order to annul the leasing agreement for the runways. Court proceedings, which Kamenshchik consistently lost, lasted for more than three years. It seemed that nothing could prevent the state from taking away the airport. In February 2008, the Federal Arbitration Court of the Moscow Region ruled the runways rental contract void, and the court ruling swiftly came into force. However, it became clear that the airport would have to be shut down immediately after that, since the operating company had no legal authority to keep things going. Within a day, the Federal Property Management Agency wrote and signed a substitute contract "to ensure the continuous operation of the airport," which allowed it to keep the situation in limbo. However, at the crucial moment, luck favored Kamenshchik: his appeal reached the Presidium of the Supreme Arbitration Court—his last legal chance—whose newly appointed chair, Anton Ivanov, convinced the parties to sign an amicable agreement stipulating a thirtyfold increase in rental payments. Although the Federal Property Management Agency later tried to challenge this agreement, all it managed to achieve was another fourfold increase in rental charges in 2012.

Though Kamenshchik was able to repulse an attack and defend his rights, his company faced continuous challenges. The FSB, tax authorities, and technical and transportation inspectors visited the airport, launched criminal investigations, and brought him to court on a variety of pretexts. By 2014, according to Kamenshchik, the number of court hearings involving his companies exceeded 3,100 facts in dispute, nearly 200 of which involved decisions by tax authorities. But Domodedovo's employees were not prosecuted, and all the inspections conducted by the government agencies ended in favorable reports.

On January 24, 2011, a suicide bomber detonated an explosive device inside Domodedovo airport, killing 37 people and injuring more than 170. Four days after the attack, before the investigation had yielded any results, President Dmitry Medvedev appeared to have figured it all out, and blamed the airport's management for the attack: "What happened shows that obviously there were violations in guaranteeing security. And it should be answered for by those who make the decisions there and by the management of the airport."[126] Although the law neither required nor authorized airport managers to search people entering the terminal, one month later Medvedev went even further by proposing to hold the airport owners responsible and by publicly asking the prosecutor general: "In Domodedovo . . . have you dealt . . . with the owner of the airport?"[127]

Meanwhile, in March 2012, the criminal case initiated against the airport managers and police officers right after the attack was closed. But two months later, it was reopened, only to be closed yet again in August 2015. (It seems that this was done to relieve the police officers of liability.) On July 25, 2015, Russian Investigative Committee chairman Aleksandr Bastrykin made an unexpected statement: "They [the airport owners] have been avoiding responsibility—financial, not criminal—for five years, they have not tried to hide, they have been in Moscow. But they have never made amends for the damages caused as a result of the terrorist attack. If you do not want to pay compensation for material damages, then you will be held criminally liable as the owners and managers."[128] As it turned out, a short time before his remarks, investigators had opened a new criminal case—this one charged the owners and managers of the airport alone, accusing them of providing unsafe services. Three airport managers, who were arrested in February 2016, and Dmitry Kamenshchik, who was placed under house arrest, were the defendants in the case.[129]

Although bizarre criminal cases are not uncommon in Russia, the case against Domodedovo's owner and managers stands out. The criminal case did not stand up to scrutiny from a legal point of view; under Russian law, even the police were not required to screen people entering the airport at that time. The odd thing about this case is that the prosecutor general's office openly, and successfully, confronted the Investigative Committee, categorically demanding that the criminal case be closed—which it was, in late September 2016.[130] This surprising move raised two interesting questions: Why did this new criminal case against Domodedovo airport take place? And who was acting as Kamenshchik's protector?

Most experts answered the first question in more or less the same way: the company that Kamenshchik had created was too attractive and too profitable to be allowed to remain in his hands. Moreover, from 2011 to 2013 Kamenshchik had been negotiating with a number of Russian investors about the possibility of selling all or part of his business. Putin's crony Arkady Rotenberg and his partners (who a few years later found a simpler and much cheaper way to establish control over another state-owned Moscow airport, Sheremetyevo), Viktor Vekselberg, and Rosneft, in partnership with a company owned by a person close to Rosneft CEO Igor Sechin, were among the potential buyers. It is possible that one of them attempted the well-worn method of using arrests and criminal cases to bring down the ultimate sale price of the business.

The answer to the second question, however, is not so obvious. Kamenshchik is neither a friend of the Russian president nor one of the business owners who have been enjoying the regime's good graces. He once made such a strong statement at a government meeting on the development of the Moscow air hub that officials refrained from inviting him to participate in other such discussions for more than a decade. In another case, Kamenshchik refused to carry out a demand by Deputy Prime Minister Sergey Ivanov to provide free fuel to planes belonging to a bankrupt company. He once openly stated in an interview that the main reason for the existence of a property structure based on the use of offshore companies was the lack of trust that Russian law and law enforcement practice could protect people's property rights. He also was not afraid to ask for permission to speak at a meeting with President Putin and state a point of view that contradicted the one supported by all officials, as well as the president himself. He has a reputation for being a straightforward and tough person, unwilling to forsake his principles in any circumstance.

How does a businessman who has been under sustained attack for the past fifteen years by everyone from the powerful secret police to the highest-ranking officials manage not just to survive but to protect his property as well? The explanation Kamenshchik himself offers seems the least plausible: "Very good lawyers work for my company, and they are successful in the courts." He did indeed have good lawyers, who were skillful and resourceful in defending his rights. To be sure, sometimes their tenacity played an important role. Faced with stubborn resistance, the attackers' motivation waned and attentions switched to different objectives. However, many Russian companies have good lawyers, but few lawyers are successful when the courts knowingly abuse the law for the sake of someone's vested interests.

In today's Russia, one can oppose administrative power or judicial arbitrariness only with the aid of a protector from some other sector of the state authorities. There are precious few situations in which the prosecutor general's office obstinately argues with the Investigative Committee during a trial, claiming that the defendants' actions lack the essential elements of criminality and requesting that the charges be dropped. Kamenshchik himself says that he does not have such protectors. It is, however, hard to believe that his letters reached the desks of the president and the prime minister, soon followed by instructions to curb attacks against him, without his having a protector.

Those protectors could be the idealists among high-ranking Russian officials, like Economic Minister German Gref, who actively opposed Domodedovo's nationalization in 2004–06. However, there are fewer and fewer such people in the Russian government every year, as the cynics and opportunists continue to push them out. It is easier to imagine that Kamenshchik had secret protectors who were in conflict with his enemies and were thus ready to undermine their actions. As the saying goes, the enemy of my enemy is my friend.

If one is inclined to conspiracy theories, one might suggest that Kamenshchik received indirect support from Vladimir Putin himself, who had noticed the young go-getter who had transformed the Moscow airport faster and better than the government had with airports that belonged to it. Yet one must keep in mind the well-known saying by Felix Dzerzhinsky, the founder of the Cheka—the first Soviet secret police, the ancestor of the KGB: "The fact that you are still free is not your achievement, but rather a failure on our side." Putin did not slap the *siloviki* on the wrist. Could it be that in Kamenshchik's case, they merely failed?

In the end, the situation played into Kamenshchik's hands. By all appearances, he was meticulously following all legal requirements, or so read the history of his legal arguments with the tax authorities. Then again, perhaps this is also his weakness: even the smallest mistake on his part could result in a fall, and in his enemies winning. Nevertheless, Dmitry Kamenshchik keeps walking the tightrope.

BUT ONE CLAW SNAGGED, THE BIRD IS BAGGED

One might think that the aforementioned stories of corporate raiding by the Russian authorities, be they from the government, state-owned companies, or just men in uniform, are sui generis cases having to do with the Kremlin's wish to establish control over strategic assets. Or perhaps one might believe that, in the worst-case scenario, these incidents, as in the case of Evroset, were the result of criminal actions by dishonest policemen. But both explanations are mistaken. Incidents similar to the ones described above have been a regular occurrence throughout Russia. Companies large and small, foreign and domestic, manufacturing and service-oriented, have fallen victim to the state and its representatives. Although state takeovers of large companies receive coverage in the media, the plundering and seizure of small and medium-sized businesses are typically not widely publicized. At best, they are covered by local newspapers and discussed by business owners in private forums. However, the methods used to wrest control of these businesses is the same.

Starting in the late 1990s, Nikolai Kudelko, a Lithuanian businessman, owned a company specializing in the wholesaling of coffee in Russia. By Russian business standards, his was a medium-sized company, with an average annual revenue ranging from 10 million to 50 million rubles (U.S. $500,000 to $2 million). In November 2006, three men dressed in civilian clothing, who introduced themselves as representatives of the Russian Interior Ministry's Economic Security Department, arrived at his company's warehouse to conduct an inspection. It was suggested that the businessman pay $50,000 to "expedite" a "problem-free" inspection, and he was offered protection against any future demands by criminals or any governmental agencies. Failing that, they promised to paralyze the company for at least three months. After considering the company's contracts and commitments, Kudelko agreed to the terms.

Less than a year later, the same policemen returned and removed from the warehouse more than thirty truckloads of coffee worth more than U.S. $2 million. They demanded that Kudelko pay $500,000 to get his goods back, and promised to return the coffee after the receipt of half that amount. Although Kudelko did pay the extortionists $200,000, he never got his coffee back. Moreover, the policemen threatened to destroy the goods unless they received the entire amount.

Kudelko sent a claim to the Interior Ministry's internal security service complaining of the illegal actions by the police officers. A criminal case was opened—but against Kudelko, not the extortionists. Kudelko was charged with illegal business activities based on the results of fraudulent expert analysis claiming that the coffee was uncertified and of substandard quality. The court's verdict was tough: six years in jail. Soon after the businessman's arrest, the coffee that had been confiscated was destroyed; according to official documentation, it posed a health hazard. However, a few days later this coffee reemerged from its notional ashes and was sold in the Moscow suburbs.

Kudelko's luck changed a little. Several members of the Russian parliament, the Russian ombudsman, and the embassy of Lithuania intervened on his behalf. Media reports and requests to the Investigative Committee and the prosecutor general's office resulted in the court softening its position while considering Kudelko's appeal; his sentence was reduced to three years. This was the exact amount of time the businessman had spent in pretrial custody during the investigation and trial. Furthermore, five police officers who had acted as secondary perpetrators received prison sentences. The police officer who had masterminded, led, and most probably been the main beneficiary of the attack on Kudelko was the son of Svetlana Orlova, then deputy speaker of the Federation Council, the upper house of the Russian parliament, and now governor of Vladimir region. Not long after Kudelko's sentence was reduced, this individual voluntarily resigned from the police force to become adviser to the state-owned Olympstroy, the corporation responsible for the construction of the venues used for the Sochi Olympics.[131]

YOU CANNOT HIDE BEHIND PROPERTY PAPERS!

On the night of February 8–9, 2016, heavy construction machinery was brought to the central squares of Moscow. Workers began using it to demolish stalls and convenience stores, a multitude of which had emerged in the early 1990s. In one night, ninety-seven storefronts were demolished.

In Soviet times, the ground floor of residential buildings did not have spaces for stores or offices of service companies. In the first half of the 1990s, municipal authorities across the country realized that this problem needed solving. One solution approved by Moscow authorities was to build light-duty pavilions in city squares near metro entrances. More precisely, this was an initiative pursued in parallel by both business and government. Ambitious entrepreneurs took it upon themselves to build the pavilions first and seek property rights later, by hook or by crook. It cannot be said that these constructions always beautified the city, but they certainly solved many day-to-day problems experienced by Muscovites.

In the summer of 2015, the Russian parliament adopted a law giving municipal authorities the right to demolish buildings and facilities that had been built without an official permit. Most importantly, this law deprived the owners of the right to judicial protection by permitting authorities to arbitrarily determine what constituted unauthorized construction, and what buildings and facilities should be demolished. Based on this law, in December 2015 the Moscow government decided to demolish 104 buildings in the city; these facilities were claimed to be dangerous to Muscovites because of their location near utility lines and over metro utility areas.[132] The owners of these buildings were outraged, as they had dutifully registered their property with government authorities.[133] Many went to court to defend their property rights, to no avail. Having stated that the buildings marked for demolition "had been built in the 1990s with the obvious connivance or assistance of the officials," Moscow mayor Sergey Sobyanin ordered their destruction. Faced with strong media criticism of his actions, Sobyanin made a statement that was astonishing in its cynicism, and that illustrated his attitude toward property rights: "You cannot hide behind property papers that have been acquired in an obviously fraudulent way."[134] Although Article 35 of the Russian constitution states that "no one may be deprived of property other than by a court decision," in April 2016 Russia's Supreme Court justified the actions of the Moscow mayor's office. In late August 2016, Moscow authorities demolished eighty more buildings. Needless to say, no investigation was conducted of the bureaucrats who issued property documents "in an obviously fraudulent way".

In September 2016, having considered the claim submitted by a group of State Duma members challenging the law passed in the summer of 2015, Russia's Constitutional Court washed its hands of the matter. On the one hand, the court confirmed citizens' right to defend their property rights in court. On the other hand, the Constitutional Court rejected the claim as inadmissible from a legal point of view, and thus demonstrated its unwillingness to defend property rights in Russia.

Notes to Chapter 7

1. Grigory Vygon, *Evaluation of Tax Burden Borne by Russian Oil Companies in 2000* (Moscow: Financial Research Institute, 2002). See also Anna Skornyakova and Aleksey Efimov, "YUKOS zaplatil slishkom mnogo nalogov" [Yukos paid too much in taxes], *Nezavisimaya Gazeta*, July 14, 2003.

2. Yukos shareholders eventually appealed to the European Court of Human Rights (ECHR) and an international court of arbitration in The Hague to defend their rights. The ECHR approved the shareholders' claim, ordering the Russian government to pay 2.7 billion euros, but the Russian Constitutional Court announced that this decision contradicted the Russian constitution, thus allowing the government to avoid paying this sum. The arbitration court in The Hague later decided in favor of the Yukos shareholders as well, in a $50 billion judgment. This ruling was later overturned on appeal, but the case may yet come before the Supreme Court of the Netherlands.

3. Theoretically, this was possible but unlikely. It could have happened if Gazprom had refused to convert the debt into stock and chosen not to participate in the forthcoming stock issue that had been scheduled to consolidate Hungarian chemical enterprises purchased by Goldovsky's companies.

4. President of Russia, "Vstupitel'noye slovo na soveshchanii po voprosam razvitiya gazovoy otrasli" [Introductory speech at the meeting dedicated to the development of the gas industry], news release, Novy Urengoi, November 20, 2001 (http://kremlin. ru/events/president/transcripts/21406).

5. A few days later, Sheremet was released without charges. Within six months, he was fired from Gazprom.

6. Goldovsky received U.S. $95 million and later claimed that the estimated value of the sold assets amounted to U.S. $700 million. But it should be remembered that a considerable part of these assets had been bought with leverage, and thus it is impossible to find out the discount on their real price.

7. Interfaks-Ural, "'Tobol'sk–Polimer' budet zapushchen v 2013 godu" ["Tobolsk-Polymer" will be launched in 2013], *Kommersant*, April 4, 2013.

8. Dmitriy Dmitriyenko, "Mikhelson pokupayet u Gazprombanka polovinu 'Sibur kholdinga'" [Mikhelson buys half of Sibur Holding from Gazprombank], *Vedomosti*, December 23, 2010.

9. Olga Mordyushenko, "Esli iz desyati proyektov vystrelyat khotya by tri, eto khorosho" [If at least three projects out of ten work out, it will be good], *Kommersant*, August 8, 2015.

10. Olga Mordyushenko, "SIBUR dobilsya deneg FNB" [SIBUR has got money from the Sovereign Wealth Fund], *Kommersant*, June 19, 2015.

11. Gazprom, "OAO 'Gazprom' i Royal Dutch Shell podpisali Memorandum o

vzaimoponimanii po obmenu aktivami v ramkakh proyektov 'Zapolyarnoye-Neokom-skiye zalezhi' i 'Sakhalin-2'" [JSC Gazprom and Royal Dutch Shell signed a Memo-randum of Understanding on the exchange of assets in the framework of the projects "Zapolyarnoe-Neocomian deposits" and "Sakhalin-2"], press release, Moscow, July 7, 2005 (http://www.gazprom.ru/press/news/2005/july/article55382/).

12. Igor Khoroshilov, "Ekspertizu otmenili vakhtovym metodom" [Examination was canceled by rotational method], *Kommersant*, July 27, 2005.

13. Denis Rebrov, "Sergei Stepashin obschital 'Sakhalin-2'" [Sergey Stepashin evaluated Sakhalin-2], *Kommersant*, October 7, 2006.

14. "Proverki 'Sakhalina-2' vyyavili narusheniy na pyat' ugolovnykh statey" [In-spections of Sakhalin-2 revealed five criminal violations], Lenta.ru, October 25, 2006 (https://lenta.ru/news/2006/10/25/sakhalin/).

15. "Sakhalin Energy ne pustyat k vode" [Sakhalin Energy will not have access to water], *Kommersant*, November 15, 2006 (http://www.kommersant.ru/doc/722003).

16. Denis Rebrov and Natalya Grib, "'Sakhalin-2' otsenyat s ekologicheskim dis-kontom" [Sakhalin-2 will be valued at an environmental discount], *Kommersant*, De-cember 18, 2006 (http://www.kommersant.ru/doc/731063).

17. Minren, "Amurskoye BVU Rosvodresursov priostanovilo deystviye 12 litsen-ziy na vodopol'zovaniye, vydannykh OOO 'Starstroy', vypolnyayushchemu raboty v ramkakh proyekta 'Sakhalin-2'" [The Amur River Basin of Rosvodresursov sus-pended the 12 water use licenses issued by Starstroi LLC, which is carrying out work on the Sakhalin-2 project], news release, Moscow, December 7, 2006 (http://mnr.gov.ru/news/detail.php?ID=15828).

18. "Royal Dutch Shell soglasilas' prodat' 'Gazpromu' dolyu v 'Sakhaline-2'" [Royal Dutch Shell agreed to sell Gazprom a stake in Sakhalin-2], Lenta.ru, Decem-ber 11, 2006.

19. Dmitriy Butrin and Maksim Shishkin, "'Sakhalin-2' kupyat ne glyadya" [Sakhalin-2 will be purchased sight unseen], *Kommersant*, December 23, 2006.

20. Denis Rebrov, "Shell dali tri mesyatsa chtoby dogovorit'sya s 'Gazpromom' o 'Sakhaline-2'" [Shell has been given three months to agree with Gazprom on Sakhalin-2], *Kommersant*, December 13, 2006. Carter Page, the foreign policy adviser in Donald Trump's electoral campaign, was on the Merrill Lynch team that within twenty-four hours prepared and signed the so-called fairness opinion that was delivered to the Gazprom board of directors. Page claimed that this deal was the "key Gazprom trans-action" on which he was advising.

21. President of Russia, "Vyderzhki iz stenograficheskogo otcheta o vstreche s akt-sionerami kompanii 'Sakhalin Enerdzhi'" [Excerpts from the transcript of the meet-ing with Sakhalin Energy shareholders], news release, Moscow, December 21, 2006 (http://kremlin.ru/events/president/transcripts/23971).

22. MINREN, "20 marta 2007 g. v MPR Rossii postupil 'Plan-grafik priro-

dookhrannykh meropriyatiy po ustraneniyu zamechaniy i trebovaniy Rosprirodnad-zora, ukazannykh v predpisaniyakh i aktakh proverok soblyudeniya prirodookhrannogo zakonodatel'stva pri stroitel'stve truboprovodov po proyektu "Sakhalin-2"'" [On March 20, 2007, the Ministry of Natural Resources of Russia received a "Schedule of environmental measures to eliminate comments and requirements of Rosprirod-nadzor, specified in regulations and certificates of compliance with environmental legislation in the construction of pipelines for the Sakhalin-2 project"], news release, Moscow, March 20, 2007 (http://www.mnr.gov.ru/news/detail.php?ID=15943).

23. MINREN, "11 dekabrya sostoyalas' torzhestvennaya tseremoniya nagrazh-deniya laureatov premii Minprirody Rossii 'Luchshiy ekologicheskiy proyekt goda'" [On December 11, the solemn ceremony of bestowing the laureates of the Ministry of Natural Resources of Russia award "The Best Environmental Project of the Year" took place], news release, December 12, 2008 (http://www.mnr.gov.ru/news/detail.php?ID=17006).

24. Natalya Grib. "'Gazprom' vernulsya na Kovyktu" [Gazprom returned to Kovykta], *Kommersant*, June 19, 2007.

25. Natalya Grib and Natalya Skorlygina, "'Gazprom' zashel po-angliyski" [Gaz-prom took French leave], *Kommersant*, June 25, 2007.

26. Such "compensation" could have stemmed from the fact that the Russian side of TNK-BP was represented by Mikhail Fridman's Alfa Group and Viktor Veksel-berg's Renova Group, both companies owned by influential oligarchs who were ab-solutely loyal to the Kremlin. Because Fridman and Vekselberg did not in any way "violate the rules of the game" and eagerly demonstrated their loyalty to the regime, the Kremlin did not see any need to punish them or nationalize their assets on artificial pretexts.

27. Ed Crooks, "Gazprom Looks to Fuel Growth," *Financial Times*, December 9, 2008.

28. Olga Mordyushenko, "Krizis zamorozil Kovyktu" [The crisis froze Kovykta], *Kommersant*, February 4, 2009.

29. The fully state-owned Rosneftegas was established in 2004 for the then-planned absorption of Rosneft by Gazprom. However, in late 2004, Rosneft purchased Yukos's flagship asset, Yuganskneftegas—and all discussion of this deal ceased. In 2005, to protect Rosneft from claims by Yukos shareholders, all state-owned Rosneft shares were vested in Rosneftegas. That same year, Rosneftegas bought 10.74 percent of Gazprom from companies affiliated with the gas monopoly. In effect, Igor Sechin runs Rosneftegas and manages its financial resources.

30. Olga Shkurenko, "Trudnaya sud'ba Kovykty" [The difficult fate of Kovykta], *Kommersant*, March 2, 2011.

31. Olga Mordyushenko and Kirill Melnikov, "'Rosneftegazu' perekryli gaz" [Rosneftegaz was cut off from gas], *Kommersant*, March 2, 2011.

32. At the time, Russian license-granting procedures rigorously specified the volumes of annual natural resource extraction. Any deviation could be seen as a violation of the license agreement and result in sanctions, including withdrawal of the license.

33. "Russneft extracted 16 million tons instead of 15.94 million tons, and this is what the company's president—not the heads of affiliated companies—is accused of," Gutseriyev commented angrily. "This is stupid." See Anna Gorshkova, " 'Chto posle etogo mozhno dumat?' " ["What is one to think after that?"], *Vremya Novostey*, May 5, 2007.

34. The companies were accused of making numerous par value transactions between themselves involving Russneft's shares in order to avoid paying taxes. Anna Gorshkova. "Fiskal'nyy press dlya Gutseriyeva" [Fiscal press for Gutseriyev], *Vremya Novostey*, June 21, 2007. In April 2008, the Plenum of Russia's Supreme Arbitration Court prohibited the use of this norm contained in the Civil Code in tax disputes. By October 2008 the Tax Service had withdrawn its claims. See Olga Pleshanova and Denis Rebrov, " 'Russneft' vyshla na svobodu" [Russneft released], *Kommersant*, October 9, 2008.

35. Ekaterina Karacheva, "Smeshnyye den'gi" [Ridiculous money], *Vremya Novostey*, April 12, 2007.

36. In Soviet times, the Republic of Ingushetia, together with neighboring Chechnya, constituted the Chechen-Ingush Autonomous Soviet Socialist Republic (Chechen-Ingush ASSR). Ingushetia was strategically important for the Kremlin's counterterrorism activities in Chechnya. The Kremlin accused Ingushetia's charismatic and popular leader, the Afghanistan war hero Ruslan Aoushev, of supporting Chechen militants—a claim that led to Aoushev's dismissal.

37. Alla Barakhova, "Zhizn' prodolzhayetsya" [Life goes on], *Kommersant*, April 30, 2002.

38. Nikolay Gorelov, "Ne fontan" [Not very well indeed], *Vremya Novostey*, April 5, 2002.

39. " 'Russneft' otritsayet fakt pokupki 50% 'Zapadno-Malobalykskogo' " [Russneft declines the purchase of 50% of Zapadno-Malobalykskoye], Neft' i Capital, August 9,2005. See also " 'RussNeft' zavershila sdelku po pokupke 50% doley v Zapadno-Malobalykskom" [Russneft finalized the purchase of 50% shares in Zapadno-Malobalykskoye], *AK&M*, September 15, 2005 (http://www.russneft.ru/pressabout/?id=200034); and " 'YUKOS' obrusel. 'Russneft' Mikhaila Gutseriyeva priobrela 49% aktsiy Transpetrol" [Yukos became a little Russian. Mikhail Gutseriyev's Russneft acquired 49% of the shares of Transpetrol], *Kommersant*, February 7, 2006.

40. Mikhail Gutseriyev received U.S. $3 billion, and the buyer assumed Russneft's debts (valued at around $2 billion). See Natalya Grib, Alek Akhundov, Denis Rebrov, and Olga Pleshanova, "Mikhailu Gutseriyevu naznachili vykhodnoye posobiye" [Mikhail Gutseriev was awarded severance pay], *Kommersant*, July 30, 2007.

41. Denis Rebrov, "'Russneft' dlya russkikh" [Russneft for Russians], *Kommersant*, September 8, 2009.

42. Denis Rebrov, "'Russneft' vernulas' k Mikhailu Gutseriyevu" [Russneft was returned to Mikhail Gutseriev], *Kommersant*, January 11, 2009.

43. Although the government owned a 20 percent stake in the design bureau, as a precondition for the merger it requested retaining its 37 percent stake nondiluted.

44. These newly created organizations included Rosatom, Rostec (formerly Rossiyskiye Tekhnologii), Rosnano, and the Bank for Development (Vnesheconombank, VEB).

45. Rosvooruzheniye was a much larger company involved in the export of arms.

46. Before Chemezov, another Putin friend from his East German days, Andrey Belyaninov, had served as the director of Rosoboronexport. In 2004, Putin appointed Belyaninov head of the Federal Defense Order Service, and in 2006 head of the Federal Customs Service.

47. Elena Kiseleva, "MERT narushil gospaketnoye soglasheniye" [Ministry of Economic Development and Trade violated state agreement], *Kommersant*, April 10, 2008.

48. Elena Kiseleva, "Aleksey Kudrin raskryl skrytuyu privatizatsiyu" [Alexey Kudrin reveals hidden privatization], *Kommersant*, June 10, 2008.

49. Elena Kiseleva, "'Rostekhnologii' vyvodyat iz stroyki" [Construction is stopped on Rostekhnologii], *Kommersant*, May 22, 2008.

50. This holding, established by President Putin's decree in April 2008, was named the United Engine Corporation (UEC).

51. Vladislav Tyumenev, "Sdacha 'Saturna'" [Giveaway of Saturn], *Expert*, December 2, 2008.

52. Lastochkin later described the events: "As the head of the company and its majority shareholder, I was receiving offers from a group of people to sell the controlling block of shares. . . . The negotiations took a long time, more than eighteen months, with offers following one another on a nonstop basis. Eighteen months is a long enough time to come to an agreement, but we failed to do so because these people wanted to receive the factory as a gift. . . . Eighteen months later, however, I agreed to sell since these people felt so strongly about it, but I insisted that everything be carried out under normal market conditions. In mid-2008 Saturn's capitalization reached around U.S. $900 million. The price of its controlling stake was more than half of this amount. Of course, no one wanted to pay this price. . . . And so the negotiations with state officials continued. . . . They were not very fruitful since no one wanted to pay. Everyone believed that since they represented the state they should get a special, preferential treatment." See Yuriy Lastochkin, "Posledneye slovo. Rastrata" [The last word: Embezzlement], *Odnazhdy v Rybinske*, August 15, 2015.

53. "Ukaz Prezidenta RF No. 497, 'O dal'neyshem razvitii OAO Obyedinennaya promyshlennaya korporatsiya "Oboronprom"'" [Decree of the president of the Russian Federation No. 497, "On further development of the publicly held company

United Industrial Corporation Oboronprom"], Garant.ru, April 16, 2008 (http://www.garant.ru/products/ipo/prime/doc/93146/#ixzz4jWfVYCyy).

54. Later, the court determined that Saturn had overpaid taxes in the amount of 45 million rubles, and consequently rejected the Tax Service's claim.

55. Alisa Gritskova and Elena Kiseleva, "'Saturn' popadet v 'Oboronprom' cherez VEB" [Saturn will get into Oboronprom through VEB], *Kommersant*, November 1, 2008.

56. Government of Russia, "V.V. Putin provel soveshchaniye v NPO 'Saturn' v gorode Rybinske [V. V. Putin held a meeting at the NPO Saturn in the city of Rybinsk], news release, Moscow, December 2, 2008 (http://archive.premier.gov.ru/visits/ru/6087/events/2634/). According to the media, Lastochkin and his partner sold their stakes in Saturn and the Ufa factory for 1.6 billion rubles (approximately U.S. $60 million at the then-current exchange), which was less than 15 percent of the shares' price in early 2008. It seems impossible to adequately estimate the values of these shares at the height of the crisis.

57. Government of Russia, "V.V. Putin posetil OAO 'Avtodizel'" [V. V. Putin held a meeting at Avtodiesel], news release, Moscow, December 2, 2008 (http://archive.premier.gov.ru/visits/ru/6087/events/2636/).

58. Svetlana Izrayleva, "Yuriy Lastochkin: 'Ne smeshite moyu ZH'" [Yuriy Lastochkin: "Don't make my a-- laugh"], *Rybinskaya Nedelya*, February 3, 2015.

59. According to the most plausible version, Tetyukhin sent numerous letters to Putin asking for state protection against Vekselberg's actions. In the summer of 2003, Tetyukhin and Brecht met with a Kremlin official, who realized that it was a corporate conflict—a common occurrence at the time—and declared that the Kremlin would not get involved. During the meeting, Brecht said that Tetyukhin and he were the actual co-owners of the controlling stake. This piece of news came as a surprise and alarmed Tetyukhin. A few days later, Brecht was to celebrate his fiftieth birthday at the VSMPO cultural center—an idea proposed by Tetyukhin a few weeks before. However, on the eve of the celebration, Tetyukhin forbade it out of fear that it might considerably increase Brecht's influence in the company, since no one manager had ever celebrated a birthday in the cultural center before. Moreover, Tetyukhin suspected his partner of trying to establish personal control over the company using methods he could not comprehend. For his part, Brecht was deeply offended by his partner's decision, since the cancellation of the celebration had been publicly announced without warning or personal conversation, which put Brecht in an extremely embarrassing position. He began to suspect Tetyukhin of playing unfairly.

60. Mariya Cherkasova and Mariya Molina, "VSMPO perevodyat na 'zolotuyu' aktsiyu" [VSMPO is transferred to the "golden" share], *Kommersant*, January 29, 2005.

61. Mariya Cherkasova and Vyacheslav Sukhanov, "Viktor Vekselberg ne titanovyy" [Viktor Vekselberg is not made of titanium], *Kommersant*, May 4, 2005.

62. The initial plan consisted in attracting Boeing as a shareholder. The U.S. com-

pany began seriously considering the idea of buying shares but hesitated, because at some point its risk was not hedged. The shares that had been put in the trust could not be pledged.

63. At the same time, Brecht signed a tag-along agreement with Renaissance Capital, according to which the parties pledged to sell the company's shares together and at the same price. This agreement later came in handy for Brecht.

64. Evgeniya Sergeyeva. "Chto zhdet rossiyskiy titan ili who is 'Professor Ti'?" [What's the future for the Russian Titan, or who is "Professor Ti"?], Nakanune.ru, June 27, 2005.

65. Without revealing details, Tetyukhin said that "it was clear that the state had set its mind on a complete dominance and a 100 percent control. I have formulated my position as follows: A man's life has a limit, whereas a state is limitless. One can have a dialogue, argue with the state up to a certain point. Then a conciliatory position comes in. I had an opinion that if an enterprise belongs to the state and it takes care of it, then this is not such a bad option. Brecht had a different view, though he, as a pragmatist, also realized that there were no other options." See Nadezhda Ivanitskaya and Pavel Sedakov, "Kak drug Putina vzyal pod kontrol' i privatiziroval titanovogo monopolista" [How a friend of Putin took under control and privatized a titanium monopolist], *Forbes*, May 20, 2013.

66. In a well-established tradition, after the nationalization of VSMPO, the Moscow Arbitration Court refused to support the tax authorities' claims.

67. Brecht interview with the author, June 11, 2017.

68. Evgeniya Chernozatonskaya, "Titanicheskoye usiliye" [Titanic effort], *Harvard Business Review*, September 14, 2016.

69. "Gendirektor VSMPO-AVISMA prodayet 26% aktsiy Rosoboroneksportu" [General Director of VSMPO-AVISMA sells 26 percent of shares to Rosoboronexport], RIA Novosti, October 18, 2006.

70. Many stories have been written about this remarkable partnership. It is best described in Alexander Khinshtein's book, *Oligarchs*.

71. Such a large number of employees could be explained by two factors: low levels of productivity and the fact that VAZ was a "full cycle" enterprise, which meant that principal car parts were being manufactured in its facilities.

72. Sergey Vologodskiy, "Udavka dlya AvtoVAZa" [Noose for AvtoVAZ], *Sovershenno Sekretno*, February 1, 1998.

73. Aleksandr Malyutin and Gleb Pyanykh, "Vladimir Kadannikov: Predel general'-nosti" [Vladimir Kadannikov: The limit of generality], *Kommersant*, March 25, 1997.

74. "Nature abhors a vacuum," as a famous saying goes. After Berezovsky's departure from VAZ, his place was soon taken by the SOK Group of local business owners. The group began by consolidating the supplies of 50 percent of parts to the factory, and later signed a long-term contract to manage sales networks.

75. Vardanyan described the events plainly and cynically: "We went to Artyakov [then Chemezov's deputy in Rosoboronexport] and made him an excellent offer: we would use a market scheme to unloop shares, and the state would obtain a big block of shares as good as for free. Who would ever refuse such an offer?" He added, "I am proud of my deal with VAZ. . . . We attracted a strategic investor, returned the blocking stake to the state, and made money ourselves." See also Ivan Vasilyev, Elena Vinogradova, Vladimir Shtanov, and Irina Gruzinova, "Kak drug Chemezova investiroval v avtoprom" [How Chemezov's friend invested in the auto industry], *Vedomosti*, May 23, 2016.

76. Vladimir Shtanov. "'Svoy biznes — eto illyuzornaya svoboda' — Sergei Skvortsov, upravlyayushchiy direktor 'Rostekha' po investitsiyam" ["Your own business is an illusory freedom": Sergey Skvortsov, Rostec's managing director for investments], *Vedomosti*, July 1, 2013.

77. When journalists later asked Kadannikov about the reasons for his departure, he said, "You know them as well as I do." See Nikolay Semenov, Ekaterina Emel'yanova, and Dmitriy Belikov, "AvtoVAZ ne poydet na otkat" [AvtoVAZ is not going to roll back], *Kommersant* 242, December 23, 2005, p. 13.

78. Elena Kiseleva and Dmitry Belikov, "Vchera" [Yesterday], *Kommersant*, August 22, 2007.

79. Yuliya Fedorinova and Gleb Stolyarov, "Konsolidatsiya 'AvtoVAZa' i GAZa neizbezhna" — Boris Aleshin, prezident gruppy 'AvtoVAZ'" ["The consolidation of AvtoVAZ and GAZ is inevitable": Boris Aleshin, president of the AvtoVAZ group], *Vedomosti*, September 18, 2007.

80. Sergey Skvortsov claimed that Rosoboronexport purchased this block of shares from Troika: "The price was considerably lower than the one at which we sold the blocking stake to Renault." See Shtanov, "'Svoy biznes — eto illyuzornaya svoboda'" ["Your own business is an illusory freedom": Sergey Skvortsov, Rostec's managing director for investments].

81. Troika sold its remaining stake to Renault in the spring of 2013 for U.S. $600 million. See also Vasilyev, Vinogradova, Shtanov, and Gruzinova, "Kak drug Chemezova investiroval v avtoprom" [How Chemezov's friend invested in the auto industry].

82. Until the late 1980s, the Soviet Union did not have any tax system at all. Financial relations between state-owned enterprises and the budget were based on individual requirements established by the supervising ministry. An income tax for private companies was not codified by law until the mid-1990s, but the Soviet Union had never had time to establish a proper tax service.

83. According to estimates, in 2004 the Russian cell phone market reached U.S. $4–$4.5 billion. The cost of customs intermediaries' services for retailers amounted to 3 to 7 percent of the cell phone price. Thus, intermediaries' aggregate annual revenue

went from U.S. $150 million to $300 million, with a part of this amount ending up in the pockets of customs officials.

84. Dmitry Kryazhev and Rodion Levinskiy, "Oplata po kontrafaktu" [Payment for counterfeit goods], *Kommersant* 57, April 1, 2006, p. 1.

85. As a result of a trial that took place four years later, Valery Kuzmin, deputy head of the Sheremetyevo customs, was sentenced to nine years in a prison colony. See "Zamnachal'nika tamozhni Sheremet'yevo osuzhden na 9 let za kontrabandu" [Deputy head of Sheremetyevo customs office sentenced to nine years for smuggling], Vesti.ru, April 1, 2009.

86. Igor Ivanov, "Ogon', voda i telefonnyye trubki" [Hell, cell and high water], *Forbes*, November 3, 2009.

87. The aggregate cost of cell phones imported into Russia and cleared by customs grew twentyfold in one year.

88. Dmitry Zakharov and Rodion Levinskiy. "MVD popalos' na kontrafakte" [The Ministry of Internal Affairs came across counterfeit goods], *Kommersant* 59, April 5, 2006, p. 1.

89. Ibid.

90. All subsequent efforts to find information that would shed light on the reasons behind the incident brought no results: it was most likely a mistake on the part of the police officers.

91. Zakharov and Levinskiy, "MVD popalos' na kontrafakte."

92. Dmitry Kryazhev and Dmitry Zakharov, "Telefony Motorola prevratili v pyl'" [Motorola phones turned into dust], *Kommersant* 74, April 26, 2004, p. 15.

93. According to Yevgeny Chichvarkin, in 2006 the K division officials similarly seized large shipments of cell phones and household appliances being imported into Russia by other companies. Unlike Evroset, these companies did not dare openly confront the police and used loans to buy out the confiscated goods for 30 percent of their actual price. Unable to pay off their debts, these companies soon went bankrupt.

94. Aleksey Sokovnin, "Delo — trubka" [The deal is off], *Kommersant* 114, June 29, 2010, p. 4.

95. Nikolay Sergeyev, "Na balans 'Evroseti' postupil prigovor" [The balance of Evroset received a sentence], *Kommersant* 185, October 6, 2010, p. 5.

96. According to Chichvarkin, intermediaries regularly approached him, first asking to drop charges against the police officers and later openly threatening him and his employees.

97. Vladislav Trifonov and Aleksandr Igorev, "'Teper' ya ponimayu, nado bylo vse delat' po zakonu'" ["Now I understand, it was necessary to do everything according to the law"], *Kommersant* 220, November 27, 2010, p. 4.

98. "Kak presledovali Evgeniya Chichvarkina" [How they pursued Yevgeny Chichvarkin], *Kommersant*, February 17, 2011.

99. According to Yevgeny Chichvarkin, the attack on his person and his company had been launched and backed by the Kremlin to force the sale of the company at a reduced price. "There was a takeover attempt, which the buyers had nothing to do with. They were not the ones who lowered the company's cost," he said in an interview two and a half years later. "I do not, however, have any other proof to support this theory and I am inclined to believe that the reduced price came about as a result of hasty negotiations because of the urge to save the bulk of the fortune. Besides, one should not forget that the deal was made at a time when the global financial crisis had reached Russia, and market prices had begun spiraling downward. See "Chichvarkin ne sobirayetsya osparivat' stoimost' prodazhi 'Evroseti'" [Chichvarkin is not going to dispute the price of Evroset], *RAPSI*, January 26, 2011.

100. Ivanov, "Ogon', voda i telefonnyye trubki."

101. Vladislav Trifonov, "Pod Evgeniyem Chichvarkinym zashatalas' mebel'" [The furniture rumbled beneath Yevgeny Chichvarkin], *Kommersant* 15, January 29, 2009, p. 1.

102. Nikolay Sergeyev and Vladislav Trifonov, "Vse taynoye stanovitsya pensiyey" [Everything hidden becomes a pension], *Kommersant* 15, January 29, 2011, p. 1.

103. "Londonskiy sud zakryl delo ob ekstraditsii Chichvarkina v Rossiyu" [The London court closed the case of Chichvarkin's extradition to Russia], *RAPSI*, March 14, 2011.

104. "Chichvarkin gotov vernut'sya v RF, esli k vlasti pridet novaya elita" [Chichvarkin is ready to return to Russia if new elite comes to power], *RAPSI*, January 26, 2011.

105. Sergeyev and Trifonov, "Vse taynoye stanovitsya pensiyey."

106. In the late 1990s, a domestic cell phone call cost $0.50; by 2010, this cost had decreased tenfold.

107. The numbers kept growing over the next few years: more than 166 SIM cards per 100 people by the end of 2010, and almost 194 by the end of 2015.

108. Meanwhile, Svyazinvest lost control over its daughter enterprises in Moscow and St. Petersburg. The companies were transferred to MegaFon. See Igor Korolev, "Novyy federal'nyy sotovyy operator: Polnyy reyestr aktivov" [New federal mobile operator: Full asset register], *Cnews Telecom*, December 31, 2013.

109. Anna Chernikova, "Operatory stoyat na svoyem" [Operators won't budge], *Kommersant-Voronezh*, September 30, 2011.

110. Oleg Salmanov, "Kak raspredelyayutsya chastoty v rossiyskoy svyazi" [How frequencies are allocated in Russian telecomunications], *Vedomosti*, October 10, 2011.

111. Ibid.

112. Tele2, "Tele2 AB: Jere Calmes Appointed New CEO of Tele2 Russia and Steps Down as Non-Executive Board Member," press release, February 5, 2015 (http://www.tele2.com/media/press-releases/2013/tele2-ab-jere-calmes-appointed-new-ceo-of-tele2-russia-and-steps-down-as-non-executive-board-member/).

113. Ilya Khrennikov and Adam Ewing, "Fridman Considers Making $4 Billion Bid for Tele2 Russia," *Bloomberg*, March 28, 2013.

114. VimpelCom, "MTS and VimpelCom express joint interest in acquisition of Tele2 Russia," press release, March 28, 2013.

115. Alexey Mordashov, whose net worth *Forbes* estimates at $17.5 billion, became Yury Kovalchuk's loyal associate and a co-investor in many of his projects (including REN-TV, National Media Group, and Bank of Russia). One can only speculate as to his role in all these projects: he may be a disproportionate investor, financing a greater share of expenses for a lesser share of the project's capital; he may also be a figurehead investor, fronting for the real owner.

116. Rostelecom is one example of state inefficiency. Even with such a large number of operator licenses, the company managed to create functioning businesses in only thirty-one out of seventy-one regions. See Korolev, "Novyy federal'nyy sotovyy operator."

117. " 'Rostelekom' i Tele2 Rossiya sozdali 'T2 RTK Kholding' " [Rostelecom and Tele2 created T2 RTK Holding], *Vesti Finance*, February 6, 2014.

118. Dar'ya Trosnikova and Oleg Salmanov, "Gosudarstvo pomozhet Tele2 vyyti v Moskvu" [The state will help Tele2 go to Moscow], *Vedomosti*, January 28, 2015.

119. Tele2 was the only mobile communications company to receive such a loan. The government refused to provide the same assistance to both the private MTS operator and the state-owned Rostelecom. See Andrey Frolov, "Pravitel'stvo otkazalo 'Rostelekomu' i MTS v l'gotnykh kreditakh na summu 31 mlrd rubley" [The government refused Rostelecom and MTS preferential loans in the amount of 31 billion rubles], Vc.ru, April 30, 2015.

120. Because of Russia's vast territory, most imported goods arrive first in Moscow and are shipped throughout the country from there.

121. The parties obtained equal shares in the newly created company, in which the state-owned company had brought its title to the old passenger terminal and Kamenshchik's companies had invested money.

122. Oleg Galkin, "FSB otchitalos' o zachistkakh v 'Ist Layne' " [The FSB reported on the sweeps on the East Line], *Kommersant*, September 30, 2000.

123. Vladislav Trifonov, "Aviakompaniyu 'Ist-Layn' prigovorili k konfiskatsii" [East Line was sentenced to confiscation], *Kommersant*, November 6, 2001.

124. In 2003, Boris Gromov, governor of the Moscow region, expanded the territory surrounding Domodedovo that was not subject to development more than twentyfold—enough space to build eight more runways. Kamenshchik's companies purchased a piece of this land. Although the remaining land plot was owned by the Moscow region, it received a special status. Nothing could prevent the airport's development any longer. See Government of the Moscow Region, "O vnesenii izmeneniy v postanovleniye Pravitel'stva Moskovskoy oblasti ot 07.10.2002 No. 446/38 'O

merakh po dal'neyshemu razvitiyu mezhdunarodnogo aeroporta Domodedovo' (utratilo silu na osnovanii postanovleniya Pravitel'stva Moskovskoy oblasti ot 21.02.2017 No. 117/7)" [On the Introduction of Amendments to the Resolution of the Government of the Moscow Region of October 7, 2002, No. 446/38, "On Measures for the Further Development of the Domodedovo International Airport" (expired on the basis of the Moscow Region Government Decree No. 117/7 of February 21, 2017)], No. 591/37, October 6, 2003 (http://docs.cntd.ru/document/5808845).

125. Vladimir Solovyov, today a notorious Kremlin propaganda mouthpiece, colorfully described the story and the nature of the FSB's and the Kremlin's involvement in the legal prosecution of Domodedovo on his 2008 radio show, "'Domodedovskoye delo' i kadrovik Kremlya Viktor Petrovich Ivanov s sotovarishchami" [The "Domodedovo case" and Kremlin personnel officer Viktor Ivanov with his associates], Kompromat.ru, March 11, 2008.

126. President of Russia, "'Eto terakt, eto gore, eto tragediya.' Prezident otvetil na vopros zhurnalistov o tragedii v aeroportu Domodedovo" ["This is a terrorist attack, it's sadness, it's a tragedy." The president answered journalists' questions about the tragedy at Domodedovo Airport], news release, Moscow, January 25, 2011 (http:// kremlin.ru/events/president/news/10141).

127. President of Russia, "Koordinatsionnoye soveshchaniye rukovoditeley pravookhranitel'nykh organov" [Coordination meeting of heads of law enforcement agencies], news release, Moscow, February 21, 2011 (http://kremlin.ru/events/president/news/10397).

128. Nikolay Sergeyev and Oleg Rubnikovich, "Chas vyleta rasplaty nastal" [The hour of departure of reckoning has come], *Kommersant*, July 25, 2015.

129. According to Kamenshchik's lawyers, the investigator initially had signed an order to place Kamenshchik in custody, but suddenly changed his decision on the day of the trial, requesting that Kamenshchik be placed under house arrest.

130. This happened three months after an official request had been sent by the acting prosecutor general to the Investigative Committee demanding that the criminal case be closed. Under Russian law, such a decision is considered final and is not subject to appeal. It is also worth noting that, along with the criminal case, more than seventy victims of the terrorist attack and members of their families filed civil lawsuits against Domodedovo demanding compensation for damages. Under an unofficial amicable agreement, Dmitry Kamenshchik and Domodedovo, without admitting their guilt, created a charitable foundation to aid the bombing victims. See Nikolay Sergeyev, "Dmitriya Kamenshchika opravdali bez prava na obzhalovaniye" [Dmitry Kamenshchik was acquitted without the right to appeal], *Kommersant*, September 28, 2016.

131. Irek Murtazin, "Khozyain temy" [Topic master], *Novaya Gazeta*, September 23, 2013; and Nataliya Zverko, "Kak i za chto biznesmen iz Litvy otsidel 3 goda v rossiyskom SIZO" [How and for what reason the Lithuanian businessman has spent

three years in a Russian pretrial detention center], Ru.Dwlfi, December 22, 2016 (http://ru.delfi.lt/news/economy/kak-i-za-chto-biznesmen-iz-litvy-otsidel-3-goda-v-rossijskom-sizo.d?id=73192628).

132. The downtown of any large city has a huge number of underground utilities (such as water pipelines, sewer lines, and communication lines) that often exist in multiple overlapping layers. Few land plots have no utility facilities underneath.

133. Delovaya Rossiya, a union of entrepreneurs, checked fifty buildings out of 104 on the mayor's list and declared that all the checked facilities had proper ownership registration papers, and the owners of twenty-seven of them had successfully proved in court that their properties had been built after all the necessary permits and approvals had been obtained.

134. Sergey Sobyanin, personal blog, VKontakte, February 10, 2016 (https://vk.com/mossobyanin?w=wall265870743_15755).

Eight

NOTHING PERSONAL, JUST YOUR BUSINESS

Long before becoming president, Vladimir Putin got to know the power of the Russian oligarchs who had built their wealth in the 1990s. As deputy mayor of St. Petersburg, and during his subsequent career in Moscow, he saw how easily they gained access to the offices of top Russian officials, and how easily they arranged beneficial decisions. Perhaps, deep down, he envied them: many of them had managed to build such enormous fortunes in such a short time! Whereas he, working as a "galley slave," as he once described himself, remained a modest government official. All he owned was an apartment (questionably obtained) and a small house in the St. Petersburg suburbs.[1]

Having become prime minister, and having witnessed his first State Duma election campaign in December 1999, Putin saw that many lawmakers elected in majoritarian districts had strong connections with different business groups. Vladislav Surkov described this situation: "Ambitious amateur business executives in some cases replaced state authorities. It is not a secret that entire ministries, regions, and parties were placed under the control of certain financial groups—that is, under their direct and definite control." A new player in the federal political arena, Putin was worried that the oligarchs might join forces and, at best, limit his influence by imposing decisions from which they could profit. At worst, they might even oust him from power. And so, a few days after his inauguration in May 2000, Putin invited Russia's top business owners to an informal meeting at which he proposed an agreement: government structures would not dig into their past if the oligarchs agreed to "distance themselves, not to loaf about the Kremlin, not to hang about the corridors of the ministries, and not to solve problems that did not fall within their competence."[2]

Although those present at that meeting accepted Putin's proposal immediately and without debate, the Kremlin decided to demonstrate its seriousness. In the following two months, the *siloviki* sent an unequivocal message to Russian business. The state initiated criminal cases for tax fraud against Vagit Alekperov, the CEO and principal shareholder of Lukoil, Russia's second-largest oil company.[3] Both the CEO and the president of the automaker VAZ, Alexey Nikolayev and Vladimir Kadannikov, soon faced similar charges of tax fraud.[4] Vladimir Potanin, the main shareholder of Norilsk Nickel, received a letter from the deputy prosecutor general suggesting he make an additional payment to the government for the privatization sale of the company, which had been finalized four years earlier.[5] Another criminal case was opened in connection with the privatization of the TNK oil company, which belonged to Mikhail Fridman's Alfa Group; company offices were raided and searched.[6] Several other major firms also fell victim to catastrophes: Vladimir Vinogradov's Inkombank went bankrupt in February 2000; Aleksandr Smolensky's banking group lost state support and never recovered from the 1998 financial crisis; and the Kremlin orchestrated a full-scale attack against Vladimir Gusinsky's Most Group, during which Gusinsky was arrested. It was evident that the Kremlin was targeting all Yeltsin-era oligarchs.

It would be naïve to think that the business owners did not understand the message. One way or another, they came to an agreement with the Kremlin,[7] and consequently the aforementioned state pressure campaigns came to a swift halt. At his meeting with President Putin, Vladimir Potanin volunteered that if the state decided it needed his stake in Norilsk Nickel, he was prepared to part with it as soon as possible—no need for any arrests or criminal prosecution. Many Russian business owners made similar statements in the following years. In 2007, RUSAL's major shareholder, Oleg Deripaska, known for his absolute loyalty to the Kremlin, said, "If the state says that we have to give RUSAL away, we will give it away. I do not separate myself from the state." In 2014, Putin's crony Gennady Timchenko declared, "I can say in all earnestness: if need be, I will give everything to the state as soon as tomorrow."[8] When the state took the oil company Bashneft away from AFK Sistema, its main shareholder, Vladimir Yevtushenkov, said, "I understand the rules of the game. . . . This [nationalization] could happen to anyone. . . . Such incidents sooner or later take place somewhere."[9]

Although Vladimir Putin never openly opposed the market economy, as a former operative of the Soviet secret services he merely tolerated the concept of private property, rather than believing it to be the foundation of Russia's economic system. From his early years in the KGB, two well-known phrases etched themselves into his mind. One of them—"Property is theft!"— belongs to the nineteenth-century philosopher Pierre-Joseph Proudhon, whose theories on property and ownership influenced the development of anarchism. The other was uttered by Felix Dzerzhinsky, the founder of the Cheka, the first Soviet secret police agency and the predecessor of the KGB: "The fact that you are free is not your achievement, but rather a failure on our side."

Putin was absolutely certain that all large fortunes in modern Russia had been built on the foundation of Soviet assets, and that the oligarchs had just gotten lucky. He recognized that the oligarchs were willing to sacrifice their property to the Kremlin to satisfy its financial appetite. Realizing this allowed him to take a critically important step by preventing the principle of the inviolability of property from taking hold in the public imagination. Putin laid down an informal rule for Russian big business, according to which business owners were only "authorized to use" their firms' assets, rather than owning them outright. In other words, they were free to manage and benefit from their businesses but were not authorized to make independent decisions concerning their sale, merger, or expansion. The state granted all rights to manage and receive profits from a business, and consequently the state—at Putin's sole discretion—could grant, withdraw, or transfer this right (or keep it for itself). Thus all large business deals had to be coordinated with the Kremlin.[10]

It is difficult to overestimate the importance of this decision for Russia's long-term economic prospects. By the early 2000s, Russian society had realized that even though Yevgeny Primakov's pro-communist government had come to power with the support of the leftist majority in the Russian parliament, the state did not try to (or was not able to) review property rights. It also had not begun a large-scale reexamination of the privatization of state assets—a process that many believed had been unfair. Throughout the Soviet Union's seventy-five-year existence, the concept of private property had not been recognized at all; this history should have provided the strongest possible incentive to cement the principle of the inviolability of property ownership in the public's mind. But this did not happen. In fact, Vladimir Putin created the exact opposite system, one in which the Russian state yet again obtained virtually total control over all property in the country. It would hardly be an exaggeration to say that this was one of the most important "railroad junctions" where Putin flipped the switch that helped send Russia backward.

Putin has never believed in the power of competition and private initiative. He did not see these factors as contributing to the growth of the Russian economy, and at the same time he was certain that state officials were best placed to determine the country's long-term economic interests. This was why Putin's state could admit no mistakes. Whenever the state made a decision—whenever it put a company or a sector of the economy under its control, or introduced new restrictions, or intervened in business decisions of any kind—its role was always strictly positive. And so Putin soon began to support the acquisition of private companies by state-owned ones.[11] Most important, this process would almost always be accompanied by the use of pressure tactics on business.

The aforementioned business cases are similar in that every one of them showed an example of an infringement of the law and of wrongful rulings by courts that would not dare to contradict the Kremlin. In the case of attacks on private owners, the state augmented official pressures with threats of arrest against the owners or their employees (that is, hostage-taking). Once the state had achieved its goal, the many and varied claims against the businesses would just evaporate.

The fundamental difference between the Yeltsin and Putin eras is that *si-*

loviki are now "routinely" involved in practically every state action targeting Russian business owners as well as opposition politicians.[12] The prosecutor general's office, the tax police (eliminated in 2003), the Interior Ministry, the Investigative Committee, the Antidrug Service, and, most important, the FSB—which historically has been at the top of the Soviet and Russian law enforcement systems—appear in every story.

In Soviet times, all *siloviki* agencies, including the KGB, were under civilian (albeit specific) control through Communist Party structures. During Boris Yeltsin's era, the Russian constitution placed law enforcement agencies under the president's direct supervision, and the Kremlin realized its control over *siloviki* by continuously rotating the heads of law enforcement agencies. In the eight years from 1992 to 1999, six different people headed the FSB[13] and five people held the post of prosecutor general. This regular turnover of personnel helped prevent stable "groups of interests" from forming within agencies. The situation changed dramatically when Vladimir Putin came to power. In the eighteen years since Putin's first inauguration, the heads of both the FSB and the prosecutor general's office have been replaced only once each.

In the Yeltsin era, neither the state nor state-owned companies pursued the goal of expanding business by acquiring private companies. On the contrary, privatization was one of the main themes of Russian economic policy. Even though a group of prominent business owners labeled "oligarchs" emerged in Yeltsin's time, none of them was related to President Yeltsin or the heads of *siloviki* agencies by either blood or marriage.

On December 20, 1999, while giving a speech in the FSB's headquarters, Prime Minister Putin joked that "the first order for a complete takeover of power has been executed. A group of FSB officers has successfully infiltrated the government." There is a grain of truth in every joke. At the time of the speech, Putin knew that Yeltsin had decided to leave office before the end of his term; Yeltsin himself had told Putin so. And so a few weeks later, when Putin was the acting president, it came as no surprise to anyone that former KGB and FSB generals and officers began to receive top appointments to key government agencies and state-controlled companies. There is a well-known saying in Russia that there is no such thing as a former Chekist (KGB/FSB official). Having become president of Russia, Vladimir Putin—a former head of the FSB and a former Chekist himself—realized the FSB's political potential. As he was willing to use the FSB to strengthen his power, he made sure to maintain a personal control over the powerful Russian secret police. This tactic eliminated any kind of civilian control over the activity of this organization. It also is symbolic that the FSB was first used as an instrument of coercion against business in May 2000, less than one week after Putin's inauguration, when the prosecutor general's office, the FSB, and the tax police searched the Moscow offices of Vladimir Gusinsky's Media-Most company.[14]

Until the Yukos case, such incidents had been relatively rare, while the destruction of the biggest oil company was carried out in such an ostentatious way that Russian businesses soon understood that they would have no hope of legally defending their interests in court if they came under attack from the state. It also served as model for the regional and local authorities, who realized that they could seize any assets they fancied as well. Meanwhile, this practice became widely used not only in the rare cases of nationalization, but mainly in situations in which government officials were motivated solely by an interest in enriching themselves, their families, or their partners. Large companies and small businesses alike came under assault.

The new practice of "law-enforced asset-grabbing," in which the courts and *siloviki* agencies supported state-led corporate takeovers and property redistribution, became widely used across Russia. The courts denied shareholders their voting rights during shareholder meetings, which allowed the owners of minority stakes to form management bodies under their control. The registering authorities introduced changes to charter documents that effectively transferred property to new owners. With the help of *siloviki* operatives, the attackers took over facilities and offices and established control over companies. Government-sponsored racketeering, in which a business owner's refusal to pay a bribe or to sign away—that is, sell, often for peanuts—part or all of the business would lead to criminal prosecution, became widespread.

Russian businesses quickly came to fear the mass employment of criminal law in economic disputes. Under Russian law, arbitration courts were supposed to review and rule on economic disputes between companies. However, from the mid-2000s a new practice emerged in the Russian legal system. As described by Sergey Ivanov, who was Kremlin chief of staff at the time, "Law enforcement operatives initiate a criminal case against an entrepreneur, impounding documents, hard drives, other valuable items, and goods in warehouses in the context of the investigation. There is no saying how long law enforcement officials will keep these things. The law does not stipulate this; it does not in any way regulate this. Meanwhile, the company's activity, naturally, comes to a halt; the business is destroyed or, truth be told, is taken over."[15] Russian courts of ordinary jurisdiction began to authorize the arrests of business owners and managers in the context of criminal cases, even though the disputes on which these cases were based were at the same time being considered (or had already been considered) by an arbitration court.

After the 2008 crisis, when Russian banks confronted large amounts of "bad loans," two state-owned banks, Sberbank and VTB, regularly began to file fraud charges against managers of the borrower companies who were unable to maintain their payment schedules. On the grounds of those claims, the prosecutor general's office and police initiated criminal proceedings against business owners. As a result, a large number of business assets were transferred to banks or to companies with close ties to the banks' management. Ivanov was familiar with this practice as well: "Businessmen who simply failed to fulfill their commitments stipulated in agreements or contracts are being punished for fraud. There are many reasons for this, and they do not fail to fulfill them out of malice but due to the circumstances. For example, the market situation or the business climate has changed, competition has increased, partners or contractors went bankrupt. . . . It is also common that the entrepreneur himself makes a mistake, takes an unjustified risk, fails to calculate the consequences and turns out to be guilty" The Kremlin was well aware of this problem but did nothing, allowing many business owners to be charged with fraud.

Figure 8-1 shows that the number of criminal cases initiated against Russian business owners each year during the period 2008–17 reached the hundreds of thousands.[16] Only 15 percent of such cases reach the courts, which usually convict the defendants, whereas in 80–85 percent of cases, the accused business owners, who are often deprived of their freedom during the investigation, end up losing their businesses.

Repressions against business owners subsided somewhat during Dmitry Medvedev's presidency. At the beginning of his term, Medvedev himself uttered a wonderful statement: "Both our law enforcement agencies and our

FIGURE 8-1. Criminal Cases and Sentences against Entrepreneurs, 2008–17

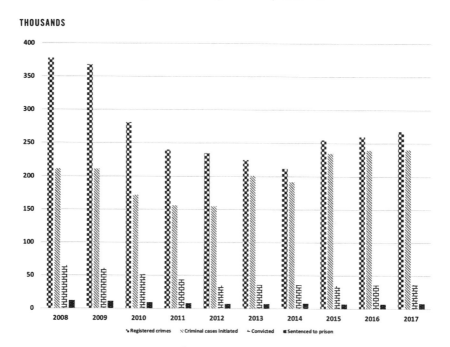

Source: Presidential Commissioner for Entrepreneurs' Rights,"Doklad Prezidentu RF-2018" [Report to the President of Russia-2018] (http://doklad.ombudsmanbiz.ru/doklad_2018.html)

government agencies should stop causing nightmares for business." However, with Putin's return to the Kremlin, the number of criminal cases brought against business owners increased rapidly. Consequently, since 2012, Russian businesses have reacted to this situation by cutting their investments; if the state has no intention of protecting private property, there is little reason to build or develop it. This decline in investment activity caused a sharp slowdown in Russia's economic growth beginning in 2013—a time when the average oil price was U.S. $108 per barrel, Crimea still belonged to Ukraine, and there was no talk of economic sanctions against Russia. Investments are a kind of fuel for economic growth. Any company needs investment to maintain existing business volume, much less increase it. As soon as Russian businesses decided to stop investing in development, the economy began to falter.

Not long after, collapsing oil prices and Western sanctions over Ukraine resulted in a two-year recession in the Russian economy.

Back in 2008, Vladimir Putin had recently changed seats with Medvedev to become Russian prime minister. In this new position he not only faced significant economic problems but also had to personally lead the struggle to respond to the economic crisis. At the time, he frequently heard from the owners and managers of large, medium, and small private and state-controlled businesses, listening to them complain about bureaucratic red tape and other obstacles to business growth in Russia. Many told him that the poor investment climate was the main obstacle to running a business in Russia and that Russia's drop in global competitiveness rankings had alienated foreign investors and increased the cost of capital for Russian businesses. In 2011, Putin decided to address the problem, announcing the goal of making Russia achieve one of the top twenty rankings in the World Bank's Ease of Doing Business index by 2018.[17]

In the summer of 2011, Putin established and personally led the supervisory board of the Agency for Strategic Initiatives (ASI), an autonomous nonprofit organization dedicated to improving Russia's business environment. The ASI's main objective was to raise Russia's position in the World Bank ranking, and the World Bank's quantitative approach to bureaucratic obstacles considerably simplified this task: business owners and ASI officials joined forces to single out the trouble spots that had caused Russia's low ranking. They discovered two particular causes for the slowness of many bureaucratic processes in Russia. In some cases, the absence of time limits on decision-making in statutory documents stalled progress on new initiatives. In other cases, the system struggled with the fact that certain decision-making processes had been inherited from the Soviet era, and the post-Soviet Russian state had not taken advantage of modern technologies to improve these processes. ASI developed eleven "road maps" to simplify, decrease the cost of, and speed up existing procedures regulating the relationship between the business and the state.

Putin's efforts bore fruit: Russia began climbing up in the World Bank's rankings (see figure 8-2). However, this purported improvement did not actually change the Russian investment climate and did not lead to an increase in investments for one simple reason: there were no meaningful changes in key areas of the relationship between businesses and the state. Among all the indicators that the World Economic Forum's Global Competitiveness Index (GCI) uses to characterize the investment climate, there are a few that most closely measure the key economic concern for investors, the protection of property rights. On all of these indicators, Russia had shown little, if any, progress.

Figure 8-3 shows that, although Russia's position on the GCI's Institutions subindex has risen rapidly, its progress reflects improvements in important but not crucial components, such as judicial independence and reliability of police services. Meanwhile, there have been only minor improvements to crucial components, such as protection of property rights. Even though the numbers look better on paper, Russia still remains a less than attractive country for investment.

FIGURE 8-2. Russia's Position in the World Bank's Ease of Doing Business Ranking and Global Competitiveness Index

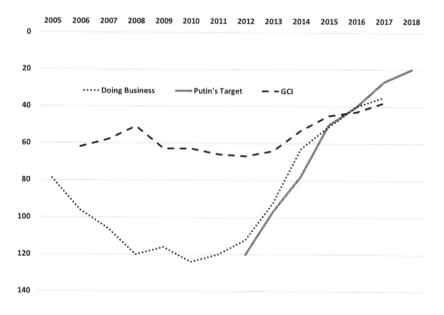

Source: World Bank, World Economic Forum.

Note: In both rankings, the higher a country's ranking, the better its position. From 2005 to 2017 the number of countries evaluated in the World Bank's Ease of Doing Business ranking increased from 155 to 190. From 2006 to 2012 the number of countries on the World Economic Forum's GCI list first increased from 125 to 148, then dropped to 138.

Vladimir Putin is well aware of the practice of using criminal prosecution of business owners to seize property. In his December 2015 address to the Federal Assembly, he talked about the scope and scale of the practice and the need to fight against it. However, these good intentions have not been realized. On the contrary, as table 8-1 demonstrates, the FSB's actions against business continue to increase, even as the total number of reported crimes has declined.

In 2000, Putin opened a proverbial Pandora's box by using the FSB to pressure the courts to destroy Vladimir Gusinsky's media empire. Soon after, he forced business owners to accept the Kremlin's right to manage their property, and by destroying Yukos he erased the boundary between state interests and the interests of individual government officials. Today, the state's

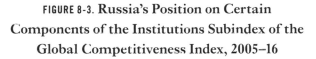

FIGURE 8-3. Russia's Position on Certain Components of the Institutions Subindex of the Global Competitiveness Index, 2005–16

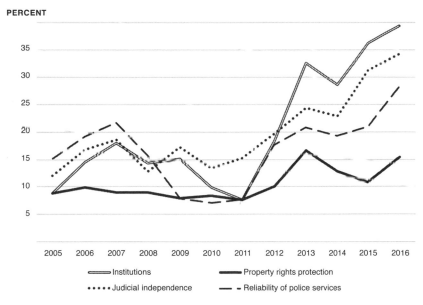

Source: The World Bank, World Economic Forum.

Note: Due to the constantly changing number of countries evaluated in the ranking, the indicators are shown in percentage terms. The smaller the indicator, the lower a country ranks. For instance, a value below 10 percent indicates that a country falls in the lowest 10 percent of the ranking.

TABLE 8-1. Growing Activity of the Secret Police in Russia, 2011–17

NUMBER	2011	2013	2015	2016	2017	First 6 months of 2018 (percentage of first 6 months of 2017)
New crimes recorded by all agencies	2,404,807	2,206,249	2,388,476	2,160,063	2,058,476	992,966/ (−3.6%)
Number recorded by FSB	6,354	8,634	13,159	15,950	17,994	9,778/ (+5.7%)
Economy-related crimes	202,454	141,229	112,445	108,754	105,087	68,737/ (+3.4%)
Number recorded by FSB	1,541	2,056	2,926	3,635	4,112	2725/ (+22%)

Source: Interior Ministry of Russia, "Sostoyaniye prestupnosti" [The situation with crimes] (https://mvd.rf/ folder/101762).

use of law enforcement resources to redistribute property and the absence of an independent judicial system that would protect citizens' rights are the main obstacles to the development of the Russian economy.

Putin has paid lip service to attempts to limit the scope of this problem, if not to eradicate it outright. But one cannot put toothpaste back into the tube. At any rate, the solution is obvious: the Russian court system must become independent, and law enforcement resources should not be used to maintain Putin's hold on power. This means that the vertical of power that he has built since his earliest days as Russia's president has to be destroyed. The course that Vladimir Putin chose for Russia eighteen years ago has to be recognized as wrong.

In the spring of 2014, Putin's foreign policy decisions drastically changed the external environment for the Russian economy. On February 23, 2014, he ordered the annexation of Ukraine's Crimean Peninsula. Five days later, Crimea's parliament building was occupied by "little green men"—soldiers in unmarked green army uniforms. Held at gunpoint, the parliament appointed a new pro-Russian government and instituted a so-called independence referendum on Crimea, which later was reformulated into a referendum to join the Russian Federation. On March 16, 2014, this referendum took place in Crimea, and the Crimean parliament asked to join Russia. Two days later, Russia annexed Crimea.

Three weeks after the annexation, Russian-speaking units without insignia began trying to foment revolts in several cities in eastern and southern Ukraine. In July, as the Ukrainian army made gains against these uprisings and the revolt was nearly suppressed, Russia deployed regular troops with heavy weapons in parts of Donbas and supported the establishment of the self-proclaimed Donetsk and Luhansk People's Republics. Those two territories comprise 17,000 square kilometers, approximately equal to the area of Kuwait, or twice the size of Israel. They have not been recognized by any country, including Russia. The bloody conflict in this region has resulted in more than 10,000 deaths, and no progress has been made toward its resolution.

The European Union and the United States imposed economic sanctions on Russia for its aggression in Ukraine. Russian state-controlled banks and companies were prohibited from raising capital in Western markets; Western companies were prohibited from supplying technology and participating in deep-sea and shale oil projects in Russia; and dozens of Russian politicians,

Putin cronies, and military officers were banned from receiving visas to EU countries and the United States, and their assets in those countries were ordered to be frozen. The initial impact of economic sanctions, which coincided with the unrelated fall in oil prices, was strong: the Russian ruble collapsed in December 2014. But by mid-2016 the sanctions were no longer having a significant effect; the Russian economy had adjusted to lower oil prices and returned to moderate if unstable growth. Though Russian politicians, including Vladimir Putin, are optimistic in assessing their country's future economic growth, the radical shift in the Kremlin's foreign policy has created significant obstacles for the Russian economy.

One aspect of the Western sanctions cannot be measured by any short-term statistics. Although financial sanctions may have substantially increased the cost of capital for the Russian economy, the external political pressure on Russia has dramatically increased the political risks of doing business in Russia for both Russian and foreign business owners. Political risks in Russia have effectively reached prohibitive levels, and nearly all Western investment projects and plans in Russia have been put on hold, if not canceled. In the modern world, technology transfer is an essential part of foreign direct investment flows, as is the transfer of managerial expertise. In the medium and long run, the Russian economy is much more sensitive to the lack of access to technology and human capital. Russia, like the Soviet Union, has historically been dependent on technology imports for all industrial sectors, and the present-day Russian economy requires massive injections of new technologies in order to stay competitive. In August 2018 one of Putin's closest lieutenants, Nikolai Patrushev, former FSB director and currently secretary of the Russian Security Council, recognized this problem, saying, "The financial and technological problems imposed by the U.S. and its allies on Russian energy companies demonstrated the vulnerability and dependence of the national energy sector on foreign capital, technologies, and software."[18]

If economic sanctions against Russia remain intact, the persistent political risks will inevitably increase the isolation of the Russian economy, widen the technology gap, and contribute to deteriorating competitiveness and lower growth rates. These effects cannot be seen today, but in five to seven years they will become the main sanctions-related burden for Russia and will undermine its long-term economic prospects.

Notes to Chapter 8

1. Although Putin is believed to have profited from corruption during his years at St. Petersburg city hall, no one has ever found any proof of his ill-gotten wealth. Perhaps his fortune was not so big at the time and easily fit into that "briefcase" with his family's savings that was destroyed in the fire at Putin's dacha in 1996. Or maybe Putin was as unsuccessful in defending his property interests as he was in defending the interests of city hall, having signed many contracts that privatized public revenues but left the government on the hook for large losses.

2. Vladislav Surkov, "Osnovnyye tendentsii i perspektivy razvitiya sovremennoy Rossii" [Main trends and prospects for the development of modern Russia] (Moscow: Sovremennaya gumanitarnaya akademiya, 2007), p. 19.

3. Aleksandr Igorev, Sergey Topol, Petr Sapozhnikov, and Irina Reznik, "Prishli za Alekperovym" [They came for Alekperov], *Kommersant* 125, July 12, 2000, p. 1.

4. Aleksey Ivanov, "Ushli ot Kadannikova" [They left Kadannikov], *Kommersant* 142, August 4, 2000, p. 1.

5. Gleb Pyanykh, "Vladimir Potanin uzhe pishet pis'ma" [Vladimir Potanin is already writing letters], *Kommersant* 124, July 11, 2000, p. 1.

6. Petr Sapozhnikov and Andrey Elizarov, "V TNK prishli za dokumentami trekhletney davnosti" [They went to TNK for the documents from three years ago], *Kommersant* 116, June 29, 2000, p. 4; and Petr Sapozhnikov, "'My ne umeyem dogovarivat'sya'" ["We do not know how to negotiate"], *Kommersant* 134, July 25, 2000, p. 5.

7. Thus, according to numerous sources, Potanin paid the required U.S. $140 million, even though the block of shares that he had purchased from the state had cost him $170 million. According to Kakha Bendukidze, in late July 2000, during his meeting with business owners, Putin asked to raise money for a charity fund for veterans of the secret services. Those present at the meeting immediately raised tens of millions of dollars. See Roman Kutuzov, "Oligarkhi" [Oligarchs], Forbes.ru, October 20, 2010. In July 2001, Vladimir Kozhin, head of the Control Directorate of the presidential administration, announced that a foundation had been created to restore the Konstantinovsky Palace near St. Petersburg and convert it into a presidential residence. The target funding amount initially was set at U.S. $200 million, with a minimal contribution of $20 million. Although the cost of the reconstruction later increased by 50 percent, Kozhin claimed that not one cent came from the government's budget. See also Andrey Smirnov, "Investitsii v prezidenta" [Investment in the president], *Kommersant* 143, August 11, 2011. According to Mikhail Khodorkovsky, Kremlin officials often approached him on Putin's behalf asking him to finance different projects, and when he asked Putin to confirm these requests, the latter always answered in the affirmative. Khodorkosky's interview with the author, August 13, 2017.

8. Andrey Vandenko, "Gennadiy Timchenko: za vse v zhizni nado platit'. I zaznakomstvo s rukovodstvom strany tozhe" [Gennady Timchenko: For everything in your life you have to pay. And for acquaintance with the leadership of the country, too], TASS, August 4, 2014.

9. Elizaveta Osetinskaya, Roman Badanin and Irina Malkova, "Vladimir Evtushenkov — RBK: 'YA vse pravila igry ponimayu' " [Vladimir Evtushenkov—RBK: "I understand all the rules of the game"], RBK, June 23, 2015.

10. Khodorkovsky confirmed that he personally sought and received approval from Putin at least twice for a proposal to merge Yukos and another Russian oil company, Sibneft. Afterward, he also sought preapproval from Putin to sell a large stake in this consolidated company to the U.S. oil and gas company Exxon (Khodorkosky interview). From 2002 to 2004, Potanin's Interros had been denied several requests to sell certain company components: a stake in the power generation equipment manufacturer Silovye Mashiny to the German company Siemens; Permskiye Motory to the U.S. company Pratt & Whitney; and a 10 percent stake in the small oil company Verkhnechonskneftegaz to the Chinese company CNPC. The oil company TNK-BP was created under the continuous control of the Kremlin, and the documents establishing it were signed during Putin's official visit to Great Britain.

11. Slightly later, in 2006 and 2007, when the Russian budget received unexpected revenues because of the dramatic increase in world oil prices, Putin began supporting the creation of state corporations in the hope that they might become the equivalents of South Korean chaebols.

12. During Yeltsin's rule, there was perhaps only one time when the Kremlin used law enforcement agencies against business owners. In early December 1994, Presidential Security Service head Aleksander Korzhakov authorized an operation led by law enforcement operatives against Vladimir Gusinsky. However, this was an attack on a political opponent, not an attempt at taking over a private business.

13. Russian Ministry for Security from 1992 to 1993 and the Federal Counterintelligence Service from 1993 to 1995.

14. Three weeks later, the court recognized some of the searches as illegal; such rulings soon became so rare as to be almost unimaginable. See Dmitry Pavlov, " 'Media-Most' zasudil Genprokuraturu" [Media-Most sued the Prosecutor General's Office], *Kommersant* 99, June 3, 2000, p. 1.

15. President of Russia, "Zasedaniye rabochey gruppy po monitoringu i analizu pravoprimenitel'noy praktiki v sfere predprinimatel'stva" [Meeting of the Working Group on Monitoring and Analysis of Law Enforcement Practice in the Field of Entrepreneurship], news release, Moscow, March 23, 2016 (http://kremlin.ru/events/president/news/51556).

16. Anastasiya Kornya, "Kak zashchitit' biznes ot ugolovnogo presledovaniya" [How to protect business from criminal prosecution], *Vedomosti*, April 10, 2017.

17. The World Bank's Ease of Doing Business ranking and the World Economic Forum's GCI are two key rankings for evaluating the conditions for doing business in a country. Vladimir Putin chose the World Bank's ranking for a reason: it is based on technical criteria (such as the number of days it takes to complete a certain bureaucratic procedure, or the number of procedures one has to complete in order to obtain a permit or a license), whereas the World Economic Forum's index is based on polls conducted among business owners from different countries, thus producing a more qualitative evaluation.

18. InfoOrel, "V Orle sostoyalos' vyezdnoye soveshchaniye Sekretarya Soveta Bezopasnosti RF v TSVO" [The out-of-office meeting of the Secretary of the Russian Security Council in the CFD (Central Federal District) took place in Orel], August 3, 2018 (www.infoorel.ru/news/v-orle-sostoyalos-vyezdnoe-soveshchanie-sekretarya-bezopasnosti-rf-v-cfo.html).

Nine

LOOKING FORWARD

The history of Vladimir Putin's counterrevolution—the story of how one man altered the trajectory of an entire country—is not a particular outlier in the global history of the past 100 years, Russia's uniqueness and its mysterious soul notwithstanding. During that same period, many nations moved toward democracy, only to backtrack. For some, this regression happened only once; others made two, three, or more attempts. Antidemocratic transformations can happen suddenly, often in the form of a military coup, or they can happen over an extended period, as those who resist democratic norms progressively gather all the powers of the state and remove their rivals from the political scene. Such transformations have their own characteristic trends and patterns, and the events of twenty-first-century Russia fit this template well.

When the Soviet Union collapsed at the end of 1991, Russia had no historical memory of democratic practice on which it could draw. Its republican period had been brief, lasting only a few months in 1917, until the Bolshevik revolution dispersed the elected Constituent Assembly. After the subsequent seventy-five years of communist rule, there was no one left in Russia who had actual experience, rather than just theoretical knowledge, of how a market economy worked. Moreover, the country also lacked a strong civil society, one capable of opposing authoritarianism and forcing the government to grant concessions to protect civil rights. The movement toward democracy had been initiated from above, not below, by Soviet leader Mikhail Gorbachev, and in the new post-Soviet era its momentum was fragile and uncertain.

But Russia got lucky. As the Soviet empire crumbled, a politician came to power whose main objective was to move the country away from its totalitarian past. Boris Yeltsin's education and career differed little from that of other senior Soviet officials. After he became president of a newly independent country, his actions were guided not by precise calculations and a clearly formulated vision of Russia's future but by political intuition and a choice to resolve conflicts through compromise and negotiation rather than violent suppression. Even after the failed putsch of August 1991 and the acrimonious political conflict with parliament in the autumn of 1993, Yeltsin did not seek to persecute his opponents but freed them from criminal prosecution and allowed them to participate in the political life of the country.

The decisions that Yeltsin made were never part of any kind of plan. In fact, his actions frequently seemed erratic. But judging from the end result of his presidency—Russia in 1999 versus Russia in 1991—it must be said that the country moved in a clear direction throughout that period. The new market economy experienced severe crises but did not collapse under their weight. An independent judiciary was created, in which judges overturned presidential decrees and suspended laws and government regulations without fear of reprisal. Disagreements between the two chambers of parliament, whose opposing sides frequently were unable to find mutually acceptable concepts of law, were seen as the normal state of affairs. It also was considered normal practice for the president to exercise his right to veto laws passed by parliament, and for parliament to override such vetoes.

I do not mean to imply that everything was rosy in the 1990s. I am well aware of the spike in crime, the unfairness of the privatization process, the corrupt judiciary, the arrears in state employee pensions and salaries, and the 1998 default. But when analyzing the Yeltsin era, or that of any politician in any country, one must look at the progress that the country made toward its goals. By that measure, with each new step Yeltsin's presidency made Russia freer, its economy more stable, and its future prospects clearer.

Yeltsin naturally wished to find a successor who would carry on his legacy. With the benefit of hindsight, we can see clearly today that the communists' peak popularity hit in 1995–96. With the Duma under their control in 1999, they had the clout to insist that the president compromise on his choice of prime minister. But Yeltsin's inner circle at the time believed that the communists had a good chance of winning the next presidential election.

One could, of course, fault Yeltsin for choosing Vladimir Putin, a man who swiftly changed the course of Russia's trajectory, leading it into the proverbial swamp in which it is now mired. But at the time, Yeltsin did not have much of a choice in his candidates. His two options were Putin and Sergey Stepashin. Yeltsin had known Stepashin for much longer, had seen his work in various positions and situations, and knew him to be a loyal supporter. But he did not see Stepashin as a strong leader and had little confidence in his choices or authority. The second candidate was a newcomer to Yeltsin's inner circle, and almost nothing was known of his political views. But Putin had always expressed himself clearly and was prepared to defend his position with well-reasoned arguments. It was a difficult choice, perhaps an impossible one. The factor that tipped the scales in Putin's favor was the opinion of influential members of Yeltsin's inner circle, who felt that Putin's electoral chances were much higher.

Appointing Putin was not Yeltsin's biggest error but it gave the green light to using the power of the government to persecute and dismiss Prosecutor General Skuratov and to attack Gusinsky's media empire in spring 1999. It was a watershed moment in Russian political history: the Kremlin employed *siloviki* against political opponents and their business allies. Putin, then the head of the FSB, had carte blanche to use his agency's resources against disloyal actors. He faithfully completed the task set before him and learned from the experience that it was both permissible and effective to use such methods in political battles.

After Putin became prime minister and was designated Yeltsin's successor in 1999, he quickly adapted to his new circumstances. In this new life, it was no easy task to find his stride. He had no experience with public politics, and his only ally was the Kremlin administration. It was during the concurrent Duma election campaign—the results of which would in large part determine Putin's political future—that he was first described as a "strong hand."

After the instabilities and uncertainties of the Yeltsin years, many Russians had been seeking such a quality in their leader. But this campaign was being managed by experts that Putin did not know well, and likewise, he was only dimly acquainted with the deputies on the Unity party list drawn up by the Kremlin's staff. After the elections, he would have to trust his fate to both these groups. His experience in the KGB, meanwhile, had not accustomed him to trusting unfamiliar people. In this situation, his desire for a powerful, dependable ally—one who, above all, would be loyal to him alone—was rational. Putin's choice of ally was the FSB, the Russian secret police, the organization in which he had spent a quarter century. It was an organization for which the ends always justified the means, whose actions were never restricted by law, and which was accustomed to carrying out the Kremlin's orders without question. It was an organization whose forceful intervention could alter the balance of power in the country. It was an organization that could grant its ally the power to rule by force, undermining the rule of law.

The alliance was cemented without delay. Within days of Putin's inauguration, the FSB arranged the attack on the media tycoon Vladimir Gusinsky, deprived him of his holdings, and forced him into exile. It directly threatened the governors of Russia's regions with arrest when the presidential draft diminishing their power was being debated in parliament. Before long, Putin's inner circle was populated by people whose careers had originated with the secret police, and he soon appointed them to leadership positions in many government structures and state-owned companies. There was no place in Putin's circle, either before or after the elections, for intellectuals or politicians who could have helped him develop a strategic objective and vision for Russia's future. What his administration did have was plenty of people who applauded the idea of building a strong state.

This idea that Putin had inherited a weak, failing state from Boris Yeltsin was pushed from the earliest days of acting president Putin's tenure in the Kremlin. Putin spent most of his working life in a hierarchical system with no checks and balances and no democratic procedures, where the word of a superior was greater than the law. When Putin secured his position in the Kremlin, it seemed perfectly natural to him that he should build a hierarchical system of governance in Russia. "The governance vertical is destroyed; we need to restore it" was one of his first messages.[1] Hierarchy and subordination to superiors were synonymous with order for him, and order was the sign of a strong leader. Anyone who criticized the manner in which order was established—or, God forbid, opposed it—was immediately accused of attacking the state and became Putin's enemy.

Putin wasted no time in compiling his list of enemies. Vladimir Gusinsky and Boris Berezovsky were two of them, as the new president ominously indicated in June 2000 when he spoke of those who "not only got very wealthy, but acquired . . . more influence in the political sphere . . . than was useful for the country . . . and [tried] to influence the political leadership. These people will, naturally, be put in their place."[2] The media were another target: "[The media's] economic ineffectiveness makes them dependent on the commercial and political interests of the owners and sponsors of these news resources. This makes it possible to use the media to attack competitors, and sometimes even transform them into a resource for the dissemination of mass disinformation. That's why we must guarantee journalists' actual, not just superficial, freedom."[3] Yet another group of enemies were regional elites, who "began to test the stability of central authority," weakening the government by "competing [with the center] for authority," and whose desire to construct a federative system of relations was deemed a fight that would lead to "mutually assured destruction" and the creation of a "decentralized state."[4]

Well aware of the difficulty of fighting on several fronts simultaneously, during his first years in office Putin constantly had to build coalitions to combat those who presented the greatest threat. This was the case with Gusinsky: to bring down the media magnate, the Kremlin joined forces with Berezovsky, who became its next target once the first was out of the picture. In his clash with the Federation Council and the governors on it, Putin formed an alliance with the liberals and communists. Later on, Putin used the support of the liberal parties in the Duma to obtain full control over the judiciary. Putin had no love for this continual need to form temporary coalitions; he saw it as a sign of weakness. He therefore deployed the resources of the government to find former opponents who were willing to become temporary allies. One crucial historical junction for Putin was the final dismantling of the governors' bloc and the formation of a new party, United Russia. After that, the majority in the State Duma came under the Kremlin's control, and Putin had little need to worry about coalition-building on the federal level. Once that concern was settled, Putin established full control over the regional elites by assigning to himself the right to nominate regional governors and by manipulating election legislation; United Russia subsequently dominated all regional legislatures. Putin underlined this political success with the nationalization of Yukos in the mid-2000s, sending an unmistakable warning to the Russian business world about what would happen if they were to support any party besides United Russia. The Kremlin would view any attempt to promote the election of lobbyists for business to parliament as an attack on the stability of the state.

The Kremlin falsified election results on a large scale for the first time during the 2003 State Duma elections, undermining the basic principle of democratic elections: one person, one vote. From then on, seats in parliament would be filled not through polling stations but by the decision of the presidential administration. After that, Putin's political opponents had a choice: agree to be co-opted into the Kremlin-built system under the Kremlin's conditions or become an enemy of the Kremlin and face the full arsenal of state power. To those who chose the first option, the Kremlin guaranteed the chance to participate in elections at all levels and offered consolation prizes: a gubernatorial post for each parliamentary party, or an agreement not to put forward United Russia candidates in majority districts. As payment for their loyalty, the "systemic opposition" received state financing and guaranteed access to state-controlled television news channels. Those politicians who failed to swear allegiance and eternal loyalty to Vladimir Putin, however, were simply tossed out of politics by the Kremlin, in effect depriving them of the right to participate in elections. The main instrument for this was a permanent modification and tightening of the electoral legislation, the law regulating the activities of political parties, and its enforcement (see table 9-1).

This purge of the political scene in Russia intensified significantly during Putin's second presidential term, instigated by his unconcealed desire to extend his stay in power indefinitely. As he said in 2007: "The constitution prohibits a president from being elected to more than two consecutive terms. After a term out of office, at some future point—yes, it is theoretically possible under the law."[5] But to come back to office after skipping a term, Putin would have to weather a dangerous period: four years of another person in the Kremlin. The "color revolutions" that had swept through the countries

TABLE 9-1. Number of Changes to Laws Regulating the
Russian Electoral System and Political Competition

Law and Year When Adopted	Presidential Term			
	2000–04	2004–08	2008–12	2012–18
Law on Basic Guarantees of Electoral Rights and on the Right to Participate in Referenda for the Citizens of the Russian Federation (1997, 2002)	6	18	26	39
Law on Election of the President of the Russian Federation (1999, 2003)	3	7	14	13
Law on Elections of the Deputies of the State Duma and the President of the Russian Federation (1999, 2002, 2006, 2014)	6	11	13	19
Law on the Formation of the Federation Council (1995, 2000, 2012)	1	3	3	10
Law on Basic Principles of Organization of Legislative and Executive Bodies of the Subjects of the Russian Federation (1999)	6	24	39	68
Law on Political Parties (2001)	5	11	17	16
Law on Assemblies, Meetings, Demonstrations, Marches, and Picketing (2004)	—	1	3	7

Source: Information and legal portal Consultant.ru (http://www.consultant.ru/).

of the former Soviet Union demonstrated to him how easily a president could lose power in the face of combined parliamentary opposition and street protests. As a result, there could be no place in Russia for strong nonloyal opposition or street demonstrations. "Regarding change of power, of course, it should take place," Putin declared. "Of course, in those processes, a healthy competition should take place, but it should be among people nationally oriented, oriented toward the interests of the Russian people."[6] Naturally, Vladimir Putin alone would have the right and power to decide which politicians were oriented in the proper way—and to ensure that those who were oriented in wrong ways would be repressed.

In the 1930s, Stalin used public trials to literally destroy real and potential political opponents. During these trials, key Soviet political and military figures such as Leon Trotsky, Nikolai Bukharin, Grigory Zinoviev, Lev Kamenev, Alexey Rykov, Mikhail Tukhachevsky, and dozens of other Soviet party members, generals, or economic leaders were wiped out. Putin's system employs subtler methods of government pressure, forcing political opponents to flee Russia out of fear of criminal prosecution and prison terms, or indirectly depriving them of the right to be elected to public office. Garry Kasparov, Mikhail Khodorkovsky, Ilya Ponomarev, Vladimir Ashurkov, Sergey Guriyev, and dozens of other Russian citizens who took an active role in Russian politics are now living abroad. Sergey Udaltsov and Eduard Limonov, both of whom served time in prison, and Alexey Navalny, now twice sentenced to probation, are prohibited by law from running for public office for a lengthy period.

Under Putin, Russia's political transformation moved in a consistent direction. Each time he faced a decision on political reforms, he chose to further restrict freedoms. He has never agreed to concessions, opting instead to go on the attack and increase pressure on his opponents. His practice of destroying the opposition in Russia led to the destruction of political competition, without which there can be no rule of law or independent judiciary. The rule of law is the principle that laws should apply equally to everyone, and that one group cannot use the law to violate the rights or property of others. Without political pluralism, existing Russian institutions could not and would not curb the increasingly widespread abuses of the law.

The desire to hold on to power is a natural one for many politicians. Some employ democratic methods to win elections, and some wait for the right moment to change the rules of the game, drawing their country farther away from political equality. Putin chose the second path, and was helped along this path by a collection of circumstances that, according to political scientists, tend to create authoritarian leaders. At the start of the twenty-first century, Russia lacked any political or public leaders who were capable of consolidating public pressure on the state in the defense of democratic rights. At the same time, the political costs for suppressing democracy and political pluralism in Russia were low; the public had no control over the secret police and other *siloviki*, which meant that the government could easily intimidate any opponents. The history of the world has demonstrated that in countries moving toward democracy, significant reserves of raw materials often destabilize the process of building state institutions. Regimes whose economies are based on natural resources have much less need to cooperate with businesses. Thus the global spike in oil prices, which brought Russia nearly $3 trillion in additional oil revenue in 2003–17, worked in Putin's favor, helping him to buy off the masses.

Nondemocratic regimes rarely have successful economies and often pursue policies inconsistent with their countries' actual long-term interests, fearing that the "creative destruction" of business development could cause political instability. At the turn of the fifteenth century in China, for example, the emperors began to prohibit international trade and banned merchants from making overseas expeditions—preventing, in the rulers' view, threats to their political stability. In the seventeenth century, the regent Oboi of the Kangxi Emperor of Qing went even further, forcing the entire population of a region to move inland in order to prevent them from interacting with foreigners. These kinds of decisions left China on the sidelines of the international exchange of ideas and technologies. By the nineteenth century, China had fallen far behind European nations in terms of economic development. It took this country two centuries to restore its place in the global world.

In the first half of the nineteenth century, the Russian and Austro Hungarian empires made a conscious decision to delay the construction of railroads. Their reasoning was that the railroads would further economic industrialization, concentrate the population in cities, and increase the rates of education, all of which would threaten their governments' stability. Around the same time, Russian finance minister Yegor Kankrin shut down the Commercial Bank established by his predecessor, which had been issuing loans to industry, and reopened the State Loan Bank, which had been closed ten years before. This reopened bank relaunched lending to landowners, who used their land and serfs as collateral for the loans. As a result, Russia's emerging industry lacked funds for its development while the financial resources of the country were used for the preservation of the inefficient economic structure.

It took Russia another fifty years to experience, during the reign of Aleksandr II, a period of intensive institutional reforms, industrialization, and railway construction, leading to rapid economic growth.

In this sense, Putin is no exception. His interference in economic matters often creates waste and inefficiency. As prime minister, he lied to the International Olympic Committee about the scale of government financing that would be used to prepare for the 2014 Sochi Olympics and approved a process for Olympic construction financed by loans from the state-owned Vnesheconombank. The lending for the Olympics effectively broke the bank; an injection of hundreds of billions of rubles from the federal budget and the central bank was needed to keep Vnesheconombank afloat. Likewise, to punish its rebellious neighbor Ukraine, Putin supported Gazprom's plan to build gas pipelines that would circumvent Ukrainian territory. Now, although the total capacity of Russia's gas export pipelines exceeds Russian gas export volumes by 70 percent, the gas monopoly is pursuing the construction of two more pipelines.

In 2014, when the government was promoting the transformation of the existing Russian pension system, the Ministry of Finance insisted on freezing the mandatory pension savings funds. Despite its initial promise to funnel those funds into the pension system, the government spent that money—in contravention of the law—to make up for the decline in revenues from the falling oil prices. (At the time, the government could have gone with another option: using its fiscal reserves to make up the difference and leaving the pension system untouched.) It again froze pension savings funds in 2015, 2016, and 2017, after which it de facto eliminated the mandatory pension savings plan. This bad decision had three consequences. First, it completely discredited the concept of mandatory pension savings, making it necessary for the government to come up with another structure for the national pension system, which has yet to be created. Second, it drained resources from the financial market, making it much more expensive for Russian business to borrow money needed for growth. Third, the lengthy break in accumulating pension funds will require Russia to preserve for another ten years the current inefficient solidarity pension system that drains resources from the federal budget.

The six biggest Russian oil companies are responsible for 75 percent of all oil production in the country. Each also holds numerous small or poorly performing fields that are unprofitable to develop. Liberalizing regulations for small companies working in this sector and transferring unused fields to them could sharply increase oil production in Russia and, correspondingly, federal budget revenues. Over the years, however, the Kremlin has blocked all proposals to liberalize the industry because it sees energy as a strategic sector and therefore one that should be kept under tight control. In addition, rapid growth in the small business sector is a constant worry for the Kremlin, as it would lead to a new and rising class of entrepreneurs who would demand more political rights and freedoms.

It is easy to provide many other examples of Putin's economic policy mistakes, but they all pale in comparison to the lack of protection for property rights, which is the main obstacle to stable economic growth. This diagnosis was delivered long ago and is well known to everyone—even Putin. He regularly brings it up in speeches to the Federal Assembly, where the president traditionally discusses key matters of domestic and foreign policy. In 2000, he said, "The foundation of government regulation in the economy . . . is the protection of private initiatives and all forms of property. . . . It's important to establish a legal framework for the rights of private property." In 2001, he admitted, "Unfortunately, we still have poor protections for property rights." In 2003, he declared, "Russia should be and will be a country . . . where property rights are reliably defended." In 2005, he stated, "The inviolability of private property is the cornerstone of any business dealing. Government regulations in this sphere should be clear to all, and, essentially, stable." In 2006, he warned, "If we . . . do not strengthen property rights, it is unlikely that we will be able to meet the economic objectives we have set within the planned timelines." Upon his return to the presidency for a third term in 2012, he said, "Economic freedom and private property should be at the center of the new model for growth. . . . The best way to make business patriotic is to ensure effective guarantees for the protection of property." That same year, he reminded the Assembly, "Again, the role of law enforcement and the judicial system is to . . . defend the rights, property, and dignity of all those following the law and conducting their business honestly." By 2016, he was openly admitting the real source of the problem: "In last year's address, I spoke of pressure on business from certain representatives of law enforcement bodies. Such actions often lead to the failure of successful businesses, and people's property is taken from them."[7]

But these words have never translated into action. The state continued to take businesses away from their owners and helped others to do the same under state protection. There was talk about "dishonest officials" and the "ineffective work of law enforcement," but the Kremlin did everything it could to ensure that this problem was never resolved. Election laws were changed to minimize the possibility of political pluralism developing. The suppression of speech and political repression became the state's main tools to combat the rise of popular opposition. The Kremlin kept a tight grip on the judicial system, giving the government free rein to abuse the law. Russian courts no longer defended citizens' basic rights, such as property rights, the right to a fair judiciary, and the right to elect the government.

All of this presents an obvious question: If Putin has known all along about the problem with regard to the protection of property rights, why hasn't he been able to resolve it after eighteen years in power? The answer to that question is simple: as a politician, Putin represents and defends the interests of a broad coalition uniting the top government bureaucracy, the *siloviki*, and commodity exporters, whose positions would be weakened by rapid economic growth. Institutional reforms with greater protections for private property would increase the number of well-off Russians who are not dependent on the state and who would then demand their own political representation at all levels of the government. Any movement toward an independent judiciary inevitably would undermine the Kremlin's ability to seize property and also make it impossible to falsify election results, which in turn would increase the level of political competition in Russia and destroy the power vertical that Putin began building as soon as he set foot in the Kremlin. Eventually, Putin, or his successor, would lose power in free elections.

In the kind of state that Vladimir Putin sees as the only true and correct one, the kind he has built over the course of eighteen years, that future must never come to pass.

It is not difficult to predict Russia's future course for Putin's next presidential term—which he easily orchestrated in March 2018—because the political regime he has created in Russia has played out many times over the past sixty years. Political scientists frequently refer to such regimes as authoritarian; occasionally, they are called dictatorial or undemocratic. Having come to power through elections or through coups d'état, leaders of such regimes solidify their claims to long-term rule by removing from the political stage those who could restrict or usurp their powers. Such regimes tend to be stable because they rely primarily on force, whether exercised through the army or the secret police. (Table 8-1 shows how the FSB's activity is permanently growing in Russia, including in the economic sector, where the Russian secret police has arrogated to itself the right to be tremendously involved.) These regimes can indeed fall, but for a limited number of reasons: as a result of losing a war to a stronger neighbor, because of their destructive economic policies, or through a coup d'état. An authoritarian regime may also be brought down as a result of a popular uprising, but this rarely happens on its own without one or more of the above conditions being present.

I see no reason to adjust my predictions for Russia's future course. I would like to think that Vladimir Putin is not planning a war against NATO or China. His economic policy does not undermine the foundations of the market economy: the absence of price regulations allows the economy to restore equilibrium even after the strongest of external shocks, as seen in the wake of the 2014–16 crisis. Putin has removed from his inner circle almost all his old friends who might have had serious political ambitions. Instead, he has surrounded himself with young technocrats whose ascent to the top was so rapid that they will be content with what they have achieved for a long time to come.

Therefore, nothing and no one will prevent Vladimir Putin from advancing the policies he considers right, and it is not that hard to predict what these policies will be in broad outline. He will spend his entire current term contemplating what will happen afterward. Should he go for a referendum that will extend his powers for one or possibly two more terms? Or should he step aside, leaving his place in the Kremlin to a political successor? In either case, he will play the role of a "Russian Deng Xiaoping"—the man whose approval will be required for any important decision. But whatever scenario Putin chooses, he needs the Russian political situation to remain under his complete control so that no one can prevent him from making his choice.

This means that Putin the politician will still have the same goal: holding on to power by all possible means, so that no one has any reason to doubt his leadership abilities. That is the goal that will inform his decisions and actions, and that is why we should not expect his policies to change. In fact, it has been Putin's main goal for the past eighteen years.

This means that pressures on freedom of speech in Russia will continue, since freedom of speech inevitably will chip away at the myth of the Great Leader and the idyllic situation in the country. This means that Russia will still be governed as a unitary state, with no serious powers granted to the regions or municipalities, and the governors will still come to the Kremlin to beg for money to solve regional problems. This means that Russia will not have free and fair elections on the federal and regional levels, since such elections could produce strong independent politicians. This means that the election law will be manipulated, that formal and informal barriers for nominating political candidates and running election campaigns will become stricter, and that election results will be massively rigged again. This means that there is a risk of rising repression against political opponents and defenders of freedom of speech in Russia.

All of the above means that there will be no positive changes for the Russian economy, and that property rights will remain a fancy constitutional term devoid of real meaning. Economic growth will be slow and unsteady. Russia's economy will lag further behind that of developed countries in terms of technological development and will continue to rely on raw material exports. However, none of this will threaten the stability of Vladimir Putin's hold on power—and thus it won't concern him all that much.

Notes to Chapter 9

1. Vladimir Putin, *Ot pervogo litsa* [First person] (Moscow: Vagrius, 2000; New York: PublicAffairs, 2000), p. 123.

2. President of Russia, "Interv'yu germanskim telekanalam ARD i ZDF" [Interview with German television channels ARD and ZDF], transcript, Moscow, June 9, 2000 (http://kremlin.ru/events/president/transcripts/24205).

3. President of Russia, "Poslaniye Federal'nomu Sobraniyu Rossiyskoy Federatsii" [Address to the Federal Assembly of the Russian Federation], transcript, Moscow, July 8, 2000 (http://kremlin.ru/events/president/transcripts/21480).

4. Ibid.

5. President of Russia, "Interv'yu Iranskomu gosteleradio i informatsionnomu agentstvu IRNA" [Interview with the Iranian state television, radio and information agency IRNA], transcript, Moscow, October 16, 2007 (http://kremlin.ru/events/president/transcripts/24603).

6. Oliver Stone, *The Putin Interviews* (Visit 3, day 3, May 11, 2016) (Moscow: Alpina, 2017).

7. The quotations are from Putin's presidential addresses for the years cited.

Index